BODY IMAGE

A surgical perspective

BODY IMAGE
A surgical perspective

FREDERICK M. GRAZER, M.D., F.A.C.S.

Associate Clinical Professor of Surgery (Plastic),
University of California School of Medicine, Irvine, California

JEROME R. KLINGBEIL, M.D.

Associate Clinical Professor of Surgery (Plastic),
University of California School of Medicine, Irvine, California

With 1,026 *illustrations, including* 49 *in color*
Drawings by **Denis Dykes Sperling**

The C. V. Mosby Company

ST. LOUIS • TORONTO • LONDON   1980

Cover illustration from Dürer's studies in proportion

The C. V. Mosby Company
11830 Westline Industrial Drive, St. Louis, Missouri 63141

Library of Congress Cataloging in Publication Data

Main entry under title:

Body image.

    Bibliography: p.
    Includes index.
    1. Surgery, Plastic. 2. Abdomen—Surgery.
3. Extremities (Anatomy)—Surgery. 4. Buttocks—
Surgery. I. Grazer, Frederick M. II. Klingbeil,
Jerome R. [DNLM: 1. Body image. 2. Surgery, Plastic.
WO600 B668]
RD119.5.B63B63   617'.95   79-23858
ISBN 0-8016-1965-3

C/CB/B 9 8 7 6 5 4 3 2 1   02/B/273

Contributors

Sections on anatomy and clinical research (co-author)

DARRYL J. HODGKINSON, M.D.

Fellow in Plastic and Reconstructive Surgery, Mayo Clinic, Rochester, Minnesota

Section on anesthesia

WILLIAM A. MATHEWS, M.D.

Vice Chairman, Department of Anesthesia, Hoag Memorial Hospital, Presbyterian, Newport Beach, California

Section on patient counseling

MARY MATTIELLO, B.A.

Department of Psychology, Pepperdine University, Newport Beach, California

Sections on patient care

JANE G. WILSON, R.N.

Associate Professor, Faculty of Nursing, University of Toronto, Toronto, Ontario; Doctoral candidate, University of California Medical Center, San Francisco, California

Acknowledgements

It is difficult to fully acknowledge all who deserve our thanks for their help in producing this text. We must thank the following because their efforts were so freely given:

Peggy Carlson, R.N., Operating room supervisor, Hoag Memorial Hospital, Presbyterian, Newport Beach, California

Contributing gynecologists, particularly **Richard Jonas, M.D.,** and **Lawrence Kline, M.D.**

Beatrice De Araujo, R.N., extraordinary circulating nurse, Hoag Memorial Hospital, Presbyterian, Newport Beach, California

Jean Galloway, R.P.T., Hoag Memorial Hospital, Presbyterian, Newport Beach, California, whose tireless effort in instruction and patient ambulation has refined our results

Stanley Greiwe for his talent with the camera, providing not only the surgical but also all infrared and fluorescein photography

Martin Hansen, M.D., for his surgical assistance on many of the procedures

George Hart, M.D., for his willingness to share his extensive knowledge about the use of hyperbaric oxygen

Sue Hinsey and **Helen Suzuki** for long hours of typing and proofreading

Cecilia Hodgkinson and **Frances Ishii** for the hours spent in bibliographical research

Owen Mapp for his interest and input about tattooing and the Maori of New Zealand

Nuclear Medicine Department, Hoag Memorial Hospital, Presbyterian, Newport Beach, California, for the isotope studies

Owen Seffern, M.D., for his ability to translate the German language—even old script

Denis Dykes Sperling, University of California, Los Angeles, medical arts honor graduate, for her unrestrained efforts in her phenomenal illustrations

Preface

Like all our predecessors in the specialty of plastic surgery, we not only recognize our obligations to our patients as well as the thrills and challenges of the surgery itself, we also hope to make some contribution to the lore of our profession. Together with our ideas about surgical problems, patient care, and operative techniques, we have tried to bring into perspective some of the various factors that created the need for plastic surgery. The importance of thorough investigation, accurate reference, and an increasing realization of our human fallibility increased our desire to accurately document our research efforts. The earlier literature concerning dermolipectomy of both the abdominal wall and the extremities has been replete with errors and misreference; however, we recognize that verifying every early reference is both time-consuming and expensive. Therefore we have attempted to correct and verify as much of the available literature as possible despite limited sources. Translation of articles in foreign languages is difficult and can also be extremely expensive, regardless of the home country of the author. No criticism or derogative implication of other authors is intended by our efforts to provide corrected reference data. It is certain that we too have made mistakes.

The realm of cosmetic surgery in the area of the abdominal wall, buttocks, and extremities involves a different approach and attitude than do the more visible areas of otoplasty, rhinoplasty, and rhytidectomy. Prolonged exposure to this field necessitates more than a superficial awareness of the patient's regard for the whole body, which has been characterized by others as "body image" and the surgery associated with it as "body sculpture."

The term *body image* has two applications. The individual views the body as a total unit but visualizes and regards the different parts separately. Apparently many illogical and symbolical associations result from this dual concept. Congenital, traumatic, and/or psychopathological defects become woven into the individual's overall regard for self. Long-standing hidden personality problems, which in the past were lessened by strong family ties and/or strict religious beliefs, today surface far more easily. It has become apparent that society as a whole as well as individually cannot handle periods of affluence as well as times of stress and conflict, in which personality problems are sublimated to other needs. In an era of accelerating cultural change, the restraints of moral and religious attitudes rapidly diminish, and the inner conflicts demand attention. Problems brought to the plastic surgeon are many and varied; insight into the personal goals of the patient is an important ingredient for proper total care. Decreasing discipline and individual freedom, however desirable, have an effect on all levels of social interaction. Of importance to the plastic surgeon is the burgeoning of cosmetic surgery during these periods. History tells of similar periods during which ornamentation of dress or the body parallels the trends we see in cosmetic surgery today.

To understand this subject matter, we believe it is important not only to know the anatomy of the involved surgical areas, the biochemistry and physiology of involved vascular phenomena, and the totality of all surgical aspects and implications, but also to become aware of the feelings of the patients and the ancillary contributions to body change made by clothing, painting, scarification, mutilation, and tattooing. Although each of these subjects could provide material for a complete text or even several texts, we searched these areas for material that would give greater depth to our understanding of the surgery as well as the psychological needs of our patients.

We trust that *Body Image: A Surgical Perspective* will be both informative and interesting to our readers.

We also realize that the technical data we present are merely another addition to the information whole. If we have done our job as well as we hope, this text may make the problems of other surgeons and their patients more understandable and possibly contribute to better results.

Frederick M. Grazer
Jerome R. Klingbeil

Contents

BODY IMAGE
A surgical perspective

CHAPTER 1

History of body change

The human body is a wondrous entity and, whether ascribed to a creator or a developmental evolutionary process, cannot be regarded as less than a fantastic accumulation of an unlimited number of intricate processes. Constantly functioning are numerous basic inorganic chemical interactions, as well as an interchange of the most complex chemical structures not yet totally understood. Not only do the body's anatomical structures have a myriad of functions, the potential scope, flexibility, and judgment of the human mind cannot be matched by any computer yet built. When combined into single human beings, these magnificent systems become enigmatic creations, no two of which are identical in any way or react in the same manner. With such a great potential for variance, it is logical that the standards individuals set for themselves as to what is desirable or beautiful are dissimilar. Therein begins our story about body form, body image, and the ways humans have tried to achieve their own goals of beauty. To understand today's patient who seeks body change, we must understand the humans of history, the attitudes they had toward their bodies, and the ways in which they tried to change their bodies.

Nature endows all creatures with special physical characteristics and attributes that tend to ensure mating and survival of their species. The cobra has its fangs and venom; the lion, its mane; and the pelican, its magnificent beak. No creature other than the human tries to or can change its physical features. Only humans are capable of altering the way in which they have been created. Men, like other creatures, have chosen in their strivings from their very beginning to make themselves attractive to their mates. In like manner, women also try to alter their appearance to make themselves attractive to their mates.

The evolution of humans' regard for the appearance of their bodies does not reflect a progressive, healthier, more stable existence. Instead, the image parallels the path of the political, social, and religious wanderings of people. No one can deny that politics, religion, and social behavior have varied from the highest idealistic level to the most depraved levels imaginable, sometimes simultaneously and at other times independently of each other.

Clothing may have been introduced as a necessity for people to live together in groups. Men's external sexual organs may involuntarily indicate interest in the opposite sex, and women need to disguise the effects of menstruation. Most societies protect children against the onset of sexual aggression; clothes disguise the appearance of pubic hair and prolong that protection.

In Garland's treatise,[2] *The Changing Form of Fashion*, the author graphically states that "the concept of modesty comes and goes through the centuries as the cat came and went through the branches of the tree in *Alice in Wonderland,* each time appearing in a different place, totally lacking in some periods but at others an essential ingredient of the current mode. Each time it selects a different part of the body as proper for exhibition or concealment, and what passes without comment in one country or period is considered indecent in another."[2,p.26]

The ancient Egyptian's ideal of female beauty was exemplified by Nefertiti, the mother-in-law of the famous Tutankhamen. The qualities she possessed then are equally admired today. A professional plastic surgery society whose members specialize in aesthetic surgery today use her profile as the central theme of the society's logo. However, between the time of Nefertiti (2500 BC) and today, history has recorded that in all cultures almost any imaginable variation in the shape of the human body has been touted as the most desirable.

Even before Egypt and its pharoahs, the Etruscans bequeathed us body forms whose standards are similar to those of today. In a tile mosaic from the Piazza Amerini Villa, Sicily, of third to fourth century AD, a svelte young girl wearing the equivalent of today's bikini swimsuit is depicted as competing in games.[1]

Without the capability of surgical alteration, the measures employed to alter body form were many, varied, and often bizarre. Ancient or primitive cultures made distortions of the anatomy the norm of the culture. The lips of the Ubangi African were expanded by discs until they became huge and rounded. To the Mangaians of Polynesia, the sexuality of women was the shape of their genitals. The width of the pelvis was once the criterion of value for the woman. Understanding primitive humans' need for survival and reproduction, such a standard becomes less bizarre.

How an individual regards himself as a physical entity is a product of the many forces around the individual. This regard is formed essentially by the family social structure into which the baby is born and in which the child is reared.

The rank of individuals wearing certain articles was accentuated by making them of different colors. One of the less popular ideas of why clothing was developed and worn was that feelings of inferiority had to be overcome, kinship with the animal world covered, and a juxtaposition with the world of gods reinforced. Modesty was not the reason for clothes but, contrarily, the elevation of one's own self-image. In some countries only prostitutes go completely clothed.[2] Modesty came later with the development of more complex social and religious forms. In today's world, modesty may have become the main or at least one of the major modifiers of clothing.

The ebb and flow of any society's cultural attitudes creates a similar fluctuation in morality standards, as well as in personal attitudes toward body shape and activity. Early Christianity separated the opposed body from soul. As the complexities of religious doctrine built a hatred of the body, usually a similar attitude developed toward women. Shame or modesty was so intensified that women and their bodies were degraded. At one time, even dyeing clothes to give them various colors was considered sinful. Primitive tribes in various places in the world even today impart to various parts of the body social significance that differs markedly from the average Eurasian cultures.

For many centuries before the mid-1880s, it was assumed, particularly in Western civilization, that the chief reason for clothing was modesty. On almost the same level was the belief that humans began to wear clothes to cover their bodies from the elements.

Today there are tribes in cold climates who wear no clothes and desert tribes such as the bedouins who wear relatively large quantities of clothing in the face of intense heat. The implication is that neither heat nor cold created the need for clothing. Therefore we must assume that either or both a religious or decorative function was the responsible force. This is amplified when we learn that in history body painting, along with its two counterparts, body scarification and/or tattooing, preceded the use of clothing. The wearing of amulets or jewelry made of animal teeth by primitive tribes amplifies this judgment. Of course, vanity and the enhancement of social status contributed to the formation and use of clothing, allowing for repeated use without the time consumed in reproducing the painting process or the discomfort of tattooing and scarification.

The more primitive our ancestors, the less logic and reason existed for many aspects of day-to-day living. So much was not understood in ancient times that existence was dominated by general thinking primarily about survival, witchcraft, magic, and spirit worship. Survival of the species was the central core of living, and sexual matters were most important. Sterility was a condition to be feared, and all things implied to be sexually enhancing were used, worn, and even stolen when possible to be admired and worshiped. Even today the emotional needs of all persons have a strong sexual basis, which is imparted to the individual's appraisal of self and body form.

CLOTHING

Historians generally ignore both dress and body contour, preferring to discuss architecture, literature, art, and sculpture. Costume and body image go hand in hand and often reflect the political, religious, and social attitudes of both the time and a particular culture. Often these decorations disguise physical deformity. The baldness of Queen Elizabeth's red hair was covered by one of 80 wigs, which passed the fashion of wigs on to her court. Until the paintings of Diego Velázquez brought understanding of and insight into the painting of the deformed and dwarfed, most small people were disguised as clowns or children. To discuss body image without discussing dress is historically bad manners and incompletely addressing a complex subject.

There were times when many items of dress were initiated for reasons of modesty or decency, but changing attitudes allowed people to use items for sexually highlighting a particular area. The best example of such efforts is the codpiece worn in the 1500s and 1600s.

Text continued on p. 12.

3

Idealized body form in the ancient world

Mesopotamian
3000 BC

Mesopotamian
1900 BC

Egyptian
1900 BC

Egyptian
1900 BC

Egyptian
1800 BC

Minoan
1800 BC

Greek
Fourth century BC

Mycenaean
1800 BC

Assyrian
600 BC

Ancient Greek

Greek and
Etruscan

Ancient
Greek

Greek and
Roman

300 to 1500 AD

Byzantine
300

Early Christian
400

Byzantine
500

German
1000

Flemish
1100

Spanish
1200

English
1310

Italian
1300

Italian
1400
(Note doublet and codpiece)

French
1400

Mayan
1500

American Indian
(Florida)
(Note tatooing)

1500 to 1700 AD

French
1500

English
1515
(Note codpiece)

Flemish
1520

Spanish
1520

English
1520

Spanish
1521

Italian
1530

American
Pilgrim
1600

English
1536

French
1530 to 1630

French
1625

American
Puritan
1625

French
1675

1700 to 1850 AD

Scottish
1700

French
1740 to 1770
(Note hooped slip)

French
1762

French
1770

French
1780

English
1780

French
1800

French
1798

French
1814

English
1820

French
1850

Bloomers
1851

Bloomers
1853

English
1853

1850 to 1900 AD

Italian
1850

French
1855

Bloomers
1855

1867 to 1900

1870

1875

1876
"Bustle"

Bathing suit

French
1880

Yachting
1886

Hunting
1887

Bicycling
1890

Tennis
1895

1900 to 1950 AD

1900

1905

1910

1912

1920

World War I

1919

1920

1926

1930

1945

1948

1954

1950 to present

1953

1956

1957
Navy

1958
Sack

1960
Mini

1964

1978

Contemporary

Jeans

1979

1979
Contemporary

Traditional dress

Iran

Vietnam

Spain

India

Japan

Ethiopia

Russia

Austria-Germany

Balearic islands

Philippines

Norway

China

Hawaii

Algeria

Poland

Throughout history, the appearance of women has been of far more interest than that of men. In various cultures at various times male appearance and dress became more important, but these episodes are few in relation to those of the woman.

The beauty of women seems to be a complexity of varying factors of size and shape such as the mouth, hair, eyes, neck, breasts, waist, thighs and buttocks, legs, and finally the feet.

The eyes and neck preoccupied the Egyptians, whereas the breasts intrigued the ancient Syrians; tiny waists, the Minoans; and smiles, the Etruscans. Greek women had firm feet, whereas Chinese bound the feet of their women to make them tiny. Statues of the women of ancient Crete exposed bare breasts. Extraordinary coiffures characterized fashionable Rome. S-shaped figures, large stomachs, tiny breasts, and large feet were fashionable in the fifteenth century. The Renaissance replaced the ripe mature figure with angular grace and the body lines of the young. Walter Plunkett designed for the role of Catherine de Medici in the recent movie *Diane* a costume in which the skirt had a 17-inch waist. In the court of Henry VIII, women wore headgear that covered both hair and ears, as exemplified in the art of Holbein. Dressmakers of the Elizabethan era designed dresses to highlight and frame the face and neck. Titian and Tintoretto painted large-limbed, full-breasted, broad-shouldered women, accentuating roundness and fullness of form that was so desired in the sixteenth and seventeenth centuries.

In the eighteenth century, women who were petite, corseted, and coquettish became the models of the day. Long flowing hair reached its zenith as an object of beauty as best exemplified by Winterhalter's portrait of Empress Elizabeth of Austria.[2] The bustle beneath dresses accentuated the buttock area at the beginning of the 1900s. Small waists, sleek shoulders, and fine bosoms with the lower body completely covered then became the mode. Tennis was played in long skirts. Just before World War I, a breakdown of moral restraint resulted in the exposure of legs, thighs, and breasts. This trend also brought to the fore the similarity in dress between the sexes, especially in areas like Berlin, as portrayed in the famous musical, *Cabaret*. Painted faces, sleek hair, flat chests, and frilly see-through dresses accompanied the jazz era.

Movies have had a tremendous impact on the present-day wearing apparel of women. In a sense, they have also tended to confuse the fashion world and its trends. The ancient, medieval, Renaissance, and Victorian eras are all now revealed to the public simultaneously through films, resulting in the wide variety of nondefinable costumes seen. The onset of television even further accelerated the process. Fashion trends today change at a progressively rapid pace. The lack of strong religious restraints as well as breakdown in national feeling tends to eliminate costume standardization and regional conformity. Only in strong regionalistic areas such as the Alpine regions of Switzerland, Austria, and Germany are clothes distinctive and relatively unchanging. In cities the world over, people are dressed alike to some degree.

Sexual attraction is a force in which a body structure and the clothes worn are intimately conjoined. Of course, it is recognized historically that limitation of materials and untoward climatic conditions are natural modifiers and restraining influences. Nudity and its acceptance have not necessarily been related to sexuality, neither by far are the standards of contour similar. The sexual application to dress may also be one of disguise or rejection of one's own sex.

Even in the Bible, a certain mystical power is given to hair, as exemplified by the story of Samson and Delilah. This belief may have come from the so-called power of hair to grow even after death. Fraternization of the women of a country with its enemies has often led to the cutting off of their hair as a symbol of degradation. Covering of the head by women in church and of the church was meant to prevent desire of these women by men. However, in some areas of the world today, women wear headgear at all times to cover baldness resulting from malnutrition, the aftermath of World War II.

The changing hairstyles have also allowed women to cut their hair short to attain the gamin or boyish look. Carrying that further, women have styled not only their hair but their clothing to underline equality with men. Conversely some men now style their hair in the current fashions of women.

Forms similar to shawls or cloaks existed as the earliest clothing until a bone, wood, or stone needle was created primarily to shape or fix pieces of animal hide together. This development seems to date back to the era known as the Upper Paleolithic period. Until the fourteenth century, simple moccasins, tunics, pants, and capes constituted the primary kinds of clothing. Even the sophisticated Egyptians from 3000 BC wore essentially the same type of clothing for many centuries. Exposure of the body apparently had much less stigma attached to it then. Breasts were often exposed, and many activities were conducted with a minimum of cloth covering.

Examples of modern dress in various areas of the Western world where the female breast is highlighted are the dirndls of the Austrian and German Alps, as well as current braless, deep-cleft blouses of today's haute couturieres.

Throughout history, the artist has given culture a look at what was most desired at the time: from the tomb of Tutankhamen, Nefertiti and her long graceful neck and facial beauty; from the middle of the fifteenth century, the same striking features are seen in Rogier van der Weyden's *Portrait of a Woman*.

The so-called Greek period (Hellenic) costume differed from its predecessors in that the entire body was covered. This is not to imply that nudity was unacceptable. In the early days of Athens and Rome, the costumes of both men and women were essentially similar. In the so-called Dark Ages, the more primitive tribes (Teutons, Goths, Huns) that defeated and followed the Romans also wore the simplest of costumes. Beginning in the fourteenth century, women began to use clothes to attract and influence men. Exposure of the bosom, the use of corsetlike lacing to emphasize the waist, and the use of various hairstyles and hair coverings were mechanisms of the change in emphasis. These costume usages were essentially restricted to the well-to-do and royalty.

As time passed, changes occurred in men's attire to include items previously worn by women and vice versa. In the sixteenth century, hose was developed and worn by men. This hose led to today's stockings and panty hose for women; likewise, men's doublets became women's blouses of today.

The one costume variation of women that never seemed to be used by men was that of distending a portion of dress by so-called hoops. Hooped skirts eventually reached a diameter of 18 feet. The hoop almost disappeared by the end of the eighteenth century, being replaced by pads or cushions attached to the hips and back. At the same time, the change from the fancy costumery of the French court was described as a trend back to nature. At that time fashionable women had dresses in which the bodice was cut very low, and dresses were often split up the sides, exposing either flesh-colored tights or the skin itself. Sometimes the material of the dress was so diaphanous that it was practically transparent.

The nineteenth century introduced prudery as a reaction to the era of exposure: long sleeves, high necklines, and multiple petticoats appeared. However, by the 1840s the necklines again began to drop, exposing shoulders, and the hooped skirt came back into vogue.

Exposure of legs and the use of divided skirts or pantaloon types of costumes by women has sometimes been blamed on the bicycle. Apparently, Mrs. Bloomer made her contribution to the history of costume about the middle of the nineteenth century. The narrow waist and the mutton sleeve found their niche in the Victorian era. Very short skirts with resultant exposure of women's legs occurred in the 1920s during the so-called flapper era. This trend for exposure continued until the 1960s, when Rudy Gernreich, a designer of women's clothes, revealed the completely transparent blouse. Today's minibikini swimsuit provides approximately total body exposure, but nude beaches and camps eliminate even the most meager gestures toward body costume.

In this modern age we see the tremendous impact of television on the standards of body proportion and dress. Earlier it was the movies, and before that the "live" theater. Because of almost worldwide instant communication today, changes in mores and dress happen much more rapidly than in the past. In the relatively modest, almost Victorian Soviet Union, blue jeans have become a fad and are increasingly desired by the younger age group. The stolid, thick-limbed picture of the Russian peasants who tilled the land and required bodies structured for labor is no longer the norm, having been replaced by the slimmer, more graceful figure of athletic types who can wear blue jeans.

The economic status of the environment is often reflected in the dress of the people. Often the more flamboyant the dress of those in "high places," the greater the stress of the majority. Corpulent bodies covered with furs, lace, and jewels often mean that hunger and poverty are the lot of the multitude. Prosperity tends to decrease the need for ostentation in clothes and to increase the desire for a slim figure. When disease, starvation, and tragedy are rampant, the hardy woman and the rugged man are the desired types if the family is to survive. So it has been since time began. Humans have a great subliminal urge to ensure their survival.

If we believe Francis Bacon in his Essays XLIII of Beauty, then "there is no excellent beauty that hath not some strangeness in the proportion." Clothes became a most important adjunct to modifying body image to current standards, that is, until plastic surgery offered a more permanent remedy to physical aberration. We can add to or take away. What we add can sometimes be the patient's own tissue from other areas or foreign material such as silicone. What we take away can sometimes be transferred to other areas to meet current standards of proportion or simply be discarded.

The success of such endeavors is not always predictable, but on the whole the relative number of successful surgeries is much greater than that of the failures.

BODY TATTOOING, SCARIFICATION, AND PAINTING

As we continue to try to understand the need for, the problems of, and the intricate nuances of the basis for body image, we make many nonfactual assumptions about areas other than cosmetic surgery. Our preconceived ideas are often incorrect. Among these misconceptions certainly is the realm of painting, tattooing, and scarification of the body. Probably body painting was the first attempt to cover or clothe the human body. Forms of body image change existed for thousands of years preceding the relatively narrow confines of the 6,000 years or so of recorded history. In all primitive cultures, body tatooing, painting, and scarification have been used. To identify and classify the motivation for these procedures would require an extremely large volume, which would discuss individually the multiple cultures, areas, and subcultures that exist and have existed throughout the world. The techniques and the practices of all three methods of body marking seem to have followed the migration of various cultural groups as they wandered over the earth in the dim history of the past. The basis for this assumption is the similarity of the various forms that body marking takes. The significance of body scarification, tattooing, and painting in each separate culture or subculture and area is or should be regarded as a constantly changing entity. Some practices began having religious significance, and some authors believe that a great connection exists between body marking and sexual impulse.

Certainly tattooing may be regarded as a good measure of sexual attraction. This concept is emphasized when one realizes that the more sophisticated the ability to produce such items as clothing and jewelry, the less evident is body marking. Numerous cases have been recorded of prostitutes with bizarre subjects tattooed on their bodies that were designed to increase the commercial aspect of their profession. The usual sites on extremities were traded for an area near the genital region, particularly the anterior abdomen, which emphasizes the importance of tattooing as a means of expressing emotion. Emotional immaturity has often been brought out as the hallmark of those being tattooed. The practices of painting, scarification, and tattooing are coexistent and coextensive.

Great doubts existed in the mind of the primitive person regarding survival of self and that of family and species. The correlation between tattooing and sexual significance, along with the mysteries of life, death, and birth, is very important. In the Pacific area, the influence of the missionaries was tremendous; alteration in the rituals associated with tattooing occurred that changed markedly with the presence of the missionaries. In addition, other rituals associated with puberty and marriage changed. One of the more impressive areas of tattooing was in New Zealand where the Maori practiced the art in an extensive manner, particularly in the late 1700s and early 1800s, when fine specimens of the tattooed skin of bodies and faces of the dead were extremely popular in European museums. In their eagerness to transact business, the Maori often did a great deal of both scarification and body-puncture tattooing of unmarked individuals even after death. This procedure had essentially no religious significance.

The term *tattoo* was not the common term given to their body pigmentation by the Maori; rather it was and is known as *moko*.[3] The Maori *moko* was analogous to European heraldry, with the difference that *moko* attested to the merits of the individual wearing *moko* and not to the merits of ancestors. Early historians have said that *moko* lines were blue or black in color. However, some examples in early photographs appear to be green or green-blue. Generally the whole face, buttocks, and thighs were the only areas with *moko*, but exceptions occurred in women. Tattooing occurred in most Pacific areas, but designs varied. The chisels used were usually bird-wing bone with serrations; however, stone or jade was used occasionally. The grooves or serrations held the dye. Soot, the primary dye, was mixed with shark liver oil. Vegetable dye was used at times, as was dog's fat with which to mix it. Two sets of iron chisels are displayed at the New Zealand National Museum, but these we believe to be rare.[5]

South Americans tattooed extensively, with the types of procedures varying among the many diverse areas and cultures, as would be anticipated. One of the main purposes of investigating the history of tattooing is to understand what the primitive person really wanted from the tattoo.

A great amount of interest remains in this practice; body marking apparently is a laborious copying process that is transmitted from culture to culture. Tattooing among the Haida and Thompson Indians of British Columbia was quite extensive and complex. Tattooing on the trunk was confined to men, but both men and women were tattooed on their extremities and faces. The needles originally used were from bone, cactus spines, or porcupine quills, and the pigment was powdered charcoal. The tattooing was designed to make the young courageous.[4]

In the past the color had considerable significance. Black apparently signified evil or death, whereas red had the opposite meaning. Much of body painting was ornamental, but religion also played an important part. Precise significance of particular designs has long since passed into oblivion.[3]

Very few tribes with primitive cultures have older individuals who can relate the significance of their particular tattoos. Therefore many ethnologists believe that the significance we currently attach to the origin and derivation of many of the tattoos may be unreliable. Another factor that somewhat confuses our comprehension of the significance of tattoos is the fact that many of the primitive tribes actually do not understand all of the present religious rite and rituals of their own culture and their significance to the individuals involved. In some instances, evidence exists that tattooing was used as a form of passport, particularly of one primitive tribe traveling through the land of another primitive tribe, which indicates friendliness or perhaps the opposite. It is interesting that the Haidas, whose home was about 500 miles north of Vancouver Island, traveled as far as Mexico and South America by canoe.

Although the influence of missionaries of the European civilization on a particular pagan culture tended to reduce and change the body-marking procedure, there are instances, for example, in which some of the Eurasians of the Malabar Coast who have been exposed to the Roman Catholic religion have a bird tattooed on the forearm as a symbol of the Holy Ghost. Serbians and others are often tattooed with the sign of the cross. Certainly, in the earlier cultures, the marking of individuals in some manner was used as a form of punishment.

As cultures have intermingled and passed from one generation to another, the importance and sequence of their rituals have changed tremendously. The rituals were often a form of punishment or a mechanism to maintain one's own social or class benefit or as a designation of one's higher and higher class. Because the primary purpose of this aspect of the text is to clarify the reasons for and the place of body marking in the realm of body image, the technique itself is only briefly mentioned. Historically, the actual mechanism of ancient body tattooing is poorly known.

REFERENCES

1. Boucher, F.: 20,000 years of fashion, New York, Harry N. Abrams, Inc.
2. Garland, M.: The changing form of fashion, New York, 1970, Praeger Publishers, Inc.
3. Robley, M. G.: Moko or Maori tattooing, London, 1896, Chapman & Hall, Ltd.
4. Teit, J. A.: Tattooing and face and body painting of the Thompson Indians of British Columbia, fascimile ed., Seattle, 1972, The Shorey Book Store.
5. Webb, S.: Heavily tattooed men and women, New York, 1975, McGraw-Hill Book Co.

CHAPTER 2

Motivation for body change

A movement is occurring around the world to emphasize youthful, trim, healthy-looking bodies. Interest in athletics has intensified. A great deal of importance has been placed on "getting into shape." Interest in physical fitness is substantiated by the increase in the number of health clubs. New interest is occurring in some very old sports such as running, swimming, skiing, and indoor and outdoor tennis, along with one of the latest crazes, racquetball. Americans seem determined to get their bodies into shape at any cost.

To smoke is negative, to be overweight is unhealthy, and to grow old quietly is no longer tolerated.

In the past, after a woman married and had children, it was an accepted fact that she would probably acquire the matronly look: a little overweight, never quite getting back into shape because, after all, now she had a family, and things were different for her.

A self-awareness is sweeping across the country. Women are setting goals for their own growth and development. The woman's liberation movement calls it the rising consciousness of women. Women, motivated by newly acquired ambition, are pursuing careers, but they are faced with many obstacles in the work world. Perhaps one of the strongest is lack of self-assurance, as well as the competition that must be faced. Women now have the opportunity to make choices for themselves. They are in a position to make their own income, which allows them to take care of their own needs. The one area that a woman has control over and may change is her body.

The media are always dictating what an attractive body should look like and the positive things that will happen to one with an attractive body. Advertising has infiltrated every aspect of the literature, as well as all media. High fashion and a trim body have been made to be the key to happiness and success. To women who once had a shapely figure but have undergone childbirth or abdominal surgery, this advertising is a constant reminder that they now live with an acquired deformity. The number of persons desiring body contouring is rapidly increasing, making it evident that the need is emotional as well as physical.

The human race throughout history has tried to beautify the body. Anthropological studies on the concepts of beauty are infinite. Medicine men were part of primitive cultures, performing rituals varying from wound repair to exorcism of psychic demons. Aesthetic appearance, either through ceremonial rites or surgical procedures, was of universal importance. The course by which today's cosmesis is performed has changed radically, but the discomfort and expense that patients are willing to endure is simply fulfilling the emotional dictation of the times as did our ancestors.[2]

PROCEDURE OF STUDY

In the initial phase of our study, 50 women were interviewed postoperatively as part of a larger follow-up program of patients who have had abdominoplasties. All patients had been operated on by one of the authors (F. M. G.), and the postoperative period ranged from one to ten years, with a mean of three years. A list of structural questions was prepared for the patients, allowing them open-ended answers, not forced choices. After the "Long-Term Results of Abdominoplasty" survey was completed, the study was continued to include interviews with all patients interested in abdominoplasty.[3] Patients were seen preoperatively and were observed while in the hospital. Direct attention was given to the patients' attitudes toward and level of understanding of the surgery. It was found repeatedly that the patients heard only half of what was told to them. About 40% of the patients learned of the surgery from their obstetrician-gynecologist, whereas the remainder learned through friends. The interaction between the patients and their spouses or whoever took care of the patient was observed for the presence of emotional and physical support. Most patients were attended to by their husbands. Often it was found that husbands would agree with whatever their wives wanted without showing much enthusiasm. At times it was noted that the husbands found it difficult to watch their wives in postoperative discomfort, and it was distressing for the husbands to attend to everyday household functions.

The behavior of the patient toward office and surgical ward staff members was also regarded as useful information. These employees are in key positions to be extremely helpful to the patient. Many times the patients would share their dispositions and outlook with a staff member rather than with the physician. The patient too often places the physician on a pedestal and deliberately goes out of her way not to disappoint him by showing her own fears or anxiety.

If patients share their true feelings and fears, it is usually during the postoperative period that they feel free enough to express themselves. The preestablished relationship between the patient and interviewer allows the patient more liberty. All the questions that were never asked before the surgery are asked now. The information that the patient was too excited to hear about, such as swelling, pain, discomfort, drains, tapes, and number of days in the hospital, are often re-asked. It is not unusual to encounter husbands or children shocked to see their loved ones bruised or swollen. All of this needs to be handled delicately. The best a physician may offer is to continue to go over the information and to realize that the patient will not really hear the answers until the surgery is completed. Reassurance from the physician is imperative.

SPECIFIC GROUP CHARACTERISTICS

The study group consisted of 128 patients with the following characteristics:

Age (years)	Average	39
	Range	23 to 73
Marital status	Married	101
	Divorced	17
	Single	5
	Widowed	5
Average number of children*		2
Employment	Homemakers	78
	Employed outside home	50

At the time of the surgery 40 women could be considered to be within normal range of weight for height and body build, 83 were 5 to 20 pounds overweight, and 5 were greater than 20 pounds above the desired weight.

If patients are putting on weight around the time of their consultation, it is often a cue that they are encountering extreme emotional problems. The consultation becomes an important time to discover patients' specific expectations.

At the time of the abdominoplasty 95 patients had combined procedures. Of these, 58 had additional cosmetic surgery; 8, face-lift; 12, blepharoplasty; 2, rhinoplasty; 30, augmentation mammaplasty; and 6, breast-reduction. The surgical needs were 20 vaginal hysterectomies, 3 bladder repairs, 7 tubal ligations, and 7 abdominal hysterectomies.

One patient who had a breast reduction and an abdominoplasty became pregnant a year later and delivered a healthy son. Her abdomen stretched, the plication appeared weak, and some ptosis of her breasts occurred as results of the pregnancy. She underwent an abdominal wall revision and revision of the breasts, obtaining excellent results.

Attitudes toward the abdomen

The patients identified their abdomen as an acquired deformity. All patients showed a tremendous dislike for their abdominal area and thought it had emotionally affected their self-image.

During the follow-up interview, these women retrospectively defined the following reasons for having surgery: a recent life change was about to take place; they were experiencing a period of transition; or perhaps a sense of inadequacy or loss of self-esteem was building up inside them. In general they appeared to be satisfied with life-style situations; they placed the focus of their concern on the abdomen while the life changes were taking place. Divorce, widowhood, a recent move (a move into southern California would place a great deal more emphasis on body image), the husband's change in job, and in-

---

*Of the 128 women, 13 had no children.

crease in income, children leaving home, or a new love relationship beginning are all underlying motivations for body contouring. (These reasons could also be applied to women seeking thighplasty.)

Some patients in the study had placed themselves on a rugged exercise and diet program, but problems with striae and diastasis remained. Swimsuits, normal year-round attire in southern California, also became an emotional concern. Sexual relationships often became hampered because of the patient's embarrassment about her unshapely abdomen, which lead to depression and a sense of inadequacy.

A great many patients seeking surgery have unrealistic expectations. They never fully accept the acquired deformity and fantasize that the plastic surgeon has a kind of magic that will restore them to their natural state. (Some patients actually believe that the plastic surgery will leave no scar). Unless the patient grasps precisely what the surgery will entail, a buildup of resentment and displeasure is likely to erupt.[5]

Attitudes toward the interview

The initial response from the patients who were invited to come in and talk about their surgery was a willingness to be helpful. If patients came in on the long-term survey, they were happy to share their past experiences.

Preoperative patients thought that the interview was helpful. It gave them another avenue for reassurance and guidance. It also allowed them to ask questions that they would not have asked the physician. The counselor met the patient on the first day of consultation, letting the patient know that someone was there to answer any additional questions. The patient was seen again by the counselor on each office visit, as well as during the postoperative period in the hospital. These times together build up a level of trust for the patient and allow the counselor to obtain important messages from the patient.

Attitudes toward the operation

At the time of the consultation, the patient is usually so highly motivated to have an elective surgery that it seems she has made up her mind before she has even come into the office to have the surgery. Once she finds out something can be done, she perpetuates in total blind trust, surrendering herself completely and putting the physician in charge. The interview reveals that the patient has no fear of the risks that she is taking with her healthy body. The term "tummy tuck," which is frequently used by women's magazines, becomes implanted in the patient's mind and gives her the illusion that the surgery is a minor one. If the patient is having a thighplasty, she wants to look good in clothes and does not care about the scars. The idea of complications or death rarely occurs to any patient. In the study each patient was given the option to view the actual operative technique in the *Operation Bikini* movie.[4] After the film was viewed, the patients were found to have total dependence on the physician, whom they believed to be infallible.

Postoperative attitudes and conditions

The long-term patients had a great deal of information to offer in terms of what conditions their bodies were in, whereas the more recent patients had more to say of their emotional states. Long-term patients usually found that the scar had faded into a white line and that the abdomen was still firm. Any weight gained seemed to stay immediately above the suture line; some patients were still experiencing numbness in the midline section, and they felt better in clothes and bikinis. Patients who had had this surgery many years ago were not able to recapture their emotions of that time. Some made it sound effortless, forgetting the time of the postoperative depression and anxieties. They had little recall of the discomfort once experienced. The mind has the wonderful property of allowing one to forget pain.

Recent patients remembered postsurgical details more on an emotional level than did long-term patients. Almost everyone experienced postoperative despondency and needed understanding and reassurance from the family and nursing staff. The plaster splint and the drains came as a surprise to some patients, although they had been informed of their use preoperatively. Some found walking and getting around more restrained than they had anticipated. Many patients concerned themselves with the swelling and continually needed to be reassured that it would go away.

DISCUSSION

A surgeon knows neither exactly how the patient really feels, nor the impact of the patient's childhood experiences and attitudes formulated over the years. One thing is certain: the patient who is having abdominoplasty is not having the surgery because of childhood persecution.

The patient looks at the abdomen as an acquired deformity. The body change that takes place after childbirth is a common line to every woman regardless of the part of the world she is from. This thread runs through all patients who seek abdominoplasty. After having children, a woman must experience the body change whether or not she wants to. For years it was believed that a woman who had children or an abdominal surgical procedure had to live with the striae and diastasis with which she was left. Often the result is certainly not what she bargained for when she decided to have a family. It is important to understand that the psychological reasoning of someone who has chosen to have an abdominoplasty is different from that of those seeking other cosmetic surgeries. A fair amount has been researched on the psychological makeup of patients choosing to undergo a rhinoplasty, a rhytidectomy, or augmentation mammaplasty.

Three basic methods of understanding women requesting rhinoplasty involve conscious, preconscious, and unconscious factors. Consciously women desire beauty, needing to be recognized as being attractive and wishing to change cultural stereotyping. Preconscious awareness has been observed, a letting go of previous rigid, restrictive attitudes toward being female. Finally the unconscious begins to unlock, and a socially active, participating woman begins to emerge.[6]

The emotional trauma of the aging process usually surfaces as a women reaches her fifties. It is a time of great concern for the patient. She resents aging. Having a tremendous need to change herself, often she looks to her plastic surgeon for help.[1]

Augmentation mammaplasty stems from the desire to have physically acceptable breasts. Present-day beauty standards place nicely formed breasts high on the list and are thought of as a mark of beauty by many men. It is no wonder that many women who have the opportunity to change the size of their breasts will not hesitate to have an augmentation.

At the same time, it is not surprising that a woman who is willing to change the upper part of her body will, given the opportunity, change the bottom half as well.

The image of oneself must be a total overall view. The extent of what one will do and just how much one will subject oneself is fascinating.

Candidates seeking thighplasty or brachioplasty are limited in number. Thighplasty patients may be motivated by many factors. Generally their motivation stems from a tremendous weight loss, from which the skin loses all its elasticity, or from a great desire to look good in clothes. For women who have the "riding britches" syndrome, no amount of self-maintenance will help. The patients who were interviewed believed they had reached a point at which they wanted very much to change their appearance. The resulting scars did not seem to matter, as long as the look was satisfying in clothes.

One patient wrote her reactions right after the surgery:

> When the doctor and nurse helped me to stand up, I looked into the mirror to see the reflection of my profile. I couldn't believe it, the image staring back was really me. I tried hard to fight back tears of excitement and joy. My reaction was happiness . . . ; all the pain was worth that one lone anticipated glance that flashed back at me in the mirror.

Usually age or a tremendous weight loss dictates the reason for wanting arm surgery. The number of patients interviewed for this surgery was limited; the resultant scars are an obstacle in brachioplasty. One patient who plays golf finds the scar hampering. Although she knew exactly where the scar was to be placed, she did not think it would really show. Understanding patients' expectations cannot be stressed enough.

Most patients feel so self-conscious about their appearance that they will spend a tremendous amount of time and money putting themselves through a major surgery so they can feel better about themselves. Trading the excess skin for an incredible scar seems to be a reasonable tradeoff.

It is extremely important that the physician give patients positive verbal feedback to help them formulate a sound attitude about themselves and their choice of surgery. It is essential that the physician build a level of trust with the patients. The communication is an intricate part of a successful surgery and a happy patient. Every patient has a story; it is helpful if the physician encourages patients to talk, allowing them to express their motivations and especially their expectations. An alert physician will watch for messages from the patient: the way in which the patient sits and moves, facial and postural shifts, expressions, shrugs, gestures, voice pitches, emotional overtones or inflections, rapidity of speech, stuttering, sighs, pauses, or yawns. The best results for effective communication and trust start with the initial interview, which, aside from the actual surgery, is the most important time.

Two techniques have become useful tools for both patients and physicians. First, the surgeon marks the site of the incision on the patient and then asks her to go home with the lines left on her body to allow her to see just where the scars will be after the surgery. The patient is encouraged to try on a bikini and to be sure to show her husband where the scar will be so that he too can have a better understanding of what the results will entail.

The second useful approach in dealing with the patient is to allow the patient to bring her husband or very close friend to the second consultation. Good friends will listen, especially if they are the ones who will be taking care of the patient postoperatively. Often it is they who remember what is going to take place, not the patient. Patients have stated postoperatively that they were grateful to have someone who knew what to do because they could not remember.

Although the discussion and interviews were directed at women, many of the motivating forces for such procedures are the same for men.

SUMMARY

The examination of patients' psychological aspects is as vital as that of their physical defects. Surgeons must always keep in perspective their own biases and the true needs of the patients. When a crippling psychological handicap becomes apparent, the plastic surgeon should not hesitate to use psychosocial services. Regardless of the plastic surgeon's awareness and skill, the physician has no choice but to stay within the boundaries of the patient's age, skin texture, physical structure, and general health. However, with effective communication the plastic surgeon has the power to allow the patient a positive surgical experience.

REFERENCES

1. Edgerton, M. T., and Knorr, N. J.: Motivational patterns of patients seeking cosmetic (esthetic) surgery, Plast. Reconstr. Surg. **48:**551, 1971.
2. Gifford, S.: Cosmetic surgery and personality changes: a review and some clinical observations. In Goldwyn, The unfavorable result in plastic surgery, Boston, 1972, Little, Brown & Co.
3. Grazer, F. M., Klingbeil, J. R., and Mattiello, M.: Long-term results of abdominoplasty, Boston, 1980, Little, Brown & Co. (in press).
4. Grazer, F. M.: Operation bikini, film, Minneapolis, 1974, The Filmmakers.
5. Knorr, N. J., Hoopes, J. E., and Edgerton, M. T.: Psychiatric-surgical approach to adolescent disturbance in self image, Plast. Reconstr. Surg. **41:**248, 1968.
6. Meyer, E., and Jacobson, W. E.: Motivational patterns in patients seeking elective plastic surgery. I. Women who seek rhinoplasties, Psychosom. Med. **22:**193, 1960.
7. Sachs, B. C.: This bosom business, changing emphasis on the breasts, Med. Asp. Hum. Sex. **3**(4):49, 1969.

CHAPTER 3

Anatomical considerations

The incisions and shaping in body contour surgery are made in the skin, subcutaneous tissues, and muscular fascia. Techniques often demand extensive undermining so that excessive folds of skin and subcutaneous fat can be mobilized, trimmed, and repositioned to achieve the more pleasing contour desired by the patient. Incisions are placed inconspicuously, hidden in the briefest swimwear or concealed in skin creases or natural folds. Incisional site and length must be limited.

Aesthetic surgery of the abdomen, thighs, buttocks, and arms involves three separate systems—superficial vessels, nerves, and lymphatics—in the superficial fascia that may need to be cut or retracted to allow sculpturing of the tissues to achieve the desired body shape. The surgeon may use the underlying fascia over skeletal muscle to tighten relaxed muscles and may reduce tissues, repair fascial defects, and excise bulging accumulations so that the skin and subcutaneous tissue, when mobilized, drape into a more pleasing underlying armature.

The purpose of this chapter is to review the anatomical features of concern to the body contour surgeon in the abdomen, buttocks, thighs, and upper arm.

TOPOGRAPHICAL ANATOMY

Topographical anatomy is the cornerstone of the body contour surgeon; it is the nucleus through which all surgery begins. The surgeon must be able to see the intended surgery in relationship to the final cicatrix. It is of utmost importance that the physician be able to visualize the patient's scar without clothing as well as in clothes. The type of clothing the patient expects to wear without exposing any significant amount of scarring must be taken into consideration.

The surgeon must be aware of the current swimsuit styles with regard to incision placement. The chapters on surgical technique will relate to this. The following photographs of a patient in a string bikini (Fig. 3-1, A) in a French one-piece bathing suit (Fig. 3-1, B) would call for a different selection of incision sites. Note that the French design cut is higher by as much as 2 to 3 inches in the inguinal area.

When considering a patient for a thighplasty or buttockplasty, it is important to note that much of the lower gluteal area and infragluteal fold is exposed. No incision should mar this natural anatomical roundness (Fig. 8-1). Incision should be made above the lower aspect of the swimsuit line with enough margin to account for the eventual descent of the cicatrix (Fig. 3-2).

Other topographical anatomical considerations are shown in Figs. 3-3 to 3-7.

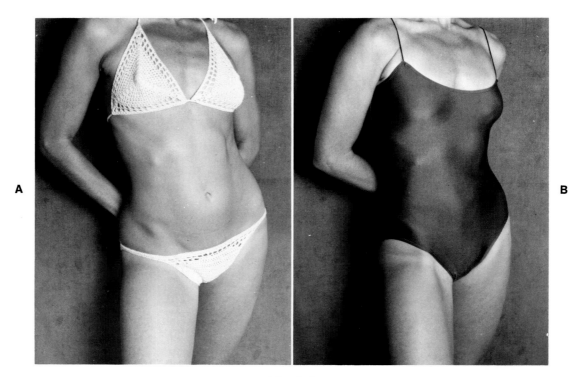

A   B

Fig. 3-1

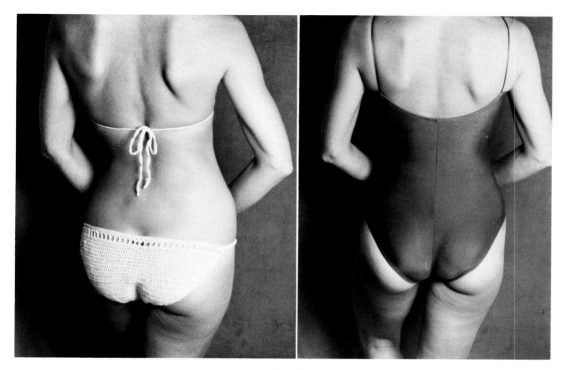

Fig. 3-2

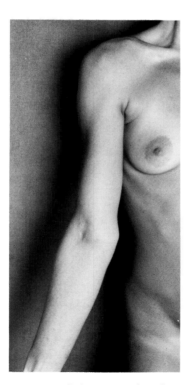

Fig. 3-3. The topographical anatomy of the arms is of utmost importance. This is the only area of body contouring not always covered by clothing. To be as inconspicuous as possible, incisions should be confined to the medial posterior aspect of the arm.

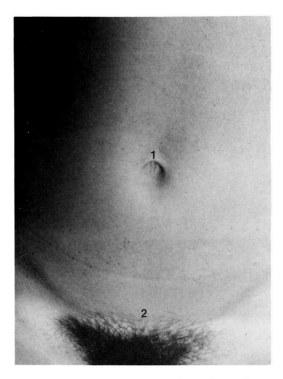

Fig. 3-4. *1,* Natural anatomical hooding effect; *2,* escutcheon.

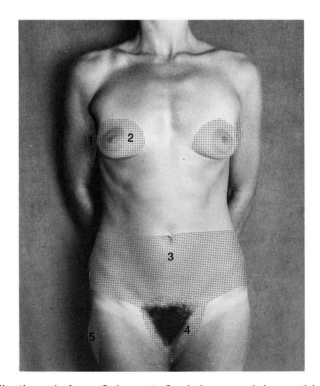

Fig. 3-5. Fat distribution. *1,* Arm; *2,* breast; *3,* abdomen; *4,* inner thigh; *5,* lateral thigh.

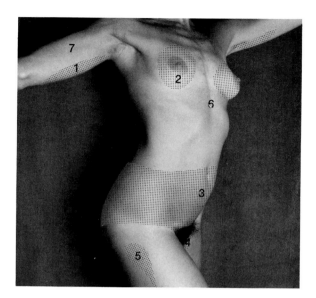

Fig. 3-6. Fat distribution: *1,* arm; *2,* breast; *3,* abdomen; *4,* inner thigh; *5,* lateral thigh. Anatomical landmarks: *6,* xiphoid; *7,* brachial sulcus.

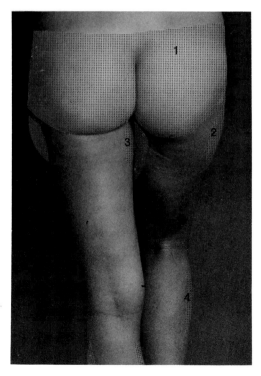

Fig. 3-7. Fat distribution of buttocks. *1* and *2,* Lateral thigh; *3,* inner thigh; *4,* calves; *5,* infragluteal fold.

INTERNAL ANATOMY
Abdominal wall
Circulation

In elevation of the abdominal panniculus, multiple bleeding points are encountered that have considerable anastomotic connections and originate from three different sources: (1) segmental perforating musculocutaneous branches of the subcostal, intercostal, and lumbar arteries; (2) superior and inferior epigastric perforators through the rectus abdominis muscular sheath; and (3) superficial branches of the femoral artery that ascend to supply the skin and subcutaneous tissue of the lower abdomen (Figs. 3-8, A, and 3-9). Fig. 3-8, B, shows the venous circulation.

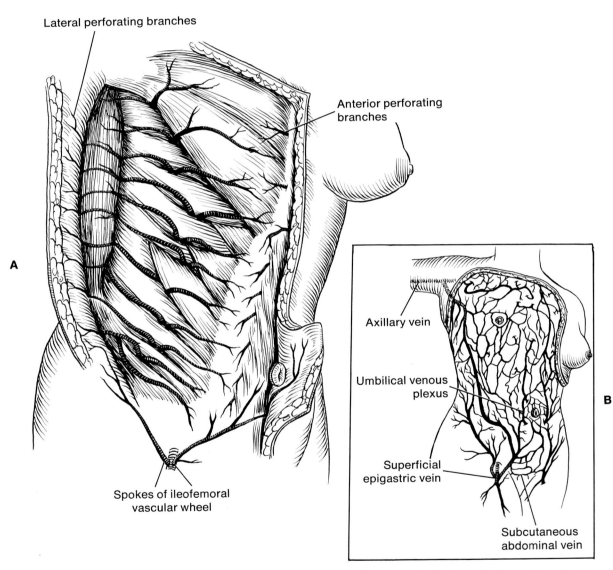

Lateral perforating branches

Anterior perforating branches

A

Spokes of ileofemoral vascular wheel

Axillary vein

Umbilical venous plexus

Superficial epigastric vein

Subcutaneous abdominal vein

B

Fig. 3-8. A, Present concept of the cutaneous vascular supply of the anterior abdominal wall. B, Superficial veins of the anterior thorax and abdomen. (A modified from Brown, R. G., Vasconez, L. O., and Jurkiewicz, M. J.: Plast. Reconstr. Surg. **55:**416, 1975; **B** modified from Pansky, B., and House, E.: Review of gross anatomy, New York, 1968, The Macmillan Co.)

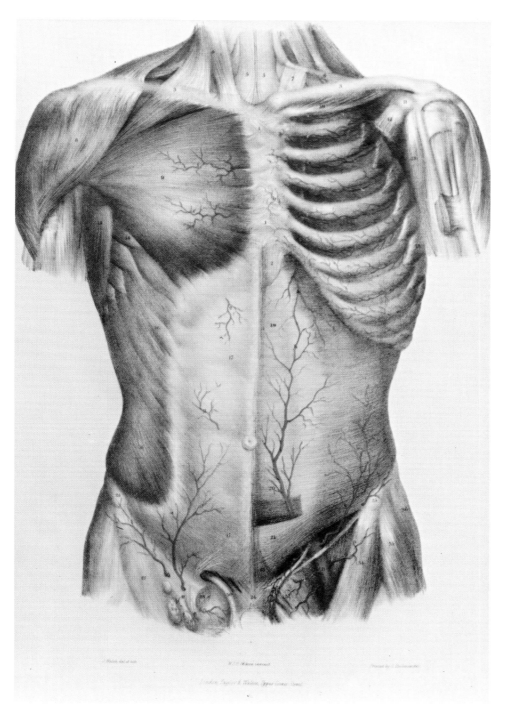

Fig. 3-9
(From Quain, J., and Wilson, W.: Vessels of the human body, New York, 1837, Appleton.)

The segmental arteries arise from the thoracic and abdominal aorta (Figs. 3-11 and 3-12) and include the previously named intercostal, subcostal, and lumbar arteries, which pass posteriorly from the aorta to eventually lie on the transverse muscle of the abdomen. These arteries form two branches, a posterior and a lateral cutaneous. The lateral branch penetrates the internal and external oblique muscles near the anterior margin of the latissimus dorsi and runs forward until it terminates by anastomosing with the perforating branches of the deep epigastric vessels, which have appeared through the rectus sheath (Fig. 3-13). The posterior branch of the intercostal artery disappears to supply skin and subcutaneous tissue on the back.

Recently Daniel, Kerrigan, and Gard[5] have outlined in detail the anatomy of these intercostal vessels. They divide the course of the intercostal vessels into vertebral, costal, intermuscular, and rectus (Fig. 3-10). The costal segment has large musculocutaneous branches; the lateral cutaneous branch pierces the intercostal musculature to travel anteriorly in the subcutaneous tissue almost to the lateral border of the rectus sheath (Fig. 3-11).

Preservation of the branch that emerges near the end of the costal margin may be difficult if extensive undermining is necessary over the costal margin or posteriorly.

Such detailed understanding of the intercostal nerves and vessels has aided in the development of large, innervated intercostal flaps based on these structures for use in torso reconstruction.[5]

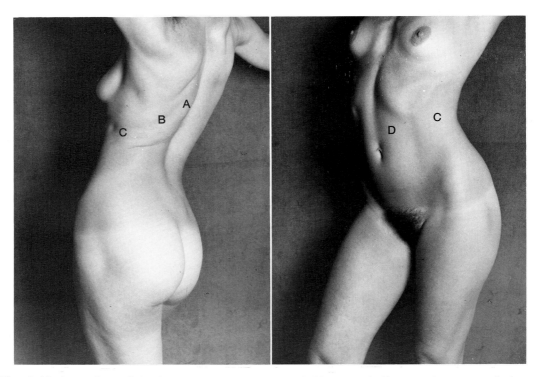

Fig. 3-10. Location of the intercostal segments. *A*, Vertebral; *B*, costal groove; *C*, intermuscular; *D*, rectus.

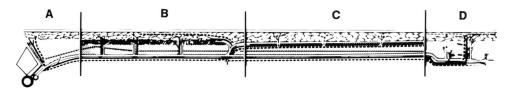

Fig. 3-11. The four intercostal segments of the intercostal neurovascular bundle. *A,* Vertebral; *B,* costal groove; *C,* intermuscular; *D,* rectus. (From Daniel, R. K., Kerrigan, C. L., and Gard, D. A.: Plast. Reconstr. Surg. **61:**653, 1978.)

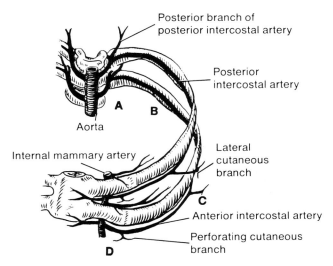

Posterior branch of posterior intercostal artery

Posterior intercostal artery

Aorta

Internal mammary artery

Lateral cutaneous branch

Anterior intercostal artery

Perforating cutaneous branch

Fig. 3-12. Oblique cross section showing the relations of the intercostal arteries to the ribs and the intercostal spaces. *A* to *D,* Intercostal segments (Fig. 3-11).

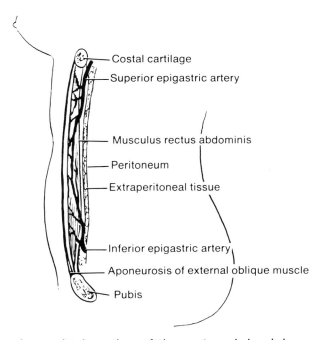

Costal cartilage

Superior epigastric artery

Musculus rectus abdominis

Peritoneum

Extraperitoneal tissue

Inferior epigastric artery

Aponeurosis of external oblique muscle

Pubis

Fig. 3-13. Diagram of a sagittal section of the rectus abdominis muscle and its blood supply.

On entering the abdomen, the internal mammary artery divides into the musculophrenic and superior epigastric vessels. The superior epigastric artery continues on into the rectus sheath, where it lies posteriorly on the posterior rectus sheath to anastomose with its fellow, the inferior epigastric artery, a branch of the femoral artery. The epigastric vessels through the rectus muscle sheath send numerous perforating musculoctuaneous vessels to supply the overlying skin (Figs. 3-12 and 3-13). The appreciation of the nature of these perforating vessels has led to extensive use of upper and lower rectus abdominis myocutaneous flaps[8] and medially based transverse abdominal flaps in difficult reconstructive procedures.[2] Elbaz has noted about 30 perforating vessels on each side.[6] The perforating vessels through the rectus abdominal sheath appear less dense below the umbilicus than above it. These perforating vessels are the main ones ligated or cauterized during abdominoplasty (Fig. 3-8).

The superficial epigastric arteries below the umbilicus pass upward from the femoral artery toward the umbilicus in the subcutaneous fat; the circumflex iliac vessels pass anterolaterally toward the anterior superior iliac spine[13] (Figs. 3-9 and 3-13). These vessels form the vascular architecture of the groin flap[12]; their detailed anatomy has been reviewed by Harii and Ohmore.[17]

The importance of the vascular supply and the danger of skin necrosis with combinations of abdominal incisions has been reviewed by Masterson[11] and Nahai et al.[14] and must be kept in mind, since the abdominoplastic surgeon so often has to dissect beneath an abdominal wall with multiple prior incisions or entertain a vertical midline incision. The venous drainage of the abdominal wall, although somewhat more variable than the arterial, retrogradely follows the arterial supply (Fig. 3-8, *B*). The superficial subcutaneous veins below the umbilicus drain through vessels that terminate in the saphenous vein beneath the inguinal ligament.

Above the umbilicus, drainage is toward the superior epigastric system within the rectus sheath and laterally to tributaries of the axillary vein, commonly the lateral thoracic vein, which enlarges as an important collateral in vena caval obstruction. The umbilical veins in the ligamentum teres offer potential for portosystemic shunting; they enlarge to form caput medusae in portal hypertension from cirrhosis of the liver (Fig. 3-8, *B*).

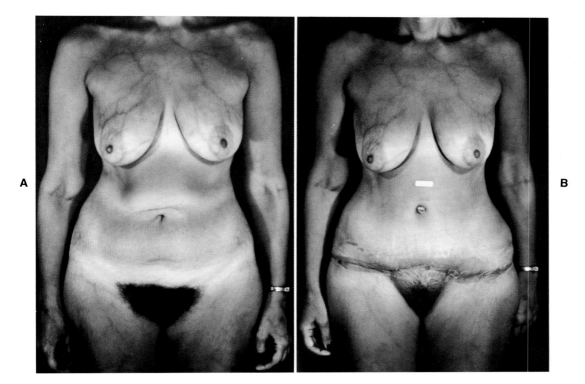

Fig. 3-14. A, Infrared photographs aid in delineation of the superficial vessels of the anterior abdominal wall. **B,** Postoperative abdominoplasty. There appears to be increased dilatation, since many of the perforating vessels have been severed.

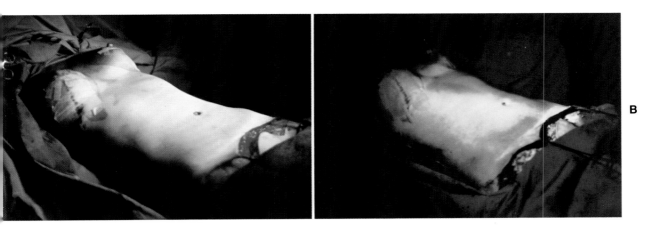

Fig. 3-15. A, Complete undermining of the abdominal panniculus, prior to fluorescein administration. **B,** Fluorescein photograph taken 15 minutes after the intravenous administration of 1 g of fluorescein, confirming the adequacy of the circulation.

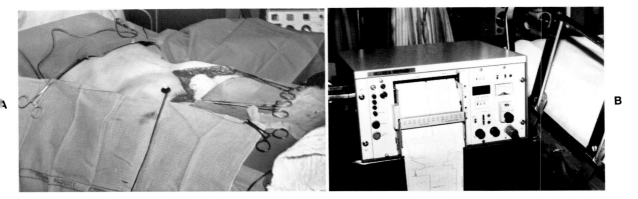

Fig. 3-16. A, Noninvasive percutaneous Po_2 monitoring is another avenue by which to confirm the adequacy of the circulation to various flaps. **B,** Litton instrument.

Superficial nerves

The cutaneous nerve supply of the abdominal wall is from the intercostal nerves (spinal segments T6 to T12) and the L1 segmental anterior nerves, the ilioinguinal and iliohypogastric (Fig. 3-17, *B*). Segmental nerves give off large lateral branches that penetrate the oblique muscles near their interdigitation with the serratus anterior muscle; these branches emerge at a lower point along the anterior border of the latissimus dorsi muscle. The lateral cutaneous branches of the last thoracic nerve and the iliohypogastric nerve descend over the iliac crest to the anterolateral aspect of the buttock. In abdominoplasties, low bikini–line incisions extended laterally, since sculpturing supratrochanteric fatty deposits may result in damage to these nerves and subsequent sensory loss over the upper lateral part of the buttock (Fig. 3-21, *A*). The remainder, T6 to T11, continue on to supply the skin anteriorly in the abdominal walls (Fig. 3-17, *B*). The anterior branches of the intercostals continue in the intermuscular plane and eventually penetrate the rectus sheath, supplying it and sending cutaneous twigs through the rectus sheath to supply sensation to the ventral midline skin. Vertical and oblique abdominal incisions may intersect these anterior rectus muscles. The lateral cutaneous nerve of the thigh (L2 to L3) is subject to injury from cautery in low lateral sculpturing incisions as it emerges through the inguinal ligament at a point that is usually close to the anterosuperior iliac spine (Fig. 3-17, *A*). Patient complaints of numbness on the lateral aspect of the thigh may be present for several months until recovery. Since the nerve is deep to the fascia, the most likely cause of damage to it is cautery conduction. After abdominoplasty, the dermatome distribution is altered[4] (Fig. 3-18, *A* and *B*).

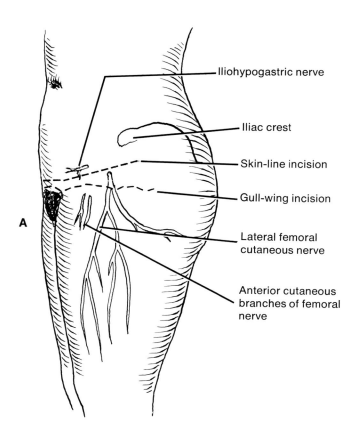

A

- Iliohypogastric nerve
- Iliac crest
- Skin-line incision
- Gull-wing incision
- Lateral femoral cutaneous nerve
- Anterior cutaneous branches of femoral nerve

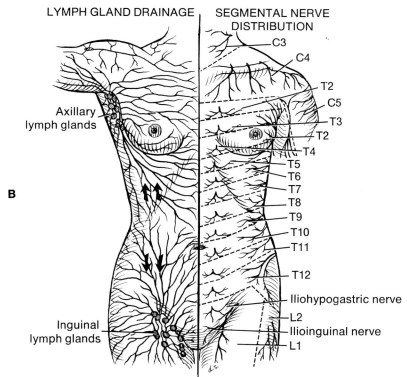

B

LYMPH GLAND DRAINAGE

SEGMENTAL NERVE DISTRIBUTION

Axillary lymph glands

Inguinal lymph glands

- C3
- C4
- T2
- C5
- T3
- T2
- T4
- T5
- T6
- T7
- T8
- T9
- T10
- T11
- T12
- Iliohypogastric nerve
- L2
- Ilioinguinal nerve
- L1

Fig. 3-17. A, Relationship of superficial nerves to abdominoplasty incisions. **B,** Anterior abdominal wall lymphatics and segmental nerves.

Lymphatics

The superficial drainage of the abdominal wall is to the axillary nodes above and below the umbilicus to the superficial inguinal nodes (Fig. 3-17, *B*). The abdominoplasty incisions sever connections to these nodes and can result in swelling of the flap inferiorly. The rerouting and reestablishment of the lymphatic drainage will usually resolve this swelling within several weeks[2] (Fig. 3-18, *C* and *D*).

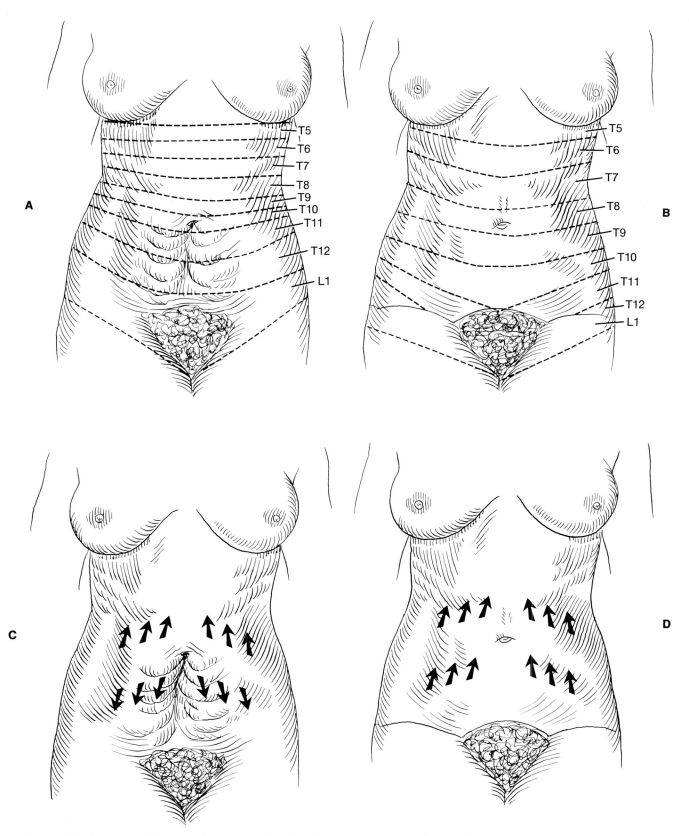

Fig. 3-18. A and **B,** Segmental nerve distribution before and after abdominoplasty. **C** and **D,** Lymphatic drainage before and after abdominoplasty. (Modified from Carvalho, C. G. S., Baroudi, R., and Keppke, E. M.: Aesthet. Plast. Surg. **1:**217, 1977.)

Superficial fascia

Two layers of fascia exist in the anterior abdominal wall (Fig. 3-19). Superficially is the fatty layer (Camper's), and deeper, a more fibrous dense fascia (Scarpa's), which fuses to the fascia lata just beneath the inguinal ligament. These two layers may not be as distinct as was once thought; what were considered two distinct layers may in fact be merely overlapping and compression of connective tissue lamellae.[8]

Some surgeons believe the deep areolar tissue layer covering the aponeurosis should not be incised[17] (Fig. 3-20).

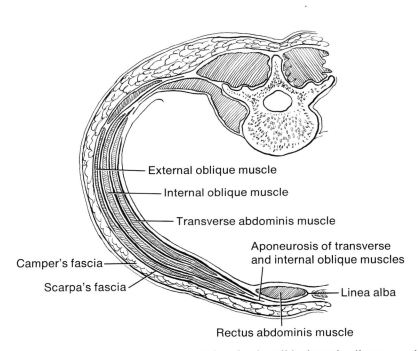

External oblique muscle

Internal oblique muscle

Transverse abdominis muscle

Aponeurosis of transverse and internal oblique muscles

Camper's fascia

Scarpa's fascia

Linea alba

Rectus abdominis muscle

Fig. 3-19. Transverse section through the abdominal wall below the linea semicircularis. (Modified from Callander, C. L.: Surgical anatomy, Philadelphia, 1939, W. B. Saunders Co.)

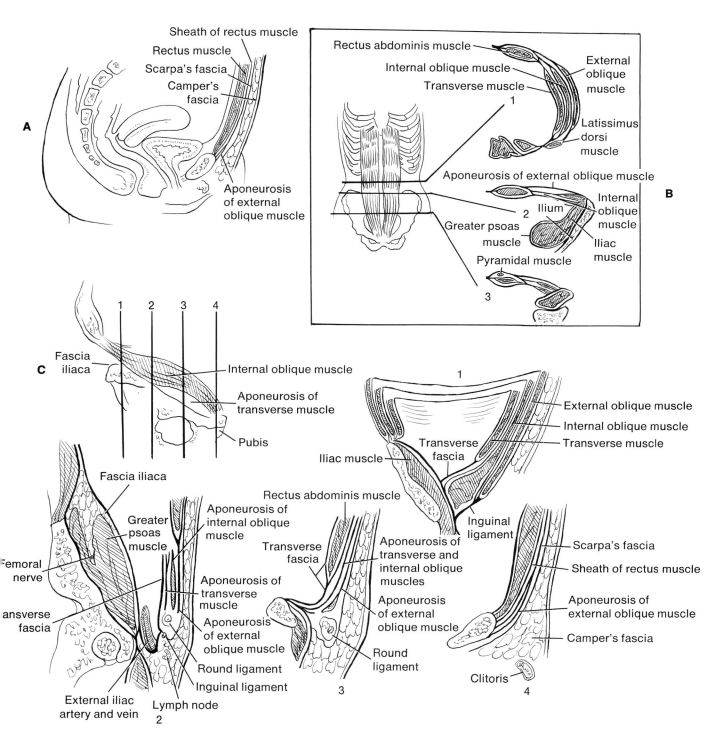

Fig. 3-20. A, Midline sagittal section with particular reference to the abdominal wall and rectus muscle. **B,** Orientation showing muscles of the anterior abdominal wall. *1* to *3,* Transverse sections. **C,** Orientation for sagittal sections through the inguinal canal and anterior abdominal wall. *1* to *4,* Sagittal sections. (Modified from Gardner, D., Grey, D., and O'Rahilly, R.: Anatomy—a regional study of human structure, Philadelphia, 1960, W. B. Saunders Co.)

Buttock and inner thigh

The blood supply to the skin and subcutaneous tissue of the buttock is derived from numerous perforating vessels that exit on the superficial surface of the muscles as described by Manchot.[11] The skin over the lower buttock and posterolateral thigh is supplied by the cutaneous branches of the descending branch of the interior gluteal artery, the cutaneous branches of the medial and lateral circumflex femoral arteries, and the first perforating branch of the deep femoral artery. Superficial venous drainage follows the arterial supply, but a major portion drains to the greater saphenous system medially (Fig. 3-21, *A*).

The cutaneous nerves in the buttock region include the superior cluneal nerves from the dorsal rami of L12 and 3 and some minor contributions in the region posterior to the anterosuperior iliac spine from the subcostal and iliohypogastric nerves (Fig. 3-21, *B*).

Medially and inferiorly, the cutaneous supply is from medial cluneal nerves from the dorsal branches of S12 and 3. Several branches from the posterior cutaneous nerves of the thigh (S12 and 3) turn upward below the gluteus maximus muscle and supply skin on the lower aspect of the buttock. Lymphatic drainage follows the vascular drainage to the inguinal nodes (Fig. 3-17, *B*).

The superficial fascia of the buttocks is loaded with fat that contributes significantly to the shape of the buttock. This fascia is continuous with the fascia of the lower back thigh and perineum. In the saddle-bag deformity a peritrochanteric fatty collection is distinct in the subcutaneous fat from any other fatty collection, which is removed in toto to correct this deformity (Fig. 3-21, *C*).

The thicker deep fascia envelops the gluteus maximus and tensor fascia lata muscles. At the gluteal crease the deep fascia sends multiple dense septae into the superficial fascia; these connections must be severed to reposition the gluteal crease (Fig. 3-21, *B*).

In the inner thigh the arterial perforators from the internal pudendal and perineal arteries are sparse. Superficial veins coursing to the saphenous system may be encountered. In this rather avascular area the superficial fascia is also thinner than in the buttock but may be sagging and loaded with fatty collections. Inner thighplasty exposes the origin of the long or adduct and gracilis muscles in this area. It is important to carefully delineate the inner upper thigh from the labia majora because incisions that are placed too high may encroach on the labia and cause introital widening after the inner thighplasty (Fig. 3-21, *D*).

Cutaneous nerves from the perineal branch of the posterior cutaneous nerve of the thigh (S12 and 3), the ilioinguinal nerve, and the genital branch of the genitofemoral (L12) nerve may be encountered in the inner thigh dissection. However, because of the abundance of sensory cross-over, sensory loss is not a problem.

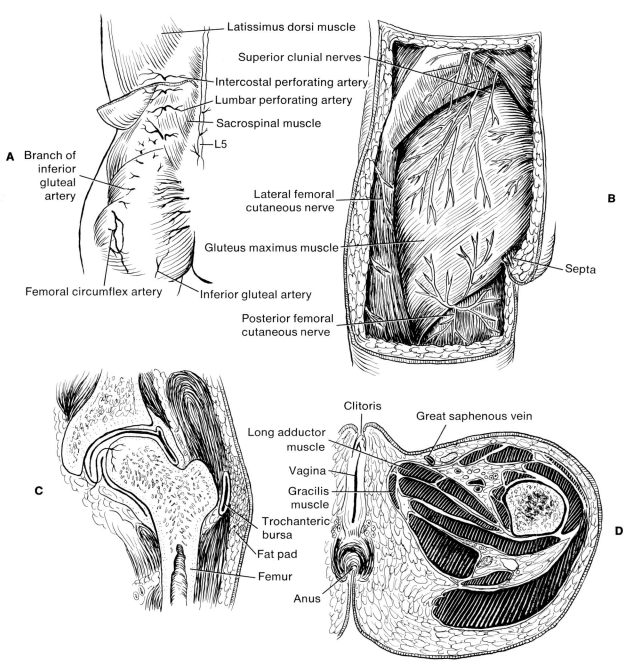

Fig. 3-21. A, Vascular supply to the lumbosacral region. **B,** Superficial structures of the gluteal and posterior region of the thigh. **C,** Frontal section through the hip showing the fat pad over the trochanteric bursa. **D,** Cross section of the upper thigh and perineum. (**A** modified from Hill, H. L., Brown, R. G., and Jurkiewicz, M. J.: Plast. Reconstr. Surg. **62:**177, 1978.)

Upper arm

The superficial fascia is often laden with fat (Fig. 3-6) in which run the cutaneous nerves and branches of the cephalic and basilic veins. The deep fascia (brachial fascia) is attached to the epicondyles of the humerus and sends medial and lateral intermuscular septae between the flexor and extensor muscles to attach to the humerus (Fig. 3-22, *B*).

Superficial veins and cutaneous nerves predominate in the region (Fig. 3-23), since there are no main named arterial branches of the brachial artery in this dissection. The cephalic vein, which passes in front of the elbow, is not seen; however, the basilic vein appears in the lower one third of the arm prior to its penetration through the brachial fascia. Care must be exercised not to injure the basilic vein. The exit of the medial antebrachial cutaneous nerves (C8 to T1) occurs at almost the same point as that of the entry of the basilic vein and is at the junction between the brachial and triceps muscles posteriorly. Many cutaneous nerves are seen in the medial aspect of the arm. The skin is supplied by the medial brachial cutaneous nerve (C8 to T1) of the arm and by numerous intercostobrachial nerves (T2 to T3). In the lower one third of the upper arm, branches of the medial antebrachial cutaneous nerve supply the skin (Fig. 3-22, *A* and *C*).

Lymphatic vessels of the medial aspect of the arm are numerous, piercing the deep fascia to terminate in the axillary nodes. The supratrochlear node is also present along the course of the basilic vein above the medial epicondyle (Fig. 3-22, *C*).

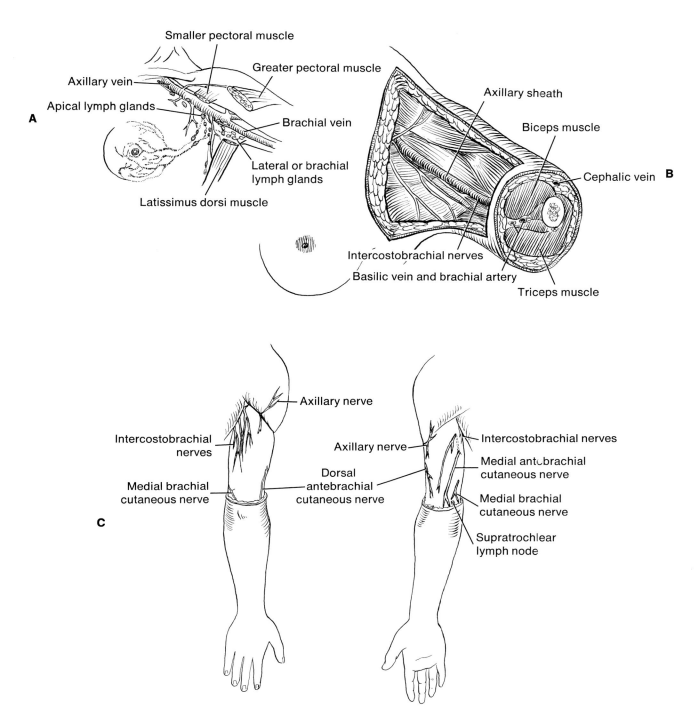

Fig. 3-22 A, Dissection of the axilla showing lymphatic distribution. **B,** Cross section of the arm. **C,** Cutaneous nerves of the upper arm.

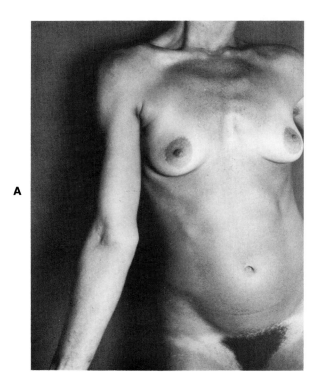

Fig. 3-23

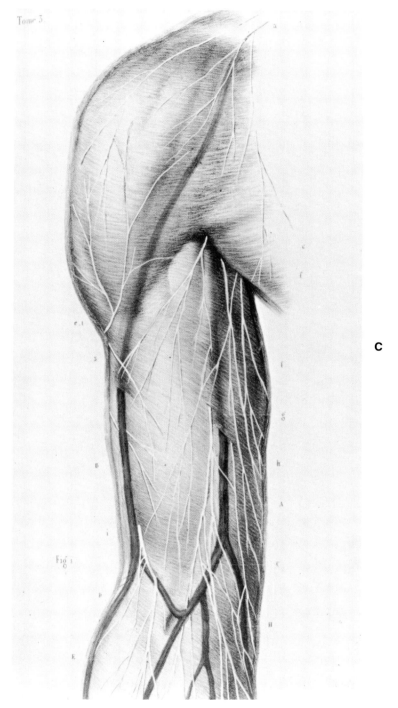

C

Fig. 3-23, cont'd
(**C** from Bourgery, J. M., and Jacob, N. H.: Anatomie de l'homme,
Paris, 1836, C. DeLaunay.)

REFERENCES

1. Anson, B.: Surgical anatomy, Philadelphia, 1958, W. B. Saunders Co.
2. Brown, R. G., Vasconez, L. O., and Jurkiewicz, M. J.: Transverse abdominal flaps and the deep epigastric arcade, Plast. Reconstr. Surg. **55**:416, 1975.
3. Callander, C. L.: Surgical anatomy, Philadelphia, 1939, W. B. Saunders Co.
4. Carvalho, C. G. S., Baroudi, R., and Keppke, E. M.: Anatomical and technical refinements for abdominoplasty, Aesthet. Plast. Surg. **1**:217, 1977.
5. Daniel, R. K., Kerrigan, C. L., and Gard, D. A.: The great potential of the intercostal flap for torso reconstruction, Plast. Reconstr. Surg. **61**:653, 1978.
6. Elbaz, J. S., and Dardour, J. C.: Anatomy and physiology of the arteries and veins of the abdominal wall. In Marchac, D., editor: Transactions of the Sixth International Congress of Plastic Surgery, Paris, 1975, Masson & Cie, Editeurs.
7. Elbaz, J. S., Dardour, J. C., and Ricbourg, B.: Vascularisation artérielle de la paroi abdominale, Ann. Chir. Plast. **20**:19, 1975.
8. Gardner, E., Grey, D., and O'Rahilly, R.: Anatomy—a regional study of human structure, Philadelphia, 1960, W. B. Saunders Co.
9. Hill, H. L., Brown, R. G., and Jurkiewicz, M. J.: The transverse lumbosacral back flap, Plast. Reconstr. Surg. **62**:177, 1978.
10. Hollinshead, W. H.: Anatomy for surgeons, New York, 1971, Harper & Row, Publishers.
11. Manchot, C.: Die Hautarterien des menschlichen Korpens, Leipzig, 1889, F. C. W. Vogel.
12. Masterton, J. P.: Necrosis of the abdominal wall following operations, Aust. N.Z. J. Surg. **37**:183, 1967.
13. McGraw, J. B., Dibbell, D. G., and Carraway, J. H.: Clinical definition of independent myocutaneous vascular territories, Plast. Reconstr. Surg. **60**:341, 1977.
14. McGregor, I. A., and Jackson, I. T.: The groin flap, Br. J. Plast. Surg. **25**:3, 1972.
15. Nahai, F., Brown, R. G., and Vasconez, L. O.: Blood supply to the abdominal wall as related to planning abdominal incisions, Am. Surg. **42**:691, 1976.
16. Regnault, P.: Abdominal dermolipectomies, Clin. Plast. Surg. **2**:411, 1975.
17. Harii, K., and Ohmore, K.: Free groin flaps in children, Plast. Reconstr. Surg. **55**:588, 1975.

CHAPTER 4

Anesthesia

The greatest contribution to the evolution of modern surgery has been the introduction of anesthesia and aseptic technique. The attraction of rendering the body insensitive to pain by inhalation of various agents has existed possibly since Djeber Yeber, a Middle Eastern alchemist, synthesized ether in the fifteenth century. It has been established that the inhalation of ether vapor was attempted without result by a Dr. Pearson of Birmingham, England, in 1785.[22] On April 9, 1799,[35] Humphry Davy discovered the analgesic properties of nitrous oxide and wrote, "It may probably be used with advantage in surgical operations in which no great effusion of blood takes place."

This suggestion remained in obscurity until 1844 when Horace Wells, a Hartford, Connecticut, dentist, became intrigued with the gas and inhaled it. During the next few weeks he used it in more than a dozen dental extractions, but after a few failures and struggling inductions he abandoned its use.

The first use of general anesthesia for a surgical procedure took place in Jefferson, Georgia, during March, 1842.[35] In this small village Crawford W. Long administered ether for the removal of a neck tumor from James Venable, a patient who was a habitual "ether sniffer" for its exhilarating effects. Dr. Long recorded in his practice ledger 3 or 4 more patients who were similarly anesthetized but never published the results.

The first well-documented and published account of the administration of general anesthesia for a surgical procedure was by W. T. G. Morton on October 16, 1846, in the Massachusetts General Hospital. On this auspicious day Dr. Morton administered ether through an inhalation device that had been fabricated only a few minutes before so that John Collins Warren could remove a vascular tumor of the neck. The anesthesia was completely satisfactory.

One is commonly led to believe that from this day there was a geometric and astronomical increase in the number of surgical procedures done. Such was not the case; in reality the evolution of first antiseptic and then aseptic techniques over the next forty years occurred before the number of operations increased greatly. Detailed investigations of the operating room records of the great hospitals of the United States and Europe by Greene[11,12] beautifully substantiate this and are exciting reading.

Endotracheal anesthesia as we know it today developed from the necessities of head and neck surgery and the pioneering work of Ivan Magill during and after World War I at the plastic surgery unit of Queens Hospital, Sidcup, England, while serving as anesthesiologist to Harold Gillies.[6,10,21] We could not leave the evolution of endotracheal anesthesia without noting that Friedrich

49

Trendelenburg[36] was the first to design an inflatable cuff for a tracheostomy tube almost like those in use today on endotracheal tubes. Perhaps Trendelenburg should be better remembered for this than his ungainly and unphysiologic head-down position! In any event, anesthesia owes a great debt to plastic surgery for its unique requirements that have served as a challenge to the development of anesthetic techniques.

PREOPERATIVE EVALUATION

We will discuss the preoperative evaluation in terms of preanesthetic interview, evaluation of pulmonary and cardiovascular function, and the effects of metachronously administered drugs on anesthesia.

Interview

The preoperative interview of patients for body contouring surgery is conducted with the pivotal fact in mind that these patients are dissatisfied with their bodily appearance and frequently have associated distortions of self-imagery, -concept, and -worth. These patients are therefore interviewed deliberately and without haste, allowing for interruption by any patient questions. The value of the preoperative visit has been beautifully stated by Egbert et al.[7]

The evaluation begins with a question concerning the patient's general health. Allergies are sought, and the nature of any reaction and the circumstances under which it occurred elicited. The nature of previous surgical procedures and the patient's reaction and comments concerning them are drawn out. Questions are raised in particular about any untoward reactions to anesthesia close family members may have had and, specifically, about prolonged respiratory depression that might have been related to abnormal succinylcholine metabolism and the occurrence of high fever or musculoskeletal disorders in family members that might give a hint of susceptibility to malignant hyperthermia.

The patient is queried about smoking, bronchitis, cough, sputum production, wheezing, dyspnea on exertion, and orthopnea, as well as concerning a regular exercise program and how strenuous and regular it is.

Questions are raised about the cardiovascular system, regarding hypertension, chest pain with emotion or activity, the occurrence of previous myocardial infarction, and a history of rheumatic fever. Patients are then asked if they have ever "had a heart attack" or if any physician has ever heard a murmur. They are questioned as to the nature and dosage of any cardiac drugs they may be receiving.

The occurrence of hepatitis or any liver dysfunction is questioned. The time between the most recent general anesthesia and the contemplated one is ascertained, since a possibility exists that repeated administration of halothane anesthesia within six months in adults may carry a slightly higher incidence of hepatic dysfunction.

Finally, the patient is specifically questioned about steroids, aspirin-containing compounds, and any current regimen of drugs.

After this interview, the following explanations are given to the patient: the exact manner in which nighttime sedatives will be given, the timing and nature of preoperative medication, and the exact way in which anesthesia will be induced, monitored, and maintained.

Evaluation of cardiopulmonary function

It is beyond the purview of this brief summary to discuss laboratory assessment of cardiopulmonary function in detail. If there are suggestions of cardiac disease, a twelve-lead electrocardiogram and chest x-ray study are minimal and absolute essentials. The use of diuretics in hypertension would indicate a serum potassium determination. A history of pulmonary disease or heavy smoking would indicate screening pulmonary function tests and a chest x-ray examination. More serious pulmonary disease would indicate arterial blood gas studies.

Effects of metachronously administered drugs

Finally in the preoperative assessment, one must consider the effects of metachronously administered drugs on anesthesia. The use of diuretics may deplete the body of potassium and predispose the patient to cardiac arrhythmias. A level below 3 mEq/dl is an indication to withhold anesthesia and replace potassium.

We have definite beliefs concerning the management of patients on propranolol (Inderal). The half-life of propranolol in humans is approximately 3.4 to 6 hours after discontinuance of chronic oral administration.[27] Assay of atrial tissue shows disappearance within 24 to 48 hours, thus negating the concept of a long-lasting pool.[30] If the patient is receiving the drug for hypertension, we reduce the dosage by one half two days before surgery and give half the dose the day before. In a patient with angina, the drug must never be abruptly discontinued because the increased myocardial work and oxygen consumption may initiate preinfarction angina or actual infarction.

We prefer in general to continue antihypertensive drugs, believing that a gentle, cautious induction, repletion of fluid volume with lactated Ringer's solution, and light levels of anesthesia avoid hypotensive episodes.

We continue tricyclic antidepressants except in the elderly but remain aware that these patients are sensitive to pressor amines,[4] probably because of inhibition of amine reuptake.

Phenothiazines are continued with reduced premedication, especially reduced barbiturates, and slow cautious induction.

Patients receiving levodopa are given neither droperidol nor phenothiazines, which may aggravate their parkinsonian symptoms.

Patients receiving monoamine oxidase (MAO) inhibitors such as phenelzine dihydrogen, nialamide, isocarboxazid, or pargyline have the drug discontinued at least two weeks preoperatively. In unknown manner MAO inhibitors can interact with opioids to produce hypertension and coma and have been reported to initiate malignant hyperthermia.

Many of the anticonvulsants are enzyme inducers that might increase the metabolic transformation of halogenated agents. We have found this to be of more theoretical than practical note.

Patients receiving digitalis are checked for serum potassium levels and, if indicated, serum digitalis levels.

Finally, in the framework of today's abuse of alcohol and drugs, reading of the article by Orkin, Louis, and Chen[28] on addiction, alcoholism, and anesthesia is recommended.

MONITORING

Adequate and constant monitoring is essential to the safe conduct of any anesthetic, be it regional, local or general. To be adequate, a monitoring device must measure a specific function, be easily and rapidly applied, be readily calibrated and stable, be reproducible from patient to patient, and provide a reliable signal readily interpreted by the anesthesiologist. Monitors may be divided into those which are mechanical and those which employ electronics to varying degrees. The minimal safe monitoring should include a continuous electrocardiogram, a precordial or esophageal stethoscope, and temperature measurement.

Electrocardiogram

When monitoring electrocardiographically, it is essential not only to be able to distinguish changes in rate and rhythm, but to suspect electrolyte abnormalities and to recognize the changes that are indicative of myocardial ischemia. Several hookups are possible; we prefer a system that will allow the monitoring of leads I, II, III, AVR, AVL, AVF, and a selected V lead, which is almost always V_5. This monitoring is used only in patients with known ischemic heart disease, since it allows one to electronically "look" at all aspects of the heart's surface for signs of ischemia. In most patients a simple observation of lead II for rate and rhythm is adequate. If a single electrode were to be studied for ischemia, the V_5 or CM_5 would give the highest incidence of positive results.[3] The CM_5 is very good for routine monitoring of rate, rhythm, and atrial activity, as well as evaluating ischemia: the positive lead is placed in the C_5 position; the negative, on the manubrium; and the indifferent, on the right shoulder. On a three-lead system this monitoring may be done by placing the switch in lead III position and attaching the left leg wire to the C_5 position, the left arm to the manubrial electrode, and the right arm electrode on the shoulder or right lateral chest to serve as the ground electrode. It is interesting that, by constant monitoring, many transient drops in blood pressure are accompanied by disappearance of P-waves, indicating lack of the atrial contraction that adds the final "kick" to ventricular filling.

Precordial stethoscope

The precordial stethoscope or its equivalent by neck or esophageal placement deserves to be mentioned as the sine qua non of monitoring. If only one monitoring device were available, it should be the stethoscope. Slavish attention to electronic boxes and gadgets has resulted in many misadventures that would not have occurred had stethoscopic monitoring been in use. The electrocardiogram is only a reflection of electrical, *not mechanical,* activity. Many cases have been reported of totally ineffective cardiac activity with a normal electrocardiogram for several minutes. In addition, the stethoscope will clearly demonstrate myocardial depression due to hypoxia, anesthetic agents, and hypotension much more quickly than will the electrocardiograph. The characteristic changes in the first and second heart sounds with myocardial depression are described in the classic article of Rence, Cullen, and Hamilton.[29] The heart sounds vary in three general ways:

1. While the patient is awake and in light anesthesia, the familiar *lub-dup* is heard.
2. As the myocardium is depressed mildly to moderately, the second sound becomes dominant in intensity and assumes a higher-pitched, slapping, metallic character.
3. As the depression deepens, the intensity of both sounds decreases, and they assume an equality of pitch.

The precordial stethoscope will tell of secretions, respiratory obstruction, wheezing, pulmonary edema, and whether the endotracheal tube has slipped down the right main bronchus. Thus we see the value of this inexpensive, easy-to-interpret, often-neglected device.

Blood pressure and temperature measurement

The blood pressure may be measured by such noninvasive techniques as the Riva-Roca method, a Doppler flowmeter, or finger plethysmography. Temperature can be measured accurately by an esophageal probe or by observing the color trend changes of a Jelco Temp-A-Strip placed on the forehead. The Temp-A-Strip is by no means quantitative but is a useful noninvasive tool.

EFFECTS OF POSITION

The success of most surgical procedures depends on satisfactory exposure, which in turn may involve positions that alter cardiopulmonary function and expose other body structures to injury.

Cardiopulmonary disturbances

Studies of various operative positions and the resultant changes in pulmonary function as compared with a similar study of the sitting position have yielded some dramatic results. The greatest decreases in pulmonary function occur in the 20-degree Trendelenburg position, lithotomy, and lateral decubitus.[14,19,20] The horizontal supine position is best tolerated by the anesthetized patient.[19] In body contouring the prone position is frequently required and may compromise both pulmonary and cardiovascular function. In actual practice pulmonary disturbances can be readily controlled by endotracheal intubation and assisted or controlled respiration with the exception of ventilation/perfusion ratio changes, which can be remedied by inspired oxygen concentrations of 40% to 50% in most instances. Circulatory changes caused by vena caval compression and increased mean airway pressure, both decreasing venous return, may be managed by proper use of chest rolls and positioning. Thought must be given to any position that would promote venous thromboembolic disease.

Neurological injuries

The most serious injuries are those to the nerves and eyes. The most common neurological injuries involve the brachial plexus and its subdivisions. Of particular concern is the ulnar nerve when an arm is tucked in beside the patient. Failure to place the hand palm down or neutral and close to the body and to keep it well supported may result in injury. The most common mechanism of brachial plexus injury is failure to carefully tuck the lifter sheet entirely under the mattress, allowing the arm to flex at the elbow. This position, with movement of the assistants, may cause the ulnar groove to lie directly over the attachment bar of the operating table, compressing the ulnar nerve. This injury has also been observed in the recovery room when an arm is pulled through the side rails of the bed to take a blood pressure and then left in this position while the patient is still unconscious.

We are particularly concerned with brachial plexus injuries with the arms abducted as well as in the prone position.[14,41] Jackson and Keats[14] elegantly described the mechanism of plexus injuries in a dissection of 15 fresh cadavers and in arterial pulse wave contours in anesthetized patients. They demonstrated that abduction of the arm to more than 90 degrees stretched the plexus significantly. Any position that tends to displace the shoulders posteriorly will also stretch the plexus. In the prone position one commonly sees the elbows and arms being propped up to the level of the shoulders, which is incorrect because it stretches the plexus. The shoulder should be allowed to comfortably descend forward to eliminate plexus tension.

Stand erect, abduct both arms to 90 degrees, turn the palms up, and then push the arms posteriorly. You will immediately note plexus pain, and occasionally the pulse will disappear. Remember the three elements to be avoided: abduction, palms up, and posterior displacement of the shoulders. The placement of the palms down or in neutral position is essential in the abducted arm, since the head of the humerus is rotated toward the plexus in the palm-up position.

Ocular injuries

Finally, attention must be drawn to the eyes, the site of the most common anesthetic misadventures. Simply keep them covered and avoid pressure.[2,5,33] A study of 200 adult patients undergoing general anesthesia revealed that 50% to 60% of patients will sleep with the eyes partially open.[2] Of the patients in the study who slept with the eyes partially open and uncovered, 44% showed areas of either scattered or confluent abrasion when studied by fluorescein staining. The degree was related to the duration of anesthesia and obviously the duration of exposure. The eyes are routinely lubricated with a nonantibiotic ointment, Lacri-Lube, and taped closed. During face-down positions the eyes are checked every few minutes to ensure that there is no pressure and that tapes have not slipped.

INCREASED RISKS IN THE OBESE

Although one can cite literally hundreds of references that argue the degree to and the manner in which obesity influences various disease states, no doubt exists that there is a direct correlation between obesity and increased anesthetic morbidity and mortality. For those interested in the influence of obesity on general health, the classic review of Mann[23] is amusing and informative reading. The primary function of this elaboration on the deleterious effects of obesity on anesthesia is twofold: first, to review obesity and the systems involved; second, to help the surgeon understand the sometimes elaborate and invasive monitoring techniques that the anesthesiologist may wish to employ. Patients desiring body contouring surgery will tend to be more obese than the general surgical population. Many definitions exist for obesity, but the most useful for our purposes will be that of the body mass index (BMI),[6,18] which is weight/height squared (kilograms/meters²). Excessive morbidity and mortality are associated with a BMI of more than 30.

Specific problems associated with obesity will be found in relation to the inherent personality traits of obese persons, their cardiopulmonary systems, and certain biochemical and metabolic disturbances.

Personality traits

The obese patient, although frequently outwardly jolly, is inwardly a very unhappy person with many unresolved conflicts. Characteristically obese persons have a low evaluation of self, a distortion of self-image, and usually a passive-aggressive personality; are extremely prone to depression; and are overcome by the "hopeless-helpless" syndrome. Under stress or during even moderately painful procedures, they may cry, become overtly belligerent and abusive to their physicians, and occasionally slip into a paranoid shell of seclusion. Obviously, great care is necessary in the choice of words during the preoperative interview and in thoroughly explaining all procedures as they are done.

Cardiopulmonary system

It can be assumed with reasonable certainty that certain pathophysiological alternations are associated with obesity and that these generally involve the cardiopulmonary system and also certain metabolic and biochemical changes of significance.

55

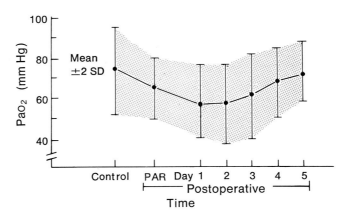

Fig. 4-1. Graphic representation of the fall in PaO₂ (mm Hg) with time postoperatively. *Solid line,* Mean; *stippled arra,* ± 2 standard deviations; *PAR,* postanesthesia room. (From Vaughan, R. W., Engelhardt, R. C., and Wise, L.: Ann. Surg. **180**:879, 1974.)

Regarding the cardiovascular system, one can expect a higher incidence of hypertension, hyperlipidemia, and coronary heart disease in obese patients. The increased body mass is associated with an elevated cardiac output and occasionally with increased total, central, and pulmonary blood volumes. It would seem prudent, therefore, to have a resting twelve-lead electrocardiogram as the minimal cardiac evaluation in every obese patient, complemented by a chest x-ray study, to evaluate pulmonary status as well.

The pulmonary effects of obesity may be more dramatic than the cardiovascular but are less easily assessed. With a BMI above 30 and a history of smoking, chronic cough, or other pulmonary disease, a screening pulmonary function evaluation and possibly a baseline arterial blood gas might be necessary. Obesity is frequently associated with early airway closure, increased work of ventilation, reduced compliance, altered ventilation/perfusion ratios, reduced functional residual capacity, and in severe cases with arterial hypoxemia. The effect of obesity on postoperative arterial blood gases has been studied by Vaughan, Englehardt, and Wise[38] and shows a decreased resting PO₂ in room air with a greater than normal decrease than that which usually accompanies aging and maximal depression on the first and second postoperative days (Fig. 4-1).

Of even greater interest is the effect of position on gas exchange.[39] A statistically significant increase in oxygenation and decrease in PCO₂ occurs with assumption of the semirecumbent position versus the supine. These changes persist for 48 to 72 hours in the obese. As part of the postoperative routine in my practice, all patients undergoing abdominal wall reconstruction and all those with pulmonary problems or obesity are maintained in semirecumbent positions and managed with incentive spirometry and at times intermittent positive pressure breathing and chest physiotherapy (Fig. 4-2).

Of particular interest in intraoperative management are observations from studies done in several laboratories[40] that an inspired oxygen concentration of

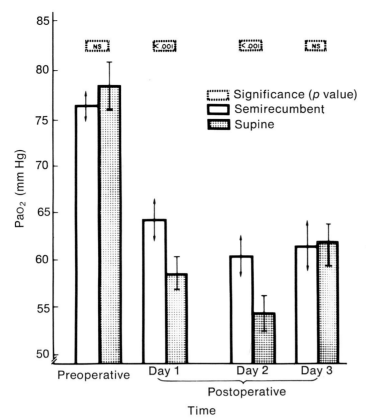

Fig. 4-2. Arterial oxygen tension (mean ± SE) in 22 obese women in the semirecumbent compared to the supine position preoperatively and on each of postoperative days one through three. Preoperatively and on postoperative day three, no positional effect on Pao_2 was demonstrable. On postoperative days one and two, however, a change to the supine position resulted in a statistically significant decrease ($p < 0.001$) in Pao_2. Significance is considered as between the two positions, not preoperative versus postoperative Pao_2 values. *NS*, Not statistically significant. All values were obtained with the patient breathing room air at rest. (From Vaughan, R. W., and Wise, L.: Ann. Surg. **182:**708, 1975.)

40% ($FIo_2 = 0.4$) does not guarantee adequate oxygenation in the obese, particularly those who are smokers or have preexistent respiratory problems.

If a head-down position is employed in the intraoperative management, the effects on the mechanics of respiration and regional ventilation/perfusion abnormalities further compound the problem.

The increased risk of silent aspiration of gastric contents in patients with hiatal hernia has recently been studied,[24] and a series of charts of patients with obesity who have had upper gastrointestinal x-ray examinations are being screened to correlate the increase in hiatal hernia with age and obesity. It would seem at this time there is a strong correlation. All patients are questioned about a history of hiatal hernia and given antacids routinely preoperatively. Vaughan, Bauer, and Wise[37] have recently demonstrated that obese patients have a lower-than-average gastric pH and higher acid volume, thus making them more susceptible to acid-aspiration syndrome.

Biochemical effects

The metabolic effects of obesity include fatty infiltration of the liver and impaired glucose tolerance with insulin resistance. Perhaps of greater significance are the effects of large fat stores on increased biotransformation of fluorinated inhalation agents. A marked increase occurs in the duration of elevation of fluoride levels in the obese versus the normal-weight patient in methoxyflurane anesthesia,[31] and some studies have demonstrated higher absolute fluoride levels in the obese. The administration of halothane to the obese patient for long periods at higher concentrations may result in significantly elevated bromide levels, which could be synergistic with postoperative narcotics and sedatives. Recently Saraiva et al.[32] have demonstrated altered pharmacokinetics of halothane with delayed awakening in the obese.

ESTIMATING AND REPLACING BLOOD LOSS

In abdominoplasty, thighplasty, and breast reduction or combined procedures, blood loss may be considerable. Various methods of estimating this loss are available from simply weighing the sponges and measuring suction contents to washing all sponges and doing hematocrits on the washed volume or even electrical conductance. Our approach is that the volume lost must be continuously estimated and certain criteria set up for management. We are not opposed to a one-unit transfusion, as has been erroneously taught, because a break point exists at which a patient will decompensate, and frequently one unit is sufficient to support the circulation. Blood loss is estimated roughly but adequately by observing the suction bottles and subtracting the volume of irrigation fluid. The sponges are observed; 4 ml are allowed for a moderately stained sponge, and 8 ml for a full one. Lap sponges are graded from 20 to 60 ml—from moderately stained to wholly soaked.

The patient's weight in kilograms × 80 is assumed as the blood volume; from 10% to 15% loss is permitted before transfusion, provided the patient can be stabilized with crystalloid and colloid. As the procedure progresses, an attempt is made to replace the blood lost with twice the volume of lactated Ringer's solution plus 4 ml/kg/hour to allow for third spacing and insensible loss. If this substitution is ineffective, we then use 5% protein solution to a volume of 10 to 15 ml/kg. There is no real reason to maintain a hematocrit higher than 30 for adequate oxygen transport, and it is uneconomical in terms of viscosity, blood pressure, and myocardial work.[42] If crystalloid and colloid have not stabilized the patient, blood is given until capillary perfusion is adequate, the blood pressure is above 90, or not less than 30% of the resting systolic pressure in a hypertensive patient, and the hematocrit is above 30%. If a catheter is in place, a urinary output of 0.75 to 1.0 ml/kg/hour is indicative of adequate microcirculatory perfusion.

EFFECTS OF LOCAL ANESTHETICS AND VASOCONSTRICTORS

In some instances the surgeon may request or require the use of epinephrine to produce hemostasis. The mechanisms by which anesthetic-adrenergic

58

arrhythmias are produced have been attributed to alpha-adrenergic stimulation, since they could be prevented by alpha blockade.[26] It would appear that the protection against arrhythmia by alpha blockade is an indirect effect caused by the prevention of hypertension and by nonspecific quinidine-like effect. With the development of beta-blocking agents, it has been shown that they will consistently abolish arrhythmias; however, the beta blockers also have local anesthetic-like action and may act in several ways.[17] Most studies have demonstrated that maximal vasoconstriction by infiltration is achieved with concentrations of epinephrine in the range of 1:150,000 to 1:200,000.[8,24] Of the anesthetics used in various studies,[15,17,25] enflurane (Ethrane) apparently has the least potential for altering the arrhythmic threshold.[43] The subcutaneous injection of epinephrine in the recommended concentrations is safe if the dosage of 1:100,000 epinephrine does not exceed 10 ml in a 10-minute period or 30 ml per hour with halothane, methoxyflurane, or enflurane.[16] Most studies have been done with epinephrine in saline and failed to consider the antiarrhythmic protection afforded by employing 0.5% lidocaine as the vehicle. The use of lidocaine may also reduce anesthetic requirements, not only by inducing a field block of the operative site, but also by its own anesthetic properties. In one study[13] the effects of variable plasma levels of lidocaine on nitrous oxide requirements in man and halothane in the dog were studied. A plasma level of 3 to 6 μg/ml decreased anesthetic requirements from 10% to 28%.

Arrhythmias will be increased by carbon dioxide retention and by hypoxia, as well as with preexistent documented arrhythmia.

It should be emphasized that most arrhythmias do not need sudden dramatic treatment when they occur. Usually decreasing anesthetic concentration and briefly hyperventilating with oxygen will suffice. If persistent runs of premature ventricular contractions or the "R on T" phenomenon occurs, lidocaine in a bolus of 75 to 100 mg should be used.

APPROACHING THE IDEAL?

No standard or supremely superior agent or technique exists to produce anesthesia for body contouring surgery; in fact, anesthesiologists should choose agents with which they are experienced and feel comfortable and should gradually refine their techniques to meet the demands of their particular teams. Following is the technique refinement of one team after a seven-year period with the same surgeon, assistant, and anesthesiologist.

Morphine is preferred for premedication, unless a contraindication exists, and is given in a dosage of 0.16 to 0.18 mg/kg along with 0.3 g of scopolamine or 0.3 mg of glycopyrrolate (Robinul) approximately 75 minutes prior to induction. Two hours before induction, 10 mg of diazepam (Valium) is given orally with sips of water. Because of its highly fat-soluble nature, the sedation of oral diazepam is superior and longer lasting than that which is injected intramuscularly. Detectable blood levels and sedation will average from 8 to 20 hours. The incidence of nausea has been decreased by this to a degree superior to ataractics and phenothiazines, which are painful on injection. When the patient arrives in the operating room, a blood pressure cuff is applied and the electrocardiographical leads placed. An intravenous infusion is begun with one of the "over-the-needle" plastic catheter systems, usually with 5% dextrose/lactated Ringer's solution as the first bottle. Patients are not preoxygenated while awake unless a medical condition so indicates.

Prior to induction, 2 to 4 mg of metocurine (Metubine) is given intravenously and followed immediately with a sleep dose of a short-acting barbiturate such as thiopental (Pentothal) or methohexital (Brevital).

Assisted ventilation with 100% oxygen is begun as the patient starts to lose the lid reflex, and enflurane is gradually introduced along with other small increment of barbiturate. Intubation is facilitated with 80 to 100 mg of succinylcholine, and a cuffed endotracheal tube lubricated with 5% lidocaine ointment is introduced. As respiration begins to return, the inhaled gases are changed to nitrous oxide oxygen, 3:2 or 2:2, with metocurine given in a dose of 0.2 to 0.3 mg/kg and enflurane at a 1 to 1.5 MAC (minimal alveolar concentration). At this point, respiration is usually controlled and neuromuscular blockade assessed by use of a nerve stimulator. Throughout the procedure the electrocardiogram, precordial or esophageal stethoscope, blood pressure, and temperature are continuously monitored. As the procedure approaches termination, enflurane is discontinued; as dressings are being applied, nitrous oxide is discontinued and neuromuscular blockade reversed with a glycopyrrolate/pyridostigmine (Regonol) combination of 0.2 mg glycopyrrolate with 10 mg pyridostigmine. Reversal may take as long as 10 minutes and is monitored by a nerve stimulator.[1] If neuromuscular function has not completely recovered, a second dose is given after 15 minutes. No patient is extubated until tidal volume is adequate and she can generate an inspiratory force of -20 cm/H_2O. Patients are transported to the postanesthesia unit with a precordial stethoscope in place and routinely given oxygen until reaction occurs. On reaction 10 mg of thiethylperazine (Torecan) is usually given intramuscularly to smooth emergence, provide sedation, decrease shivering, and prevent nausea. If emergence delirium occurs, 0.5 to 2 mg of physostigmine salicylate (Antilirium) is given slowly intravenously.

This outline is presented as a frequently used method. In every case the agents and techniques should be individualized to the patient and no "cookbook" approach employed.

SUMMARY

The contribution of plastic surgery and the impetus it has given to the development of endotracheal anesthesia are noteworthy. The increased risks of obesity, methods of monitoring, effects of position on cardiorespiratory function and nerve injuries, methods of estimating and replacing blood loss, the influence of adrenergic drugs, and a technique of anesthesia for body contouring have been presented. In the simplest terms, safe clinical anesthesia provides psychic and physical safety for the patient, with the best operating conditions for the surgeon. Each administration of anesthesia should be individualized to the patient.

REFERENCES

1. Ali, H. H., and Sauarese, J. J.: Monitoring of neuromuscular function, Anesthesiology **45:**216, 1976.
2. Batra, Y. K., and Bali, I. M.: Corneal abrasions during general anesthesia, Anesth. Analg. (Cleve.) **56:**363, 1977.
3. Blackburn, H., Taylor, H., et al.: The standardization of the exercise ECG. A systematic comparison of chest lead configurations employed for monitoring during exercise. In Karvonen, M. J., and Barry, A. J., editors: Symposium on Physical Activity and the Heart, Helsinki, 1964; proceedings, Springfield, Ill., 1967, Charles C Thomas, Publisher.
4. Boalnes, A. J., Laurence, D. R., Teoh, P. G., et al.: Interactions between sympathomimetic aminos and antidepressant agents in man, Br. J. Med. **10:**311, 1973.
5. Boyd, C. H.: Ophthalmic hypersensitivity to anesthetic vapour, Anaesthesia **27:**456, 1972.
6. Bray, G. A., Jordan, H. A., and Sims, E. A.: Evaluation of the obese patient. 1. An algorithm, J.A.M.A. **235:**1487, 1976.
7. Egbert, L. D., Battit, G. E., Turndorf, H., and Beecher, H. K.: The value of the preoperative visit by an anesthetist. A study of doctor-patient rapport, J.A.M.A. **185:**553, 1963.
8. Funakoshi, Y., Iwai, S., Kaneda, H., et al.: Hemodynamic effects of locally applied epinephrine used with various general anesthetic techniques, J. Oral Surg. **35:**713, 1977.
9. Gillespie, N. A.: Endotracheal anesthesia, ed. 3, rev. and ed. by B. J. Bamforth and K. L. Siebecker, Madison, 1963, The University of Wisconsin Press.
10. Gillies, H., and Millard, D. R.: The principles and art of plastic surgery, vol. 1. Boston, 1957, Little, Brown & Co.
11. Greene, N. M.: Personal communications, 1978.
12. Greene, N. M.: Anesthesia and the development of surgery (1846-1896), Anesth. Analg. (Cleve.) **58:**5, 1979.
13. Himes, R. S., DiFazio, C., and Burney, R. G.: Effects of lidocaine on the anesthetic requirements for nitrous oxide and halothane, Anesthesiology **47:**437, 1977.
14. Jackson, L., and Keats, A. S.: Mechanism of brachial plexus palsy following anesthesia, Anesthesiology **26:**190, 1965.
15. Joas, T. A., and Stevens, W. C.: Comparison of the arrhythmic doses of epinephrine during Forane, halothane, and fluorooxene anesthesia in dogs, Anesthesiology **35:**48, 1971.
16. Katz, R. L., and Bigger, J. T., Jr.: Cardiac arrhythmias during anesthesia and operation, Anesthesiology **33:**193, 1970.
17. Katz, R. L., and Epstein, R. A.: The interaction of anesthetic agents and adrenergic drugs to produce cardiac arrhythmias, Anesthesiology **29:**763, 1968.
18. Keys, A., Fidanza, F., Karvonen, M. J., et al.: Indices of relative weight and obesity, J. Chronic Dis. **25:**329, 1972.
19. Lincoln, J. R., and Sawyer, H. P.: Complications related to body positions during surgical procedures, Anesthesiology **22:**800, 1961.
20. Little, D. M., Jr.: Posture and anesthesia, Can. Anaesth. Soc. J. **7:**2, 1960.
21. Magill, I.: Lest we forget, Br. J. Med. **2:**817, 1930.
22. Maltz, M.: Evolution of plastic surgery, New York, 1964, Froben Press.
23. Mann, G. V.: The influence of obesity on health, N. Engl. J. Med. **291:**197, 226, 1975.
24. Mathews, W. A., and Austin, J.: Unpublished studies, St. Luke's Hospital Medical Center, Anesthesia Laboratory, Phoenix, Ariz., 1969.
25. Munson, E. S., and Tucker, W. K.: Doses of epinephrine causing arrhythmia during enflurane, methoxyflurane, and halothane anesthesia in dogs, Can. Anesth. Soc. J. **22:**495, 1975.
26. Nickerson, M.: The pharmacology of adrenergic blockade, Pharmacol. Rev. **1:**27, 1949.
27. Nies, A. S., and Shand, D. G.: Clinical pharmacology of propranolol, Circulation **52:**6, 1975.
28. Orkin, L. R., and Chen, C. H.: Addiction, alcoholism, and anesthesia, South. Med. J. **70:**1172, 1977.
29. Rence, W. G., Cullen, S., and Hamilton, W.: Observation on the heart sounds during anesthesia with cyclopropane and ether, Anesthesiology **17:**26, 1956.
30. Romagnoli, A., and Keats, A. S.: Plasma and atrial propranolol levels after preoperative withdrawal, Circulation **52:**1123, 1975.
31. Samuelson, P. N., Merin, R. G., Taves, D. R., et al.: Toxicity following methoxy-

flurane anaesthesia. IV. The role of obesity and the effect of low dose anaesthesia on fluoride metabolism and renal function, Can. Anaesth. Soc. J. **23:**465, 1976.

32. Saraiva, R. A., Lunn, J. N., Mapleson, W. W., et al.: Adiposity and pharmacokinetics of halothane. The effect of adiposity on the maintenance of and recovery from halothane anaesthesia, Anaesthesia **32:**240, 1977.

33. Snow, J. C., Kripke, B. J., Norton, M. L., et al.: Corneal injuries during general anesthesia, Anesth. Analg. (Cleve.) **54:** 465, 1975.

34. Stephen, C. R.: Influence of posture on mechanics of respiration and vital capacity, Anesthesiology **9:**134, 1948.

35. Sykes, W. S.: Essays on the first hundred years of anesthesia, vol. 1, Edinburgh, 1960, E. & S. Livingston, Ltd.

36. Trendelenburg, F.: Tamponade de trachea, Arch. Klin. Chir. **12:**121, 1871.

37. Vaughan, R. W., Bauer, S., and Wise, L.: Volume and pH of gastric juice in obese patients, Anesthesiology **43:**686, 1975.

38. Vaughan, R. W., Engelhardt, R. C., and Wise, L.: Postoperative hypoxemia in obese patients, Ann. Surg. **180:**877, 1974.

39. Vaughan, R. W., and Wise, L.: Postoperative arterial blood gas measurement in obese patients—effect of position on gas exchange, Ann. Surg. **182:**705, 1975.

40. Vaughan, R. W., and Wise, L.: Intraoperative arterial oxygenation inobese patients, Ann. Surg. **184:**35, 1976.

41. Wood-Smith, F. G.: Postoperative brachial plexus paralysis, Br. Med. J. **1:**1115, 1952.

42. Yoshikawa, H., Powell, W. J., Bland, J. H. L., and Lowenstein, E.: Effect of acute anemia on experimental myocardial ischemia, Am. J. Cardiol. **32:**670, 1973.

43. Zahed, B., Miletich, D. J., Ivankovich, A. D., et al.: Arrhythmic doses of epinephrine and dopamine during halothane, enflurance, methoxyflurane, and fluoroxene anesthesia in goats, Anesth. Analg. (Cleve.) **56:**207, 1977.

CHAPTER 5

Abdominoplasty

THE YESTERDAYS OF ABDOMINAL DERMOLIPECTOMY

Since ether anesthesia was first administered in 1846, the potential for all types of abdominal surgery has been assured. In the history of surgery, the most elusive subjects to escape early documentation have been those associated with alteration of the external anterior abdominal wall and revision of redundant skin and soft tissue of the extremities. It seems incongruous that dermolipectomy of the abdomen was apparently unknown until 1889. It is reasonable to assume that once the intra-abdominal cavity became an area for surgery, the essentially easier, less complicated external abdominal wall would become a target for surgical intervention. Such contemplation seems more logical when it is realized that the complexities of blood clotting mechanism and hypercoagulability state were poorly understood. In reality, many more surgical procedures may have been performed to remove excess fat from the abdominal wall and extremities in the nineteenth century than were reported, as a review of the early literature seems to confirm. The stigma that existed in the past toward "cosmetic surgical improvement" may have been one of the major reasons for the reluctance in reporting such cases. This stigma was a much greater retardant to activity outside the "norm" than present-day society can understand. Religion, strong family life structure, and general social peer pressures all contributed to create these restraining influences. Even opportunistic surgeons who could have been prone to publicize their services apparently were reluctant to document such procedures.

Whatever the reason for the gap in the literature, the first mention of abdominal lipectomy in medical reports seems to have been in 1889 in the *Bulletin of the Johns Hopkins Hospital*.[41] Howard A. Kelly of Baltimore briefly reported the case of a 30-year-old, 285-pound (132.3 kg) woman with an enormous development of body fat who had 14.9 pounds (7,450 g) of fat removed. This brief report also included a mention of removal of fat from the thigh, which may be the first report of a limited thighplasty. In 1901, Lindsay Peters[54] reported on Kelly's procedure in great detail. He initially discussed the difference between but equal need for surgery of a benign neoplastic lipoma and the accumulation of subcutaneous fat creating a pendulous mass. The surgery, which was performed on May 5, 1889, was a second surgery for excess fat on this patient. Apparently, sections of very large, flabby, pendulous breasts had been removed five years previously by J. W. Chambers of Baltimore. The combined weight of the two segments of breast tissue removed was almost 25 pounds

(11.3 kg). After that surgery, the abdomen began to accumulate fat, becoming so large as to hang in folds not only in front but on the sides, covering the upper portion of the thighs. The maximum circumference of the abdomen was 200 cm at a level 12 cm above the umbilicus. Under ether anesthesia, a transverse incision, 85 cm long and about 13 cm above the umbilicus, extended across the abdomen on each side to where tissue was in contact with the operating table. Dissection was made in a downward manner, separating fat from muscle. This large slab of tissue was then raised superiorly to estimate where the lower transverse incision could be made to provide a repair with tension. It is interesting that 15 vessels were encountered and ligated, some of which were about 3 mm in diameter. The resected flap reached a width of 31 cm and a maximum thickness of 7 cm, with the umbilicus centered in the mass. Closure was accomplished by an equal amount of silkworm gut and catgut sutures (a total of 56 sutures), providing a final closure of 85 cm in length. The area was dressed with silver foil, sterile gauze, and cotton maintained in position by adhesive tape strips and supplemented by an eight-tailed, circumferentially applied supportive dressing known as a scultetus bandage. Apparently two draining sites were employed, one at each of the lateral aspects of the wound. The patient was not allowed to sit up for a month after surgery, and diet was restricted to liquids for twelve days after surgery, at which time a very light, soft diet was introduced. The patient was discharged thirty-seven days after surgery with a 59-pound (26.6 kg) weight reduction. Correspondence with the patient twenty months after surgery revealed that she was alive and walking well with nervousness as the only complaint. Ten years later, Kelly reported on the same case again,[42] providing five photographs of the patient in various stages of the operations and including his personal comments about the aesthetic needs of such patients.

On February 7, 1900, James B. Bullitt[10] of Louisville, Kentucky, repaired an umbilical hernia and at the same time resected a pendulous abdominal wall. The resected abdominal wall was 7.6 to 10 cm in thickness; the excision extended from the flank area on one side to the other. The surgeon made two comments worthy of mentioning. First, although he had no knowledge of a similar procedure being performed prior to his, it undoubtedly had been done before. In addition, Bullitt thought the amount of tissue removed could have been more extensive. The line of repair was noted as 55.9 cm in length, but the weight of the tissue was not given.

In the journal, *Le Progrès Médical*, of April 5, 1890, the surgical treatment of abdominal obesity was briefly discussed and the work of Demars and Marx cited without references by a discussant whose initials were M. B.

The basic technique of resecting skin and fatty tissue in the shape of an orange wedge as shown by Kelly and others was not the only surgical procedure employed. In 1893, a surgeon named Rochay varied the shape of the area of excision.

In 1970, Ernest Maylard,[45] a surgeon of Scotland, discussed the anatomy of the abdominal wall and underlined his preference for transverse abdominal in-

Incisional history of abdominoplasty

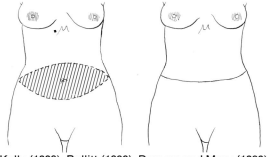

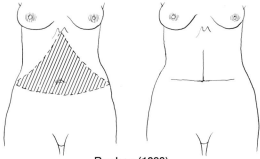

Kelly (1889), Bullitt (1890), Demars and Marx (1890),
von Schulz (1908), Jolly (1911), Shallenberger (1911)

Rochay (1893)

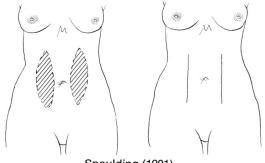

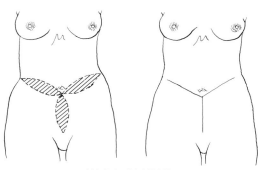

Spaulding (1901)

Weinhold (1908)

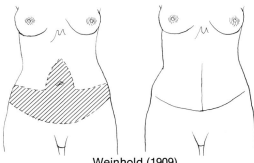

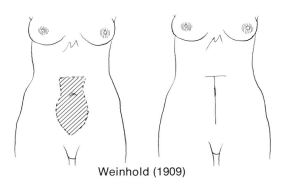

Weinhold (1909)

Weinhold (1909)

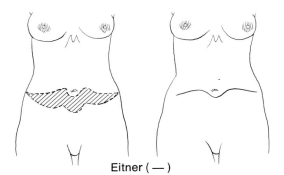

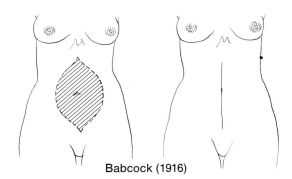

Eitner (—)

Babcock (1916)

cisions versus the vertical incisions customary for that time. In his discussion of numerous cases, Maylard reported on the repair of an umbilical hernia along with the removal of 10 pounds (4.5 kg) of fatty tissue, resulting in a transverse curvilinear incision scar line 53.3 cm in length. He also mentioned another case in which 6 pounds 2 ounces (2.8 kg) of abdominal skin and fat were removed.

Although discussion was directed at scar formation and its integrity, the casual reference to the removal of excess abdominal fat would make one think the procedure was more commonly accepted by Maylard than was reported.

In 1908, C. von Schulz[70] of Brest Litovsk, Russia, discussed the work of Demars and Marx and mentioned that he was unaware of similar cases in the literature. He went on to describe a case of a 30-year-old woman with a "large spare tire" who had had a tendency for obesity since childhood that had increased because of pregnancy and kidney disease. She could not bend to pick up fallen articles. She was of average height and weighed 217 pounds (98.5 kg). The fat also hung over the lateral aspect of the thighs. Her surgery was carefully described. There were two transverse incisions: the upper one, three fingers under the umbilicus, curving inferiorly, 36 cm on the right and 31 cm on the left. This discrepancy resulted from a visual misjudgment because the surgeon was standing on the right side. The lower incision followed the crease created by the excess pendulous abdomen and was joined to the upper on each side laterally. On the right side, the skin and fat was separated from the aponeurosis by scalpel dissection, leaving a thin layer of fat, whereas on the left it was simply pulled away from the aponeurosis, leaving it clean and free. Apparently the amount of bleeding and healing on the right was less than that on the left, with melted fat seeping from the right lateral incision after the second postoperative day. The fat was measured and found to be 2 ounces (55 g) in 24 hours.

On the third day, purulent drainage developed that necessitated removal of sutures to expedite drainage. The entire area healed by the fourth week. von Schulz retrospectively made several observations. He believed that the incisions should have been made much longer and that in the dissection he allowed two different flap thicknesses to occur with a resulting terracing at the scar line, which was not cosmetically ideal. The scalpel dissection of fat was thought to cause many problems in healing. In 1903, a second patient was operated on for a similar condition. The fat was pulled away without scalpel dissection, and the wound described was of colossal size. All vessels were tied off by ligature, and the wound drained after careful approximation of wound edges. Although some fat drainage occurred, the amount was less than that in the first case. Drains were removed on the sixth day. However, the areas of the drains became infected, necessitating suture removal for better drainage. Healing progressed, and the patient was discharged on the twenty-ninth day after surgery. The first patient was most satisfied with her results, whereas the second continued to have multiple complaints about many things and after four years had gained a considerable amount of weight. von Schulz believed the "operation" was indicated in selected cases and that postoperative pain was a consideration, but no more so than in any other skin surgery.

Incisional history of abdominoplasty

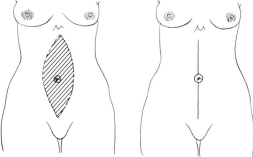

Babcock (1916) and Schepelmann (1918)

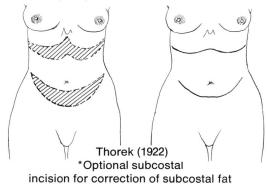

Thorek (1922)
*Optional subcostal
incision for correction of subcostal fat

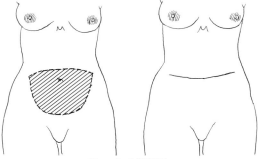

Pauchet (1925)

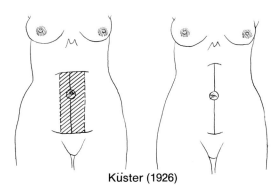

Küster (1926)

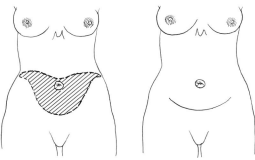

Frist (1927)

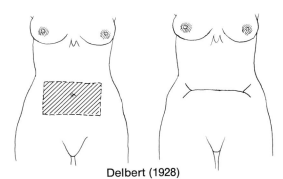

Delbert (1928)

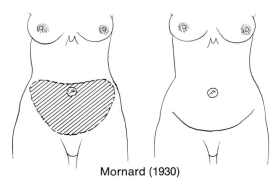

Mornard (1930)

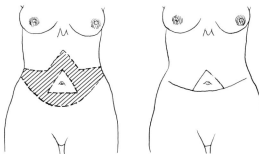

Flesch-Thebesius and Weinsheimer (1931)

In 1908, von Haberer[36] of Vienna reported the work of a Professor Baron von Eiselberg with a brief mention of von Schulz as well as Demars and Marx.

In 1909, S. Weinhold,[82] as a moderator of a discussion group, described an abdominal lipectomy he had done a year and a half previously. He stated that in the case of abdominal laparotomy or other abdominal surgery, there would be no reason not to improve the aesthetic appearance of the abdominal wall. He described three types of abdominal wall structure: that of (1) a thin person with bulging or hanging abdomen with decreased tension; (2) a fat person with tight, flat abdomen with increased tension; and (3) a fat person with bulging abdomen with decreased tension. He described the relationship of abdominal muscular tension to the type of aesthetic operation in a detailed case. Weinhold used lead plates as a buffer for the retention sutures.

In 1911, H. Edward Castle[13] of San Francisco reported on obesity and its surgical treatment by lipectomy. He discussed the need for a proper approach to general adiposity and the need for proper treatment including diet, exercise, and hygiene, as well as the psychological support necessary to prevent regression. He went on to substantiate the value of lipectomy in assisting these patients to overcome their problem. His surgical technique paralleled those of Kelly and others. Postoperative care included moist boric acid solution dressings and flexing the body to relieve tension on the suture line. Although he mentioned Kelly, Demars and Marx, Jolly, Maylard, von Schulz, Weinhold, Ballard, and Ochlechker, apparently, like many authors of that time, much of his material was taken from one or two reports. As a result, some of the reference data were in error.

In 1913, Castle[14] reported on a case of abdominal lipectomy in conjunction with an umbilical hernia originally presented before the Surgical Section of the San Francisco City Medical Society on June 18, 1912. Because of his concern for the feelings and possible embarrassment of the patient were she personally exposed, Castle made a special point of the fact that his presentation was made with lantern slides. The patient was a 42-year-old woman, 5 feet 2 inches in height (1.58 m) and mother of 8 children, who had originally been seen for the umbilical hernia. The wedgelike skin and soft tissue resection was similar to that in Kelly's report, but Castle made no mention of Kelly's procedure. He stressed caution in the dissection near the umbilicus. An interesting surgical sidelight was his use of towels soaked in hot saline solution to cover the rest of the field while the hernia was being repaired.

In 1911, W. F. Shallenberger[72] of Atlanta reported on two cases of abdominal lipectomy. His initial statement was that the operation, *although not rare*, was uncommon enough to report. In one of the cases, an appendectomy was completed during the procedure with the McBurney incision hidden underneath the transverse repair. This seems to be the first recorded multiple procedure noted other than the repair of an umbilical hernia in conjunction with a lipectomy.

In 1914, Vesco[81] also reported from the First University Clinic of Vienna on the work of Professor Baron von Eiselberg in the removal of an abdominal pan-

Incisional history of abdominoplasty

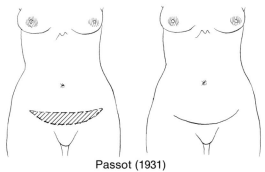

Passot (1931)

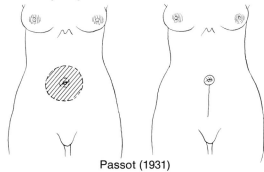

Passot (1931)

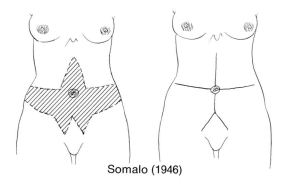

Somalo (1946)

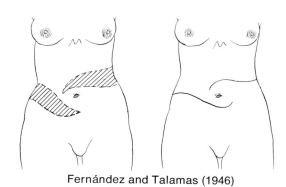

Fernández and Talamas (1946)

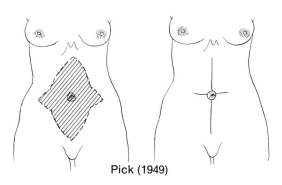

Pick (1949)

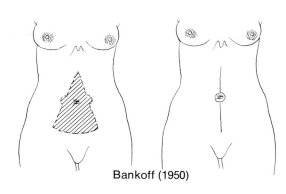

Bankoff (1950)

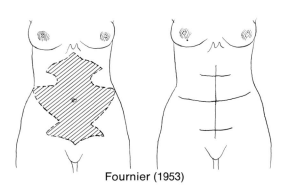

Fournier (1953)

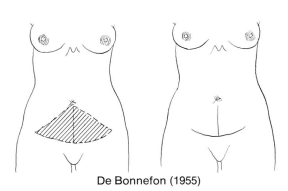

De Bonnefon (1955)

niculus, describing the case of a bartender undergoing surgery in January, 1907. He pointed out the importance of marking the patient in an upright position before surgery so that the incision lines would be in the proper place. Vesco also reported on the work of several of the previously mentioned surgeons, as had Doyen[19] of Paris in 1911.

In 1916, W. Wayne Babcock[2] of Philadelphia described the use of a silver chain in the supportive surgery for the relaxed abdominal wall. It was Babcock's opinion that a better abdominal contour may be obtained by removal of a vertical ellipse of skin with a vertical closure. Wide undermining of surrounding tissue to remove as much fatty tissue as possible was also emphasized.

On May 9, 1917, E. Schepelmann, Director of the Surgical Department of the Evangelical (Protestant) Hospital, Hamborn am Rhein, lectured on abdominal plastic surgery at the Dinsberg Military Doctors' Evening, giving special consideration to the "hanging abdomen." He stated that the kind of operation to be done depends on the type of abdominal changes present, such as a "spare tire" or a combination involving an umbilical hernia, prolapse, or surgical scar hernia. The surgical repair technique of the two conditions is essentially the same but with some slight differences. Schepelmann stated that his techniques were based on the techniques of Gersuny and Mayo. No specific references were included. The report was extensive and included references to many earlier surgeons and their work. Schepelmann noted that a case of similar surgery by Jolly on a woman who was once married was so good that she was able to remarry. He also discussed the technique of a Professor Wullstein, who carried his incisions around to the lumbar region. Schepelmann commented that the technique is not perfect if one wants an elegant form, but it is sufficient to greatly improve appearances.

In 1918, Schepelmann[68] wrote an extensive article discussing what was at that time a large number of cases of abdominoplasty with both vertical and horizontal repairs. He included drawings to demonstrate various surgical techniques, especially repair of diastasis recti abdominis and bulging of the anterior lower abdomen.

In 1921, Jochim Frist[25] described abdominal dermolipectomy in conjunction with laparotomy.

In 1922, Max Thorek[78] of Chicago reported in his excellent article, "Possibilities in the Reconstruction of the Human Form," not only on abdominal dermolipectomy but also on dermolipectomy of the thighs. His comprehension of the problems with dermolipectomy and the need for aesthetic attitudes was unusually astute compared with that of other surgeons and the state of the art at that time. Thorek stated that "we cannot consider an 'adipectomy' [as he called dermolipectomy] as mere amputation of flesh. There must be maintained a consistent effort to secure beauty of contour by eliminating superfluous adipose tissue at the same time keeping in mind the limitations that confront us."[78]

Thorek established many fundamental principles in dealing with the tissues involved in dermolipectomy that are equally valid for today's surgeon.

Incisional history of abdominoplasty

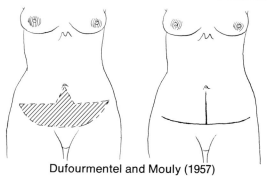

Dufourmentel and Mouly (1957)

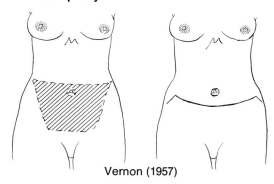

Vernon (1957)

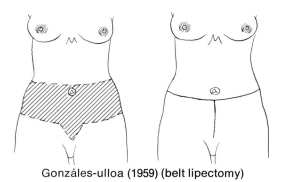

Gonzáles-ulloa (1959) (belt lipectomy)

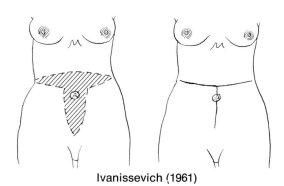

Ivanissevich (1961)

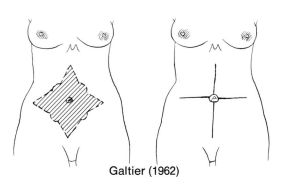

Galtier (1962)

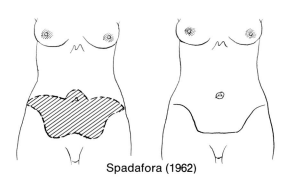

Spadafora (1962)

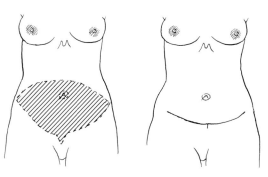

Masson (1962)

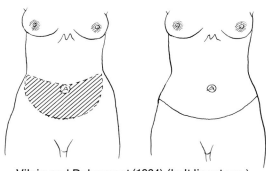

Vilain and Dubousset (1964) (belt lipectomy)

Some of these follow:

1. Fatty tissue is of low vitality and is prone to breakdown.
2. Perfect hemostasis is important; the wound should not be closed before this state is attained.
3. Gentleness during all aspects of the care of the patient from the preoperative to the postoperative state is emphasized. Crushing and tearing of tissue is to be avoided.
4. Asepsis is extremely important.
5. Tension should be avoided, and tension sutures should not be used.

In the surgical technique itself, Thorek used a knife with a large blade. The area of excision and repair was crescent shaped. The buttock surgery involved lateral tissue excision with vertical lateral repairs. From one patient he removed excess fatty tissue of the triceps areas of the arms, with repairs on the undersurface paralleling the direction of the limbs. He thereby became one of the first to discuss dermolipectomy of the extremities. He was apparently also one of the first to use electrocautery in such surgeries and to try transplantation of the umbilicus as a free graft.

Thorek's awareness of the cosmetic needs of patients was unusual; he recognized the potential of this area of surgical endeavor, as is evidenced by the following quote from his 1922 article[78]: "A vast field for research is offered in hyperadiposity." However, the section on surgery of the abdominal wall of his 1942 textbook[79] was almost totally limited to abdominal dermolipectomy in the obese patient. The text had an extensive description of the anatomy of the abdominal wall. Thorek stated that the original operation for removal of abdominal fat dates back to Kelly in 1889, but others disagree with that premise. He did not, however, cite either those who disagree or those who might have preceded Kelly. He described in detail the surgical techniques of Schepelmann, Flesch-Thebesius and Weinsheimer, and Kirchmayr, with lesser descriptions for the techniques of Küster, Weinhold, and Waltzell.

Some of the plastic surgeons of the early 1900s, such as Bettman, Kolle, Miller, and Joseph, although well known, were not in the recorded forefront of surgery for lipodystrophy.

In her book, *La chirurgie esthétique, son rôle social*[50] (1926), A. (Suzanne) Noël, the first woman costmetic surgeon of note, described and recorded photographically not only dermolipectomy of the abdomen but also of the extremities.

In 1930, Pierre Mornard[48] described and illustrated in detail what today would be considered a transposition of the umbilicus but what was titled, "A Transplantation of the Umbilicus."

Passot[52] in 1931 described several methods of abdominal dermolipectomy, including several limited resections of abdominal fatty tissue in the lower abdominal region and around the umbilicus. Also in 1931, M. Flesch-Thebesius and K. Weinsheimer[23] described a procedure whereby the umbilicus is preserved in a pyramid-shaped island of tissue that is transferred superiorly to a similarly shaped created defect as part of the resection in a lower abdominal

Incisional history of abdominoplasty

Clarkson (1966)

Peskova (1966)

Callia (1965 to 1967)

Meise (1966 to 1967)

Baaraya and Dezeuze (1967)

Castanares and Goethal (1967)

Pitanguy (1967) (vertical plication)

Serson (1971)

dermolipectomy. Interestingly, they mentioned the work of Joseph, Lotsch, and Lexer-Kraske but did not cite references.

In 1932, A. Buschke, A. Joseph, and W. Birkenfeld[11] described and illustrated several methods of abdominoplasty, including those of Passot, Schepelmann, and Flesch-Thebesius and Weinsheimer. The most interesting aspect of this text is a description of how to create a false or new umbilicus after complete removal of the original. The method described brings the skin down and fixes it to the fascia in a prescribed area. Involved are four diamond-shaped areas of skin resection and several retention sutures, including a continuous circular suture around the middle of the created defect. This is undoubtedly the first recorded reconstructive procedure.

In 1936, H. Biesenberger[9] described the inverted T type of repair in the excision of excess abdominal skin and fatty tissue.

In 1940[74] and 1946,[75] Marcos Somalo described several techniques in which both vertical and horizontal abdominal dermolipectomy are combined. He also described a circular dermolipectomy of the trunk. Somalo was apparently the first to use the term *dermolipectomy*.

Malbec[43] in 1948 used a transverse elliptical incision above and below the umbilicus, leaving it on a stalk.

J. F. Pick (1949)[55] and A. J. Barsky and S. Kahn[8] (1950) employed a shorter upper incision and a longer lower incision, which was corrected by a small, inferior V–shaped wedge excision.

In 1951, J. Fernández and M. C. Iturraspe[22] compared the incisions of abdominal lipectomy and bilateral reduction mammaplasty.

Fritz Schörcher,[69] in his extensive 1955 monograph, "Kosmetische Operationen," described and showed photographs not only of abdominal dermolipectomy but of dermal fat resection in many other areas such as thighs and hips. He described some body types and showed preoperative and postoperative photographs of subjects who had undergone abdominal dermolipectomy. Schörcher's article was the first to show many examples of extremity surgery, along with drawings for the removal of excess fatty tissue.

In 1955, Marcel Galtier[26] of Paris used a four-armed, irregular, star-shaped incision line with the umbilicus at the center, providing a less than ideal scar complex.

C. Dufourmentel and R. Mouly,[20] along with Morel-Fatio, in 1959 described a low transverse incision using the inverted T (anchor) type of repair.

In 1957, C. Claoué[17] gave a presentation by drawing several interesting variations on the surgical repair of the pendulous abdomen, one of which treated "dog ears" at the upper and lower ends of a vertical repair, ending up with a capital I–shaped scar as the result.

Also in 1957, Sidney Vernon[80] described the transplantation of the umbilicus upward, as well as an almost vertical lateral excision at the lateral margins of the transverse repair to remove the dog ears. His term, "transplantation," also was in reality transposition. His extensive use of multiple retention

Incisional history of abdominoplasty

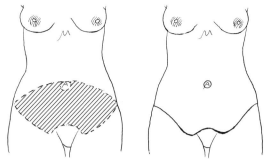
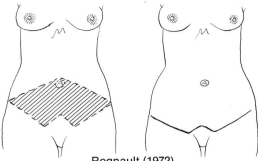

Lagache and Vandenbussche (1971)   Regnault (1972)

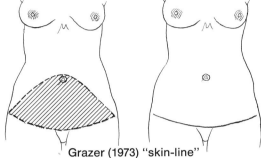
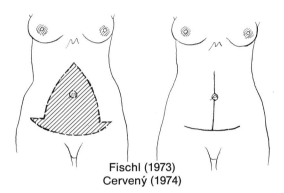

Grazer (1973) "skin-line"
(vertical rectus plication
without sheath incision)

Fischl (1973)
Cervený (1974)

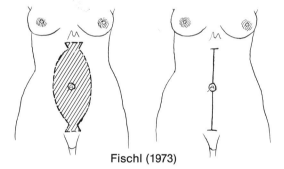
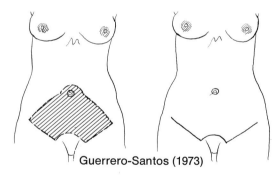

Fischl (1973)   Guerrero-Santos (1973)

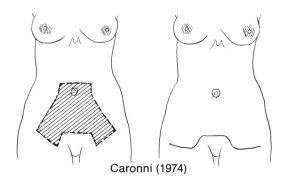
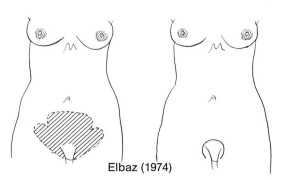

Caronni (1974)   Elbaz (1974)

sutures seemed to detract from his stated aesthetic goals. The patient reported on was treated for a pendulous abdomen after weight reduction.

In 1959, M. Gonzáles-Ulloa[28] described a dermolipectomy of the abdomen in which removal of tissue extended completely around the body, providing a vertical extension anteriorly and both upper and lower vertical extension posteriorly all at the midline with umbilical transposition. Gonzáles-Ulloa also described a procedure using the inverted T repair of Pick[55] and Barsky and Kahn.[8]

During the 1960s and 1970, surgeons such as Baron,[4] Masson,[44] Peskova,[53] and Myerowitz et al.[46,47] reported single or multiple cases of the surgical treatment. Usually they showed variations from existing techniques. Some such as Meyerowitz et al. described unusually huge amounts (83 pounds 10 ounces [38 kg]) of tissue excised as well as problems associated with such cases.

In 1961, Oscar Ivanissevich[40] described an inverted T–shaped combined horizontal and vertical abdominal dermolipectomy that left the umbilicus intact.

In 1962, Galtier[27] described the star-shaped lipectomy of his own design but also included sketches of various methods of twelve other surgeons.

In 1962, Spadafora[76] described an unusual repair whose lines of incision were actually an exaggerated W or gull-wing type of repair. On illustration the lower lines of incision seem to extend well into the anterior medial thigh areas but in postoperative drawings and photographs are low and in the abdominal region.

In 1964, K. L. Pickrell,[56] in his extensive chapter, "Reconstructive Surgery of the Abdominal Wall and Back," described in detail the anatomy, embryology, and surgical considerations of the abdominal wall. He emphasized that the type of incision will be dictated by and dependent on the variety of abdominal deformity. He advised the repair of diastasis of rectus muscles where indicated during lipectomy. Although this work was designed for review of all types of abdominal wall surgery, its contents provided much basic material for the aesthetic surgeon.

In 1966, Patrick Clarkson[18] of England described vertical and double vertical S–shaped incisions and repair lines for abdominal dermolipectomy. In view of the extensive scarring, the surgical logic involved is as difficult to justify as the resulting aesthetic deformity.

In 1967, Castanares and Goethal[12] reported on their modification of the Galtier technique with the horizontal arms of the excision extended and the vertical arms decreased but still leaving a cross-shaped scar.

In 1967, I. Pitanguy[57] presented a tremendous report on 300 cases of abdominal dermolipectomy. The incision line was swept downward at the lateral edges in an oblique manner. He illustrated the repair of the rectus sheath and introduced the use of a plaster of paris splint supplemented with sandbag pressure. Although many modifications have occurred since Pitanguy presented his original technique, it remains the prototype for all subsequent abdominoplasties. His own major difficulty with the procedure was the need to repair the dog ear deformities at the lateral edge of the repair. In 1972, Pitanguy[58] described

Incisional history of abdominoplasty

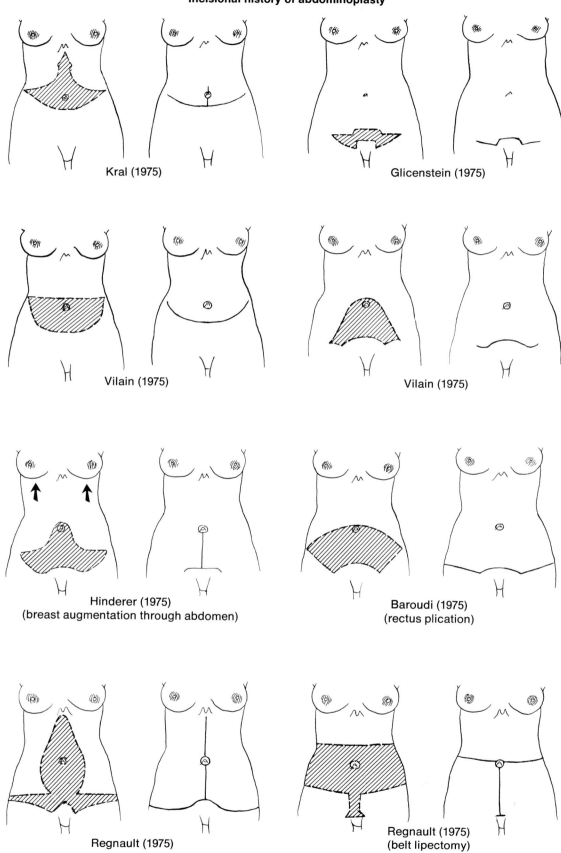

Kral (1975)

Glicenstein (1975)

Vilain (1975)

Vilain (1975)

Hinderer (1975)
(breast augmentation through abdomen)

Baroudi (1975)
(rectus plication)

Regnault (1975)

Regnault (1975)
(belt lipectomy)

several modifications of his original technique. In the foreseeable future, the standard abdominoplasty procedure will remain the basic technique, since it has stood the test of time.

In 1971, D. Serson[71] described a geometric shape of incision lines for abdominal dermolipectomy that could best be employed in mild to moderate cases. Its limitation to these cases of lipodystrophy was pointed out by an editor in a review in another publication. Serson's modification is the most interesting to follow the Pitanguy method and is more applicable for the aesthetic patient. It was introduced to eliminate the lateral extension of the incision in the linear type of abdominoplasty.

In 1972, A. Szczawiński, H. O. Oknińska, and S. Dreszer[77] stated that none of the advocated operative techniques for abdominal dermolipectomy is better than another, with the shape of the excised area needing to fit the shape of the patient. It would be interesting to know how many abdominal dermolipectomies these surgeons had completed as a background for such an all-encompassing statement.

In 1972, M. K. Chachava and T. I. Gotsiridze[16] contributed to the Russian literature. The report included references to articles from the Russian literature in 1948 and 1959, but these were not available for review.

In 1973, F. M. Grazer[31] reported on 44 cases in which a repair line was used that conformed to the area covered by a bikini swimsuit. The article emphasized the need for the surgeon to meet the psychological requirements of the patient to have a scar line covered by such garments.

In 1974, J. Cervený[15] described an inverted T–incision repair as used at the Department of Plastic Surgery in Prague, which he had modified.

In 1974, R. Baroudi, E. M. Keppke, and F. Tozzi-Netto[7] presented a report on abdominal dermolipectomy cases seen by their group over a ten-year period. This article, which is especially noteworthy for its emphasis on umbilicoplasty, was followed by an extensive, excellent article[6] by Baroudi on umbilicoplasty. Many excellent photographs demonstrated his techniques and observations.

In 1975, U. T. Hinderer[37] reported on a combined abdominal dermolipectomy and augmentation mammaplasty.

In 1975, Paule Regnault[65] of Canada reported on her "fleur de lys" technique, which appears to be a modification of Castanares and Goethal's technique. She also described her W technique, which seems to be a modification of Serson's method[71] and is indicated when the aesthetic result is most important and a vertical scar, either lateral or in the midline, is unacceptable to the patient. Regnault stated that she has used the W-plasty since 1963.

In 1975, W. D. Muhlbauer[49] described briefly an abdominal lipectomy method in which dissection extended well into the upper portion of the upper thighs.

In 1978, J. M. Psillakis[62] plicated the rectus sheath vertically in the midportion of each muscle rather than in the midline.

Incisional history of abdominoplasty

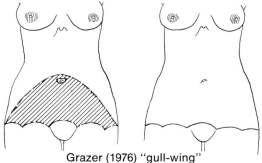

Grazer (1976) "gull-wing"
(vertical rectus plication)

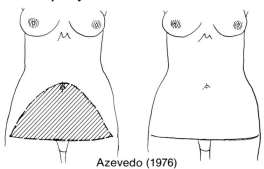

Azevedo (1976)

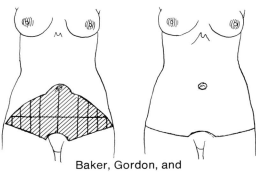

Baker, Gordon, and
Mosienko (1977) "template"

De-epithelialized

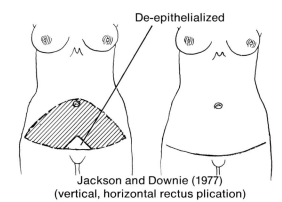

Jackson and Downie (1977)
(vertical, horizontal rectus plication)

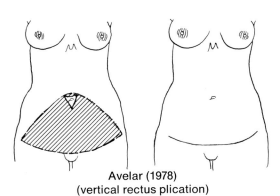

Avelar (1978)
(vertical rectus plication)

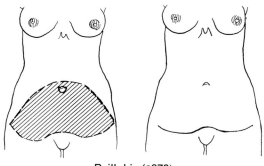

Psillakis (1978)
(three lines of vertical plication)

TODAY'S TECHNIQUES

It is important to understand that no two human bodies are alike. Therefore every surgeon has to plan for the individual patient. As a sculptor works with clay to mold and shape, the plastic surgeon needs to use artistic and aesthetic appreciation to identify the surgery that is most appropriate for the body type and sex of the patient.

At the present time and state of the art, a number of popular techniques are employed. Most of these include incisions primarily of the low transverse type and some with mixed vertical components[21] (Chapter 1).

In the past most authors have focused their primary attention on the configuration of the incision line. Although the incision is important, many other factors influence the ultimate result. The final direction and appearance of the scar line varies greatly with the experience and sensitivity of the surgeon. The kind of abdominal deformity involved also contributes to the site and shape of the scar. The surgeon must follow the natural creases in the area to obtain a scar that is as inconspicuous as possible. The lower the position of the scar or the closer to the pubic hair and inguinal crease, the easier it is to hide it with a small bikini swimsuit.

The gull-wing modification (Figs. 5-1 and 5-2), which differs fundamentally from the classic W and skin-line incisions (Figs. 5-1, 5-3, and 5-4), was introduced in 1976.[33,63,64,66] With the gull-wing design, the lateral incisions from the pubic inguinal junction are directed laterally in a convex configuration out to the plane of the anterior projection of the iliac crest, where there is an upward extension of the lateral segments.[31] The advantage of this technique is that the incision is kept much lower. The gull wing is selected for the thinner patient; the skin line is chosen for the more corpulent patient (Fig. 5-5).

Symmetry of the scar is an absolute must. Some achieve this by using a template.[3] This detail contributes greatly to a natural-appearing abdomen. The quality of a scar is related to intrinsic and extrinsic factors. The intrinsic factors are those determined by the organism itself in connection with age, race, and collagen formation. The surgery provides the extrinsic factors. A meticulous closure of the operative wound layer by layer with the least tension is a sine qua non for minimal scarring. Undermining of the dermal fat flap should be symmetrical, and the pull and resection of the stretched dermal flap must be balanced. Final tension on the suture line will therefore be uniformly distributed.

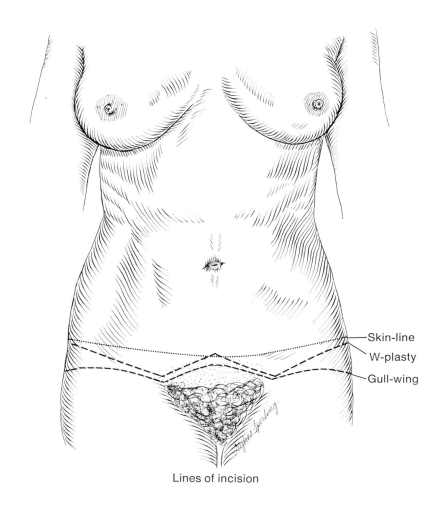

Skin-line
W-plasty
Gull-wing

Lines of incision

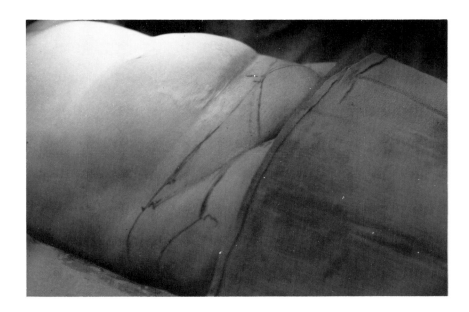

Fig. 5-1

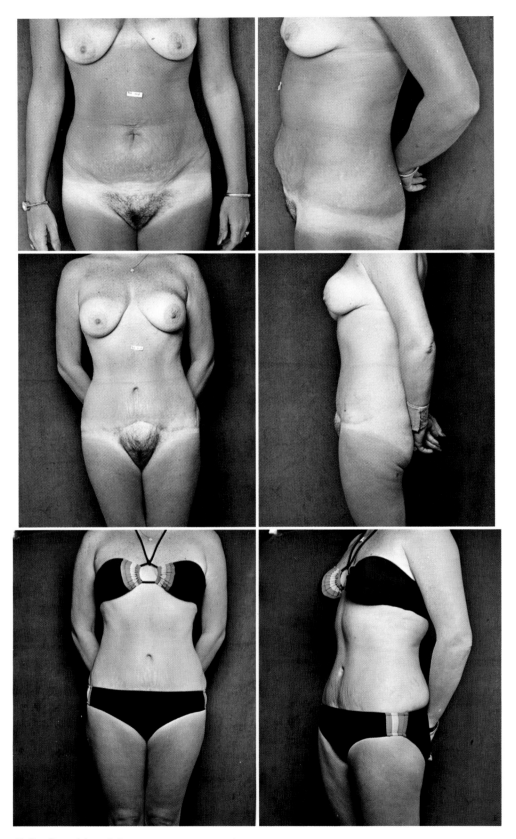

Fig. 5-2. Combined breast augmentation and gull-wing abdominoplasty. Patient is shown in her bikini two years after surgery.

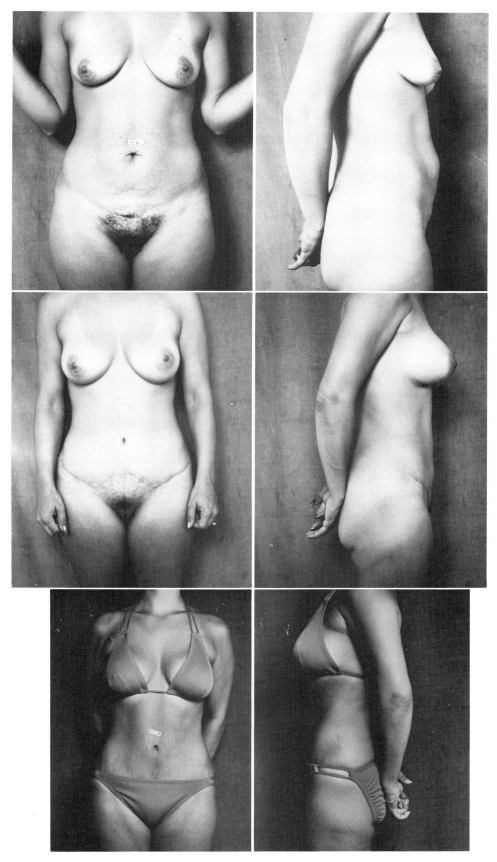

Fig. 5-3. Combined breast augmentation and classical W-abdominoplasty. Two-year postoperative result is shown in photographs with bikini.

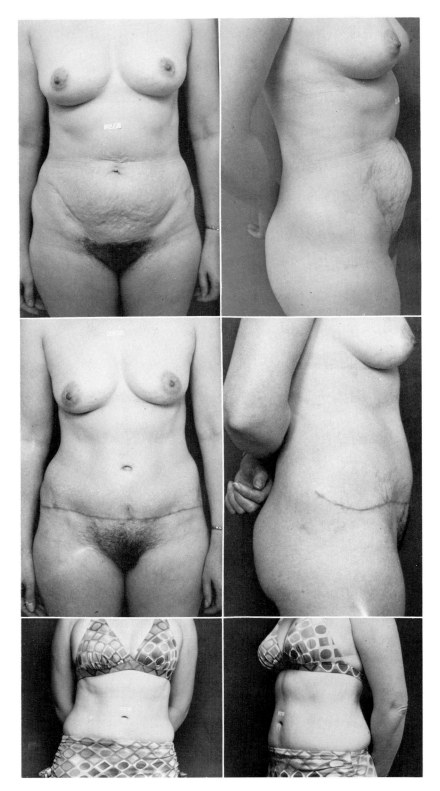

Fig. 5-4. Combined vaginal hysterectomy and skin-line abdominoplasty. Patient is shown in her bikini three years postoperatively.

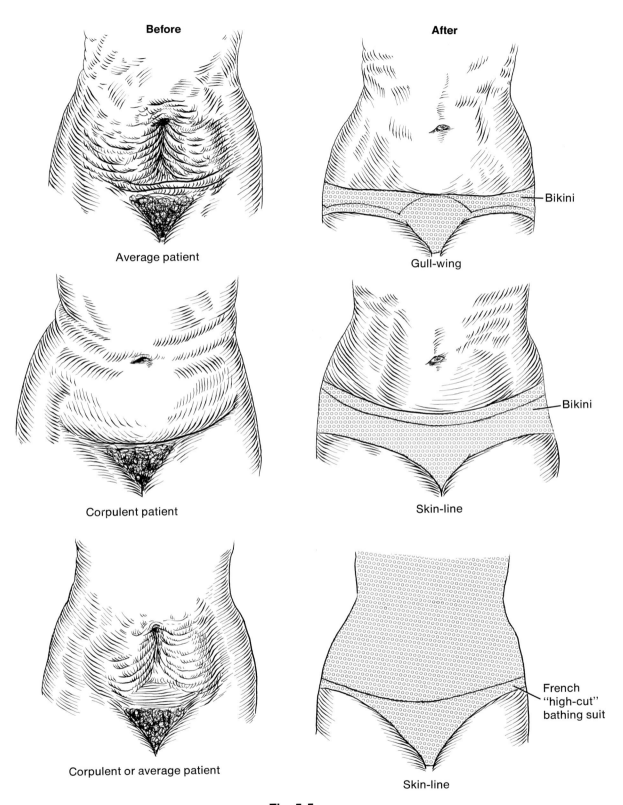

Before

After

Average patient

Bikini

Gull-wing

Corpulent patient

Bikini

Skin-line

Corpulent or average patient

French "high-cut" bathing suit

Skin-line

Fig. 5-5

Recently, various ingenious methods have been described for umbilicoplasty,* all of which try to duplicate the natural anatomical characteristics of the umbilicus as found in a young person. The best results are those showing a rounded depression of 1 to 1.5 cm diameter with a surrounding invaginated skin forming a circular fold harmoniously around the scar.[5] The umbilicus should be in the midline slightly below the waistline, dividing the abdomen into its superior and inferior segments (Fig. 5-6). Fig. 5-6 demonstrates the range and variation of the umbilical configurations, along with postoperative results. The details are described in the section on surgical technique.

*References 1, 5, 6, 24, 60, 61.

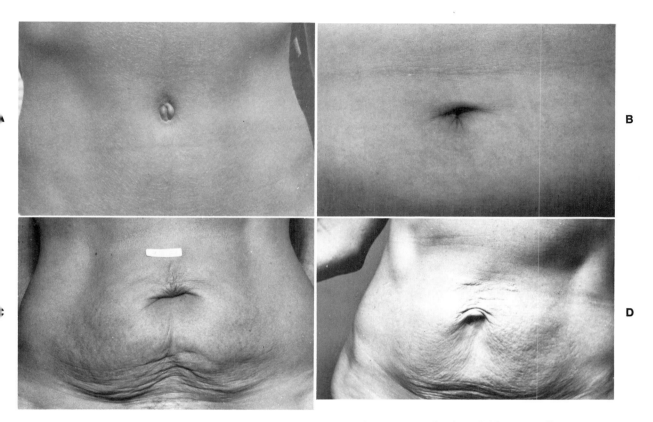

Fig. 5-6. A, Nulliparous 17-year-old girl demonstrating the vertical umbilical configuration frequently observed in this age group. **B,** Nulliparous 30-year-old woman with natural hooding that increases with age. **C,** Appearance of multiparous 34-year-old woman with old surgery scar. **D,** Transverse configuration and the advanced hooding commonly seen in multiparous women such as this 44-year-old.

PATIENT CONSIDERATIONS
Patient selection according to body type

After fifteen years of experience, it became apparent that a standard nomenclature would be helpful in selecting the appropriate operative approach and predicting operative results.

The classification of somatotypes as developed by W. H. Sheldon[73] would appear to offer such a nomenclature. He selected different body types through standard photography, concentrated on body shapes, and qualified his findings by means of three anatomical types: endomorphy, mesomorphy, and ectomorphy.[51,73]

Mesomorphy means a square, rugged-looking, heavily muscled physique with a predominance of muscle, bone, and connective tissue. This physique is normally heavy, hard, and rectangular in outline (Fig. 5-8, A and B).

Endomorphy is predominance of the abdomen over the thorax and of the trunk over the limbs, which are short and tapering with small hands and feet. This particular physique has a degree of roundness to it and a propensity to put on fat (Fig. 5-8, C and D).

Ectomorphy has a predominance of linearity and fragility; subcutaneous fat and muscle development are minimal (Fig. 5-8, E and F).

Sheldon's procedure of classification involves assigning each individual a score on a scale of 1 to 7 in terms of the degree of endomorphy, mesomorphy, and ectomorphy present: 1 indicates minimal and 7, maximal, degree of the particular body configuration (4 is the midpoint). Thus each individual body configuration is designated by a three-number score. For example, an individual receiving a score of 711 would have the maximum degree of endomorphy with minimal evidence of mesomorphy and ectomorphy.

For purposes of comparison we selected a somatotype distribution of female Oxford University students as depicted by Parnell[51] and used Sheldon's somatotype to compare the students to the patient distribution used in this text. Since the somatotypes do not change with age, we believe this is a valid comparison. The somatochart in Fig. 5-7 indicates the distribution of 671 women students (one dot = one woman).

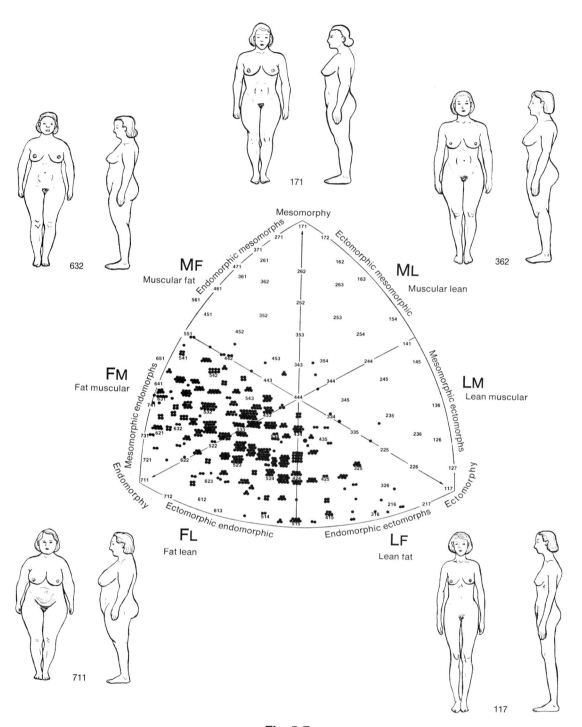

Fig. 5-7

Fig. 5-8 indicates the somatotype distribution of a hundred women whom we saw. Each patient's position on the chart was assigned by three different, independent observers employing Sheldon's descriptions of body types to analyze preoperative photographs.

Although there were extremes toward ectomorphy and endomorphy, the majority of the patients appeared to be of average body build.

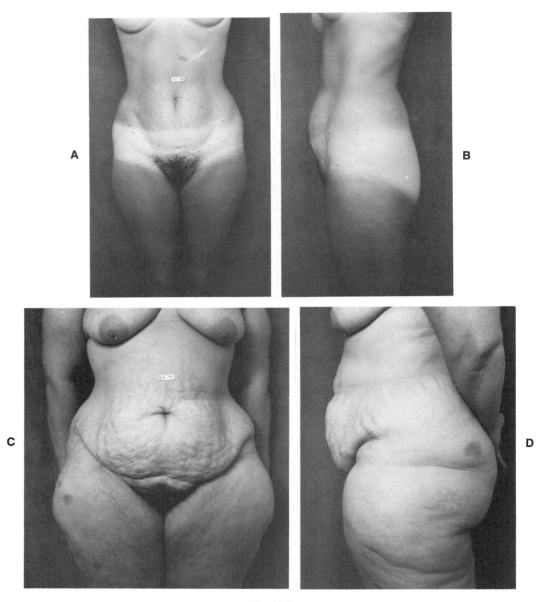

Fig. 5-8

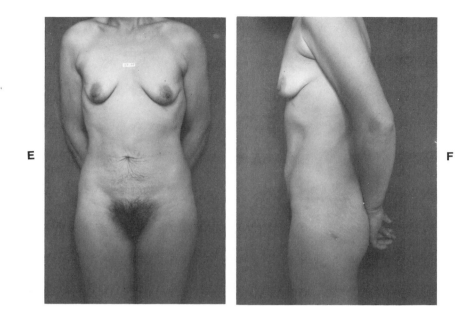

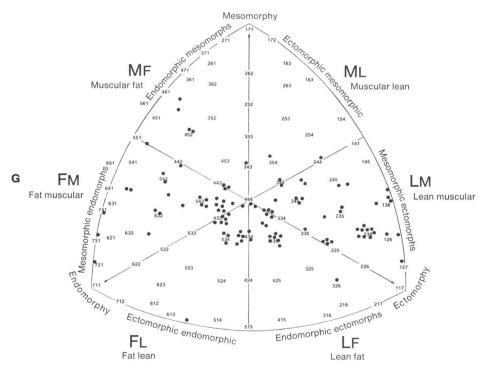

Fig. 5-8, cont'd

The ideal patient is a mesomorphic (score, 334; Fig. 5-8, *A* and *B*), or ectomorphic (score, 126; Fig. 5-8, *E* and *F*) multiparous woman whose only physical deformity exists between the xiphoid and the pubis (Fig. 5-9, *A* and *B*). The poorest candidate is the endomorphic (score, 741; Fig. 5-8, *C* and *D*), obese man or woman who is unable to lose weight by any of the usual methods (Fig. 5-9, *C* and *D*).

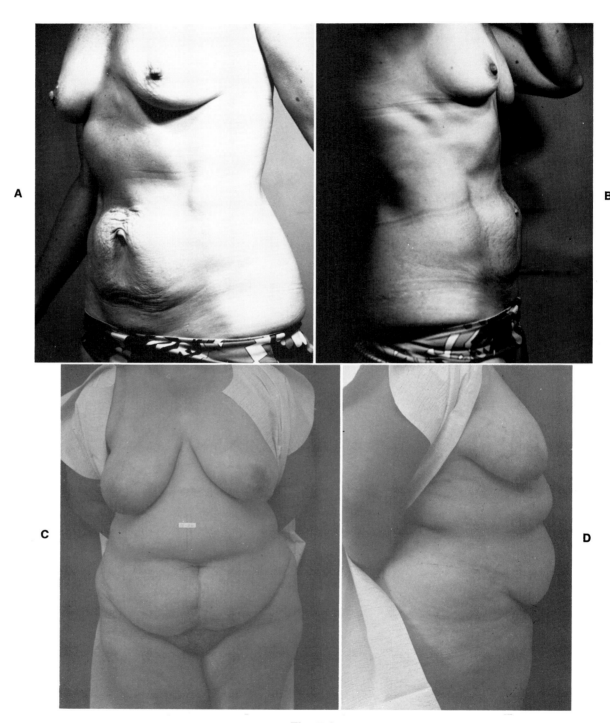

Fig. 5-9

The patient with diastasis recti is an acceptable candidate (Fig. 5-10, *A* and *B*). The thin patient with a protruding lower abdominal wall as a result of a large organ size or malposition and/or the patient with poor posture is an unacceptable candidate for this abdominoplasty (Fig. 5-10, *C* and *D*).

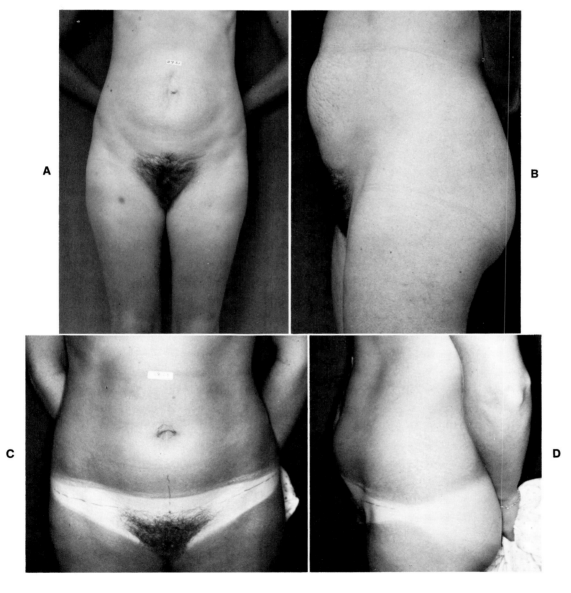

Fig. 5-10

Patients with multiple striae will not produce good scars because of loss of elastic tissue and an inability to remove all the striae (Fig. 5-11).

It is difficult in thin, tall patients with increases xiphoid-to-pubis dimensions to eliminate the umbilical defect without pulling the pubic hairline abnormally high (Fig. 5-12). Although the pubic hairline is somewhat elevated, the use of the inverted T minimizes the amount of elevation.

Patients whose previous scars cannot be eliminated often achieve less than ideal results (Fig. 5-13).

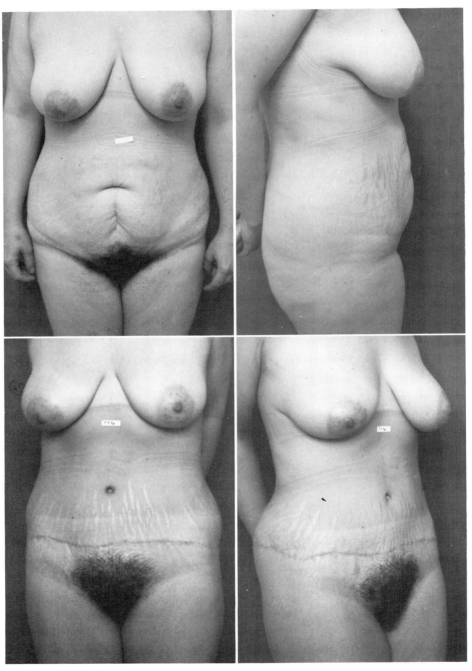

Fig. 5-11

Extreme caution should be exercised with patients who have a history of previous bowel obstruction, cardiorespiratory problems, or thromboembolic disease. Only in exceptional circumstances should a patient with diabetes or any other metabolic or autoimmune disease be considered a candidate.

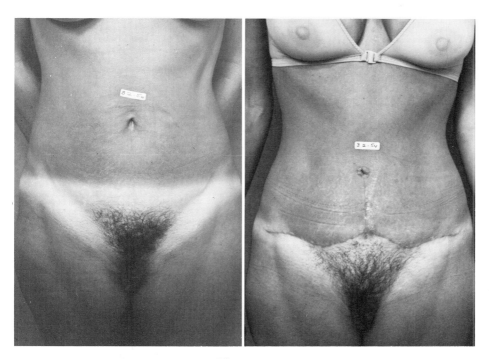

Fig. 5-12

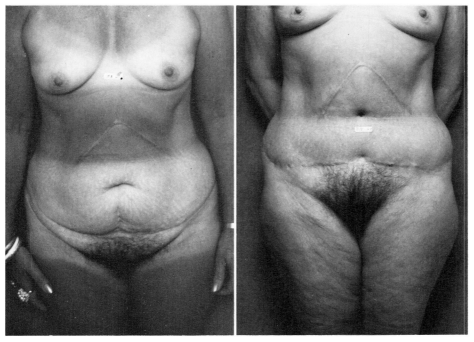

Fig. 5-13

Informed consent

Patients should be made brutally aware of the fact that they are trading one deformity, the abdominal defect, for another deformity, the resultant scar. It is patently understood that the resulting scar will be a lesser deformity, but all potential problems are thoroughly reviewed with the patient. The patient should be told that the process of recovery from an abdominoplasty is similar to that from intra-abdominal surgeries. It is anticipated that there will be some pain and discomfort, which is intensified when rectus plication is part of the procedure. The fascial repair can be compared to hernia repair in terms of healing time.

The possibility of persistent numbness in parts of the abdomen (usually the periumbilical area), skin loss, hematoma, infection, deep-vein thrombosis, and pulmonary embolus, as well as the remote possibility of death, should be reviewed in detail with the patient. They should also be told that there is a possibility of the need for a secondary scar revision.[32]

In our practices, patients are selectively allowed to view a film of the actual surgical procedure, if they so wish.[33] Patients are given a copy of "Abdomino-plasty Assessed by Survey, with Emphasis on Complications"[32] when reinforcement is desired. The patients can be shown photographs of the best and worst results as a means of assisting the development of a realistic outlook on the possible results.[38] The photographs emphasize the potential variations in the size and extent of scarring. *Caution* as to overutilization of the *best* results is emphasized. All patients undergo preliminary marking, demonstrating the bikini outline and the extent of skin resection and undermining. These marks are frequently left on so the patient may discuss the intended surgery with the spouse (Fig. 5-14).

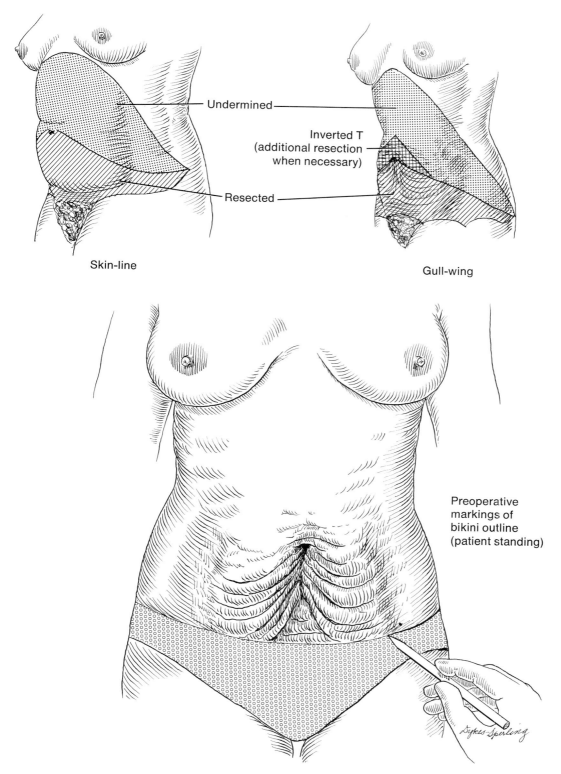

Undermined

Inverted T
(additional resection
when necessary)

Resected

Skin-line

Gull-wing

Preoperative
markings of
bikini outline
(patient standing)

Fig. 5-14

PREOPERATIVE CARE
Preparation

When unusual blood loss is anticipated, as in the obese patient or the patient who has a history of bleeding, the patient should donate blood for storage in the hospital blood bank and possible autologous transfusion at the time of surgery. This should be done three to six weeks prior to surgery. This procedure decreases the inherent risk of hepatitis transmission or blood incompatibility reaction. With up-to-date blood bank techniques, blood can be kept frozen for several years.

Baseline iodine 125–fibrinogen scans are obtained on any patient at high risk for the development of deep venous thrombosis or with previous history of thromboembolic disease (Chapter 7). This is particularly true of obese patients, patients receiving oral contraceptives, and patients with visible varicosities. As a rule routine chest x-ray and EKG studies are obtained for all patients who are over 40 years old; in addition, serum electrolyte tests are performed on patients who have been receiving diuretics.

Patients are instructed to begin showering with pHisoHex or Neutrogena soap several days before surgery. The abdominal preparation, including the shave, is not done until the time of the surgery to avoid possible infection development after trauma to the skin. When feasible, the surgeon does the preparation shave.

Since patients are usually ambulant within 24 hours after surgery, a routine bowel preparation or enemas are not ordered except for patients who think they may have problems with constipation postoperatively.

All preoperative medications are ordered by the anesthesiologist except for antibiotics, which are routinely begun on the day before surgery. Broad-spectrum antibiotics are used, preferably cephalosporin. We have observed no hematological abnormalities with this antibiotic. Heavy smokers are given intermittent positive pressure breathing (IPPB) prior to surgery. Any patient who has less than ideal respiratory function, such as chronic coughing, may require preoperative arterial blood gases and should continue IPPB after surgery.

Nursing care and education

Since the patients are frequently unfamiliar with hospital surroundings and routines, the nursing staff needs to orient the patient to the room and hospital procedures. The nurse should be alert to the patient taking any medication without the physician's knowledge and orders. On observation, any information about food or drug allergies, alcoholism, or medication that the patient has deliberately or inadvertently withheld from the surgeon should immediately be brought to the surgeon's attention. Specific preoperative preparation such as food and fluid restriction as well as the premedication should be explained. The flexed position, which the patient will need to assume postoperatively, should be demonstrated. Patients should be taught the calf and thigh exercises that will be used postoperatively to promote good venous return. It is helpful for the patient to review this demonstration and practice these exercises as well as the deep breathing exercises prior to the day of surgery. Frequently, the nurse will need to tactfully reinforce the physician's explanations about the surgical procedure and the preoperative and postoperative care. Many patients do not hear or retain all that the surgeon has told them.

Patients undergoing aesthetic procedures such as abdominoplasties have additional concern about the final postoperative appearance, since appearance itself is usually the prime motivation for surgery. Unusual anxiety prior to surgery should alert the surgeon to potential problems and the possible need for psychiatric consultation. Canceling the surgery may be in the best interest of all parties.

Patients desiring aesthetic procedures have frequently been stereotyped as vain, narcissistic, and wealthy individuals by hospital personnel as well as by the public. One of the major factors in the apparent antipathy toward the aesthetic patient on the part of many people (including physicians in other specialties) is an expressed concern that these patients divert required health care resources and personnel from other "more pressing" medical needs. Such a point of view does not recognize the importance of the quality of life as opposed to the quantity of life. Most of these patients do not get third-party compensation for their expenses. The fact that they continue to pursue aesthetic improvement, in spite of the cost, is evidence of their high level of motivation and the importance of such surgery to them.[83]

In the course of hospitalization the patient comes in contact with many different hospital personnel: admitting office staff, laboratory and x-ray technicians, housekeeping personnel, ward clerks, and nursing staff. The patient often feels the need to defend the decision to have aesthetic surgery to each of these numerous staff personnel. This defensiveness is frequently enhanced by well-meaning attempts at support for the patient with statements such as "You don't really look like you need that surgery."[33]

Because the patient's need to defend the decision is renewed with each new staff member, it is helpful to provide continuity of nursing staff when possible. This enables the patient to develop a relationship of trust with a few staff members. Such continuous experience with aesthetic patients will also enable the nurses to become comfortable with the various procedures and preoperative and postoperative requirements. Ideally, care in the same area and under the direction of the same nurses should be sought.

Care in the operating room

The patient should void immediately prior to receiving preoperative medication before going to the operating room. If there is any delay, the patient should be required to void on a bed pan immediately before surgery. Even though the patient is heavily medicated, reassurance by the operating room personnel puts the patient at ease. Discussion of such areas as materials, equipment, instruments, and techniques should be avoided while the patient is awake. Hearing is the last sense to leave as the patient goes to sleep; medical personnel should bear this in mind.

SURGICAL TECHNIQUE
Position and preparation

The patient is placed in the supine position directly over the hinge break in the operating table to obtain maximum flexion when needed during the operation (Fig. 5-15, *A*). After the intravenous solution is positioned and the patient is intubated, the cautery plate is placed either on or under the thigh or the gluteal area. If the patient is wearing elastic stockings, it is important that they are in the proper position and not pulled partially down, acting as a tourniquet. At the present time elastic stockings are not routinely used except in certain selected cases such as patients with large varicosities. The anesthesiologist or the surgeon, prior to the preparation, flexes the patient to make sure that the position on the table is satisfactory (Fig. 5-15, *B*).

Preoperative skin preparation with povidone iodine (Betadine) extends from the upper thighs to above the breast. Preparation is extended over the sides of the patient as far as the table, and frequently buttocks are pulled up to allow for preparation extension. With upper hip contouring, the patient may be rolled on her side and prepared on sterile sheets. Prior to the placement of sterile drapes, the circulating nurse and the anesthesiologist ensure that the patient is properly positioned to avoid pressure points, which could lead to nerve damage. If the patient has an indwelling cathether, as in a combined procedure, it is important that the proper drainage is established.

Draping

Sterile paper drapes are preferred. A paper laparotomy drape with its central aperture can be enlarged by cutting it with scissors to expose the entire surgical area from nipples to pubis. The prepared hairline is exposed to obtain a reference point from the midline of the genital area.

Lighting and marking

The best lighting is obtained from two separate sources: a light directly above and one angled approximately 40 to 45 degrees below the table for illumination during the creation of the flap.

Final marking of the patient on the operating table is done with the previous bikini line as reference. The marking procedure varies with the type of patient.

Skin line

For the corpulent or obese patient, the skin-line abdominoplasty technique is used. A no. 1 silk thread is stablized with a hemostat at the xiphoid process and is extended to the pubic hairline, where a marking pen is attached. A curvilinear arc, extending laterally from the pubic hairline, follows the natural skin line out to the vertical projection of the iliac spine. It is then extended laterally by freehand drawing to follow the skin line[30] (Fig. 5-15, *C*).

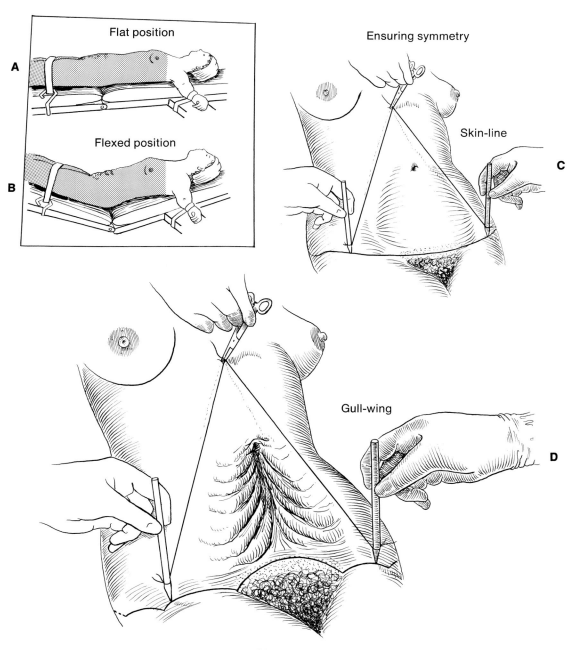

Flat position

A

Flexed position

B

Ensuring symmetry

Skin-line

C

Gull-wing

D

Fig. 5-15

Gull wing

The gull-wing procedure is chosen for the thinner, more athletic patient[28] (Fig. 5-15, *D*). The following specific points are marked (Figs. 5-16, *A*, and 5-17, *A*):

1. The center of the pubis at or below the hairline
2. The junction of the pubic hairline and the inguinal crease
3. The point directly perpendicular to the anterior vertical projection of the iliac spine
4. A slightly elevated curvilinear line extending around to the lateral hip area but well below the iliac crest
5. Dog ear extension when necessary

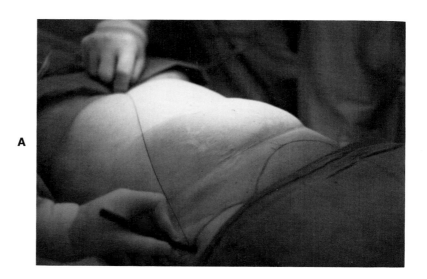

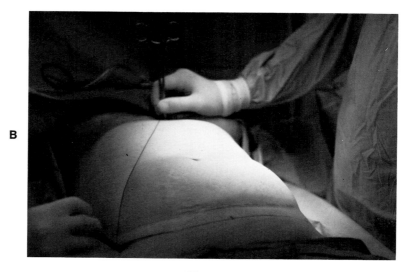

Fig. 5-16

Incision

Three different levels of incisions may be used for the skin-line technique, depending on the amount of abdominal wall relaxation (Figs. 5-16, *B*, and 5-17, *B*):

1. Higher incision with little abdominal wall relaxation
2. Middle incision with average relaxation
3. Lower incision with much abdominal wall relaxation

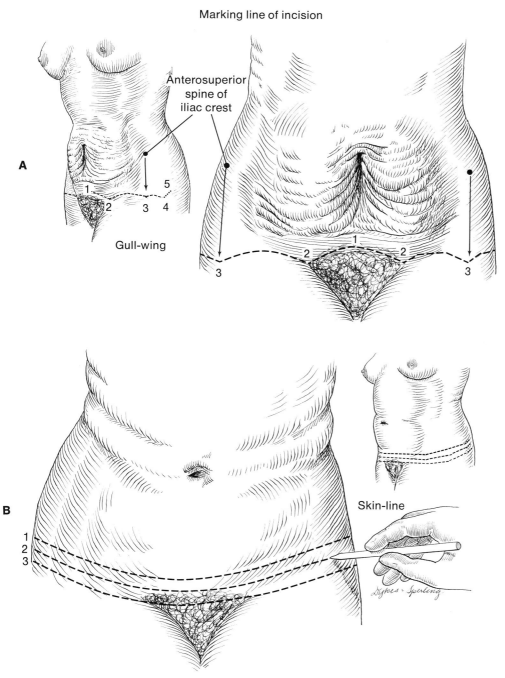

Fig. 5-17

The surgical technique for gull-wing abdominoplasty is essentially the same as that for the skin line after the initial incision, until the final resection of the flaps (Fig. 5-19, *A* and *B*). The incision is made with a no. 10 blade through the surface of the skin to the subcutaneous fat. At this point, electric cautery cutting current is used, preferably with the Valley Lab cautery or a similar unit. The incision is carried down through Scarpa's fascia to the underlying abdominal and rectus facsia. Two Kocher clamps are placed on each side of the flap to be developed. The assistant applies traction as the flap is elevated. The perforating vessels, which are larger and more prevalent in the midline area, are cauterized with an up-and-down motion of the cautery unit. Occasionally a perforating vessel must be ligated. When a vessel retracts within the substance of the rectus muscle, a figure-eight ligation to prevent immediate rectus sheath hematoma is required. Rectus hematomas that are recognized and are not corrected by ligation require immediate opening of the sheath and direct ligation of the vessel or vessels. Dissection is continued superiorly until approximately 2.5 cm from the umbilicus (Fig. 5-19, *C*). At this point the surgeon places two single skin hooks in the umbilicus and retracts it out of its pocket (Fig. 5-18). (This is similar to the technique of the gynecologist to pull the cervix down to cut around it in a vaginal hysterectomy.) With pull on the umbilicus, a circumferential incision is made in the skin (Fig. 5-19, *D*).

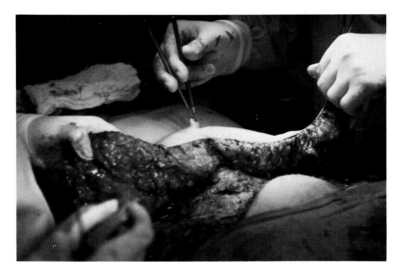

Fig. 5-18

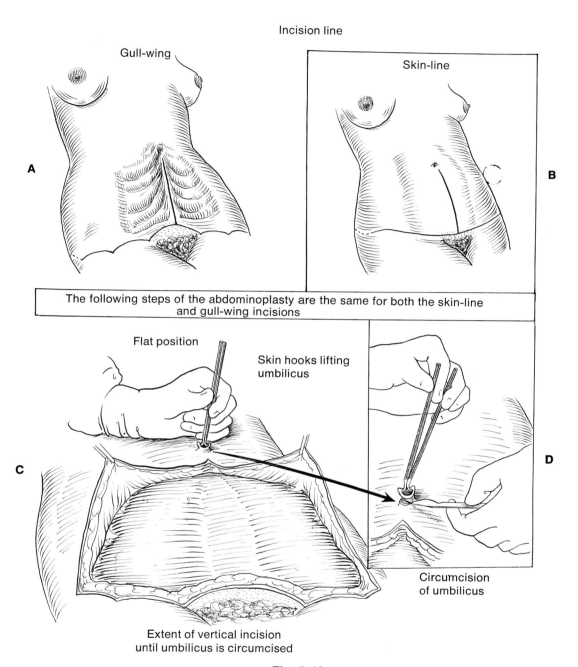

Incision line

Gull-wing

Skin-line

A

B

The following steps of the abdominoplasty are the same for both the skin-line and gull-wing incisions

Flat position

Skin hooks lifting umbilicus

C

D

Extent of vertical incision until umbilicus is circumcised

Circumcision of umbilicus

Fig. 5-19

The tension supplied by the skin hook makes this tough umbilical skin easier to incise symmetrically. The assistant continues to hold the umbilicus after circumcision and directs it out of the way of the surgeon's knife or cautery. Once the umbilical stalk is free, dissection continues up to the xiphoid and costal margin (Fig. 5-20, *A*, and 5-21). Frequently it is necessary to dissect above the rib margin. In Fig. 5-20, *B*, the surgeon's hand shows the extent of the resection above the rib margin. An extension is placed on the cautery unit to aid in dissection. After careful hemostasis, plication may begin. Maximum relaxation of the patient's abdominal wall at this point is requested of the anesthesiologist.

A
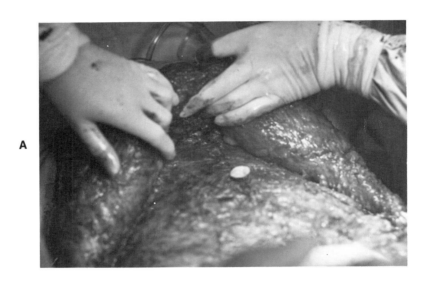

B
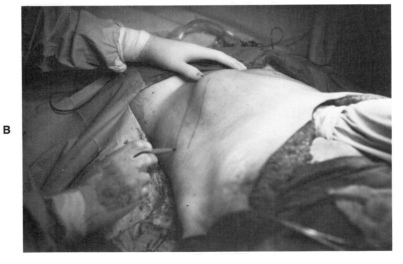

Fig. 5-20

Flat position

Dissection
by cauterization

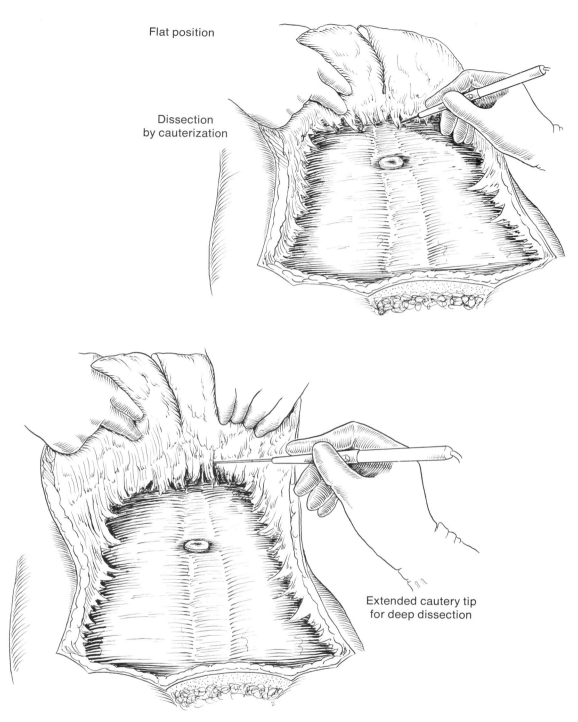

Extended cautery tip
for deep dissection

Fig. 5-21

Plication

Of the patients undergoing abdominoplasty, 95% require some plication. Beginning at the umbilicus, figure-of-eight 3-0 Tevdak sutures are used. The suture is placed through the medial edge of the rectus fascia in a figure-eight fashion. Usually from 2.5 to 5 cm in reduction of abdominal girth by plication is accomplished. The first suture begins to develop a roll of fascia that extends down to the pubis. Figs. 5-22, *A* and *B*, and 5-23, *A*, demonstrate the difference between the plicated and nonplicated areas. The sutures are placed approximately 1 cm apart. Frequently at the pubic area some fatty tissue is resected, usually prior to plication, because of the excess accumulation of subcutaneous fat and the inability to plicate without a fullness (Fig. 5-22, *C*). After the lower portion of the abdomen is plicated, plication proceeds superiorly from the umbilicus up to the xiphoid (Fig. 5-23, *A* and *B*).

After completion of the plication with the nonabsorbable sutures, the entire rectus sheath is reinforced with running, locking 0-chromic general sutures. In patients who are very thin, the interrupted sutures, which are nonabsorbable, have knots that can be felt through the abdominal wall (Fig. 5-23, *C* and *D*). The running sutures invert all the nonabsorbable sutures and provide a smooth surface[27] (Fig. 5-23, *E*).

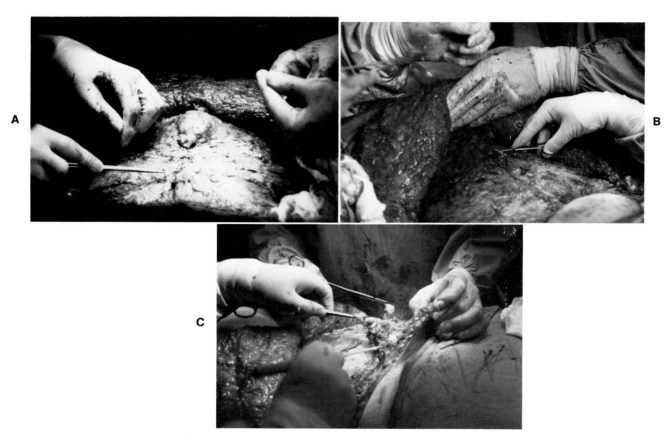

A

B

C

Fig. 5-22

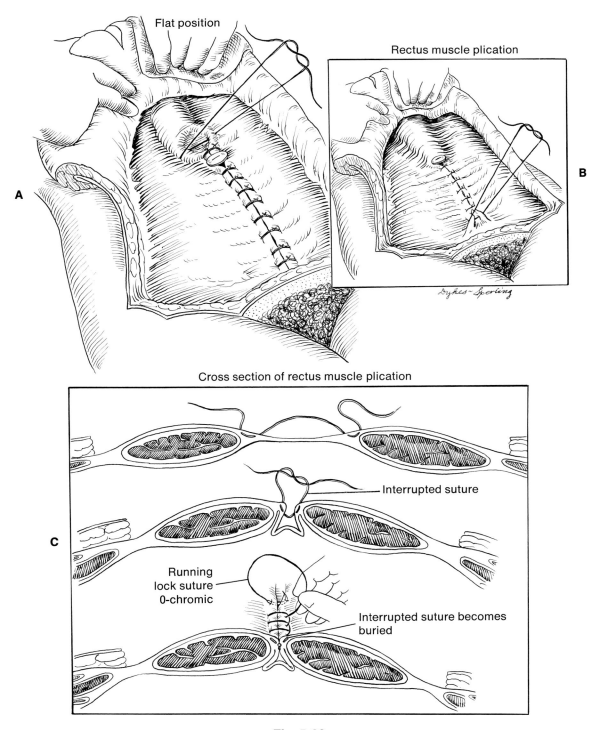

Flat position

Rectus muscle plication

A

B

Dykes-Sperling

Cross section of rectus muscle plication

C

Interrupted suture

Running
lock suture
0-chromic

Interrupted suture becomes
buried

Fig. 5-23

The rectus sheath is demonstrated prior to plication in Fig. 5-24, *A*, and after plication in Figs. 5-24, *B*, and 5-25, *A*. The running suture provides even tension along the suture line. This suture supports the suture line on extubation if coughing or musculature contractions occur, thus lessening the opportunity for deep wound separation. Frequently during plication, the patient will require additional muscle relaxation, which is the responsibility of the anesthesiologist. Placement of the patient in the flexed position prior to plication will aid relaxation of the abdominal wall. After the plication is completed and meticulous hemostasis is accomplished, the abdominal panniculus is pulled down and draped over the abdomen (Fig. 5-25, *B*).

In almost all cases where there has been plication, a puckering of the skin and subcutaneous tissue will occur in the midline over the xiphoid and costal margins (Figs. 5-24, *D*, and 5-26, *A*). It is important that the subcutaneous attachments beneath are separated, allowing the panniculus to drift laterally and drape smoothly (Fig. 5-26, *B*). This dissection is done with the electric cautery that has a handpiece with an extender of 15.24 cm (6 inches) (Figs. 5-24, *C*, and 5-26, *C*). After the abdominal panniculus is evenly draped and the patient is placed in the 45-degree flexed position, additional inspection for any signs of bleeding is mandatory.

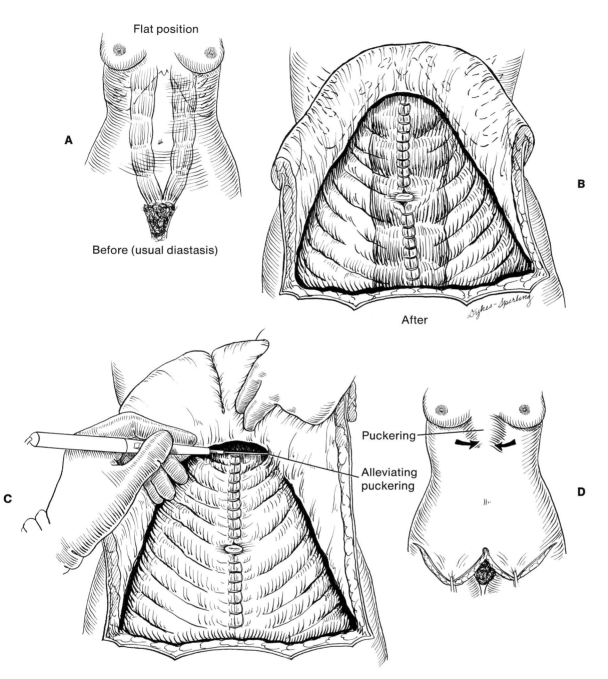

Flat position

Before (usual diastasis)

A

After

B

Puckering

Alleviating puckering

C

D

Fig. 5-24. Rectus plication.

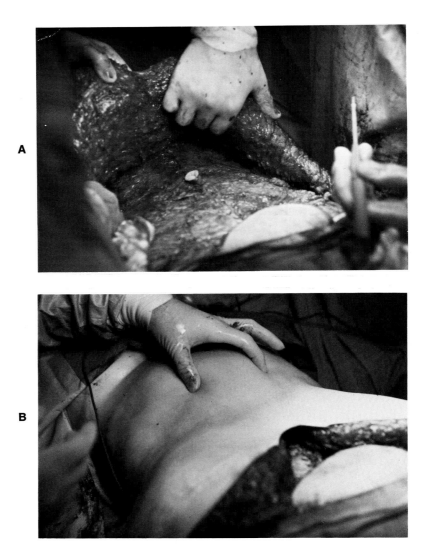

Fig. 5-25

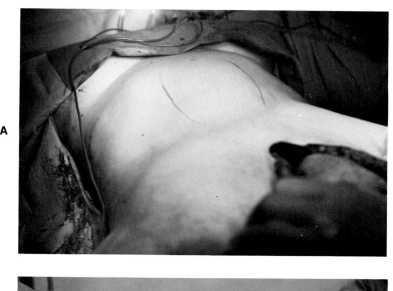

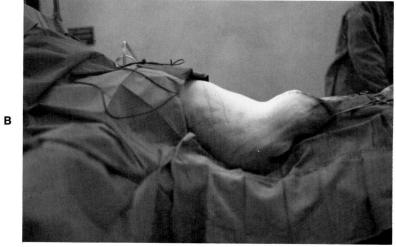

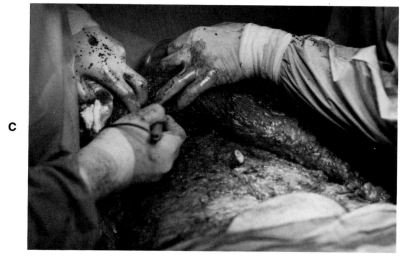

Fig. 5-26

The umbilical stalk may be trimmed of excess fat (Fig. 5-28, *A* and *B*) and may be safely shortened by additional imbricating sutures (3-0 Tevdak) (Fig. 5-28, *C*). Sutures are not placed through the stalk unless the stalk is unusually long.

A "button" is sutured onto the umbilicus to facilitate its location before the abdominal panniculus is pulled down and sutured in place (Fig. 5-28, *D*). The button consists of a small piece of rubber tubing that is cut and sutured onto the umbilicus with a 3-0 nylon suture (Figs. 5-27 and 5-28, *E*). This technique has been found to be extremely useful and accurate for finding the umbilicus in almost all patients, with the exception of those with a very thick abdominal panniculus, in whom the rubber "button" cannot be palpated.[39]

Fig. 5-27

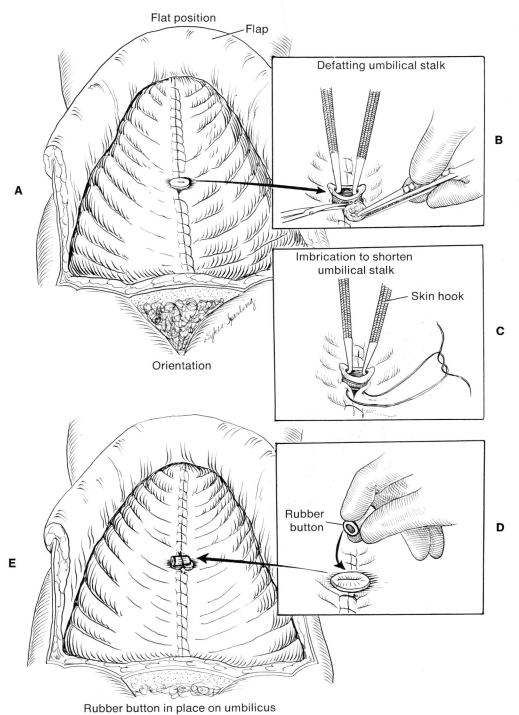

Flat position

Flap

Defatting umbilical stalk

B

A

Orientation

Imbrication to shorten
umbilical stalk

Skin hook

C

Rubber
button

D

E

Rubber button in place on umbilicus

Fig. 5-28

115

Resection

When the abdominal panniculus is pulled down, the amount of resection is determined. The amount of resected tissue removed will usually include the umbilical defect. Placing the two Kocher clamps on the lateral flaps of the abdominal panniculus, the assistant pulls down, and the surgeon adjusts proper tension. A suture is placed from the midline above the pubis to the midline of the abdominal flap.

After the initial fixation suture, the assistant puts the flap under tension. A large spinal needle is placed midway between the right or left half of the abdominal panniculus (Figs. 5-29, *A*, and 5-30, *A* and *B*) down through and, with gentle traction on the flap, to the inferior edge of the lower incision. This determines how much of the panniculus to resect. An incision is then made medially to laterally with a stay suture positioned at the site where the spinal needle was placed (Figs. 5-29, *B*, and 5-30, *C*). Excision of the flap is similar for both the gull-wing and the skin-line techniques, each following the anatomical lines of dissection. After resection is completed, the opposite side is accomplished in a similar fashion.

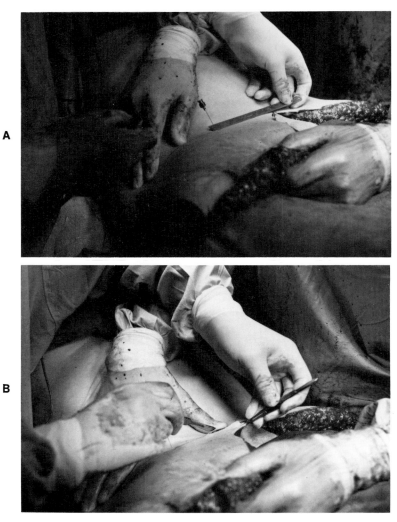

A

B

Fig. 5-29

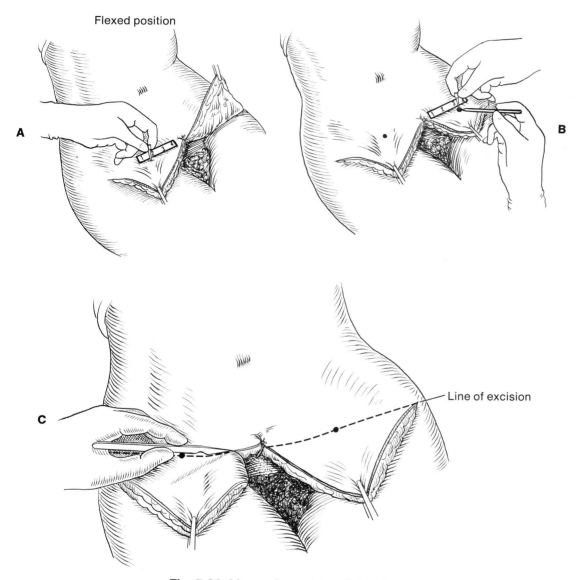

Fig. 5-30. Measuring and excising flap.

Proper tension on the flaps can be adjusted, and the flaps resected on either side with sharp scissor and scalpel dissection. Attempts are made to remove as much abdominal skin and subcutaneous adipose tissue as is possible. Frequently it becomes obvious that one can remove tissue above the umbilicus level by extending the excision, sometimes as much as 2.5 to 5 cm. In rare cases in which it is not possible to eliminate the umbilical incision site, the inverted T procedure may be used.[20,30] Occasionally the inverted T procedure eliminates central striae. Whenever the inverted T is used, the lateral extension of the incision to remove the dog ear deformity is not necessary, since the resection of the inverted T pulls the tissue into the midline area (Fig. 5-31).

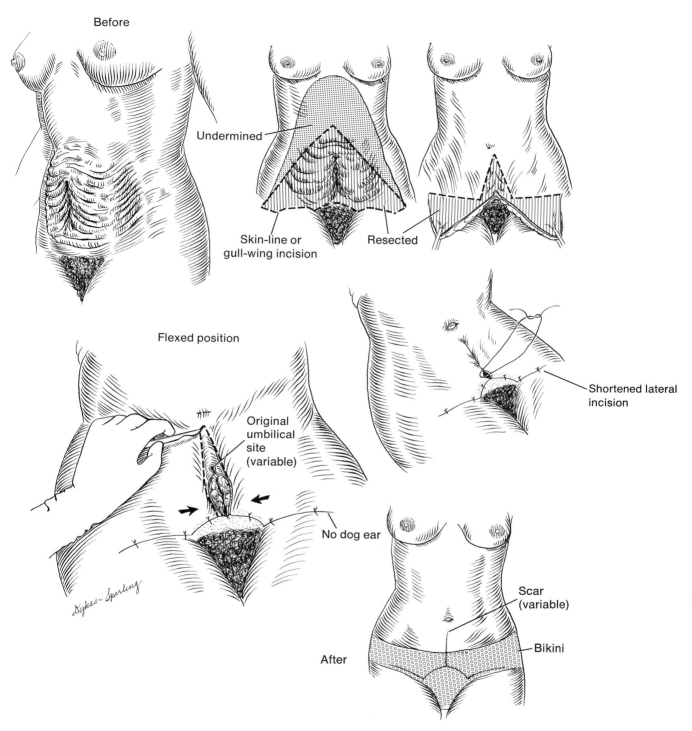

Before

Undermined

Skin-line or
gull-wing incision

Resected

Shortened lateral
incision

Flexed position

Original
umbilical
site
(variable)

No dog ear

Scar
(variable)

Bikini

After

Dykes~Sperling

Fig. 5-31. Inverted T modification.

Beveling

Depending on the thickness of the abdominal panniculus, a certain amount of beveling of the subcutaneous fat is necessary. In thinner patients beveling can be done at the time of resection of the flap (Fig. 5-33, *A*) or, in patients with thicker panniculi, after the flap resection is complete (Figs. 5-32 and 5-33, *B*).

The amount of beveling varies from the extremely thin patient requiring no beveling to the obest patient in whom beveling is carried out from the inferior portion of the flap up to the level of the new umbilicus site (Fig. 5-35, *A*). It is imperative not to defat the flap above the level of the new umbilicus because of the risk of compromising the blood supply. The beveling procedure is best accomplished with the heavy Gorney serrated scissors. After adequate resection and beveling of the flap, insetting is accomplished with multiple interrupted 3-0 nylon tacking sutures to approximate the skin.

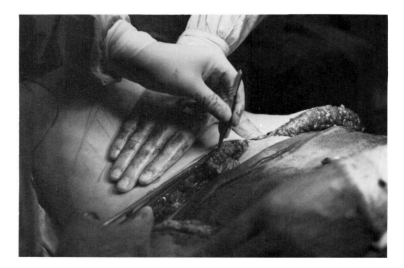

Fig. 5-32

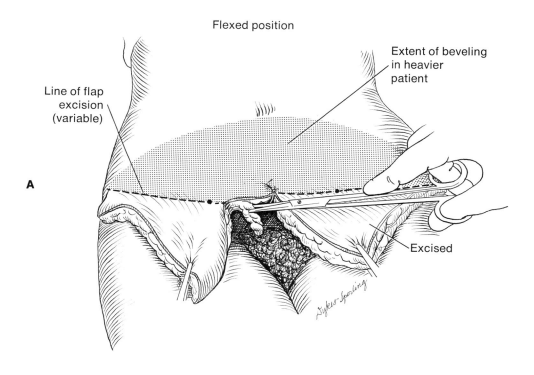

Flexed position

Extent of beveling in heavier patient

Line of flap excision (variable)

A

Excised

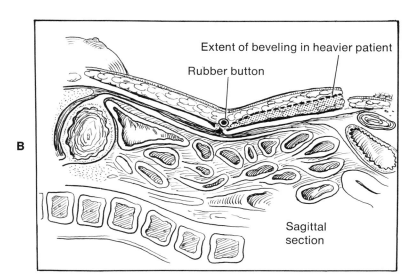

Extent of beveling in heavier patient

Rubber button

B

Sagittal section

Fig. 5-33. Beveling of abdominal flap.

Suturing

Tacking sutures are placed while the patient is still flexed. If the rubber button can be palpated, the wound is closed as far as the dog ear (Figs. 5-34 and 5-35, *B*).

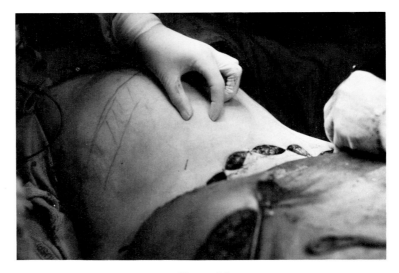

Fig. 5-34

Excision of abdominal flap

Flexed position

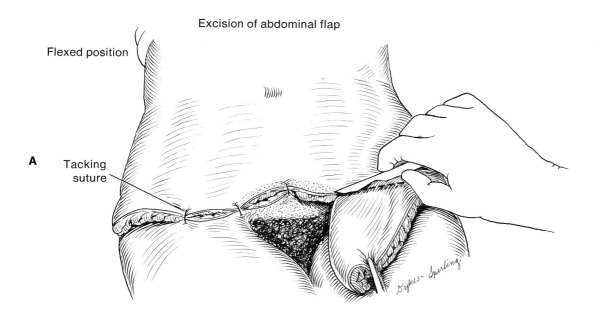

A Tacking suture

Palpation to locate umbilical button on thinner patients

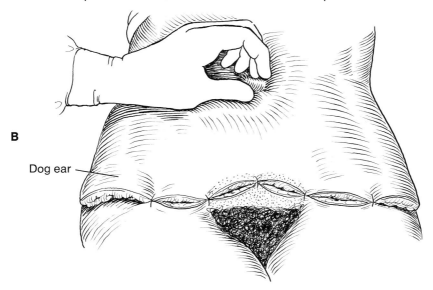

B

Dog ear

Fig. 5-35

Deep closure with 3-0 and 4-0 Dexon sutures follows. The dog ear resection is accomplished laterally with a gentle upward or downward deflection of the incision line (Fig. 5-37, *A*). This varies in many cases but is frequently extended out and down to the level of the patient's upper buttocks on the operating table to contour the hips (Fig. 5-36, *A*). It is important that the subcutaneous attachment of tissues is severed at this point lateral to the ilium to allow the dog ear area to drape evenly (Fig. 5-37, *B*). Beveling and defatting also take place here (Fig. 5-37, *C*), after which the two ¼- to ½-inch (0.6 to 1.3 cm) Jackson-Pratt drains are placed in each side of the wound, between the umbilicus and the pubes, leading out laterally through the incision (Figs. 5-36, *B*, and 5-37, *D*). Jackson-Pratt drains prevent pressure necrosis because of their soft silicone consistency. Some surgeons prefer drainage of the abdominal wound through stab wounds in the pubic area.[33]

A

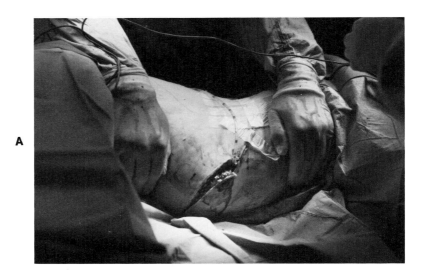

B

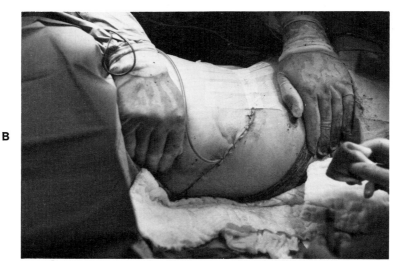

Fig. 5-36

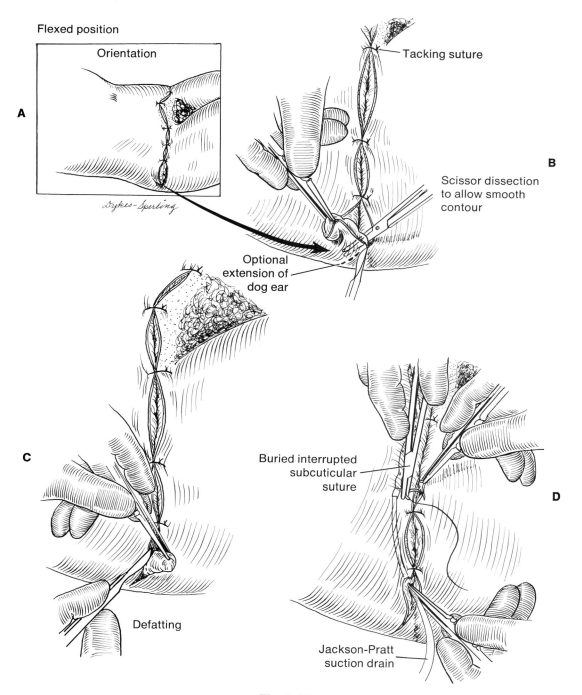

Flexed position

Orientation

A

Dykes-Sperling

Tacking suture

B

Scissor dissection
to allow smooth
contour

Optional
extension of
dog ear

C

Defatting

Buried interrupted
subcuticular
suture

D

Jackson-Pratt
suction drain

Fig. 5-37

Relocation of the umbilicus or umbilicoplasty

To locate the umbilicus, the patient is taken out of the flexed position. A transverse incision is made 1 cm in length immediately above the button (Figs. 5-38, *A*, and 5-39, *A*). The button is found and freed from the umbilicus (Fig. 5-38, *B*, and 5-39, *B*). The umbilicus is pulled through under tension to determine whether the site selected is correct. If it is, an ellipse of skin is removed inferiorly but not superiorly (Fig. 5-39, *D*). The umbilicus is then allowed to drop back in, and a core of abdominal subcutaneous fat is removed for approximately 2 to 3 cm around the umbilicus[5-7] (Figs. 5-38, *E*, and 5-39, *C*). (Some surgeons remove this core of fat from the underside before the flap is closed.) This amount of resection varies with the aesthetic eye of the surgeon, but usually amounts to 2 to 3 cm of subcutaneous fat (Figs. 5-38, *D*, and 5-39, *F*).

A

B

C

D

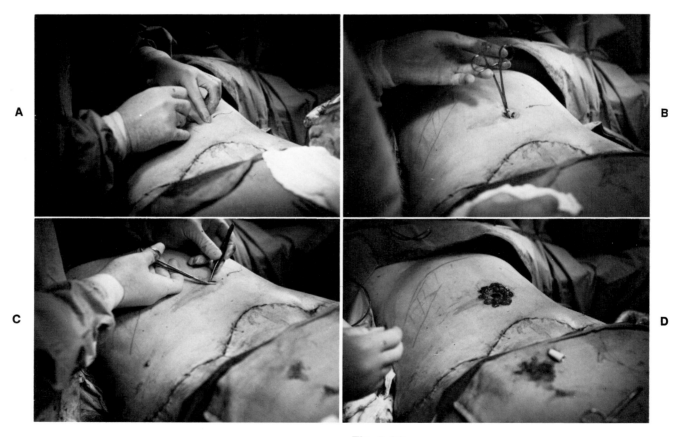

Fig. 5-38

Flat position

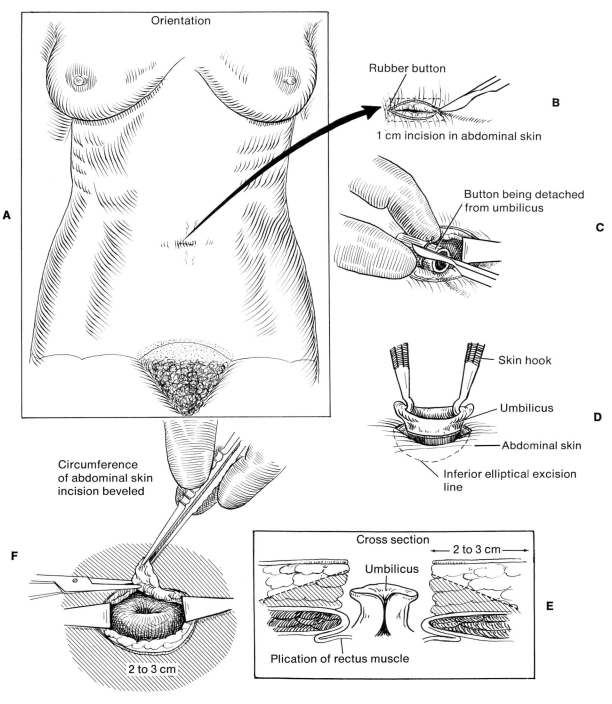

Orientation

Rubber button

B

1 cm incision in abdominal skin

A

Button being detached from umbilicus

C

Skin hook

Umbilicus

D

Abdominal skin

Inferior elliptical excision line

Circumference of abdominal skin incision beveled

F

Cross section

2 to 3 cm

Umbilicus

E

Plication of rectus muscle

2 to 3 cm

Fig. 5-39

Forceps hold the rectus fascia so that four sutures may be placed at the 6, 9, 12, and 3 o'clock positions through the skin and rectus fascia (Figs. 5-40, *A*, and 5-41, *A* to *D*). This creates an indentation of the abdominal wall with the umbilicus, as is seen in the normal, youthful adult. Occasionally, when more umbilical hooding is desired, the 12 o'clock suture is omitted. Results of this technique are shown in Fig. 5-40, *B*. When this is accomplished, the umbilicus is pulled up and through the new abdominal skin incision site and held with two small skin hooks. At this point, the anterior abdominal skin is sutured to the edge of the umbilical skin with either continuous (Fig. 5-41, *E*) or buried interrupted (Fig. 5-41, *F*) 5-0 Prolene sutures. The umbilicus appears much like a mushroom extending through the abdominal skin. A cross section is shown (Fig. 5-41, *G* and *H*). A small folded segment of Xeroform gauze is packed into the umbilicus and fixed with Steri-Strip tape, which applies pressure and promotes hemostasis (Figs. 5-40, *C*, and 5-41, *I*).

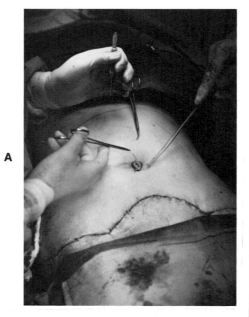

A

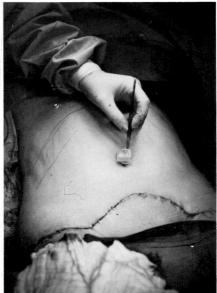

C

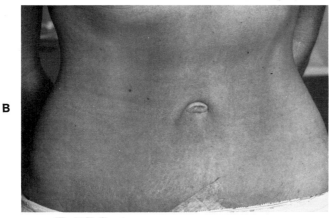

B

Fig. 5-40

Flat position

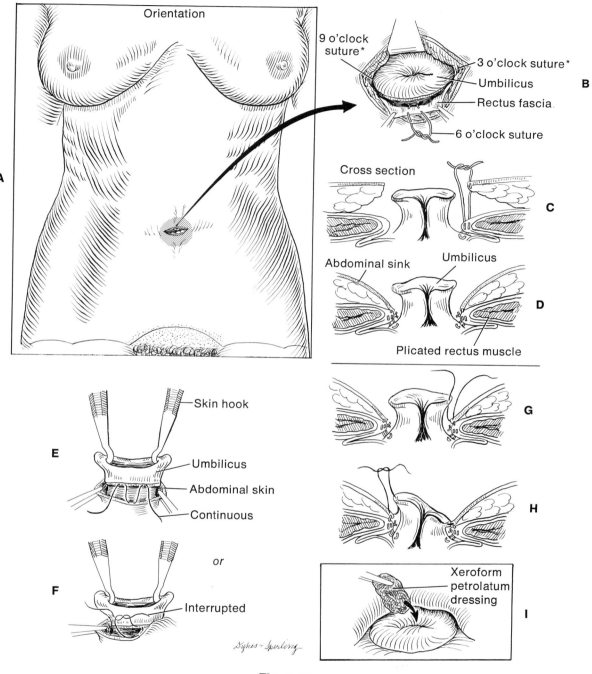

Orientation

9 o'clock suture*

3 o'clock suture*
Umbilicus
Rectus fascia
6 o'clock suture

B

A

Cross section

C

Abdominal sink   Umbilicus

Plicated rectus muscle

D

Skin hook

Umbilicus
Abdominal skin
Continuous

E

or

Interrupted

F

G

H

Xeroform petrolatum dressing

I

Dykes~Sperling

Fig. 5-41
(*Sutures to be placed.)

In the obese patient the fiberoptic-lighted instrument is used to locate the umbilicus[29,35] (Fig. 5-42). When this lighted instrument is used, the superpubic portion of the incision is left open 2.5 cm in the midline to insert the retractor (Fig. 5-43). After locating the umbilicus, the umbilicoplasty proceeds as described previously. Because of the thickness of the panniculus, the umbilicus may appear to have a deep indentation. The incision line is inspected while under tension and any necessary additional sutures are placed. The patient then returns to the flexed position and remains there for the immediate postoperative period.

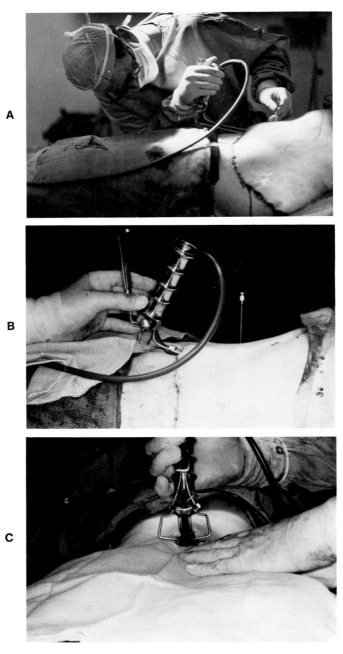

Fig. 5-42

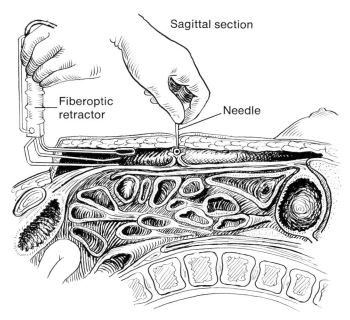

Fig. 5-43. Alternate method for locating umbilical button in corpulent patients.

Immediate postoperative period

All but a few of the skin-tacking sutures are removed (Fig. 5-44, *A*), and the suture line is reinforced with 1-inch (2.5 cm) Steri-Strip closures (Fig. 5-44, *B*). These are placed throughout the entire length of the wound. After the Steri-Strips have been applied, Jackson-Pratt drains are either taped to the patient's legs or attached to the elastic stockings with safety pins (Figs. 5-44, *C*, and 5-45, *A*). This prevents kinking of the drains or accidental removal. Removal is simplified if the drains have not been sutured in place. The abdominal skin is then carefully protected with multiple ABD dressings, which are taped to each other with 2-inch (5 cm) paper tape (Fig. 5-44, *D*). At no point is the dressing taped to the patient's skin. An operating towel is placed immediately over the ABD dressings, and a molded plaster of paris splint is fashioned to the abdominal wall contour and allowed to harden (Fig. 5-45, *B*).

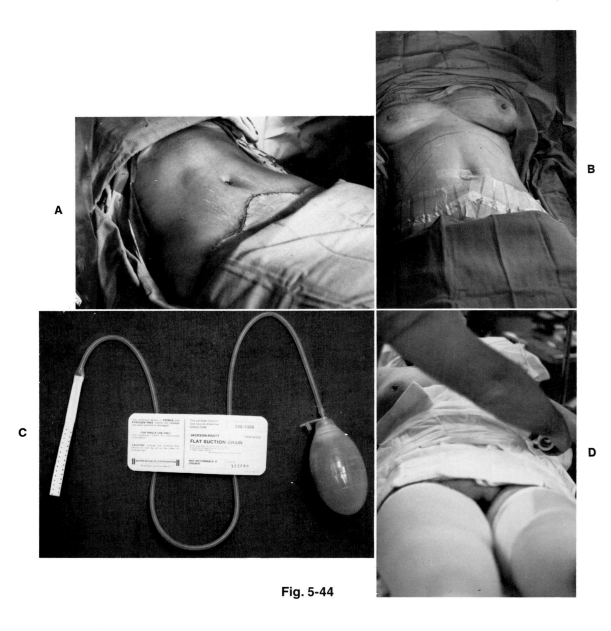

Fig. 5-44

At this point there is a need for coordination between the surgeon and the anesthesiologist, since the patient should not be extubated until the plaster has become firm enough to give support to the incision if the patient coughs or bucks but before the plaster becomes hot enough from the heat of crystallization to cause a thermal burn. As soon as the plaster splint becomes very warm, it should be *removed from the patient* and allowed to cool. It is replaced while the patient is in the recovery room.[30,33,34]

A

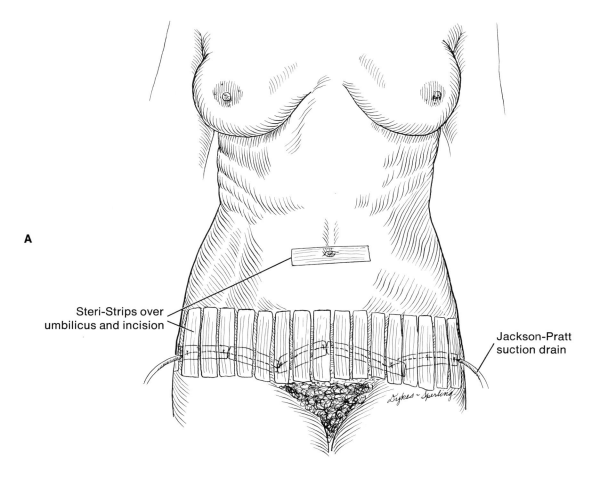

Steri-Strips over umbilicus and incision

Jackson-Pratt suction drain

B

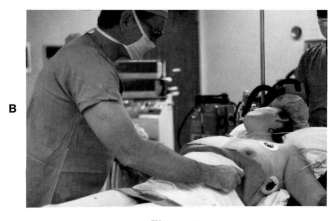

Fig. 5-45

In the immediate postoperative period, the plaster splint is preferred over circumferential pressure dressings such as scultetus binders, Velcro wraps, or Elastoplast. From a statistical standpoint, survey results indicate that fewer hematomas occur in patients to whom the abdominal plaster splint was applied. Another advantage of the plaster splint is that it allows easy inspection of the entire abdomen by simply removing the splint and elevating the nonadherent ABD dressing without having to move the patient. The other advantage of the plaster splint is the additional support it gives patients when postoperative coughing is necessary. The major disadvantage of the plaster splint is the potential for a burn.[32] Many surgeons prefer to use an abdominal binder with Velcro straps or Ace wraps. These circumferential dressings require lifting the patient during application and possess the potential to compromise circulation, since the segmental circulation enters the abdominal wall laterally. Dressings may restrict respiration, whereas the cast can move up and down (Chapter 3). There is usually a small amount of drainage from the wounds that may soil the Velcro dressing. This type of support is reserved until the first or second day after surgery when adequate circulation of the abdominal panniculus is assured.

At the completion of the procedure, while the field is still sterile, split-thickness skin grafts are taken with a hand knife from the resected abdominal apron. These grafts are stored in physiological salt solution with antibiotics added. The skin is available for use if the patient loses skin, or it may be made available later for other patients as a biological dressing (Fig. 5-46, A).

The patient usually is transferred directly to a bed that is placed in the flexed position and has an inflating and deflating mattress (Fig. 5-46, B), which we believe helps to prevent the occurrence of deep-vein thrombosis.

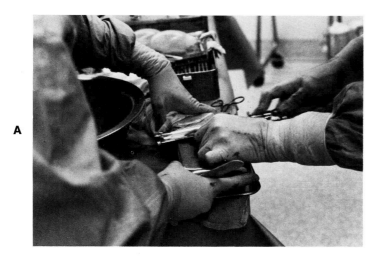

Fig. 5-46

POSTOPERATIVE CARE

The patient is awakened in the recovery room and asked to flex the calves and legs. The nurse's routine in the recovery room is to inspect the abdominal skin for signs of inadequate circulation and/or hematoma. If evidence exists of compromised circulation in the distal portion of the flap, the patient is given 500 ml of dextran 40 (Rheomacrodex) (Fig. 5-47, *A*). Although the dextran may increase the amount of subcutaneous bleeding, it also improves microcirculation of the flap.

If the development of hematoma is observed, we suggest switching from the Jackson-Pratt bulb drains to bedside suction at 125 to 130 mm pressure and irrigation of the Jackson-Pratt drains with sterile normal saline solution. In a survey of complications in abdominoplasties,[32] approximately 6% of the surgeons stated that their patients had had hematomas; however, in more than 350 abdominoplasties, neither we nor Goldwyn has had to return a patient to surgery for hematoma evacuation (Fig. 5-47, *B*).

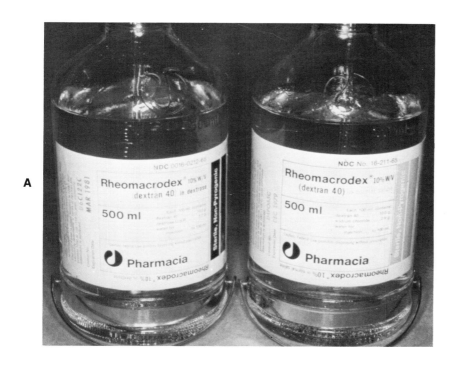

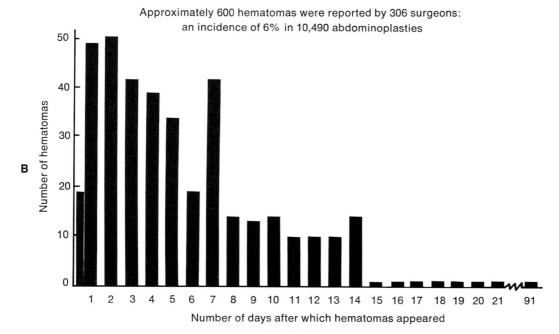

Approximately 600 hematomas were reported by 306 surgeons:
an incidence of 6% in 10,490 abdominoplasties

Number of hematomas

Number of days after which hematomas appeared

Fig. 5-47

(**B** from Grazer, F. M., and Goldwyn, R.: Plast. Reconstr. Surg. **59:**513, 1977.)

The drain reservoirs are emptied every 4 hours or whenever they become half full, and results are recorded. The usual amount of drainage is 30 to 40 ml every 4 hours, with some minimal additional drainage on the lateral wound sites. The physician should be alerted if the drainage exceeds this amount, particularly if it approaches 100 ml in 4 hours or if there is excessive drainage from the lateral wound.

Postoperative pain is usually controlled with 25 to 75 mg of meperidine (Demerol) or similar narcotic every 2 to 4 hours. It is preferable to give small doses of analgesic at frequent intervals to allow the patient continuous pain control. This will facilitate cough, deep breathing, and early ambulation. Patients tend to complain more of pain from the rectus muscle plication than from the incision site. As soon as is possible, the patients progress from a clear liquid to a regular diet. Urinary retention tends to be a problem in women after surgery. About 50% of patients need to be catheterized at least once, with approximately 25% requiring an indwelling Foley catheter for a day or two. Postoperative bowel softeners and/or laxatives help eliminate the problem of constipation.

Excessive tightening or straining of the abdominal muscles is contraindicated. Putting draw sheets on the postoperative bed often enables one or two nurses or attendants to move the patient in bed by lifting rather than asking her to push with her feet to assist in moving up in bed. Usually the first morning after surgery, the plaster splint is removed, and the wound is inspected. If drainage in the tubes is serous, which is usually the case, the Jackson-Pratt drains are removed, and the patient is either wrapped with a 6-inch (15.2 cm) Ace wrap or placed in a Velcro binder.[34] It is extremely important that the Ace wrap or Velcro binder be applied with firm, even pressure (Fig. 5-48). If it becomes wrinkled or "rides up," it should be removed and reapplied to prevent pressure that might compromise circulation to the flap. The wrapping will give the patient some support at the start of ambulation.

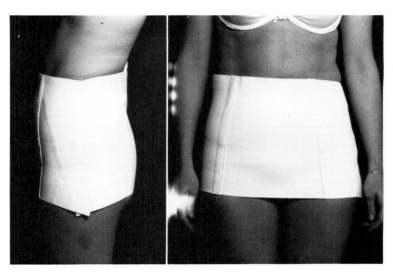

Fig. 5-48. Firmly applied binder. *Shown:* Dale Combo surgical binder (Baka Manufacturing Co., Inc., Plainville, Massachusetts).

Special ambulation instructions, including how to get out of bed, are given by the physical therapist who has been specially oriented by the surgeon. The patient bends the knees and rolls to the edge of the bed (Fig. 5-49). By placing the feet over the edge of the bed in a crawling manner and using the elbow-hand technique (Fig. 5-50, *A* and *B*), the patient can gently come to a sitting position at the edge of the bed (Fig. 5-50, *C*) with the head kept in a forward position. It is better for the patients to do this by themselves than to have someone pull or push, causing pain in areas of plication. Fig. 5-50, *C* and *D*, shows the patient in a standing position.

To return to bed, the patient sits and eases back on her hips, going down on her side. With only the head of the bed in high elevation and knees remaining flexed, the patient rolls onto her back before being repositioned with knees supported in elevation.

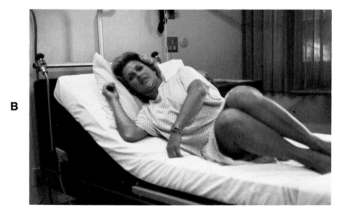

Fig. 5-49

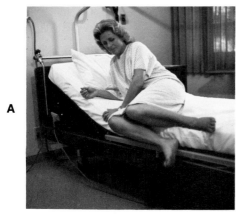

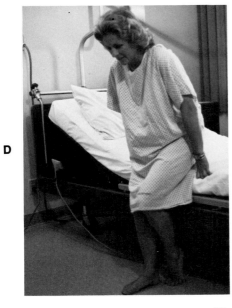

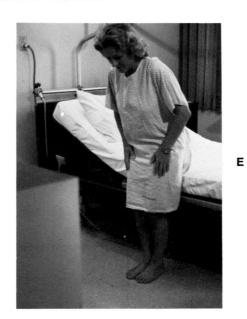

Fig. 5-50

The patient is usually discharged on the third or fourth day after surgery. When the abdominoplasty had been combined with a gynecological procedure such as a hysterectomy, the patient is usually not discharged until about the seventh postoperative day. The patient is kept on antibiotics for a minimum of five days after surgery. Because of the anticoagulant property of aspirin, no aspirin-containing medications are given; a patient should be alerted to the various over-the-counter medications that contain aspirin. Prior to discharge the patient should be instructed about progressive ambulation with abdominal support, such as an Ace bandage or Velcro binder. The patient should be warned that too much strenuous activity can result in collections of serous fluid under the flap. She should also be alerted to the fact that she will have some fatigue and that she should monitor activities accordingly. Patients have discovered that they have some postoperative depression and may, because of the fatigue and discomfort during the first few postoperative days, question their decision to have surgery. The nurse and physician need to be extremely supportive of patients at this time and remind them that things will improve daily.

When the patient is seen at the office two or three days after discharge from the hospital, the Steri-Strips and suture lines are inspected. An effort is made not to disturb the Steri-Strips that are in place. Sutures are removed depending on evidence of healing along the incision site; Steri-Strips are replaced in the areas in which sutures have been removed. In some patients blistering from the Steri-Strips has occurred; this is not an allergic reaction but results from the shearing force of the Steri-Strip on the skin. A cortisone-like aerosol medication such as betamethasone valerate (Valisone) is helpful in reducing this blistering from the Steri-Strips. The patient continues to wear an Ace bandage or Velcro binder or a snug panty girdle or body stocking of the patient's choice until the suture line appears to be well healed. The patient is advised to refrain from sexual intercourse for three to four weeks after surgery. The patient may shower three or four days after surgery and drive a car at the end of two or three weeks. Patients may begin brisk walking or activities such as swimming approximately ten days after discharge. Heavy sports such as tennis or skiing are deferred for four to eight weeks. A rule of thumb for the patient is "If anything hurts, don't do it." The patient is usually seen at monthly intervals for six months to a year, and the maturation of the suture lines observed. Hypertrophic scars are usually treated by injection of small amounts of triamcinolone acetonide (Kenalog 10). Secondary scar revision is occasionally necessary.[32]

SECONDARY SURGERY

Half of the physicians involved in the Grazer-Goldwyn survey[32] indicated that they had to revise abdominal scars; the revision was required in only 10% of the patients. The area of revision was usually at the umbilicus or at points where the scar had been pulled because of excessive tension. Such revisions are usually done six months after the original surgery under local anesthesia in the office. Tissue loss immediately after surgery usually occurs in the midline. Of the surgeons responding to the survey, 7% indicated that they had to graft for

Table 1. Scars and scar revision*

	Number	Percent
Do you revise abdominoplasty scars?†		
Yes	395	41
No	485	51
Umbilical scar contractures		
Sometimes	430	45
Always	18	2
Never	422	44
Do you end up with a midline vertical scar?		
Never	241	26
Occasionally	516	54
Frequently	156	16
Most objectionable midline scar		
Vertical	480	50
Transverse	124	13

*From Grazer, F. M., and Goldwyn, R.: Plast. Reconstr. Surg. **59**:513, 1977.
†Of the 958 physicians responding to the survey,[32] 330 indicated the need for scar revision in approximately 10% of patients.

tissue loss (Table 1). Although Pitanguy[59] indicates that skin loss occurs more frequently in patients with the inverted T incision, in our experience the incidence is approximately the same with or without the inverted T. If the defect is small enough, the necrotic area is excised with a secondary closure. If skin grafting is necessary, the graft can usually be resected six months to a year later, after the tissue has softened. When complications such as skin loss and grafting occur, the patient needs additional reinforcement, sympathy, and understanding. Every effort should be made to minimize the cost to the patient. Indications and results of secondary surgery will be discussed in detail in Chapter 6.

REFERENCES

1. Avelar, J.: Abdominoplasty—systemization of a technique without external umbilical scar, Aesthet. Plast. Surg. **2**:141, 1978.
2. Babcock, W. W.: Disease of women and children, Am. J. Obstet. Gynecol. **74**:596, 1916.
3. Baker, J. J., Gordon, H. L., and Mosienko, P.: A template (pattern) method of abdominal lipectomy, Aesthet. Plast. Surg. **1**:167, 1977.
4. Baron, H. C.: The surgical treatment of panniculus adiposus abdominis, Gen. Pract. **22**:130, 1974.
5. Baroudi, R.: Management of the umbilicus in abdominoplasty, presented at the meeting of the Society for Aesthetic Plastic Surgery, Newport Beach, Calif., March, 1973.
6. Baroudi, R.: Umbilicalplasty, Clin. Plast. Surg. **2**:431, 1975.
7. Baroudi, R., Keppke, E. M., and Tozzi-Netto, F.: Abdominoplasty, Plast. Reconstr. Surg. **54**:161, 1974.
8. Barsky, A. J., and Kahn, S.: Principles and practice of plastic surgery, Baltimore, 1950, The Williams & Wilkins Co.
9. Biesenberger, H.: Abdomen pendulous, Zentralbl. Chir. **55**:2382, 1928.
10. Bullitt, J. B.: Retrenchment of lipomatous abdominal wall combined with operation for radical cure of umbilical hernia, Ann. Surg., p. 663, 1900.
11. Buschke, A., Joseph, A., and Birkenfeld, W.: Leitfaden der Kosmetik, Berlin, 1932, Walter de Gruyter & Co.
12. Castanares, S., and Goethal, J.: Abdominal lipectomy; a modification in technique, Plast. Reconstr. Surg. **40**:378, 1967.
13. Castle, H. E.: Obesity and its surgical treatment by lipectomy, Ann. Surg. **54**:706, 1911.

14. Castle, H. E.: A recent case of lipectomy, Calif. State J. Med. **11**:58, 1913.

15. Cervený, J.: Reconstruction of the abdominal wall at venter pendulus, Acta Chir. Plast. **16**:178, 1974.

16. Chachava, M. K., and Gotsiridze, T. I.: Plastic surgery in pendulous abdomen, Vestn. Khir. **107**:89, 1972.

17. Claoué, C.: Abdominal plastic surgery, Clin. Lab. **64**:81, 1957.

18. Clarkson, P.: Lipodystrophies, Plast. Reconstr. Surg. **37**:499, 1966.

19. Doyen, E. L.: Traité de thérapeutic chirurgie et de la technique opérative, Paris, 1911, Norbert Maloine.

20. Dufourmentel, C., and Mouly, K.: Chirurgie plastique: plasties abdominales, Paris, 1959, Flammarion & Cie.

21. Elbaz, J. S., and Flaguel, G.: Chirurgie plastique de l'abdomen, Paris, 1977, Masson & Cie, Editeurs.

22. Fernández, J. C., and Iturraspe, M. C.: Dermolipectomía vertical en del delantal grasoso, Día Méd. (B. Aires), p. 1483, 1951.

23. Flesch-Thebesius, M., and Weinsheimer, K.: Die Operation des Hängebauches, Chirurg **3**:841, 1931.

24. Freeman, V. S., and Winer, D. R.: Abdominoplasty with special attention to construction of the umbilicus: technique and complications, Aesthet. Plast. Surg. **2**:65, 1978.

25. Frist, J.: Die Operation des Hängebauches, Wien. Klin. Wochenschr. **34**:266, 1921.

26. Galtier, M.: Traitement chirurgical de l'obésité de la paroi abdominale avec ptose [surgical therapy of obesity of the abdominal wall with ptosis], Mem. Acad. Chir. **81**:341, 1955.

27. Galtier, M.: L'obésité de la paroi abdominale avec ptose. Traitement chirurgical, Presse Med. **70**:135, 1962.

28. Gonzáles-Ulloa, M.: Circular lipectomy with transposition of the umbilicus and aponeurolytic technique, Cirurgia **27**:394, 1959.

29. Grazer, F. M.: Use of fiber optic bundles in plastic surgery, Plast. Reconstr. Surg. **48**:28, 1971.

30. Grazer, F. M.: Abdominoplasty, Plast. Reconstr. Surg. **51**:617, 1973.

31. Grazer, F. M.: The new image, film presented at the meeting of the American Society of Plastic and Reconstructive Surgeons, San Francisco, Oct., 1977.

32. Grazer, F. M., and Goldwyn, R.: Abdominoplasty assessed by survey, with emphasis on complications, Plast. Reconstr. Surg. **59**:513, 1977.

33. Grazer, F. M., and Klingbeil, J. R.: Abdominoplasty. In Courtiss, E. H., editor: Aesthetic surgery: trouble—how to avoid it and how to treat it, St. Louis, 1978, The C. V. Mosby Co.

34. Grazer, F. M., Klingbeil, J. R., and Mattiello, M.: Long-term results of abdominoplasty, Boston, 1980, Little, Brown & Co. (in press).

35. Grazer, F. M., and Krugman, M. E.: A new triaxial fiberoptic soft tissue retractor, Aesthet. Plast. Surg. **2**:161, 1978.

36. Haberer, von: Offizielles Protokoll der k.k. Gesellschaft der Aerzte in Wien, Wien. Klin. Wochenschr. **21**, 1908.

37. Hinderer, U. T.: The dermolipectomy approach for augmentation mammaplasty, Clin. Plast. Surg. **2**:359, 1975.

38. Hoffman, S., and Simon, B. E.: Experiences with the Pitanguy method of correction of trochanteric lipodystrophy, Plast. Reconstr. Surg. **55**:551, 1975.

39. Hoyt, J.: Panel discussion, Body Contouring Symposium, Los Angeles, 1975, University of California.

40. Ivanissevich, O.: Dermolipectomía. Técnica de Vélez Diez Canseco, Semana Med. **118**:535, 1961.

41. Kelly, H. A.: Report of gynecological cases (excessive growth of fat), Bull. Johns Hopkins Hosp. **10**:197, 1889. (Case 3.)

42. Kelly, H. A.: Excision of the fat of the abdominal wall lipectomy, Surg. Gynecol. Obstet. **10**:229, 1910.

43. Malbec, E. F.: Lipectomía abdominal, técnica operatoria, Prensa Med. Argent. **35**:1251, 1948.

44. Masson, J. K.: Lipectomy: the surgical removal of excess fat, Postgrad. Med. **32**:481, 1962,

45. Maylard, A. E.: Direction of abdominal incisions, Br. Med. J. **2**:895, Oct. 5, 1907.

46. Meyerowitz, B. R., Bruber, R. P., and Laub, D. R.: Massive abdominal panniculectomy, J.A.M.A. **224**:408, 1973.

47. Meyerowitz, B. R., et al.: From massive weight loss to abdominal panniculectomy, R.N. **37**:1974.

48. Mornard, P.: La résection esthétique du ventre en tablier avec transplantation de l'ombilic. In Pauchet, V.: La practique

chirurgicale illustrée, vol. XV, Paris, 1930, Gaston Doin.

49. Muhlbauer, W. D.: Die plastisch-chirurgische Behandlung der Fettleibigkeit (plastic surgery in the treatment of obesity), Munch. Med. Wochenschr. **117:**745, 1975.

50. Noël, A.: La chirurgie esthétique, son rôle social, Paris, 1926, Masson & Cie, Editeurs.

51. Parnell, R. W.: Behaviour and physique, London, 1958, Edward Arnold (Publishers), Ltd.

52. Passot, R.: Chirurgie esthétique pure. Techniques et résultats, Paris, 1930, Gaston Doin.

53. Peskova, H.: Plastic operations of abdominal wall, Acta Chir. Plast. **8:**127, 1966.

54. Peters, L.: Resection of the pendulous fat abdominal wall in cases of extreme obesity, Ann. Surg. **33:**220, 1901.

55. Pick, J. F.: Surgery of repair, vol. 2, Philadelphia, 1949, J. B. Lippincott Co.

56. Pickrell, K. L.: Reconstructive surgery of the abdominal wall and back. In Converse, J. M., editor: Reconstructive plastic surgery, vol. 5, Philadelphia, 1964, W. B. Saunders Co.

57. Pitanguy, I.: Abdominal lipectomy—an approach to it through an analysis of 300 consecutive cases, Plast. Reconstr. Surg. **40:**384, 1967.

58. Pitanguy, I.: Dermolipectomies crurales, Ann. Chir. Plast. **17:**40, 1972.

59. Pitanguy, I.: Thighlift and abdominal lipectomy. In Goldwyn, R. M., editor: The unfavorable result in plastic surgery, Boston, 1972, Little, Brown & Co.

60. Pitanguy, I.: Abdominal lipectomy, Clin. Plast. Surg. **2:**401, 1975.

61. Prudente, A.: Dermolipectomía abdominal com conservação de cicatrix umbilical, Anais II Cong. Latino Americano Cirurg. Plast. Kraft, p. 468, 1942.

62. Psillakis, J. M.: Abdominoplasty: some ideas to improve results, Aesthet. Plast. Surg. **2:**205, 1978.

63. Regnault, P.: Abdominal lipectomy, a low W incision, microfilm, International Society of Aesthetic Plastic Surgery, 1972.

64. Regnault, P.: Abdominal dermolipectomies, Clin. Plast. Surg. **2:**411, 1975.

65. Regnault, P.: Abdominoplasty by the W technique, Plast. Reconstr. Surg. **55:**265, 1975.

66. Regnault, P.: Abdominal dermolipectomy and body sculpture (syllabus), Edu-cational Foundation, American Society of Plastic and Reconstructive Surgeons, San Francisco, p. 162, 1977.

67. Regnault, P.: The history of abdominal dermolipectomy, Aesthet. Plast. Surg. **2:**113, 1978.

68. Schepelmann, E.: Über Bauchdeckenplastiken mit besonderer Berücksichtigung des Hangebauches, Bruns Beitr. Klin. Chir. **3:**372, 1918.

69. Schörcher, F.: Kosmetische Operationen, Munich, 1955, J. F. Lehmanns Verlag.

70. Schulz, C.: Operation for obesity. Mitt. a. d. Grenzgeb., Med. Chir. **18:**776, 1908.

71. Serson, D.: Planeamiento geométrico para la dermolipectomía abdominal, Rev. Esp. Cir. Plast. **4:**37, 1971; abstracted, Plast. Reconstr. Surg. **48:**605, 1971.

72. Shallenberger, W. H.: Abdominal lipectomy (report of two cases), Bull. Johns Hopkins Hosp. **249:**410, 1911.

73. Sheldon, W. H.: The varieties of human physique, New York, 1963, Hafner Publishing Co.

74. Somalo, M.: Dermolipectomía circular del tronco, Semana Med. **1:**1435, 1940.

75. Somalo, M.: Dermolipectomía ventral cruciforme; "incisión en golondrina," Prensa Med. Argent. **33:**75, 1946.

76. Spadafora, A.: Abdomen péndulo, dermolipectomía anterolateral baja (técnica personal), Prensa Med. Argent. **49:**494, 1962.

77. Szczawiński, A., Oknińska, H., and Dreszer, S.: Plastic operations for pendulous abdomen in obese subjects, Pol. Med. J. **11:**922, 1972; Pol. Przegl. Chir. **43:**1317, 1971.

78. Thorek, M.: Possibilities in the reconstruction of the human form, N.Y. Med. J. Rec. **116:**572, 1922.

79. Thorek, M.: Plastic surgery or the breast and abdominal wall, Springfield, Ill., 1942, Charles C Thomas, Publisher.

80. Vernon, S.: Umbilical transplantation upward and abdominal contouring in lipectomy, Am. J. Surg. **94:**490, 1957.

81. Vesco: Zur Reduction des Bauchdeckenfettes, Wien. Klin. Wochenschr., p. 155, 1914.

82. Weinhold, S.: Bauchdeckenplastik, Zentralbl. Gynaekol. **38:**1332, 1909.

83. Wilson, J. G.: Plastic and reconstructive surgery. In Moidel, H. C., Giblin, E. C., and Wagner, B. M., editors: Nursing care of the patient with medical-surgical disorders, ed. 2, New York, 1971, McGraw-Hill Book Co.

145

CHAPTER 6

Long-term results, combined procedures, and complications

We have been performing abdominoplasties for the past twenty years. This chapter is a critical review of our experience, including long-term results, the use of combined procedures,[21] and special problems and complications.

COMBINED PROCEDURES

In 1972 Grazer[7] reported on 44 abdominoplasties, two thirds of which were in combination with other procedures, such as breast augmentation (the most frequently performed associated procedure), facial surgery, abdominal or vaginal hysterectomy, sterilization procedures, and dilatation and curettage.

When other surgical procedures are contemplated in conjunction with abdominoplasty, an order of preference must be established. Following are factors to be included:

1. Ease of preparing and draping the patient
2. Potential complications, such as hematoma
3. Potential sources of contamination and infection when changing from one surgical site to another

When an abdominoplasty is performed in conjunction with facial surgery, it has been our experience that it is preferable to do the abdominoplasty first and the facial surgery second.

With breast augmentation or reduction mammaplasty, the abdominoplasty is performed second to allow time to observe for possible hematomas, which are more likely to occur in the breast than in the abdomen. The same experience is true for the armplasty (brachioplasty).[13] Brachioplasty is done first, since as a rule we do not use drains for this procedure so that the surgeon has an opportunity to observe the patient's arms for possible hematoma while the abdominoplasty is being completed. Small medial thighplasties may be performed before or after abdominoplasty if care is taken to prevent contamination from the pubic and rectal area.

Performance of major thigh reductions at the same time as abdominoplasty is not recommended because of the extensiveness of the surgery and the possibility of lymphatic disruptions.

Certain gynecological procedures, including sterilization by either laparotomy or laparoscope, dilatation and curettage, and abdominal and vaginal hysterectomy, lend themselves to combined procedures performed with other surgeons. Our experience with combined gynecological procedures dates back approximately ten years[7] with no increased morbidity in properly selected patients. Our experience at the present time is essentially the same without any significant increase in morbidity. There must be mutual respect of both the plastic surgeon and the gynecologist. Blood loss must be minimal and should not exceed 1 unit in the combined procedure unless the patient has donated 2 to 3 units of her own blood prior to the procedure. The operating time for both procedures should not exceed 5 hours of anesthesia time. If two surgical teams are used, members of each team should determine to their own satisfaction that each procedure has been performed with the least chance of complication.

One of the authors prefers not to perform combined procedures. Following is a perspective on multiple procedures.

A PERSPECTIVE ON MULTIPLE PROCEDURES

Discipline, responsibility, and honesty are as important for today's surgeon as they have always been. The surgeon's word is most often regarded as truth by patients. This trust deserves as much discipline, responsibility, and honesty as the surgeon can give. The advocacy and performance of multiple procedures are not to be lightly regarded. There seems to be a tendency to accept everything from a textbook as absolute fact and a permit to do likewise; such is not the intent of this text. Surgeons differ in technical ability and sense of responsibility. The level of sophistication and general knowledge of their patients also varies; much of this has to do with the locale of the patients.

Proceeding with complicated multiple procedures without performing all reliable tests for evaluating bleeding and clotting and determining potential peripheral vascular problems and without having the many necessary treatment modalities available is courting real disaster.

It is recommended that recognizing abdominoplasty as an extensive surgical reconstruction of the entire anterior abdominal wall with great potential for a variety of complications always be foremost in the surgeon's mind. Abdominoplasty is more than a "tummy tuck."

The willingness of a patient to undergo multiple surgeries and the surgeon's willingness to perform multiple surgeries in themselves do not constitute valid reasons for such undertakings. Because a patient trusts and believes that none of the potential complications the responsible surgeon will have related to the patient will occur does not relieve the surgeon from equating his ability and that of the hospital for treating such complications should they occur. *No surgeon should be coerced by the patient or allow himself the right to do multiple procedures without a complete, careful analysis of all aspects of what such a decision implies.*

RESULTS

The following series of patients represents our experience over the past fifteen years and is broken down into several categories with a critical analysis of each procedure.

Abdominoplasty with breast augmentation

Since abdominoplasty has been performed most frequently in conjunction with breast augmentation, we will begin with this combination, three approaches to which follow:

1. Submammary incision with submammary placement
2. Submammary incision with subpectoral implantation
3. Implantation through the abdominoplasty approach

The following cases illustrate these approaches.

Skin-line abdominoplasty with breast augmentation

The 40-year-old woman (gravida 3, para 3) shown in Fig. 6-1 has had three cesarean sections, with marked diastasis recti and scar formation. She underwent bilateral breast augmentation through the submammary incisions with submammary placement of a 175 cc Cronin teardrop prosthesis with Dacron patches. A skin-line abdominoplasty with a 5 cm inverted T was also performed. Fig. 6-2 demonstrates her postoperative appearance after a year; Fig. 6-3, after seven years.

> **Critique:** The patient's weight and muscular configuration have remained constant. The midline aspect of her scar is almost invisible. If we were doing this procedure today, we would place the incision lower by using the gull-wing configuration. We must not, however, lose sight of the fact that styles change. As one can see (Fig. 6-4), the scar position assumes less importance in a one-piece swimsuit,[7] provided the scar line does not extend below the line of the bathing suit.

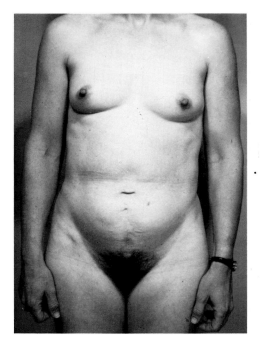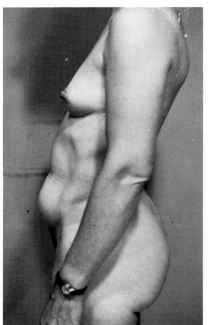

Fig. 6-1

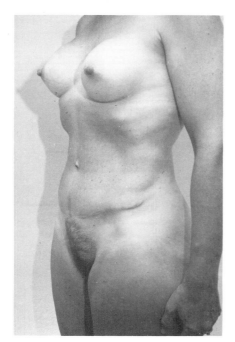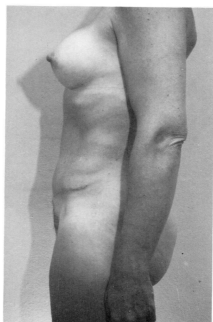

Fig. 6-2

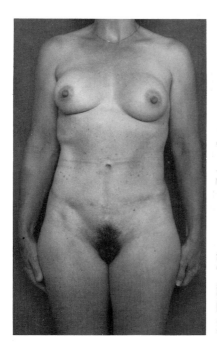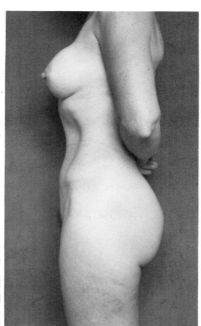

Fig. 6-3

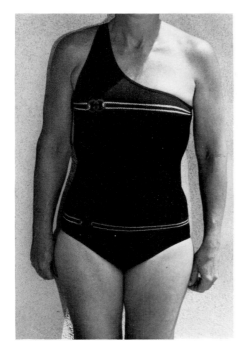

Fig. 6-4

A 40-year-old woman (gravida 4, para 4) who has had four cesarean sections and a ruptured appendix is shown in Fig. 6-5, demonstrating the previous scar contractures and the poor quality of the underlying fascia secondary to the multiple adjacent operative procedures. The patient underwent bilateral breast augmentation with a 220 cc Cronin teardrop patch prosthesis. The abdominoplasty was done with a skin-line incision and a 3.8 cm inverted T. Fig. 6-6 demonstrates the patient's appearances two months postoperatively. The width of the vertical scar is much less than the transverse aspect. Figs. 6-7 to 6-9 respectively demonstrate the patient a year postoperatively, six years postoperatively, and in her bikini.

Critique: Although the results of the combined procedure on this patient were excellent and the patient is extremely satisfied, a gull-wing incision in conjunction with an inverted T would be chosen for the procedure at this time.

Fig. 6-5

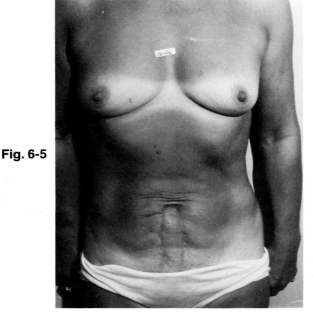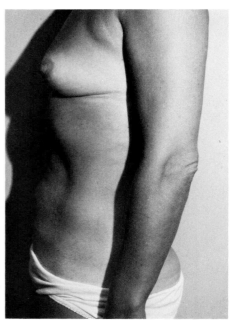

Fig. 6-6

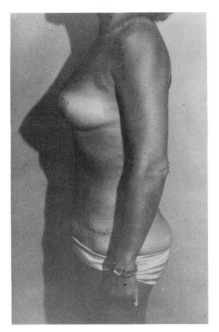

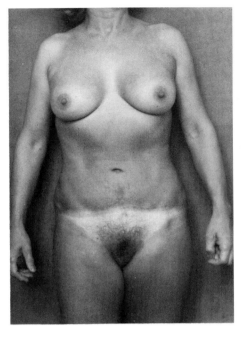
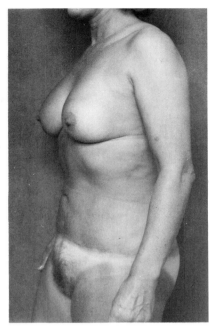

Fig. 6-7

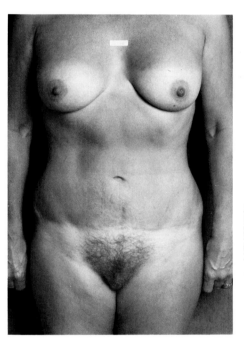
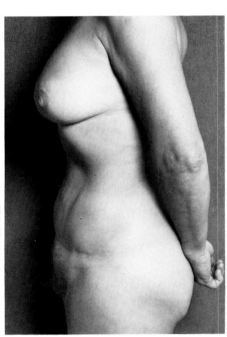

Fig. 6-8

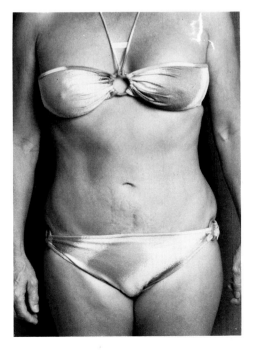
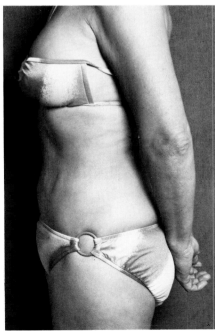

Fig. 6-9

Gull-wing abdominoplasty with subpectoral augmentation

Fig. 6-10 demonstrates the marked striae gravidarum of a 32-year-old woman (gravida 4, para 4). The patient underwent subpectoral implantation with a 340 cc McGhan gel type of prosthesis along with a gull-wing abdomino-plasty. Fig. 6-11 demonstrates the patient three months after surgery; Fig. 6-12, approximately a year postoperatively. (The mild pigment change on the patient's left side is congenital.)

Critique: This patient has had an excellent result even though the surgeon objected to the large size of breast implants that the patient desired. The patient is extremely happy. The surgeon found that the subpectoral implantation of this size of prosthesis is not technically difficult.

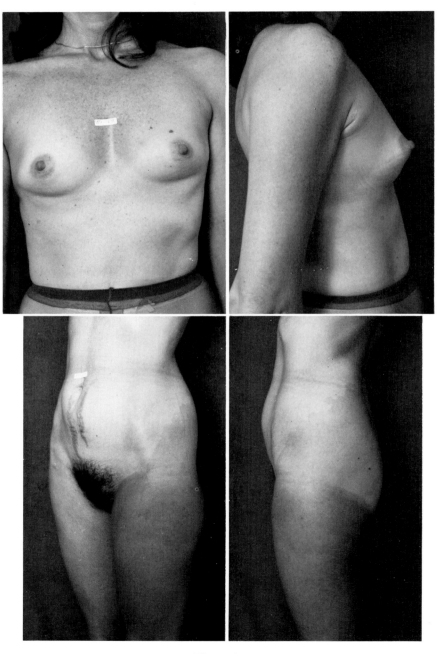

Fig. 6-10

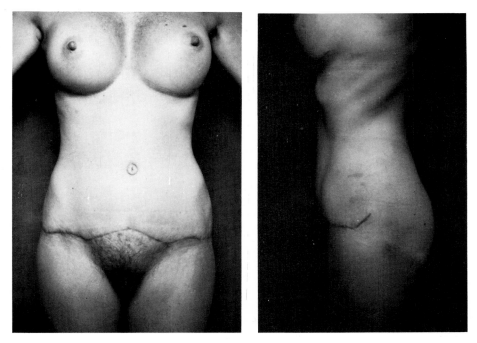

Fig. 6-11

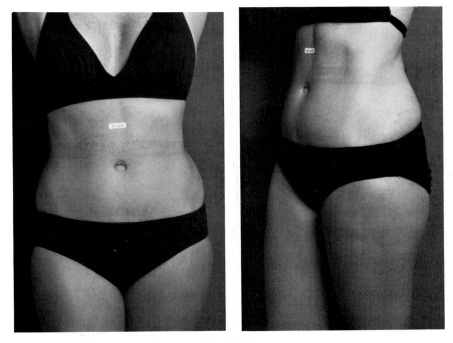

Fig. 6-12

Augmentation mammaplasty through the abdominoplasty site

The 32-year-old patient (gravida 2, para 2) in Fig. 6-13 weighed 105 pounds (47.3 kg) before surgery; she has weighed as much as 200 pounds (90 kg). The patient underwent a gull-wing abdominoplasty with breast augmentation through the abdominoplasty incision with 260 cc McGhan double-lumen implants.[15] The fiberoptic-lighted retractor (Fig. 6-14) was used to create pockets for the mammary implantation.[6,12]

Closure of the wound between the breast augmentation sites and the abdomen was accomplished with interrupted 00 general closure sutures; Jackson-Pratt drains were lead up to the mammary pocket and drained through the abdomen. The patient's appearance 2 months after surgery is shown in Fig. 6-15.

Critique: The patient obtained an excellent result. With the fiberoptic-lighted retractor, implantation through the abdominoplasty approach is not technically difficult. However, it is recommended that the communication between the breast pocket and the abdominal panniculus be securely closed with two or more catgut sutures.

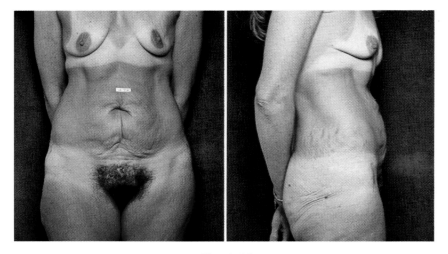

Fig. 6-13

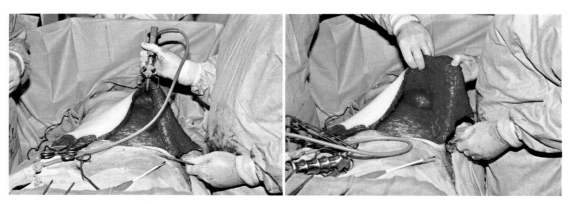

Fig. 6-14

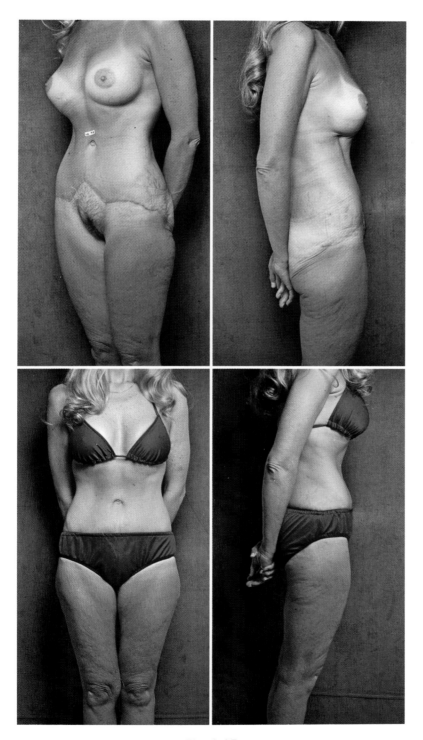

Fig. 6-15

Breast augmentation with W-abdominoplasty

Shown in Fig. 6-16 is a 39-year-old woman (gravida 2, para 2) who sustained a 50-pound (22.5 kg) weight gain during her second pregnancy. Preoperatively she had returned to her normal weight of 118 pounds (53.1 kg). The patient underwent a submammary augmentation with 220 cc McGhan gel implants, as well as a W-abdominoplasty[22] and a small inverted T. Fig. 6-17 shows the patient a month postoperatively; Fig. 6-18, two years after surgery.

Critique: The result was satisfactory. We would now recommend the gull-wing incision unless a French-style bathing suit is desired.

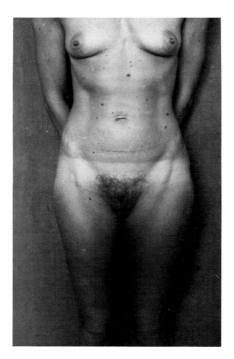
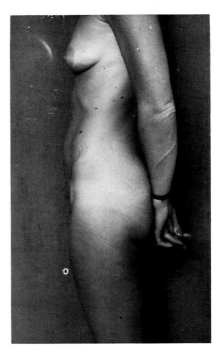

Fig. 6-16

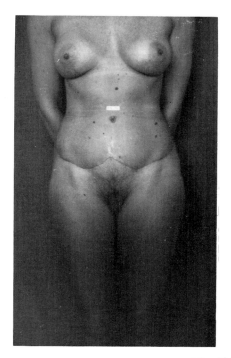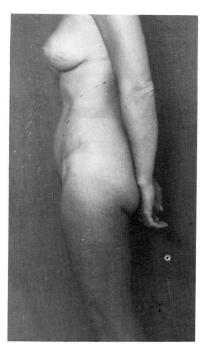

Fig. 6-17

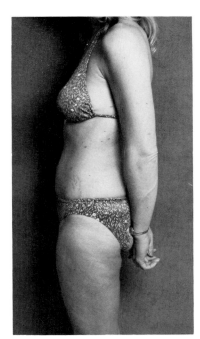

Fig. 6-18

Skin-line abdominoplasty with breast augmentation
and subsequent mastopexy

The 31-year-old woman in Fig. 6-19 (gravida 3, para 3) had undergone an appendectomy at age 5 that resulted in an extremely unattractive abdominal scar. Thus, along with bilateral breast augmentation with a 290 cc Heyer-Schulte teardrop prosthesis, she underwent a skin-line abdominoplasty with an inverted T component, which was used to reduce some of the central striae. A recommendation for mastopexy at the time of implantation was declined by the patient. Fig. 6-20 shows the patient six months after the abdominoplasty. Two years after her original abdominoplasty and breast augmentation, the patient underwent a McKissock mastopexy.[20] She is shown four months later in Fig. 6-21.[8]

Critique: This patient had an outstanding improvement in her appearance. In addition to her surgery, she gained a moderate amount of weight, which further enhanced her figure. It was readily apparent that a mastopexy was necessary for the maximum aesthetic improvement. Although the midline inverted T did not completely remove the residual striae, the procedure was vindicated by the amount of striae that was removed.

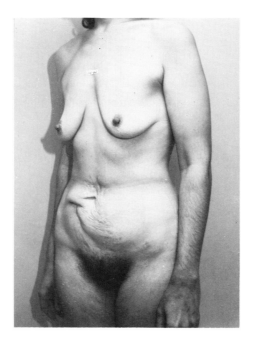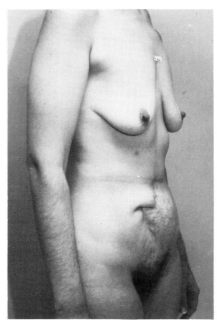

Fig. 6-19

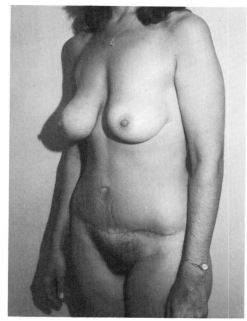

Fig. 6-20

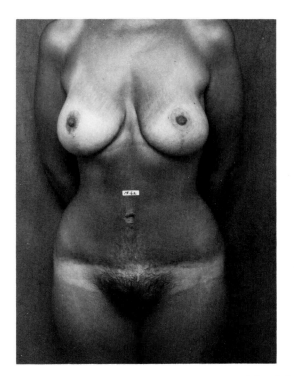
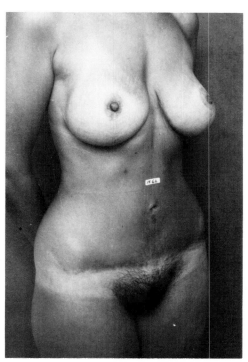

Fig. 6-21

Abdominoplasty with breast reduction
Dufourmentel mastopexy with gull-wing abdominoplasty

Fig. 6-22 represents the preoperative appearance of a 43-year-old woman (gravida 2, para 2) who six years before had undergone a hysterectomy. The patient underwent a Dufourmentel[2] skin mastopexy and a gull-wing abdominoplasty. Fig. 6-23 demonstrates the patient's postoperative results at a month; Fig. 6-24, at three months.

> **Critique:** This mastopexy/abdominoplasty is now our accepted standard procedure for a patient with this body configuration and type. We have had our most pleasing results with the Dufourmentel[2] mastopexy and our selected approach, the gull-wing[9] abdominoplasty, for this type of patient.

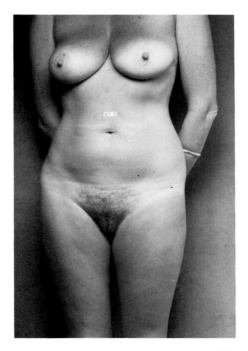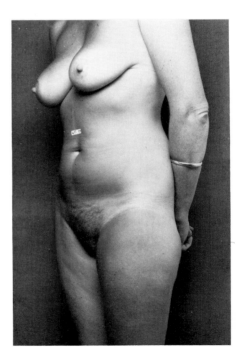

Fig. 6-22

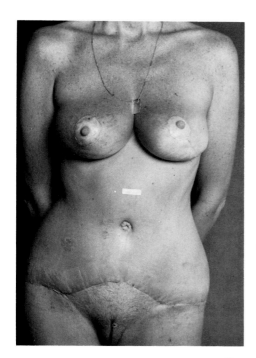
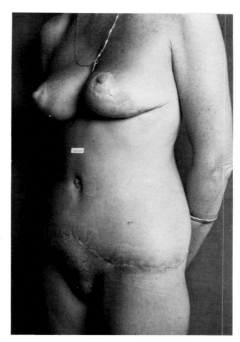

Fig. 6-23

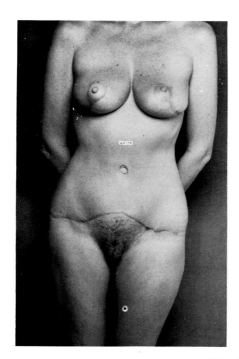
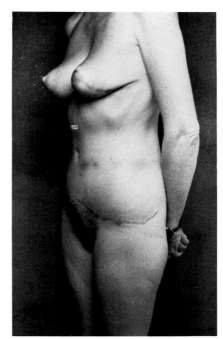

Fig. 6-24

Gull-wing abdominoplasty with McKissock breast reduction

Shown in Fig. 6-25 is a 43-year-old moderately obese woman (gravida 2, para 2) with breast enlargement, abdominal wall relaxation, and striae gravidarum. The patient underwent bilateral breast reduction by the McKissock[20] technique and a gull-wing abdominoplasty.[9] Approximately 350 g were removed from each breast. The microscopic diagnosis revealed bilateral fibrocystic disease of the breasts. A 1.2 kg abdominal panniculus was resected. Fig. 6-26 demonstrates the patient's appearance six months after surgery with the fullness over both hip areas. Figs. 6-27 and 6-28 demonstrate the appearance of the patient four months after hip revision and approximately ten months after abdominoplasty and breast reduction.

Critique: This patient obtained a satisfactory result from her combined procedure with restoration of a more normal contour. However, because of the patient's moderate weight problem, the extent of the resection of the panniculus resulted in residual fullness in each hip area, requiring the removal of an ellipse from both sides of the body under local anesthesia as an outpatient. The problem of hip fullness should be recognized preoperatively and dealt with at the time of surgery by rotating the patient from side to side and continuing the excision in the hip area.[9]

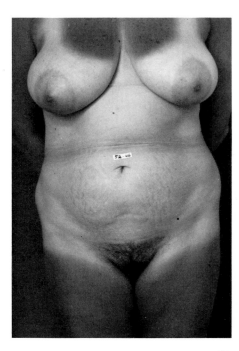 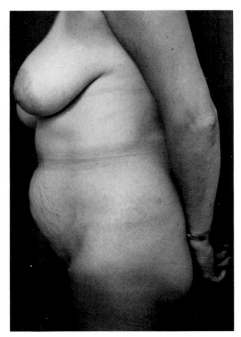

Fig. 6-25

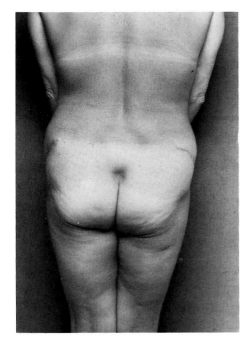 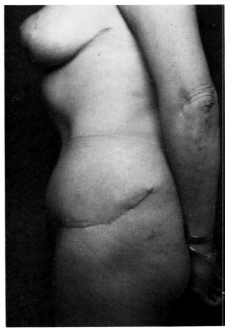

Fig. 6-26

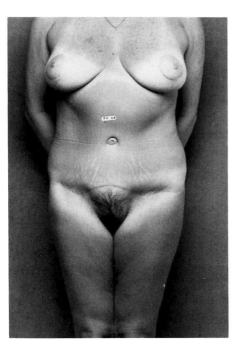 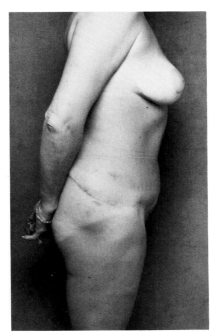

Fig. 6-27

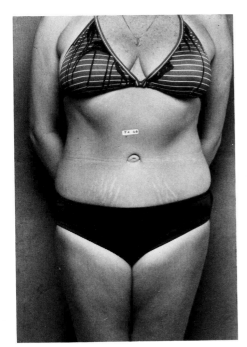 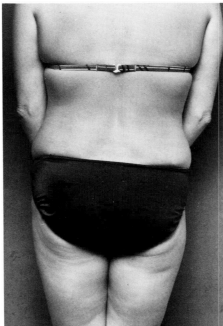

Fig. 6-28

Abdominoplasty with subcutaneous mastectomy

The 45-year-old patient (gravida 3, para 3) in Fig. 6-29 had had a previous hysterectomy. She underwent bilateral subcutaneous mastectomy for fibrocystic disease (Fig. 6-30). Three months after the first stage of the subcutaneous mastectomy, the patient's breasts were reconstructed with 260 cc Cronin gel-filled implants, and a skin-line abdominoplasty was performed. Fig. 6-31 demonstrates the patient's appearance three years after breast reconstruction and abdominoplasty.

Critique: At the present time simultaneous subpectoral implantation with subcutaneous mastectomy is preferred, thus delaying the abdominoplasty as a future surgery.[3,4]

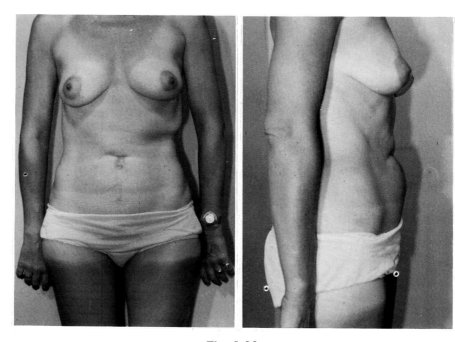

Fig. 6-29

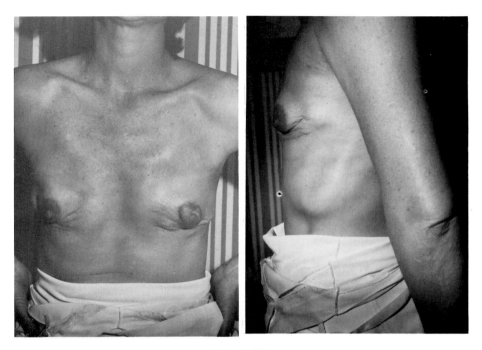

Fig. 6-30

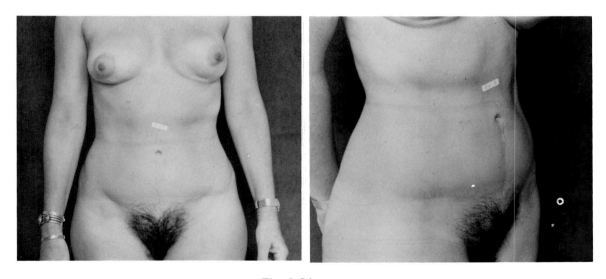

Fig. 6-31

Abdominoplasty with breast reconstruction

The 39-year-old woman (gravida 2, para 2) in Fig. 6-32 had had a modified right radical mastectomy eight months previously. Fig. 6-33 demonstrates the patient's appearance after the first stage of reconstruction of her right breast with subpectoral implantation of a 290 cc gel-filled Heyer-Schulte prosthesis. Three months later the patient underwent a left mastopexy,[20] labial areolar graft, and skin-line abdominoplasty with removal of a 700 g panniculus. Fig. 6-34, *A,* shows the patient eight months postoperatively; Figs. 6-34, *B,* and 6-35, four years after surgery, after reconstruction of the nipple; and Fig. 6-36, two months after a capsulotomy of the right breast.

> **Critique:** The only change recommended is in selection of the donor material for the areola: the perigenital region is preferred over the labia majora. This patient has developed the typical hyperpigmentation from a labial graft. She has also experienced a moderate weight gain without abnormal distribution of fat.

Fig. 6-32

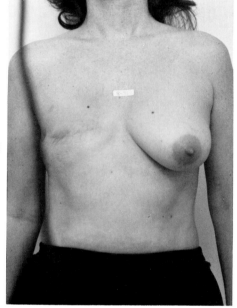

Fig. 6-33

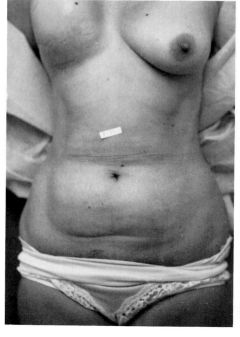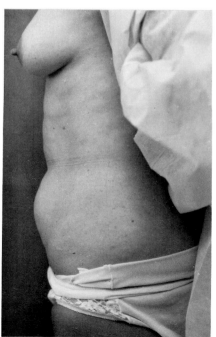

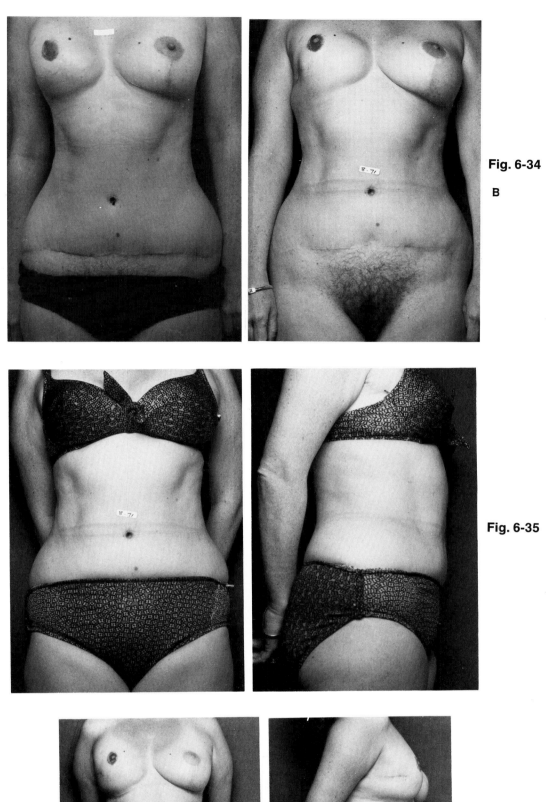

A

B

Fig. 6-34

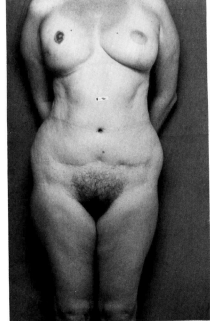

Fig. 6-35

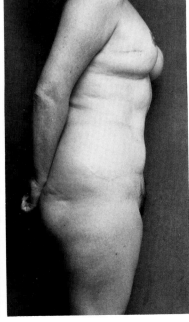

Fig. 6-36

Skin-line abdominoplasty with lower abdominal scar deformities

Fig. 6-37 demonstrates the unattractive childhood appendectomy scar of a 58-year-old woman (gravida 0). The result three years after a skin-line abdominoplasty is shown in Fig. 6-38.

Critique: Scars of the lower abdomen can be resected easily with abdominoplasty, which yields a satisfactory result. Skin-line abdominoplasty remains the preferred procedure with this patient because of her body configuration.

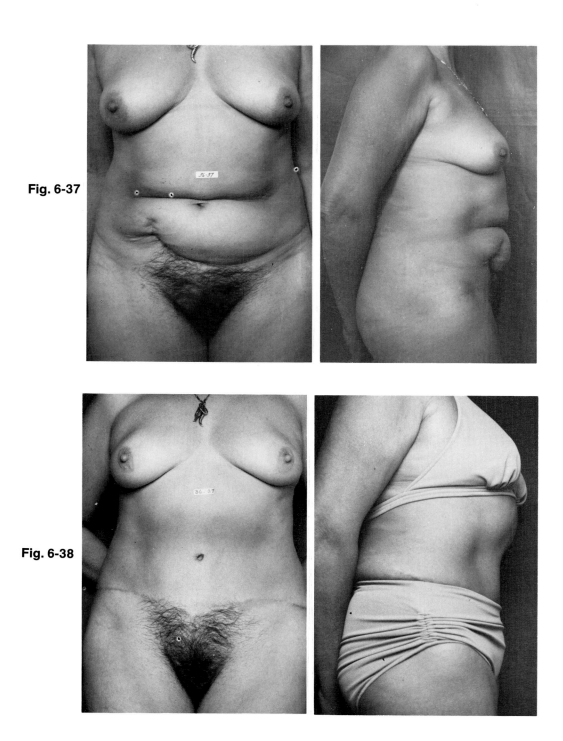

Fig. 6-37

Fig. 6-38

The 36-year-old woman (gravida 2, para 2) shown in Fig. 6-39 had had a ruptured appendix and small bowel obstruction, as evidenced by the residual scar deformity. A vaginal hysterectomy and skin-line abdominoplasty were combined. The operating time was 3 hours; the total amount blood lost, 1 unit. The patient is shown in Fig. 6-40 five years after surgery.

Critique: No increased postoperative morbidity was associated with this combined procedure. With the skin-line incision it was possible to remove almost all of the previous scar deformity. If this procedure were to be done today, a gull-wing incision would be considered.[9]

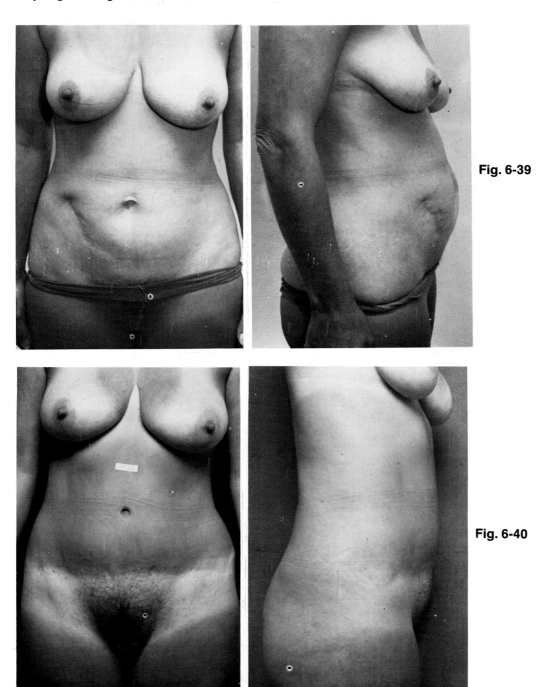

Fig. 6-39

Fig. 6-40

Skin-line abdominoplasty with extensive scar deformity

The 35-year-old woman (gravida 6, para 6) in Fig. 6-41 had, during a hysterectomy three years before, sustained a ureteral injury requiring exploration and repair by subsequent surgeries. The patient was left with a large L-shaped scar. Skin-line abdominoplasty was chosen for this patient to remove the scar deformity. Six months after surgery (Fig. 6-42), the patient had developed some hypertrophic scarring because of the tension on the suture line caused by the large amount of abdominal skin and panniculus resected to remove the original scar defect. Fig. 6-43 demonstrates the patient's appearance a year after surgery.

Critique: This patient obtained an excellent postoperative result, but, because of the amount of resection and the tightness of the wound repair, the scar became hypertrophic, and a revision was required. The patient was advised of the revision and accepted it readily. The use of either the W-plasty or the gull-wing configuration would not have succeeded in removing all of the vertical scar deformity and should not be recommended.

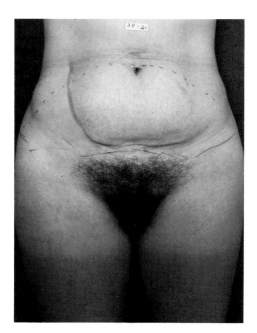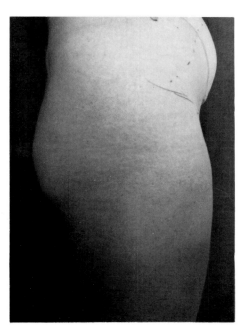

Fig. 6-41

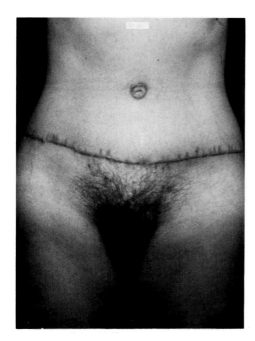
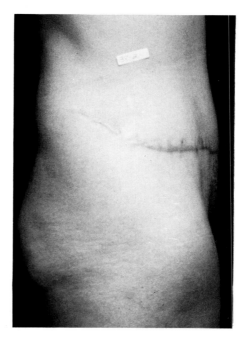

Fig. 6-42

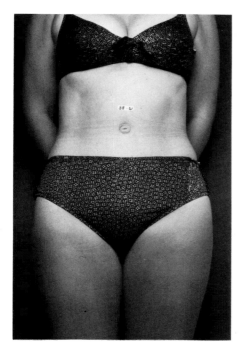
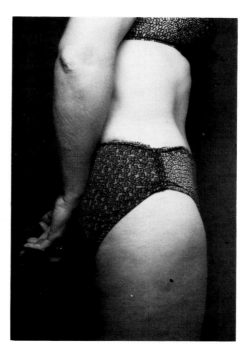

Fig. 6-43

W-abdominoplasty with midline scar deformity

A 43-year-old patient who had had a hysterectomy, appendectomy, and hernia repair, as well as seven pregnancies, is shown in Fig. 6-44. The patient was left with a marked lower abdominal relaxation and midline scar deformity. Fig. 6-45 demonstrates her appearance two months after abdominoplasty with a standard W-plasty approach.[22]

> **Critique:** This patient has had an excellent result. The only recommendation is a consultation with the patient to see what style swimsuit she wears so that the surgery would fit the style. The W type of incision lends itself well to the French-cut suit.

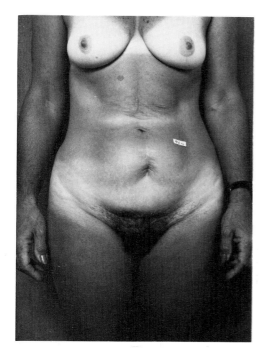
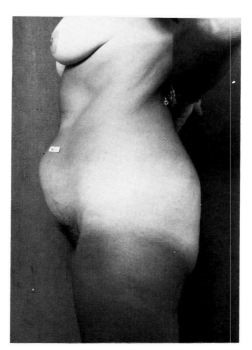

Fig. 6-44

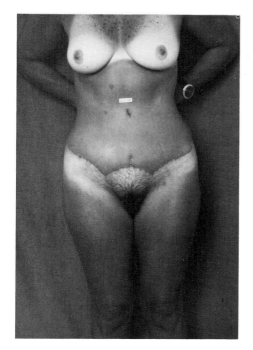
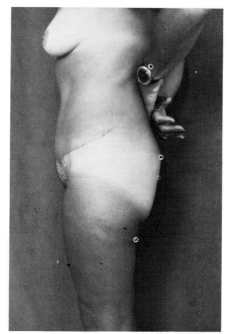

Fig. 6-45

Abdominoplasty with previous history of deep-vein thrombosis

The 42-year-old patient in Fig. 6-46 had had two pregnancies, an appendectomy as a child, and a hysterectomy seven years before this surgery. The patient's past history was significant in that eight years before she had developed deep-vein thrombosis in her leg after an automobile accident. At the time of this injury, she was heparinized. Consequently, she was given 5,000 units of heparin subcutaneously 3 hours before surgery and 5,000 units every 12 hours until she was ambulating well.[11] Her postoperative course was uneventful with the exception of a small incisional hematoma and more than the usual amount of ecchymosis. The patient is shown in Fig. 6-47 four months after abdominoplasty with a modified W approach.

> **Critique:** The use of minidose heparin contributes to more than the average amount of blood loss. The patient developed a small incisional hematoma, which resolved without further difficulty. She had no evidence of recurrent venous thrombosis.[18] It was possible to undermine and sufficiently remove all previous abdominal scars. In addition to the minidose heparin, the patient should have been monitored with fibrinogen-^{125}I scans before and after surgery.

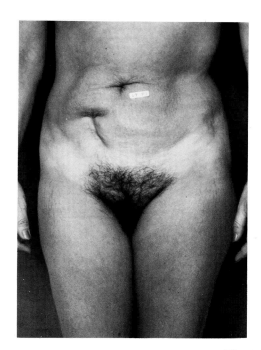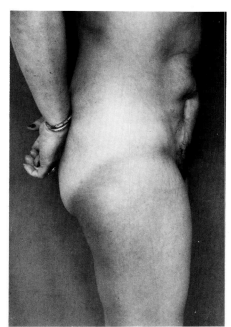

Fig. 6-46

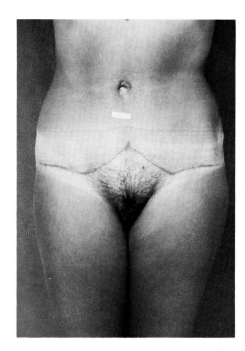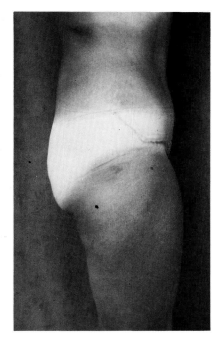

Fig. 6-47

Skin-line abdominoplasty with upper abdominal scar deformities

The 32-year-old woman (gravida 2, para 2) in Fig. 6-48, *A,* had had a cholecystectomy a year before her abdominoplasty. Fig. 6-48, *B,* exhibits the patient's appearance two weeks after surgery. The inverted T was employed to remove additional striae.

Critique: There is always a question of whether upper quadrant incisions compromise the circulation of the lower portion of the flap. In this patient, the closeness of the subcostal incision to the umbilicus and the vertical midline component resulted in no compromise in the circulation. At the present time, we would recommend the use of intravenously injected fluorescein and an ultraviolet light[5] to check on the circulation at the time of surgery or the use of a continuous noninvasive, blood oxygen monitoring device manufactured by Litton Medical Electronics.[16]

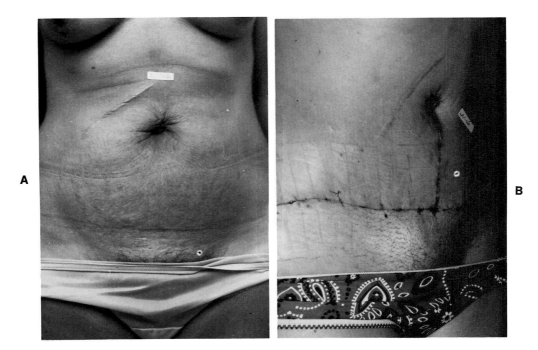

A

B

Fig. 6-48

Skin-line abdominoplasty with tubal coagulation

The 33-year-old woman (gravida 2, para 2) in Fig. 6-49, *A*, had weighed up to 200 pounds (90 kg) with her last pregnancy. At the time of surgery, the patient weighed 120 pounds (54 kg). She underwent bilateral breast augmentation with 260 cc Heyer-Schulte implants, a tubal coagulation, and a skin-line abdominoplasty. Fig. 6-49, *B*, demonstrates the patient a year after surgery; Fig. 6-49, *C*, four years postoperatively.

Critique: This patient's postoperative course was uneventful. The result was satisfactory. The patient could have had a mastopexy at the time of surgery, and a gull-wing incision along with a smaller umbilicus now would be preferred. The patient has experienced a moderate weight gain.

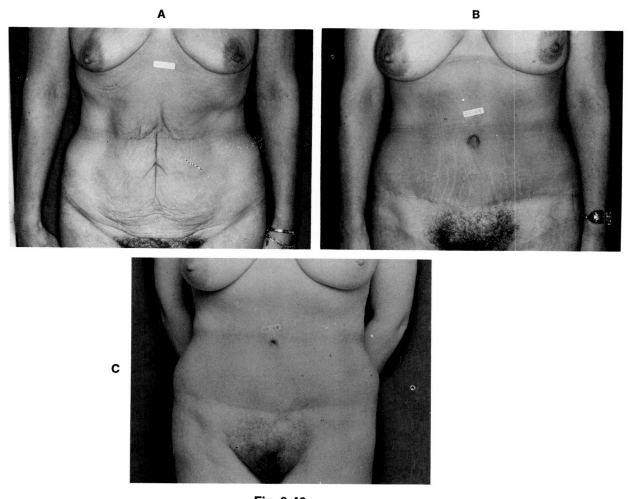

Fig. 6-49

Skin-line abdominoplasty with breast reduction and anteroposterior repair

The 53-year-old patient in Fig. 6-50 had had a hysterectomy four years previously that had been complicated by a rectovaginal fistula, which required a colostomy, bowel resection, and subsequent colostomy closure. The colostomy closure site can barely be seen to the right and above the umbilicus. She underwent an anteroposterior repair, McKissock[20] breast reduction, and skin-line abdominoplasty. A total of 630 g of tissue were removed from the breasts, and 1.2 kg of tissue were resected from the abdomen. The total blood loss was to 1.2 liter; 2 units of blood were replaced. The total operating time was 5 hours 10 minutes. Immediately after surgery, minimal evidence exists of compromise circulation to the flap between the colostomy site and the inferior closure (Fig. 6-51). This area healed primarily.

> **Critique:** The patient obtained an excellent result. No increased morbidity occurred as a consequence of combining the abdominoplasty, breast reduction, and simultaneous anteroposterior repair. The use of intravenously administered fluorescein[5] would allow for greater confidence in the distal flap circulation. This might have permitted the surgeon to do higher undermining in an effort to remove the entire residual colostomy scar.
>
> At the present time, procedures of this magnitude require the patient to donate several units of blood preoperatively for use during surgery. We were fortunate in this case that the patient did not develop a pulmonary embolism as a result of her size and the length of surgery time. Any modality that ensures reduced morbidity should be considered in future cases of this type.

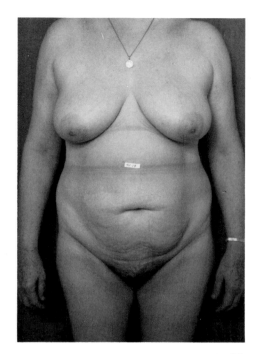
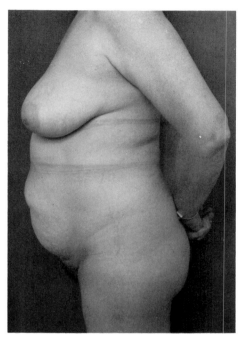

Fig. 6-50

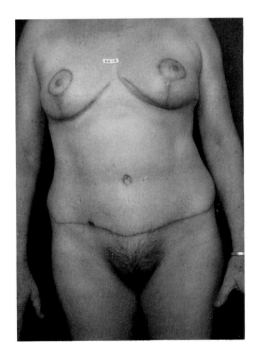
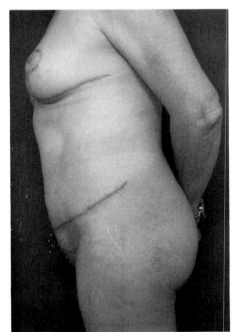

Fig. 6-51

Abdominoplasty with revision face-lift and acute injury

The 63-year-old woman (gravida 2, para 2) in Fig. 6-52, *A*, had had an appendectomy and a face-lift. The patient was admitted to the hospital for revision meloplasty and abdominoplasty. The patient stumbled in the parking lot the day she was being admitted to the hospital for surgery and sustained a fracture of her left fibula. The evening prior to surgery, the patient was seen by an orthopedic consultant who thought there was no contraindication to her planned surgery. The patient underwent application of a short leg cast by the orthopedist, followed by abdominoplasty and then by revision meloplasty. The patient is shown four years after surgery in Fig. 6-52, *B* and *C*.

> **Critique:** Criticism for combining this acute injury with elective surgery is in order. Both the surgeon and the patient were fortunate that no complications occurred as a result of her injury, including thromboembolism.

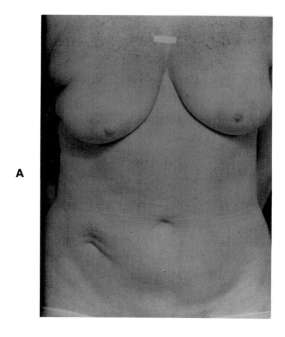

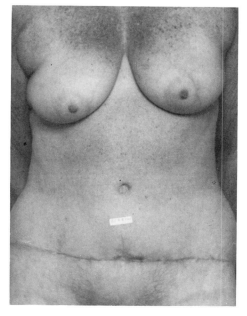

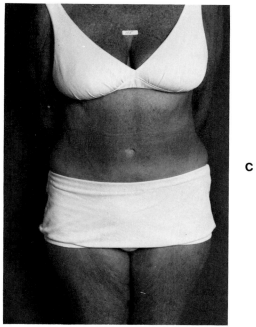

Fig. 6-52

COMPLICATIONS
Pulmonary embolism

Pulmonary embolism has been estimated to occur in more than 500,000 patients a year in the United States and is directly responsible for more than 100,000 deaths. The first pulmonary embolism resulting from abdominoplasty during our experience occurred after ten years, or approximately 200 abdominoplasties. After discussing this occurrence with several other surgeons performing abdominoplasties, we realized that this was not an isolated incidence. In 1975, Grazer and Goldwyn[10] polled all members of the American Society of Plastic and Reconstructive Surgery, including the overseas members. The survey was all inclusive with regard to abdominoplasty; however, one of the questions concerned the incidence of deep venous thrombosis, pulmonary emboli, and number of deaths. There were 958 responses, which represented a minimum of 10,460 abdominoplasties. The incidence of pulmonary emboli was 0.8%; the total number of deaths, 17. It was known to Dr. Goldwyn and the authors that there were a number of deaths that were not reported, and the incidence of pulmonary emboli is probably somewhat higher. When patients are scanned by fibrinogen ^{125}I, recognition of emboli is greatly increased. The literature reveals that the incidence of pulmonary emboli in patients undergoing major abdominal surgery, including thoracic and gynecological surgery, ranges from 11% to 65%; elective hip replacement, 48% to 54%; and emergency hip fracture surgery, 48% to 74%.

A number of high-risk factors predispose patients to venous thrombosis: advanced age; fractures of the lower limb; hip surgery; surgery of the pelvis or lower abdomen, which requires extensive dissection; previous venous thromboembolism; congestive cardiac failure; cancer surgery; obesity; and varicose vein surgery.

Of our 4 patients with pulmonary embolism, 3 were obese to a degree. None of the surgeries exceeded a 3-hour time period. The first patient had had varicose vein surgery and thrombophlebitis several years before. None of the patients had a history of pulmonary emboli, and none were on a regimen of birth control pills. The onset of occurrence was between five and eleven days. The literature indicates that a correlation exists between the weight of the patient and the length of time for surgery.[14]

As was noted in the discussion of body types (somatotypes) in Chapter 5, the obese patient is the poorest candidate for the abdominoplasty operation. However, the aesthetic results obtained with these patients must be carefully weighed against the morbidity.

Case one

The 59-year-old woman (gravida 2, para 2) in Fig. 6-53 had undergone hysterectomy thirty years before, varicose vein surgery nineteen years previously, and a laminectomy eleven years prior to abdominoplasty. The patient underwent a skin-line abdominoplasty in which a panniculus weighing 1 kg was removed. Blood loss was minimal during the operative procedure, which lasted 2 hours 50 minutes. The patient wore antiemboli stockings during and after surgery; however, because of the extent of the rectus plication, the patient was not ambulated until 48 hours postoperatively. She was discharged five days after surgery in good health. Two days later, the patient developed a sudden twinge of pain in her right calf, followed by severe chest pain and dyspnea about 45 minutes later. The patient was immediately rehospitalized. A chest x-ray study revealed pulmonary infiltration; a pulmonary lung scan confirmed the diagnosis of pulmonary embolism. The patient received therapeutic doses of heparin for anticoagulation and was discharged and maintained on anticoagulation therapy with warfarin (Coumadin).

Critique: This case, our first recognized experience with pulmonary embolism, served as an impetus to investigate the mechanism of pulmonary emboli. Some of the information gained is contained in Chapter 7. Postoperative photographs of this patient were not obtainable. The patient blamed the surgeon for the pulmonary embolus. However, her brother, a general surgeon, assured us that she has an excellent aesthetic result with no sequelae to her pulmonary embolism four years after surgery. In light of what we have learned, the obese patient with a history of varicose vein surgery would most likely be a candidate for minidose heparin[10] with preoperative and postoperative fibrinogen scans.

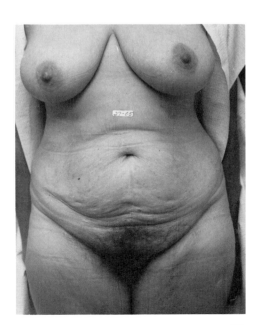
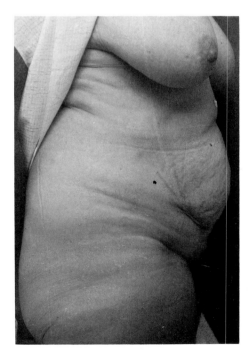

Fig. 6-53

Case two

The 37-year-old patient (gravida 1, para 1) in Fig. 6-54, who had had a hysterectomy at age 27, underwent a skin-line abdominoplasty with a resection of 760 g. Eleven days after surgery (six days after discharge), the patient was readmitted for dyspnea and chest pain. A V/W scan indicated a combined ventilation-perfusion defect at the left base. The diagnosis of pulmonary embolism was made, and the patient was immediately anticoagulated with therapeutic doses of heparin and placed on warfarin for six months after surgery. Fig. 6-55 shows the patient three and a half months after surgery.

Critique: With the exception of mild obesity, nothing in this patient's history or physical examination indicated the risk of pulmonary embolism. Consequently, we now give intravenously infused alcohol—1 liter of 5% alcohol and 5% dextrose—to all our patients as a possible deterrent to the hypercoagulable state.[11]

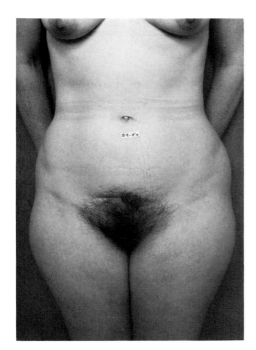
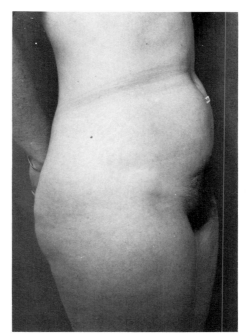

Fig. 6-54

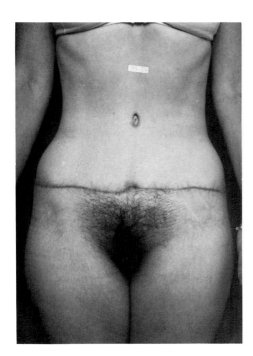
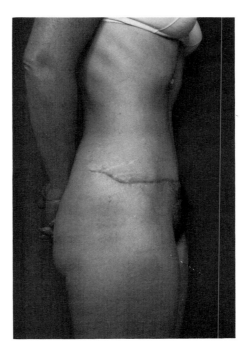

Fig. 6-55

Case three

The 40-year-old woman in Fig. 6-56 weighed over 200 pounds (90 kg). She had been pregnant six times, the last being thirteen years ago, and had had a 40-pound (18 kg) weight gain since her last child was born. She had undergone a cholecystectomy fourteen years prior to the present surgery and a hysterectomy twelve years before. A 2.8 kg panniculus was resected by skin-line abdominoplasty. During the operation the patient's legs were intermittently massaged and flexed to stimulate circulation. She was also ambulated 16 hours postoperatively. She was discharged on the fourth postoperative day, although she complained of mild right shoulder pain; however, chest examination was negative at that time. She was readmitted on the fifth day after surgery with increasing shoulder and right leg pain. A perfusion scan (Fig. 6-58) revealed evidence of pulmonary embolus; venogram (Fig. 6-59) demonstrated venous irregularities of the right calf, suggesting previous thrombophlebitis. The patient was immediately treated with therapeutic doses of heparin and discharged on a regimen of warfarin, which was continued for approximately six months. The patient, whose postoperative appearance is shown in Fig. 6-57, subsequently underwent successful thigh reduction surgery about eight months after her pulmonary embolism. She was treated with minidose heparin and intravenously infused alcohol during surgery with no postoperative sequelae.

Critique: As mentioned previously, obesity is a relative contraindication for abdominoplasty. This patient had been most appreciative of the surgical results. At the present time minidose heparin and/or intravenously infused alcohol would be considered for this patient, along with fibrogen-^{125}I scans before and after surgery.

Fig. 6-56

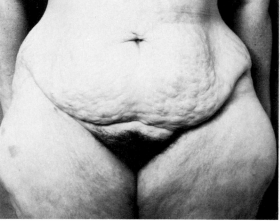
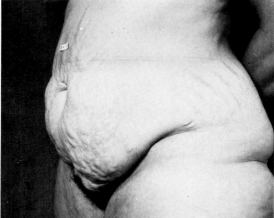

Fig. 6-57

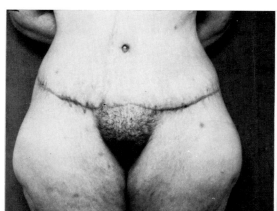
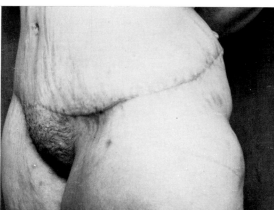

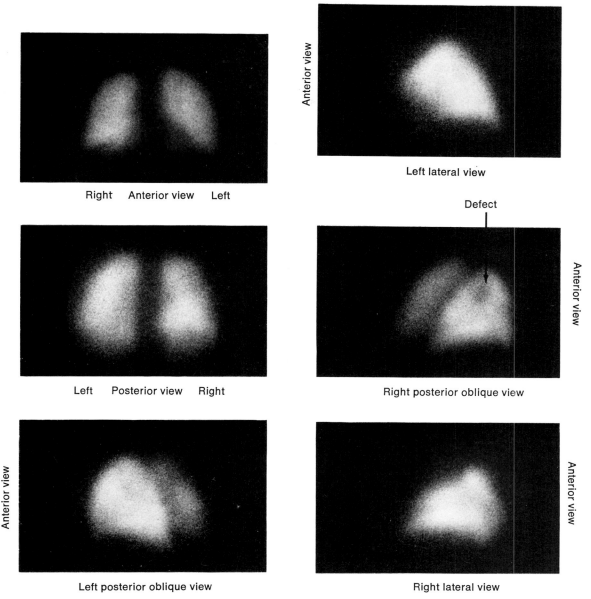

Fig. 6-58. Perfusion scan with 4 mCi of technetium 99m macroaggregated albumin (MAA). At the middle right, the scan demonstrates defects in the posterior aspect of the right upper lobe.

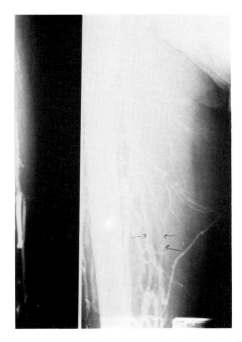

Fig. 6-59. Venogram reveals the apparent site of origin of the embolus.

Case four

Shown in Fig. 6-60 is a 41-year-old woman (gravida 2, para 2) who underwent skin-line abdominoplasty with a 600 g tissue resection. Total operating time was 2 hours 10 minutes. During the operative procedure the patient's legs were massaged while she wore antiemboli stockings. Accelerated clotting times were done in an effort to determine the hypercoagulable state. No significant change in the accelerated clotting times was observed, and the patient was discharged on the fifth day after surgery. On the seventh postoperative day the patient developed pain in her left leg and, when examined, was found to have acute thrombophlebitis of the right deep venous system with elevated temperature and dyspnea. She was readmitted to the hospital with a presumptive diagnosis of pulmonary embolus, which was confirmed by a perfusion scan (Fig. 6-61). The patient was immediately treated with heparin and maintained on warfarin therapy for six months after discharge from the hospital.[11] A year after surgery (Fig. 6-62), anticoagulant therapy was stopped and the patient has had no residual sequelae.

> **Critique:** The use of leg massage during surgery has been abandoned. Since pulmonary emboli occurred in 2 of our 4 emboli patients who were massaged on the operating table, massaging is believed to have been instrumental in the development of thromboembolic sequelae. During the past two and a half years, we have performed more than 200 abdominoplasties with no pulmonary emboli since the use of intravenously infused alcohol has been instituted during surgery and/or the use of minidose heparin for patients with presumptive history of previous thromboembolic phenomena. Clinical use of accelerated clotting times showed no correlation in predicting the formation of thrombi or emboli.

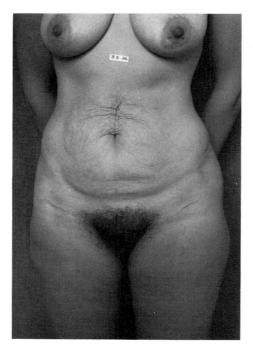
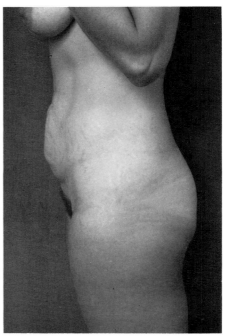

Fig. 6-60

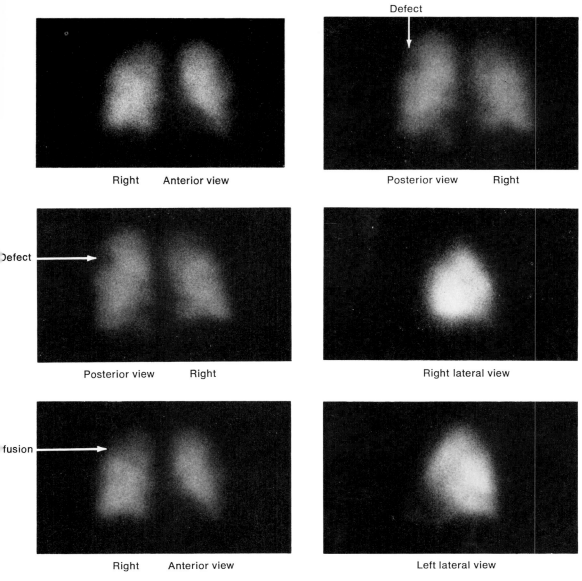

Fig. 6-61. Perfusion scan with 6 mCi of technetium 99m MAA. Bilateral pulmonary defects are apparent *(upper right* and *middle left),* as well as underperfusion of the right apex *(lower left)* and lateral scalloping along the lateral chest margin.

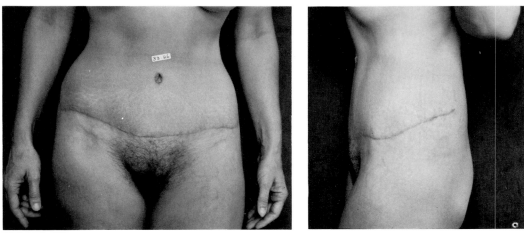

Fig. 6-62

Obesity

The 35-year-old woman (gravida 1, para 1) in Fig. 6-63 weighed 180 pounds (81 kg). During her skin-line abdominoplasty, 3.44 kg of tissue were resected. Four years after abdominoplasty (Fig. 6-64), in spite of an unfortunate 20-pound (9 kg) weight gain, the patient's abdomen had remained flat. Breast reduction and hip contouring were performed during the second surgery. Figs. 6-65 and 6-66 demonstrate the patient's appearance three months after a McKissock[20] breast reduction and upper hip reduction.

Critique: This patient has done exceptionally well for both surgeries. There were no complications during either postoperative period. It is unfortunate that the patient has remained chronically obese. Considering patients with intractable obesity for a bypass procedure remains a matter of philosophical controversy. This patient's self-image was greatly improved with the afore-mentioned procedures. Between the time of her initial abdominoplasty procedure and her second surgery, we instituted the fibrinogen-^{125}I scan. The patient's preoperative and postoperative scan[11] (Chapter 7) is shown in Fig. 6-67.

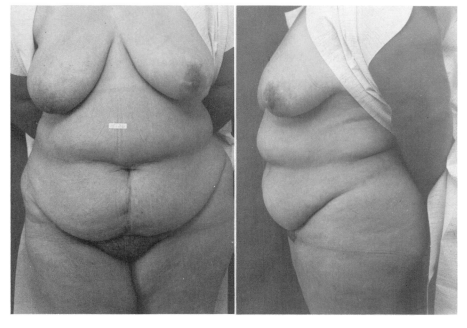

Fig. 6-63

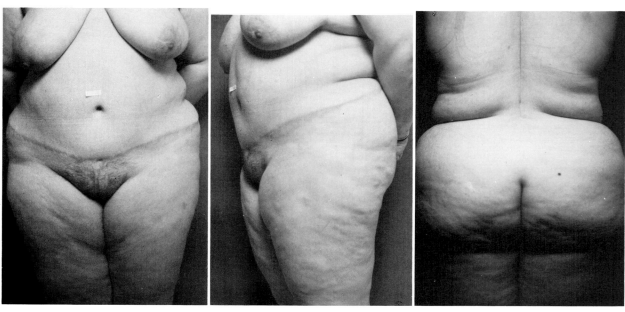

Fig. 6-64

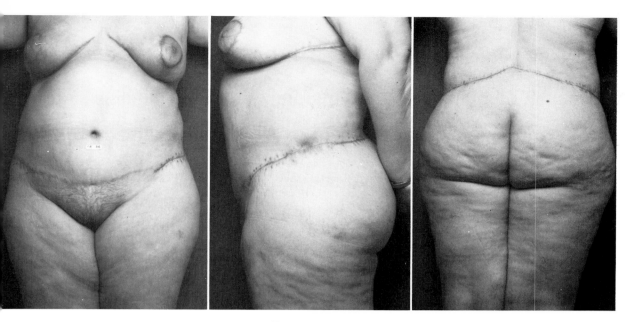

Fig. 6-65

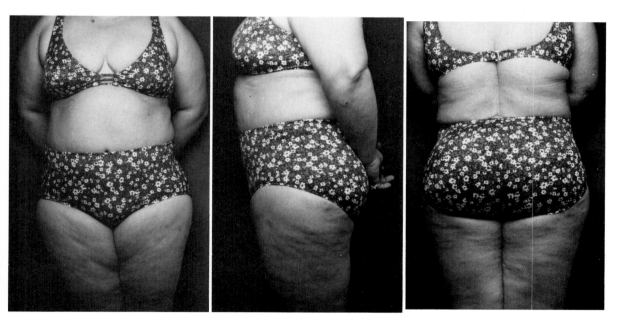

Fig. 6-66

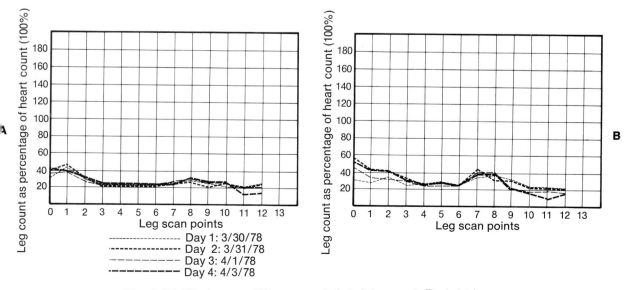

Fig. 6-67. Fibrinogen-^{125}I scans of, **A,** left leg and, **B,** right leg.

Obesity and incisional hernia

The 33-year-old woman (gravida 1, para 1) in Fig. 6-68 weighed 195 pounds (87.8 kg) at the time of surgery; she had weighed as much as 300 pounds (135 kg). Her previous cesarean section resulted in a large incisional hernia at the base of the umbilicus. A 5.56 kg panniculus was resected through a skin-line abdominoplasty. Operating time including repair of the incisional hernia was 4 hours 30 minutes. Fig. 6-69 demonstrates the appearance of the patient four weeks after surgery. Circulation around the umbilicus was compromised to a small degree during the hernia repair. The necrotic area completely healed.

Critique: The patient obtained a satisfactory result with complete repair of the incisional hernia. No specific recommendations can be made at the present time that would have prevented the soft tissue necrosis around the umbilicus. We have not obtained later postoperative photographs of this patient, but we learned by telephone conversation that there is apparently no residual deformity of the umbilicus. The patient was treated with routine intravenous infusion of 5% dextrose and alcohol at 300 ml/hour.

Umbilical loss in reconstruction

Occasionally, the umbilicus has been removed in abdominal surgery, particularly in umbilical hernias. Reconstruction can be accomplished by modifications of the umbilicoplasty technique described in Chapter 5. In the proposed site of the umbilicus the abdominal skin is incised in the shape of the umbilicus and is left attached to the abdominal wall, where it acts as a substitute umbilicus. The next steps in the reconstruction are the same as those described in Fig. 5-41 and may be used when performing a full abdominoplasty or the creation of an umbilicus.[1a]

Distortions of the umbilicus due to poor surgical technique and/or necrosis and infection may be reconstructed in a manner similar to that just described.

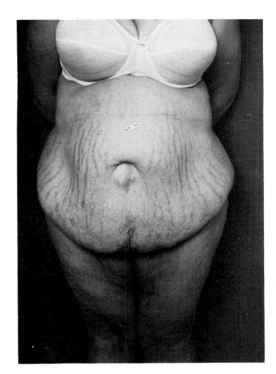
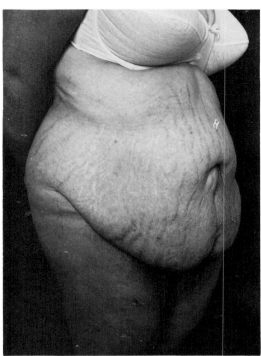

Fig. 6-68

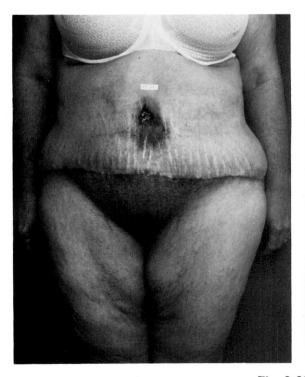
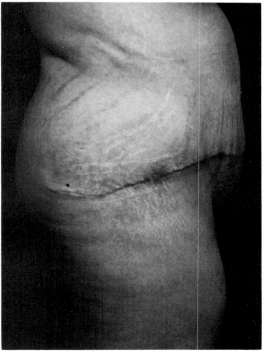

Fig. 6-69

Postural deformities

Patients with postural deformities such as scoliosis often have associated abdominal deformities. The inability to flex the back muscles as well as the abdominal muscles frequently results in increased low back pain. These patients may also complain of difficulty with proper wearing of clothing because of asymmetry in the hip contour.

The 68-year-old woman in Fig. 6-70 had undergone laminectomy for marked scoliosis three years before. She underwent a classic skin-line abdominoplasty with extension into the lateroposterior hip area to improve her hip symmetry. A total of 1 kg of tissue was resected. The patient, shown five months postoperatively in Fig. 6-71, indicates that she has been free of back pain since surgery.

Critique: This patient obtained an excellent postoperative result, and we recommend no change in technique. Because of the patient's age and obesity, she was scanned with fibrinogen ^{125}I before and after surgery (Fig. 6-72). She was also given routine intravenous infusion of alcohol. *Note:* The graphs in Fig. 6-72 show the count increasing on day two and dropping back into normal range on day three. A persistent increase of this kind of elevation would indicate propagation of a thrombus.

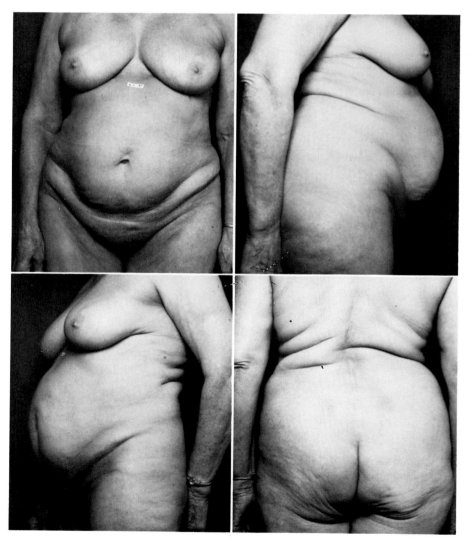

Fig. 6-70

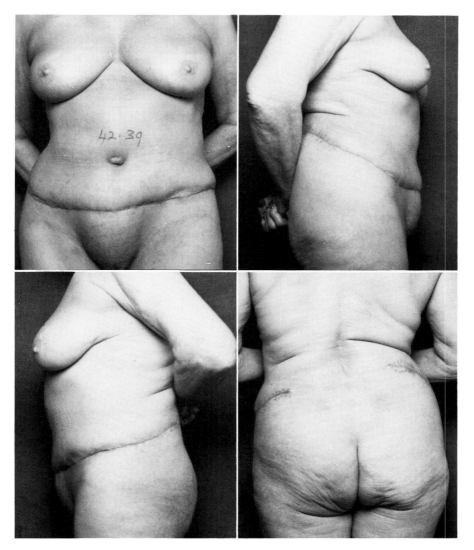

Fig. 6-71

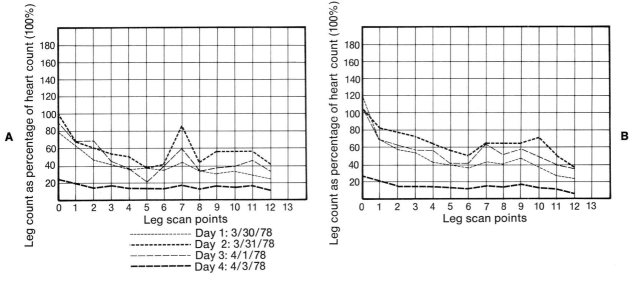

Fig. 6-72. Fibrinogen-^{125}I scan of, **A,** left leg and, **B,** right leg.

195

Surgical denervation of lower abdomen

Two years before this surgery, the 21-year-old patient in Fig. 6-73, *A*, developed a rectal prolapse and underwent a transabdominal operation for correction by a general surgeon. Postoperatively, the patient developed an anastomotic leak and subsequent pelvic abcess that required colostomy, which was closed five months later. A bowel obstruction occurred six months after the colostomy closure. The obstruction was relieved and an attempt made to repair the abdominal wall weakness before the patient was referred for possible abdominoplasty.

Marked eventration of the lower abdomen is shown in the preoperative photograph in Fig. 6-73, *B*. Ultrasound examination of the anterior abdominal wall demonstrated extreme thinning from the umbilicus to the pubic area. Preoperative electromyographic studies demonstrated denervation from T9 through T12 (Table 2). The delineation between the atrophic muscle and the normal muscle above is shown in Fig. 6-74. The patient was placed in the jackknife position. Transverse plication was begun from right to left, with closure by 2-0 nonabsorbable sutures from the upper portion of the normal fascia and muscle tissue to the shelving portion of the inguinal ligament. Good closure was accomplished from the right side to the midline and pubis. On the left side the defect was somewhat greater. Because of the significantly tighter transverse closure, reinforcement was made with a piece of Marlex mesh, 6 × 4 inches. After transverse plication, the umbilicus was positioned immediately above the pubis (Fig. 6-75). A free transplant of the umbilicus was accomplished.[23] (Fig. 6-76, *A*). Fig. 6-76, *B*, shows the marking across the iliac crest for location of the new umbilicus; Figs. 6-77 and 6-78, the patient's appearance a month after surgery.

> **Critique:** This patient presented an unusual problem. Preoperative planning included the possibility of turning down a portion of the rectus muscle sheath and employing relaxing incisions at the lateral flank area with transposition of fascia lata muscle flaps to close this defect. Postoperatively, the patient's result has been excellent. Six months after surgery some fullness of the left lower quadrant recurred. In retrospect we realize the possibility of a free fascia lata graft to support this lower quadrant could have been considered.

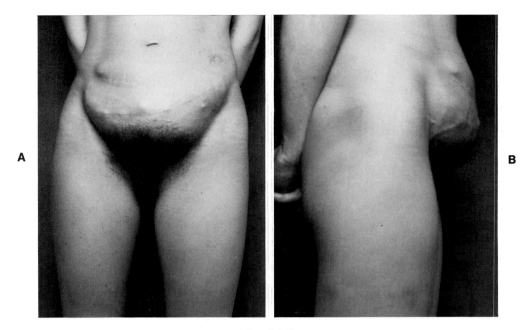

Fig. 6-73

Table 2. Nerve conduction studies

Muscles (right and left)	Nerve(s)	Electromyogram			
		Level	Fibrillations	Positive waves	Motor unit action potentials
Iliopsoas	Femoral	L2 to L4	None	None	Normal
Adductor magnus	Obturator	L2 to L4	None	None	Normal
Quadriceps femoris	Femoral	L2 to L4	None	None	Normal
Gluteus maximus	Iliogastric	L5, S1, S2	None	None	Normal
Hamstring	Sciatic	L4, L5, S1, S2	None	None	Normal
Gastrocnemius	Sciatic	S1, S2	None	None	Normal
Tibialis anterior	Peroneal	L4, L5, S1	None	None	Normal
Extensor hallucis longus	Peroneal	L4, L5, S1	None	None	Normal
Extensor digitorum brevis	Peroneal	L5, S1	None	None	Normal
Peroneus longus	Peroneal	L4, L5, S1	None	None	Normal
Abdominis (upper)	Intercostobrachial	T6 to T8	None	None	Normal
Abdominis (lower)	Intercostobrachial	T9 to T12	+1	None	No voluntary motor units

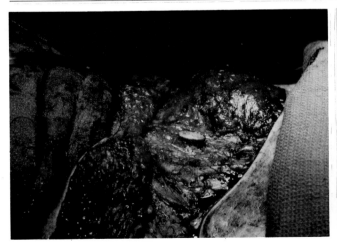

Fig. 6-74

197

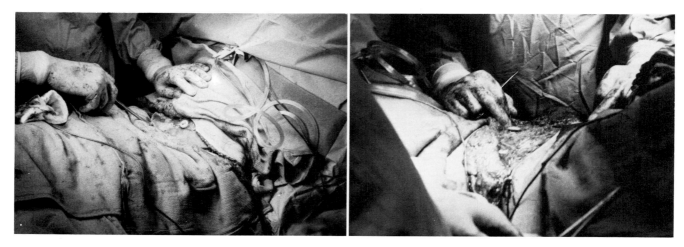

Fig. 6-75

A   B

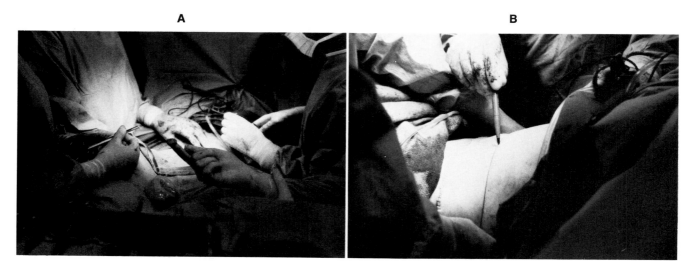

Fig. 6-76

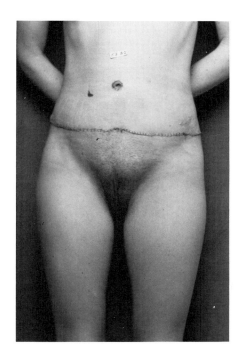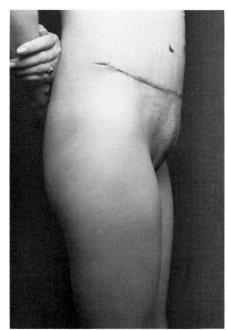

Fig. 6-77

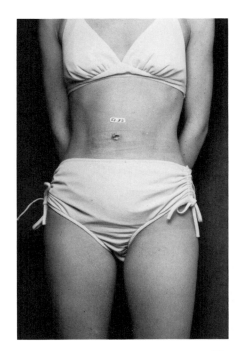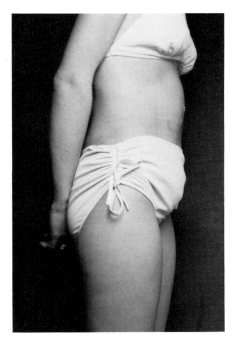

Fig. 6-78

Abdominoplasty with bypass surgery

The 36-year-old patient in Fig. 6-79 had undergone a surgical bypass procedure two years before she sought abdominoplasty. As a result of her bypass procedure, she lost approximately 150 pounds (67.5 kg), resulting in her present weight of 125 pounds (56.3 kg). A skin-line abdominoplasty was performed, with resection of 1.2 kg of tissue, as well as an arm reduction. The surgery, which was performed by the resident staff at the University of California, Irvine, was attended by one of the authors. Photographs taken a year after surgery are shown in Fig. 6-80.

Critique: The patient has had a marked improvement in her appearance. In retrospect, additional undermining over the costal margin would have resulted in a more satisfactory result. The patient has been unable to have further recommended surgery, which would include mastopexy and thighplasty. In most surgical bypass patients, the amount of skin excess cannot be completely removed during one surgical procedure. Such patients should be advised that several operative procedures will be necessary to obtain a satisfactory result. This type of surgery should be considered reconstructive surgery; therefore insurance carriers should recognize an obligation for coverage.

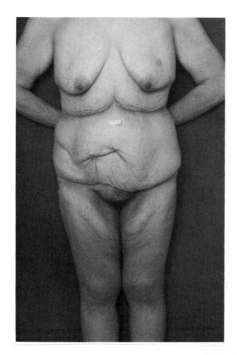
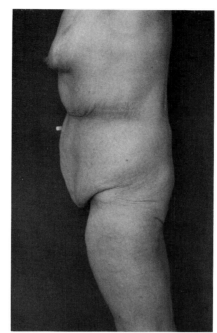

Fig. 6-79

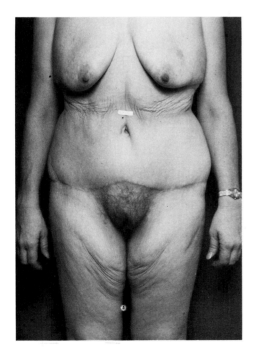
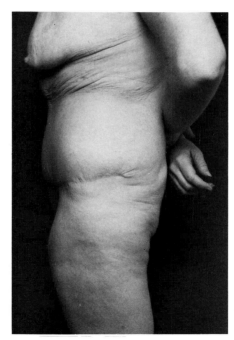

Fig. 6-80

Improper placement of incision

As pointed out in the section "Today's Techniques" in Chapter 5, too much emphasis has been placed on the type of incision; however, the exception to this is when the incision extends beyond the confines of the patient's bikini. A 45-year-old patient (gravida 2, para 2) (Fig. 6-81) preoperatively demonstrated moderate fullness of the lower abdomen. Postoperative photographs (Fig. 6-82) show an excellent result anteriorly; however, the patient objected to the upward lateral extensions of her scars (Fig. 6-83).

Critique: The patient should have been marked preoperatively in her briefest bikini attire. Possibly a gull-wing modification may have eliminated this problem.

Fig. 6-81

Fig. 6-82

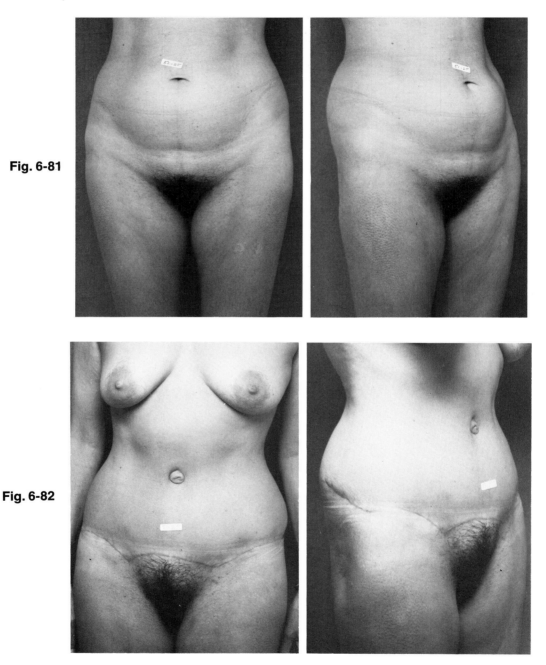

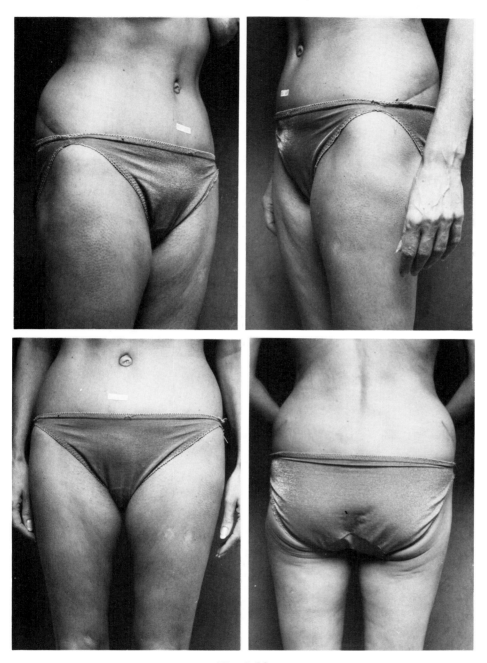

Fig. 6-83

The 26-year-old woman (gravida 2, para 2) in Fig. 6-84 underwent an inverted T gull-wing abdominoplasty along with tubal ligation and breast augmentation. Because of her small size and the location of the striae, the results of an attempt to remove the supraumbilical striae by extending the inverted T component above the umbilicus were less than satisfactory (Fig. 6-85).

Critique: Two factors should have warned the surgeon that the patient might form less than an ideal scar: the appearance of a scar in the right flank, which is elevated, and the multiple striae as well as the widened appendectomy scar. For these reasons, the use of the supraumbilical incision should be avoided.

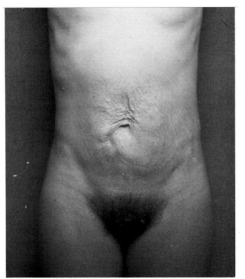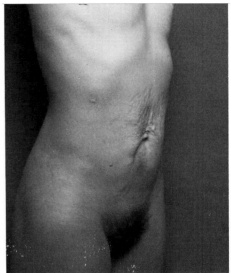

Fig. 6-84

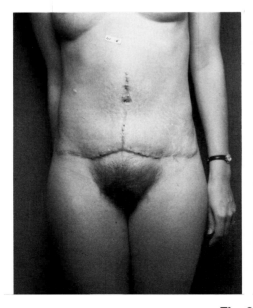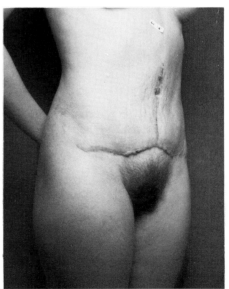

Fig. 6-85

A 35-year-old woman (gravida 2, para 2) who had undergone hysterectomy and abdominoplasty elsewhere a year before was referred for consultation. An inverted T abdominoplasty without relocation of the umbilicus had resulted in the distorted appearance of her umbilicus (Fig. 6-86).

Critique: The patient's umbilical distortion could have been avoided by relocation of the umbilicus.

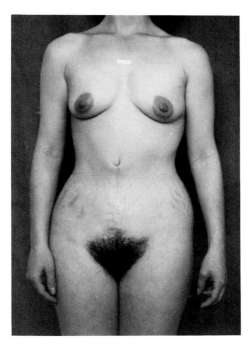

Fig. 6-86

Incomplete undermining of the abdominal flap

The 58-year-old patient (gravida 3, para 3) in Fig. 6-87 had had three previous cesarean sections. Under controlled dieting she had lost 60 pounds (27 kg) during the year before surgery. She underwent a McKissock[20] breast reduction of approximately 300 g from each breast and a skin-line abdominoplasty with 2000 g resected. The patient had donated 3 units of blood, which was given back to her and which more than adequately replaced the 1.2-liter blood loss. Fig. 6-88 demonstrates the patient's appearance a month after surgery; Fig. 6-89, nine months after surgery.

Critique: This patient has had a marked improvement in her appearance. The fullness in her upper abdomen was probably the result of inadequate undermining and plication. If a breast reduction and abdominoplasty are simultaneously performed, the use of fluorescein[5] and transcutaneous noninvasive monitoring of the P_{O_2}[16] may give the surgeon more confidence so that a more superior undermining procedure can be done.

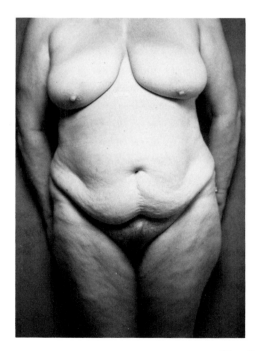 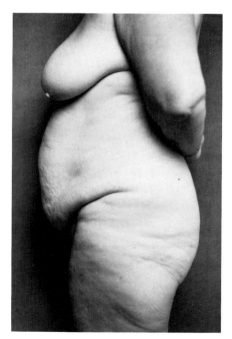

Fig. 6-87

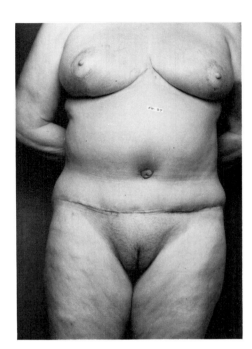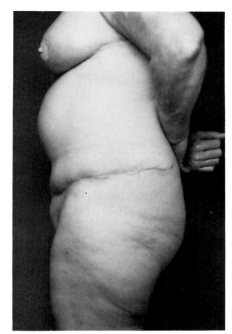

Fig. 6-88

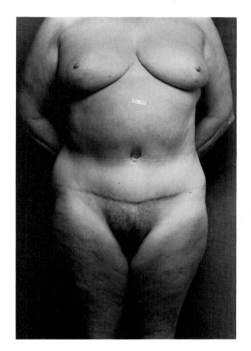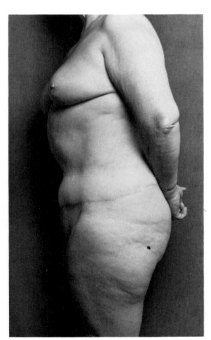

Fig. 6-89

Wound separation

Shown in Fig. 6-90 is a 42-year-old woman who had previously had an appendectomy and two cesarean sections. Four weeks after the patient underwent an abdominal hysterectomy and a skin-line abdominoplasty, a wound separation was successfully repaired under local anesthesia (Fig. 6-91). Her appearance two years later is shown in Fig. 6-92.

Critique: The abdominal hysterectomy may have contributed to the wound separation. At the present time the gull-wing incision would be preferred.

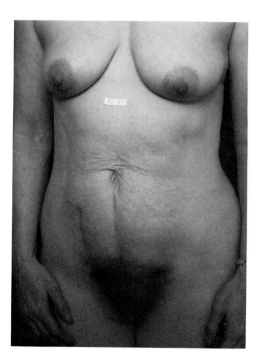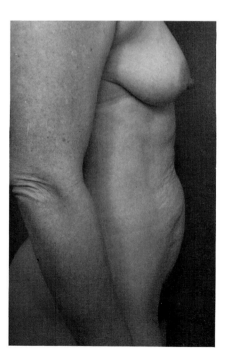

Fig. 6-90

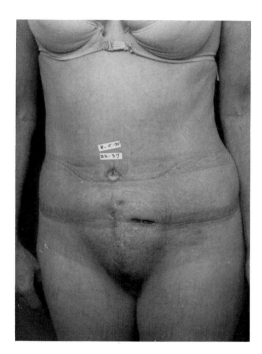
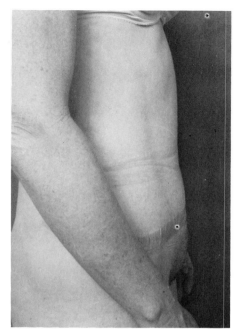

Fig. 6-91

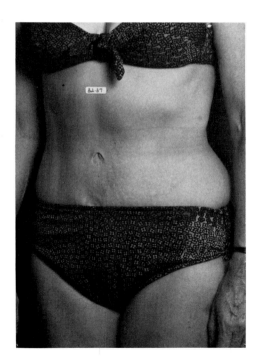
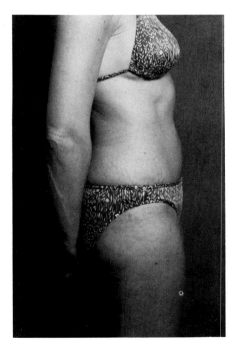

Fig. 6-92

Umbilical size

The size of the umbilicus is important to the abdominoplasty patient, since the surgical site is exposed in a two-piece bathing suit. The preoperative photograph (Fig. 6-93, *A*) of a 29-year-old patient (gravida 2, para 3) reveals a rather large, protuberant umbilicus with an accompanying small umbilical hernia. The new umbilicus (Fig. 6-93, *B*) was too large.

Critique: A reduction of the size of the umbilicus was necessary.

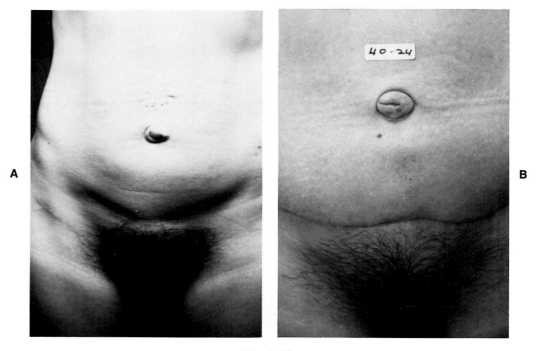

A

B

Fig. 6-93

Umbilical distortion

Umbilical distortion frequently occurs when the umbilicus is not transposed in the course of an abdominoplasty. Fig. 6-94 is courtesy of Dr. J. Kenneth Chong, who saw this patient in consultation after she had had a compromising operation elsewhere. In addition to the umbilical distortion, the sideways H operation was completely unacceptable to the patient.

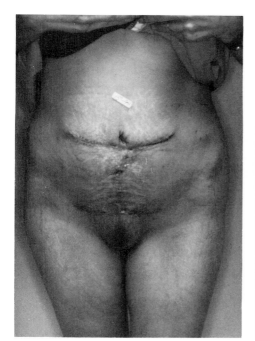
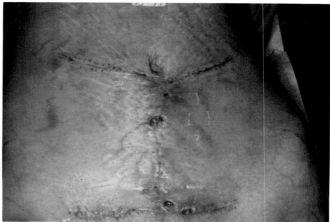

Fig. 6-94
(Courtesy J. K. Chong, M.D., Newport Beach, Calif.)

Skin loss

Skin loss is one of the perplexing postoperative complications in abdominoplasty. The Grazer-Goldwyn[10] survey indicated that 7% of the surgeons had to graft for skin loss. During the past fifteen years, the authors have each had to graft one patient. Fig. 6-95 demonstrates the area of necrosis in one patient; Fig. 6-96, the attempt at secondary closure with a tie-over bolster; and Fig. 6-97, the area that required grafting after the secondary closure. Other cases of skin loss are illustrated in Figs. 6-98 to 6-101.

Critique: The following remedial measures should be instituted at the first sign of compromised circulation: the use of dextran 40 followed by intravenously injected fluorescein to assess the circulation. If no immediate improvement occurs, the use of a hyperbaric chamber (Fig. 6-102) is strongly recommended, if available, at 2 atmospheres of oxygen per hour twice a day.[11]

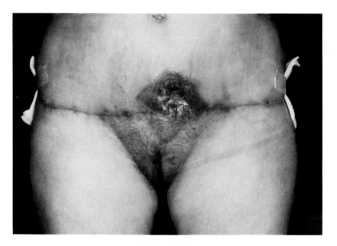

Fig. 6-95

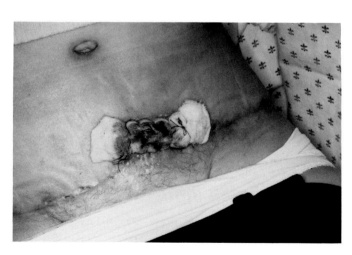

Fig. 6-96

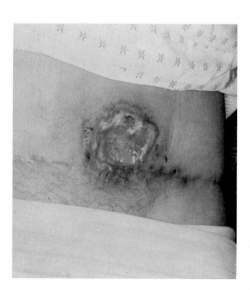

Fig. 6-97

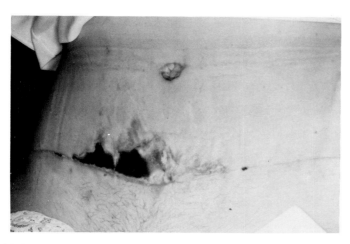

Fig. 6-98. Full-thickness loss of skin that was excised and repaired successfully two months after surgery.

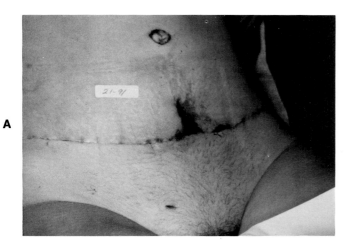

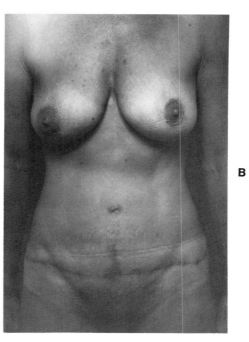

Fig. 6-99. A, This 42-year-old woman underwent abdominoplasty and developed a small area of necrosis in the midline. **B,** Postoperative view of the secondary closure and result.

213

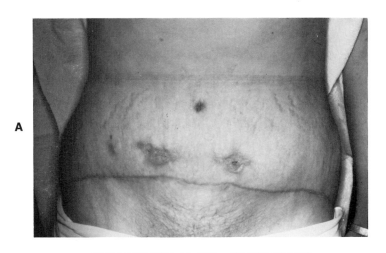

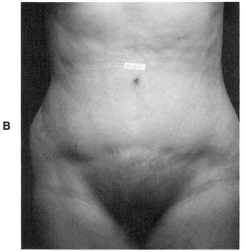

Fig. 6-100. **A,** This 33-year-old woman received a third-degree burn from a plaster of paris splint[7,11] after undergoing the Pitanguy type of abdominoplasty. **B,** Postoperative appearance of the patient four years after a secondary abdominoplasty.

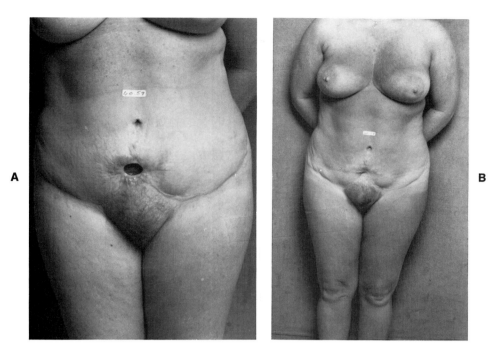

Fig. 6-101. A, This 39-year-old woman had undergone a W-abdominoplasty by a non-plastic surgeon eleven months previously. Several attempts at secondary closure were made. The patient was not allowed to bathe during the eleven months after the surgery. The defect was undermined for 5 cm all around the opening. Cultures of the area grew out *Staphylococcus aureus.* **B,** Eight weeks after the patient was examined, she was completely healed without surgery. Treatment consisted of administration of povidone-iodine complex (Betadine), use of a whirlpool, frequent bathing, and the application of homographic skin to the defect. The patient will undergo scar revision at a future date.

Fig. 6-102

MALE ABDOMINOPLASTY

In the past men have usually requested abdominal panniculectomy as a result of massive weight loss, as is demonstrated by one of the earlier patients in our series (pp. 220 and 221). However, at the present time, requests for abdominoplasty in men are increasing in number, as are those for women.

The patient in Fig. 6-103 is a 46-year-old physician who had lost 40 pounds (18 kg) during the year prior to surgery. He actively engages in outdoor sports, including water skiing, but was unable to correct his abdominal wall relaxation and panniculus with exercise. The patient underwent a skin-line abdominoplasty with a 1.2 kg reduction and is shown a year after surgery in Fig. 6-104.

Critique: Both the patient and the surgeon were satisfied.

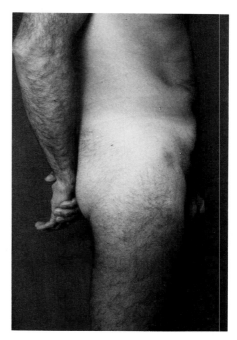

Fig. 6-103

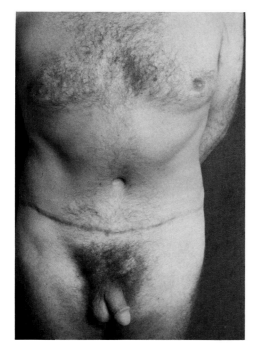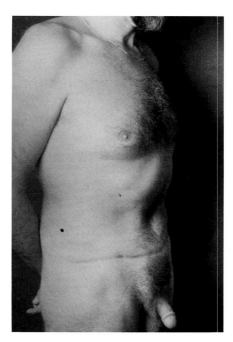

Fig. 6-104

The 49-year-old man in Fig. 6-105 weighed 183 pounds (82.4 kg) before surgery. He underwent a gull-wing abdominoplasty (1.1 kg resected), as well as the waistline stitch[17] (Fig. 6-106). Fig. 6-107 demonstrates the appearance of the patient a month after surgery with marked improvement in contour; weight is 180 pounds (81 kg).

Critique: Extensive plication and the early application of a Velcro binder probably contributed to bilateral atelectasis and ileus. The patient's condition promptly improved after administration of intermittent positive pressure breathing and relief of the tight constriction by the Velcro binder.

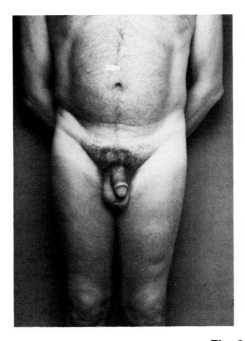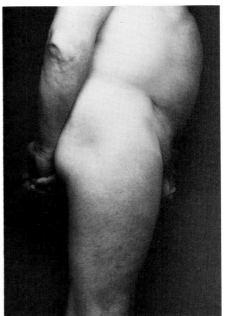

Fig. 6-105

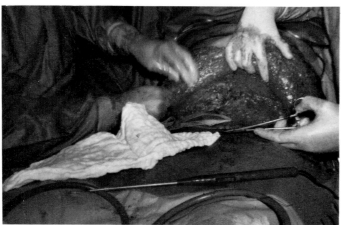

Fig. 6-106

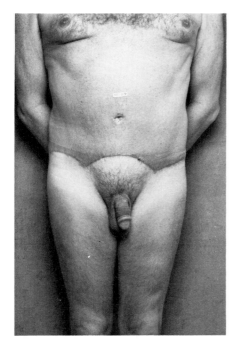

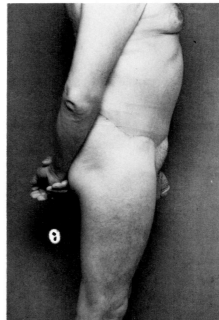

Fig. 6-107

Male abdominoplasty with bypass procedure

In 1972 Kamper[19] described the case of a 500-pound (225 kg), 42-year-old man who had lost 275 pounds (123.8 kg) on a starvation diet (Fig. 6-108). One of the authors performed an abdominal lipectomy, mons lipectomy, and mastopexy to correct the results of the massive weight loss (Fig. 6-109) and followed the case in communication with Dr. Ernest Drenick of the Wadsworth Veterans Hospital, Los Angeles, where the patient had been on the diet. Drenick indicated that the patient had regained the weight, causing an unsightly fat distribution. The patient was returned to surgery for a bypass procedure but died. According to Drenick, the patient's death was one of the very few associated with this procedure. The mortality rate for patients who are morbidly obese and have not undergone bypass surgery is probably greater than that associated with the surgical risk of a bypass procedure.

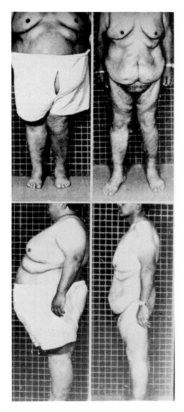

Fig. 6-108

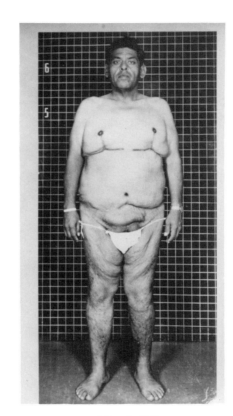

Fig. 6-109

CASTANARES' PROCEDURE[1] FOR COMBINED ILEOPEXY AND ABDOMINOPLASTY

The patient in Fig. 6-110 is 54 years of age and approximately 25 years ago had a total colectomy with ileostomy. She had a marked amount of weight loss, which complicated her ileostomy stoma. Periods of telescoping of the ileostomy site occur, and, because of the sagging of the abdominal panniculus, the patient has had difficulty applying a prosthesis bag over the ileostomy site. The adhesive has not been adhering as a result of the marked protuberance of the abdomen. Relocation of the ileostomy site in conjunction with a form of abdominoplasty was the suggested procedure for this patient. Because of the relocation of the ileostomy stoma, the Castanares procedure was selected, since it removes the greatest amount of tissue without undermining the abdominal flap. The patient's scar deformity extended up to the xiphoid area; the Castanares procedure allows for removal of the tissue in this area in the form of an anchor type of excision. The surgery (Figs. 6-111 and 6-112) was performed in conjunction with William Capps, colon-rectal surgeon, Newport Beach, California.

Critique: The Castanares procedure is believed to be the one of choice for similar cases.

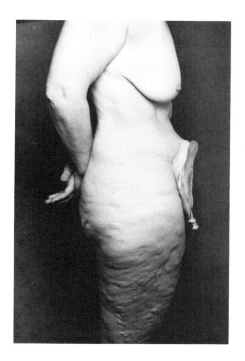

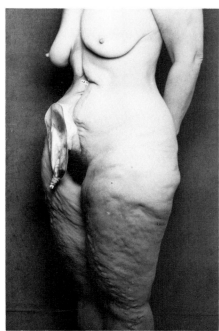

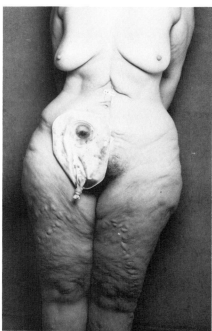

Fig. 6-110. Preoperative appearance of a 54-year-old patient who has undergone a total colectomy with ileostomy, as well as a large amount of weight loss.

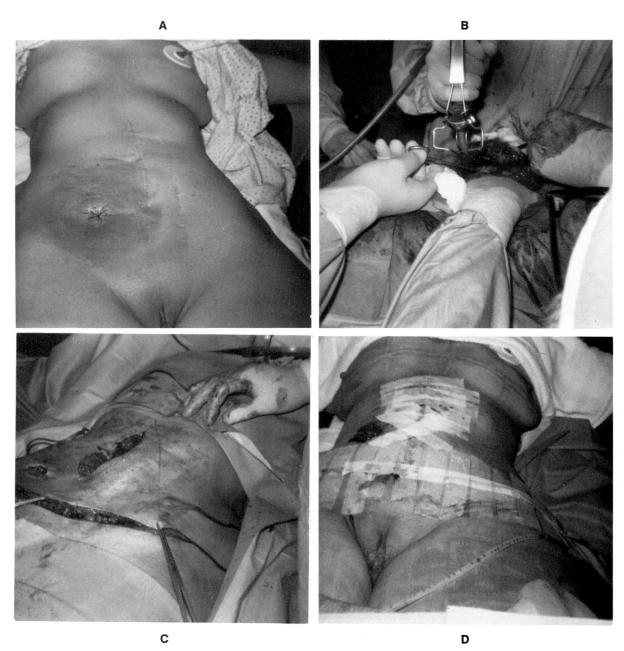

Fig. 6-111. A, Preoperative appearance at the time of surgery. **B,** Relocation of the ileostomy prior to abdominoplasty. **C,** Outline of the incisions for Castanares' abdominoplasty. **D,** Completion of the procedure.

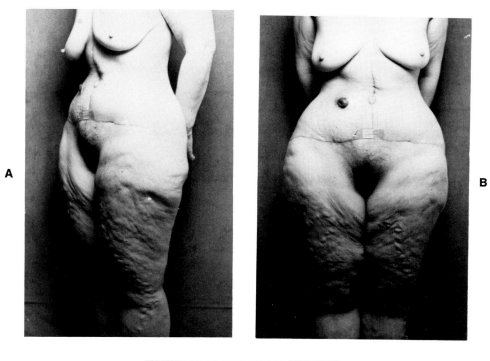

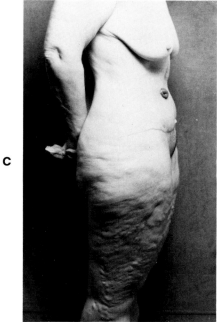

Fig. 6-112. Postoperative appearance. **A** and **B,** After tissue resection of 600 g. **C,** Note the lack of protrusion of the abdominal wall at the site of the stoma.

REFERENCES

1a. Apfelberg, D. B., Maser, M. R., and Lash, H.: Case reports: two unusual umbilicoplasties, Plast. Reconstr. Surg. **64:**268, 1979.

1. Castanares, S.: Abdominal lipectomy: a modification in technique, Plast. Reconstr. Surg. **40:**378, 1967.

2. Dufourmentel, C., and Mouly, K.: Plastie mammarie par la méthode oblique, Ann. Chir. Plast. **6:**45, 1961.

3. Freeman, B. S.: Subcutaneous mastectomy. In Georgiade, N. G., editor: Reconstructive breast surgery, St. Louis, 1976, The C. V. Mosby Co.

4. Georgiade, N. G.: Immediate reconstruction of the breasts following subcutaneous mastectomy. In Georgiade, N. G., editor: Reconstructive breast surgery, St. Louis, 1976, The C. V. Mosby Co.

5. Gibson, H. L.: Medical photography, Rochester, New York, 1973, Eastman Kodak Co.

6. Grazer, F. M.: Use of fiber optic bundles in plastic surgery, Plast. Reconstr. Surg. **48:**28, 1971.

7. Grazer, F. M.: Abdominoplasty, Plast. Reconstr. Surg. **51:**617, 1973.

8. Grazer, F. M.: Operation bikini update, film, Minneapolis, 1975, The Filmmakers.

9. Grazer, F. M.: The new image, film presented at the meeting of the American Society of Plastic and Reconstructive Surgeons, San Francisco, Oct., 1977.

10. Grazer, F. M., and Goldwyn, R.: Abdominoplasty assessed by survey with emphasis on complications, Plast. Reconstr. Surg. **59:**513, 1977.

11. Grazer, F. M., and Klingbeil, J. R.: Abdominoplasty. In Courtiss, E. H., editor: Aesthetic surgery: trouble—how to avoid it and how to treat it, St. Louis, 1978, The C. V. Mosby Co.

12. Grazer, F. M., and Krugman, M. E.: A new triaxial fiberoptic soft tissue retractor, Aesthet. Plast. Surg. **2:**161, 1978.

13. Guerrero-Santos, J.: Arm-lift. In Courtiss, E. H., editor: Aesthetic surgery: trouble—how to avoid it and how to treat it, St. Louis, 1978, The C. V. Mosby Co.

14. Hatton, R. F.: Patients at risk for postoperative pulmonary embolism, West. J. Med. **127:**423, 1977.

15. Hinderer, U.: The dermolipectomy approach for augmentation mammaplasty, Clin. Plast. Surg. **2:**359, 1975.

16. Huch, A., and Huch, R.: Transcutaneous noinvasive monitoring of Po_2, Hosp. Pract. **11:**43, June, 1976.

17. Jackson, I. A., and Downie, P.: Abdominoplasty, the waistline stitch and other refinements, Plast. Reconstr. Surg. **61:**180, 1977.

18. Kakkar, V. V., Nicolaides, A. N., Field, E. S., and Flute, P. T.: Low doses of heparin in prevention of deep vein thrombosis, Lancet **2:**669, 1971.

19. Kamper, M. J.: Abdominal panniculectomy after massive weight loss, Plast. Reconstr. Surg. **50:**441, 1972.

20. McKissock, P. K.: Reduction mammaplasty with a vertical dermal flaps, Plast. Reconstr. Surg. **49:**245, 1972.

21. Pitanguy, I., and Cavalanti, M. A.: Methodology in combined aesthetic surgeries, Aesthet. Plast. Surg. **2:**331, 1978.

22. Regnault, P.: Abdominal lipectomy, a low W incision, microfilm, 1972, International Society of Aesthetic Plastic Surgery.

23. Thorek, M.: Possibilities in the reconstruction of the human form, N.Y. Med. J. Rec. **116:**572, 1922.

CHAPTER 7

Prevention of venous thrombosis and pulmonary embolism after abdominoplasty

The problem of venous thrombosis and pulmonary embolism after surgery is of significant magnitude. Limited information exists regarding this complication after abdominoplasty.

The Grazer-Goldwyn survey[11] of 10,490 cases of abdominoplasty performed by 945 surgeons indicated an incidence of deep-vein phlebitis of 1.1% and of pulmonary embolism, 0.8%. Of the 17 patient deaths in the series, 6 resulted from pulmonary embolism. The incidence of pulmonary embolism in the cases of some surgeons has approached 5%. Recently Ubiglia and Pastacaldi[32] evaluated cardiac axis, blood gases, and lung scans before and after surgery in abdominoplasty patients with the Grazer technique. They found little physiological impairment and no thromboembolic complications. The relative incidence of 1.1% deep phlebitis and 0.8% pulmonary embolism reported in the Grazer-Goldwyn survey[11] attests to the fact that pulmonary embolism commonly occurs after acute deep-vein thrombosis; however, during the last decade it has become clear that both deep phlebitis and pulmonary embolism are far more commonly diagnosed by noninvasive tests than on clinical grounds.

Apart from death from pulmonary embolism, the long-term sequelae of deep phlebitis are a source of continuing patient morbidity. The postphlebitic syndrome of leg swelling, varicose veins, ulceration, and other skin-trophic changes is as yet one of the most intractable of surgical problems.

PATHOGENESIS OF DEEP-VEIN THROMBOSIS

The concept of venous thrombosis proposed by Virchow[33]—that blood stasis, vascular injury, and an ill-defined hypercoagulable state predispose the blood to thrombosis—is still the framework in which we can evaluate clinical venous thrombosis. A patient may be at risk to develop thrombosis because any of these three factors may be present in an abnormal state.

Perhaps the most controversial factor introduced by Virchow in the pathogenesis of a deep venous thrombosis is the question of the hypercoagulable state. Within the blood are circulating platelets and clotting factors, which may be in excessive abundance or highly active to produce the hypercoagulable state. Normally inhibitors of coagulation are present in the blood; deficiency in

227

number or activity of these inhibitors may also lead to a hypercoagulable state, which would predispose the blood to thrombosis.

The final common pathway of the extrinsic and intrinsic system of blood coagulation is the formation of fibrin from fibrinogen by thrombin, a proteolytic enzyme. The extrinsic pathway is activated by tissue thromboplastin. Tissue thromboplastin, the generic name for clot-promoting substances in tissues, brings about a set of chemical reactions, which successively involves factor VII, Stuart factor (factor X), proaccelerin (factor V), prothrombin (factor II), and calcium ions. Phospholipid is needed for thrombin production and is presumably released by injured tissue.

In the intrinsic system, Hageman's factor (factor XII), activated by glass in the laboratory, initiates a series of reactions involving plasma thromboplastin antecedent (PTA) (factor XI), Christmas factor (factor IX), and antihemophilic factor (factor VIII). The product of these reactions activates Stuart factor (factor X). The pathways coincide at this point. Calcium and phospholipids derived from plasma itself and platelets are also needed. The simplified schema shown in Fig. 7-1 emphasizes the proposed role of lipids in coagulation.

One of the mysteries of coagulation that may hold some clues concerning the true nature of hypercoagulability is what activates Hageman's factor in vivo: two suspects are collagen and soaps of saturated fatty acids. Nonesterified fatty acids in plasma have been shown to induce thrombosis.[2,3] Intravenous injection of triolein in experimental rabbits results in shortened prothrombin time for three days after the embolization, which suggests partial activation of their extrinsic coagulation mechanism secondary to release of tissue thromboplastin from damaged pulmonary parenchyma.[30]

Hypercoagulability observed in trauma victims may be in part due to a release of fat from fatty stores and fractured long bones. Traumatized tissue is

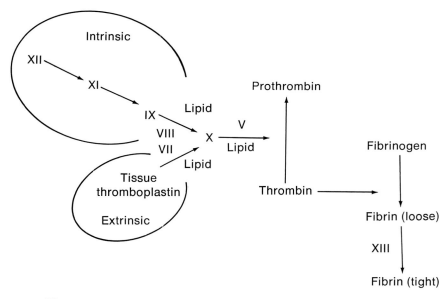

Fig. 7-1. Simplified sequence of events in blood clotting.

clot promoting[5]; studies on combat victims have shown a shortening of pro-thrombin time and partial thromboplastin time and elevation of the level of fibrinogen.[29] Perhaps fat released from manipulated tissues during surgery may initiate hypercoagulability in the surgical patient.

Fibrin clots are reliquefied by the enzyme, plasmin, whose precursor, plasminogen, exists in the plasma. The activation of plasmin is critical to the rate of dissolution of fibrin and the rate of propagation of thrombin. This deli-cate check mechanism can be a cause of the hypercoagulable state if it is not ac-tivated. Patients with fat embolism syndrome after trauma have been noted to have decreased activity in the fibrinolytic system. Antiplasmin values mea-sured in patients with symptoms of fat embolism were higher than those in pa-tients with fat embolism but no symptoms.[20] Impairment of fibrinolytic activity is also seen in association with obesity,[10] late pregnancy,[22] oral contraceptives,[25] and cancer.[31] A familial condition involving recurrent thrombosis is caused by deficiency of antithrombin III,[7] a substance with two actions that interfere with activated Stuart factor and thrombin.[17] It is an attractive idea that patients de-velop a thrombosis because an inhibitor of clotting is in short supply; some support for this theory has been found in the lower levels of antithrombin III detected in patients taking contraceptive pills.[14,18] Recently, low levels of anti-thrombin III have been shown to be associated with the postoperative develop-ment of deep venous thrombosis.[28]

The concentration of clotting factors may be increased, which may lead to an increased risk of thrombosis. In pregnancy the levels of vitamin K–depen-dent factors, Christmas factor, factor VII, Stuart factor, and prothrombin are often elevated. Fibrinogen levels have been found to be elevated after trauma[29] and in inflammatory and malignant conditions. The level of anti-hemophilic factor may be raised after surgical procedures and during preg-nancy or a regimen of oral contraceptives. The platelet count may be increased after surgical procedures or in malignant states.[23] It is known that patients with an extremely high elevation in the number of platelets, as occurs in poly-cythemia vera and after splenectomy, also have a higher risk of developing venous thrombosis.

Hence many different blood changes might be associated with a hyper-coagulable state. Screening of some of these measurable factors may lead to identification of patients who are more susceptible to thrombosis in the post-operative period, but as yet this type of screening prior to surgery is not routine. The use of anticoagulation to prevent thrombosis in the surgical patient is aimed at altering some of these blood factors.

Venous stasis is a factor in the genesis of thrombosis. Stasis occurs in pa-tients who have experienced thrombosis or who have varicose veins or conges-tive heart failure. Venous dilatation and stasis also occurs during pregnancy. Blood flow is influenced by blood viscosity; increased viscosity, especially at a low flow rate (low shear rate), may predispose to thrombosis by causing venous stasis. Blood is a nonnewtonian fluid, and its viscosity rises at low rates of shear (or low flow rate). This nonnewtonian behavior is caused by red cell adherence

229

corresponding to rouleaux formation. Raised levels of fibrinogen and increased hematocrit are known to increased blood viscosity and enhance stasis at low flow rates. Trauma has been shown to influence blood flow by elevating fibrinogen levels and hematocrit,[26] which elevates blood viscosity. The use of dextran in the postoperative period in thrombosis prophylaxis is based theoretically on its ability to lower blood viscosity.

Vessel trauma initiates thrombosis and is important in the genesis of thrombosis after hip and pelvic surgery. This factor probably does not play any part in the genesis of thrombosis in patients undergoing abdominoplasty surgery.

ABDOMINOPLASTY PATIENTS
Blood flow rates

Our patients are routinely subject to an exaggerated flexion of their hips and knees during surgery and for several days afterward. To ascertain whether this posture results in stasis of the venous flow in the lower extremities and hence might predispose to venous thrombosis, a study of 10 patients consecutively undergoing abdominoplasty was performed. In this study, the transit time of the blood from the dorsal vein of the foot to the pelvis was determined with an injection of 3 to 6 mCi of technetium. This dose was given preoperatively, as well as 24 hours after abdominoplasty with the patient in bed in the

Table 3. Isotope study in abdominoplasty

Patient	Procedure(s)	Lung scan		Transit time in seconds from ankle to pelvis	
		Preoperative	Postoperative	Preoperative	Postoperative
1	Abdominoplasty	Normal	Abnormal right lung Increased markings on chest film	12 Bilaterally	9
2	Abdominoplasty, Culp utereropelvioplasty, and anterior vaginal repair	Normal	Normal	13	14
3	Ankle cast, face-lift, and abdominoplasty	Normal	Normal	30	16
4	Abdominal hysterectomy and abdominoplasty	Normal	Normal	Left 11 Right 9	7
5	Abdominoplasty	Normal	Normal	12	14
6	Abdominoplasty	Normal	Normal	24	14
7	McKissock mastopexy and abdominoplasty	Normal	Diminished perfusion in right infrahilar area	9	20
8	Abdominoplasty	Normal	Normal	16	12
9	Abdominoplasty	Normal	Normal; slight decrease in perfusion in left base	11	12
10	McKissock breast reduction and abdominoplasty	Normal	Normal Abnormal adherence in pelvic veins	21	15

exaggerated flexed position. The results of the study are shown in Table 3. The transit time from the ankle to the pelvis increased preoperatively to postoperatively in only one patient, the seventh. From this data we do not believe that a significant degree of venous stasis in the extremities caused by the flexed position occurs after the abdominoplasty operation. Stasis, however, is present in any patient undergoing a 3- to 4-hour abdominal operation; of course, inactivity of the calf muscle venous pump may account for the report of high incidence of thrombosis in calf venous sinuses rather than in other leg veins.[13] A local deficiency of fibrinolytic activity of the soleal veins has also been proposed to explain the predilection of the calf veins for development of thrombosis during and after surgery.[24]

Risk factors

Patients underoing any type of surgery encounter innumerable risk factors for developing deep venous thrombosis. One of the major factors is the type of surgical procedure. For example, the incidence of deep venous thrombosis in persons older than 60 years undergoing general surgical procedures is 60%, compared with 18% for patients undergoing gynecological operations.[6] If a patient is undergoing abdominoplasty combined with intra-abdominal procedures, presumably the risk of thrombosis is increased. Following are other risk factors in patients undergoing abdominoplasty:

Occasional	Rare
Obesity	Congestive heart disease
Smoking	Cancer
Estrogen hormones	
Varicose veins	

Age, obesity, and smoking all increase[17] the incidence of deep venous thrombosis in the surgical patient, as does a history of previous deep phlebitis and pulmonary embolism. Oral female hormone medication and varicose veins are also risk factors that are occasionally present in patients undergoing abdominoplasty. Recently Clayton, Anderson, and McNicol[1] showed that observance of three factors—age, presence of varicose veins, and percentage of overweight—and the use of two blood tests—euglobulinolysis time and fibrin-related antigen—help identify 95% of patients who develop deep venous thrombosis. The typical abdominoplasty patient, however, usually does not have a greater degree of any particular risk factor than does the general population of her age undergoing a major operation. Careful history will indicate some patients to be a higher risk than are others.

However, some characteristics of abdominoplasty may increase the risk of thrombosis more than do other body sculpturing operations. The patient's panniculus is raised and retracted vigorously during the majority of the operation. It has been of some concern to us that this traumatized panniculus might be the source of fat globules, which enter the venous system through damaged veins and systemically might lead to a hypercoagulable state. We have not found an ideal method for detecting fat in the blood from these manipulated panniculi. During surgery, some panniculi, when squeezed, ooze free-flowing fat globules. With our technique for measuring free blood fat, we have been unable to detect this fat either in the patient's blood during abdominoplasty or when fat has been added directly to the blood.

DETECTION OF DEEP VENOUS THROMBOSIS

Clinical signs are notoriously inaccurate for detecting deep venous thrombosis[8]; and the development of noninvasive techniques such as fibrinogen-^{125}I scanning, Doppler ultrasound, impedence plethysmography, and phlebography has helped.

Of the noninvasive techniques available, fibrinogen-^{125}I scanning has proved its clinical efficacy and perhaps is the most widely used test today. After radioactive fibrinogen is administered, an actively growing thrombus takes up and incorporates the fibrinogen ^{125}I. A portable scanner is used and facilitates preoperative and postoperative scanning at the patient's bedside. Indelible marks are made on the patient's lower legs and thighs before surgery (Fig. 7-2) and remain in place for the length of the patient's hospitalization, usually five to seven days. The patient receives daily scanning during the hospitalization (Figs. 6-67, 6-72, and 7-3). The scanner is theoretically disadvantaged in that it cannot detect thrombi in the pelvic or iliac regions but, because it is so sensitive, will detect hematoma and superficial thrombophlebitis.[21] A potential complication is serum hepatitis secondary to fibrinogen; however, Kakkar[15] found no cases in more than 2,000 patients studied.

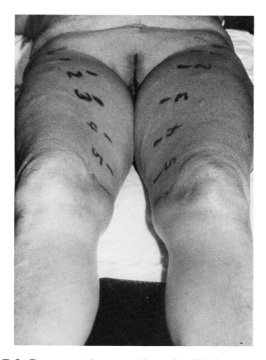

Fig. 7-2. Preoperative markings for fibrinogen scan.

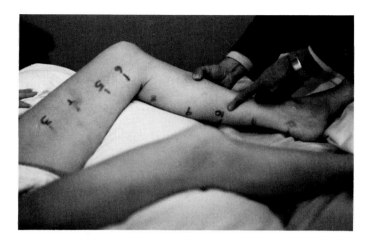

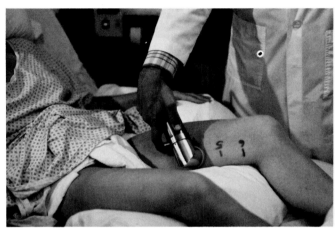

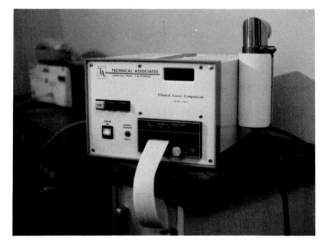

Fig. 7-3. Scanning of patient after surgery to detect deep venous thrombosis.

Approximately 20% of calf thrombi progress to the popliteal or femoral veins. Fibrinogen scanning is a convenient method of following progress of thrombosis; however, on detecting a thrombus, clinical venography is indicated and is the only accurate method of assessing proximal pelvis extension of these thrombi.

PROPHYLAXIS OF DEEP VENOUS THROMBOSIS AND PULMONARY EMBOLISM

Since half of all cases of thrombosis in the surgical patient occur in the operating room, prevention is emphasized before, during, and after abdominoplasty surgery (Table 4).

Preoperatively all patients who are considered at risk receive a fibrinogen-^{125}I scan. The proposed aim is to detect all of the deep venous thrombosis early and to initiate therapy to prevent not only pulmonary embolism but also the late-term sequelae of deep venous incompetence.

Prevention of stasis

Early in our experience we relied on elastic stockings and passive compression to try to relieve stasis in the postoperative and intraoperative phases of abdominoplasty; however, the occurrence of deep venous thrombosis in patients who had worn leggings has fortified our impression that stockings are of little value in the prevention of deep venous thrombosis.[27] All patients are placed in an alternating inflating-deflating bed immediately after the surgical procedure. Inflation approximately once a minute simulates emptying and filling of the soleal veins[3] and is continued for the duration of the patient's hospitalization. All patients are encouraged to plantar flex their feet and are mobilized the morning after surgery. Although the patients cannot fully straighten themselves on the first postoperative day, all are able to walk with the help of a physical therapist, the medical staff, and the use of a Nelson bed.* Mobilization increases daily until discharge.

*Oliver/Scientific Equipment, 5525 Wilshire Blvd., Los Angeles, Calif. 90036.

Table 4. Prevention of deep venous thrombosis

Period	Precautions
Preoperative	Medical evaluation (history of risk factors) Fibrinogen-^{125}I scan
Intraoperative	Low operating time Minimal panniculus manipulation Intravenous injection of 1 liter of alcohol
Postoperative	Alternating inflating-deflating mattress Active plantar flexion Mobilization within 24 hours Daily fibrinogen-^{125}I scanning

Prevention of hypercoagulability

When surgery commences and during manipulation of the panniculus, 5% alcohol in 5% dextrose is infused at a rate of about 300 ml/hour[12] to help clear any fat that may be in the circulation during and after the panniculus manipulation. The panniculus may theoretically be the site of origin of phospholipids and triglycerides. Alcohol, a solvent, clears away fats and may prevent the conversion of triglycerides to free fatty acids. Prior to the initiation of the alcohol regimen, 4 of our patients developed pulmonary embolisms. With the alcohol regimen, there has been no case of pulmonary embolism in the last 200 cases performed over a three-year period. Rarely, in the case of a patient who must abstain from alcohol because she is receiving disulfiram (Antabuse), intravenously injected lidocaine has been used to prevent deep-vein thrombosis. The theoretical basis for its use is not to alter the coagulant factors but to prevent endothelial damage, the initial event in the formation of a venous thrombus.[4]

Dextran 40 is not used routinely after surgery unless the patient is assessed as an extremely high risk. The value of this use is also controversial, but experimentally it has been shown to reduce platelet adhesiveness and aggregation. Dextran 40 may reduce viscosity by reducing hematocrit through hemodilution or perhaps render red cells less likely to form rouleaux and aggregate. Recently, a large clinical, double-blind trial of 831 patients undergoing major intra-abdominal surgery substantiated the effectiveness of dextran 40 in pulmonary emboli prophylaxis.[19]

Low-dose heparin has become increasingly popular in prevention of deep venous thrombosis.[16] Low, subcutaneously injected doses prevent thrombosis by enhancement of the naturally occurring inhibitor of factor X[33] in plasma. Alarming bleeding and hematoma formation are reported after small doses of subcutaneously injected heparin.[9] Bearing in mind the extent of dissection of subcutaneous tissues from the pubis to above the costal margin, we are loath to suggest subcutaneously injected heparin for deep venous thrombosis prophylaxis.

Oral anticoagulants such as warfarin, aspirin, and dipyramidole have not been used.

TREATMENT OF DEEP VENOUS THROMBOSIS

After detection of a thrombosis by fibrinogen-^{125}I scanning, the patient is immediately heparinized with intermittent doses of intravenously injected heparin (5,000 units every 4 hours). A lung ventilation perfusion scan is ordered. Medical consultation is obtained and the patient evaluated for possible long-term oral anticoagulant management. None of our 4 cases of pulmonary embolism was fatal; all resolved, and no long-term sequelae have developed.

SUMMARY

Clinical deep venous thrombosis and pulmonary embolism occur in less than 2% of cases of abdominoplasty; subclinical cases likely occur much more frequently.

All patients undergoing abdominoplasty who are considered at risk of developing deep venous thrombosis are scanned with fibrinogen ^{125}I for detection. The scanning continues daily during hospitalization. Prevention is aimed at reducing intraoperative and postoperative hypercoagulability, possibly caused by fat released from manipulated panniculi. Intravenously infused alcohol is used routinely during surgery, and intravenously infused dextran 40 is occasionally used after surgery for 24 hours. Patients are placed in an alternating inflating-deflating mattress and mobilized the morning after surgery. With the preceding regimen, no cases of clinical deep-vein thrombosis or pulmonary embolism have occurred in our last 200 cases.

REFERENCES

1. Clayton, J. K., Anderson, J. A., and McNicol, G. P.: Preoperative prediction of postoperative deep vein thrombosis, Br. Med. J. **2**:910, 1976.
2. Connor, W. E., Hoak, J. C., and Warner, E. D.: Massive thrombosis produced by fatty acid infusion, J. Clin. Invest. **42**:860, 1963.
3. Connor, W. E., and Poole, J. C. F.: The effect of fatty acids on the formation of thrombi, Q. J. Exp. Physiol. **46**:1, 1961.
4. Cooke, E. D., Bowcock, S. A., Lloyd, M. J., and Pilcher, M. F.: Intravenous lignocaine in prevention of deep venous thrombosis after elective hip surgery, Lancet **2**:797, 1977.
5. Damus, P. S., and Salzman, E. W.: Disseminated intravascular coagulation, Arch. Surg. **104**:262, 1972.
6. Dean, R. H., and Yao, J. S. T.: Hemodynamic measurements in peripheral vascular disease, Curr. Prob. Surg. **13**:1, 1976.
7. Egeberg, O.: Inherited antithrombin deficiency causing thrombophilia, Thromb. Diath. Haemorrh. **13**:516, 1965.
8. Flanc, C., Kakkar, V. V., and Clarke, M. B.: The detection of venous thrombosis in the leg using ^{125}I-labelled fibrinogen, Br. J. Surg. **55**:742, 1968.
9. Gordon-Smith, I. C., Le Quesne, L. P., Grundy, D. J., et al.: Controlled trial of two regimens of subcutaneous heparin in prevention of postoperative deep-vein thrombosis, Lancet **1**:1133, 1972.
10. Grace, C. S., and Goldrick, R. D.: Fibrinolysis and body build. Interrelationships between blood fibrinolysis, body composition and parameters of lipid and carbohydrate metabolism, J. Atheroscler. Res. **4**:705, 1968.
11. Grazer, F. M., and Goldwyn, R. M.: Abdominoplasty assessed by survey, with emphasis on complications, Plast. Reconstr. Surg. **59**:513, 1977.
12. Grazer, F. M., and Klingbeil, J. R.: Abdominoplasty. In Courtiss, E. H., editor: Aesthetic surgery: trouble—how to avoid it and how to treat it, St. Louis, 1978, The C. V. Mosby Co.
13. Hobbs, J. T., editor: The treatment of venous disorders, Philadelphia, 1977, J. B. Lippincott Co.
14. Howie, P. N., Mallinson, A. C., Prentice, C. R. M., Home, C. H. W., and McNicol, B. P.: Effect of combined estrogen-progestogen oral contraceptives, estrogen and progestogen on antiplasmin and antithrombin activity, Lancet **2**:1329, 1970.
15. Kakkar, V. V.: Deep vein thrombosis. Detection and prevention, Circulation **51**:8, 1975.
16. Kakkar, V. V., Corrigan T., Spindler, J., Fossard, D. P., Flute, P. T., Crellni, R. Q., Wessler, S., and Yin, E. T.: Efficacy of low doses of heparin in prevention of deep vein thrombosis after major surgery, Lancet **2**:101, 1972.
17. Kakkar, V. V., Howe, C. T., Nicolaides, A. N., Renney, J. T. G., and Clarke, M. B.: Deep vein thrombosis of the leg: is there a "high risk" group? Am. J. Surg. **120**:536, 1970.
18. Kaulla, E. von, Droegemueller, W., Aoki, N., and Kaulla, K. N. von: Antithrombin III depression and thrombin generation acceleration in women taking oral contraceptives, Am. J. Obstet. Gynecol. **109**:868, 1971.
19. Kline, A., Hughes, L. E., Campbell, H., Williams, A., Zlosnick, J., and Leach, K. G.: Dextran 70 in prophylaxis of throm-

boembolic disease after surgery: a clinically orientated randomized double-blind trial, Br. Med. J. **2:**109, 1975.

20. Lilienberg, G., Rammer, L., Saldeen, T., Thoren, L., and Uddenstromer, L.: Intravascular coagulation and inhibition of fibrinolysis in fat embolism, Acta Chir. Scand. **136:**87, 1970.

21. McNamara, M. F., Takaki, H. S., and Yao, J. S. T.: Venous disease, Surg. Clin. North Am. **57:**1201, 1977.

22. Menon, S., Peberdy, M., Rannie, G. H., Weightman, D., and Dewar, H. A.: A comparative study of blood fibrinolytic activity in normal women, pregnant women and women on oral contraceptives, J. Obstet. Gynaecol. Br. Commow. **77:**752, 1970.

23. Moser, K. M., and Stein, M.: Pulmonary thromboembolism, Chicago, 1973, Year Book Medical Publishers, Inc.

24. Nicolaides, A. N., Clark, C. T., Thomas, R. D., and Lewis, J. D.: Soleal veins and local fibrinolytic activity, Br. J. Surg. **59:**914, 1972.

25. Nilsson, I. M., Astedt, B., and Isacson, S.: The effect of hormones on coagulation and fibrinolysis. In Proceedings of the International Society of Thrombosis and Hemostasis, Second Congress, Oslo, 1971, Stuttgart, 1972, F. K. Schattauer Verlag.

26. Repogle, R. L.: The nature of blood sludging and its relationship to the pathophysiologic mechanisms of trauma and shock, J. Trauma **9:**675, 1969.

27. Rosengarten, D. S., Laird, J., Jeyasingh, K., and Martin, P.: The failure of compression stockings (Tubigrip) to prevent deep venous thrombosis after operation, Br. J. Surg. **57:**296, 1970.

28. Sagar, S., Thomas, D. P., Stamatakis, J. D., and Kakkar, V. V.: Oral contraceptives, antithrombin III activity and postoperative deep vein thrombosis, Lancet **1:**509, 1976.

29. Simmons, R. L., Collins, J. A., Heisterkamp, C. A., Mills, D. E., Andren, R., and Phillips, L. L.: Coagulation disorders in combat casualties, Ann. Surg. **169:**455, 1969.

30. Soloway, H. B., and Robinson, E. F.: Coagulation mechanisms in experimental pulmonary fat embolism, J. Trauma **12:**630, 1972.

31. Thornes, R. D., O'Donnell, J. M., and O'Brien, D. J.: The physiology of fibrinolysis. II. Antiplasmin, Irish J. Med. Sci. **6:**73, 1967.

32. Ubiglia, G. P., and Pastacaldi, P.: Nuovo metodo di abdominoplastica estetica, Riv. Ital. Chir. Plast. **9:**257, 1977.

33. Virchow, R.: Weitere Untersuchungen über die Verstopfung der Lungenarterie und ihre Folgen, Beitr. Exp. Pathol. Physiol. **2:**21, 1846.

34. Yin, E. T., and Wessler, S.: Heparin-accelerated inhibition of activated factor X by its natural plasma inhibitor, Biochim. Biophys. Acta **201:**387, 1970.

35. Yin, E. T., Wessler, S., and Stall, P. J.: Identity of plasma-activated factor X inhibitor with antithrombin III and heparin cofactor, J. Biol. Chem. **248:**3712, 1971.

CHAPTER 8

Thighplasty

THE YESTERDAYS OF DERMOLIPECTOMY OF THE EXTREMITIES AND BUTTOCKS

In many of the early articles on abdominal dermolipectomy, the reduction of fatty tissue of the extremities and buttocks was described in a relatively limited manner. Such descriptions were found in the literature of Kelly, Thorek, Noël, and many others. Emphasis was primarily directed at localized excision of fat without undue concern for scar location.[21]

In 1957, Lewis[13] described his procedure for removal of excess thigh fat with what he termed a *thigh-lift*. He followed this article with another in 1966.[14] The patients described were obese, and, even though scarring was prominent, improvement was spectacular. In 1977, Lewis[15] discussed removal of the excess fat of the upper arm. He emphasized the need to break up the line of incision along the inside and back of the arm by Z-plasty.

In 1960, Farina, Baroudi, Golcman, and de Castro[7] discussed "riding trousers" deformity of the thighs, pointing out the differences between the trochanteric, or pelvicrural, lipodystrophy and obesity. Although this report included a description of the surgery and a series of diagramatic drawings, emphasis seemed to be directed at differentiating the various types of fatty tissue.

In 1964, Pitanguy[17] introduced his technique for the surgical treatment of trochanteric lipodystrophy to the American literature. In 1971,[18] he pointed out that conservative treatment, that is, localized excision involving either vertical or combined vertical and horizontal incisions, does not correct deformities but leads to poor cosmetic results. He emphasized the need to place incisions in the gluteal folds. In a subsequent article in 1975, Pitanguy[19] described extensive resection of lipodystrophy of the arms, extending medially and inferiorly to the lateral thoracic wall. The lines of excision extend from the side of the elbows to the lateral aspect of the breasts on the same side.

In 1973, Delerm and Cirotteau[6] presented a technique for elevation and posterior fixation of the thigh tissue to the fibrous tissue of the ischiatic tuberosity by means of a small skin flap with the epidermis removed.

A great number of articles appeared in 1975 concerning various methods of buttock and extremity dermolipectomy. Hoffman and Simon[11] classified their cases into five groups: (1) trochanteric lipodystrophy, (2) medial redundancy, (3) ptosis and redundancy of buttocks, (4) generally obese or heavy thighs, and (5) cellulite. They pointed out that the uniformly obese patients were the most disappointed with results. They also emphasized the importance of marking

238

Text continued on p. 244.

Incisional history of hipplasty and thighplasty

Side view

Excision variable

Before   After

Kelly (1889)
Thorek (1922)
Noël (1928)

Front

Area excised

Before   After

Back

Before   After

Lewis (1957, 1966)
Barsky et al. (1964)

Side view

Before   After

Farina et al. (1960)
Barsky et al. (1964)

Back

Before   After

Side

Before   After

Side

Pitanguy (1964), Bruck and Muller (1969),
Pitanguy (1971), Mühlbauer (1971),
Pitanguy (1972)

Front

Before   After

Pitanguy (1972)

Front

Before

Front

After

Mühlbauer (1971, 1975)
(abdominoplasty with thigh contouring)

Perineum

Before   After

Ducourtioux (1971)

**Incisional history of
hipplasty and thighplasty**

Side   Side   Back   Back   Back

Flap

Before   After   Before After

Ducourtioux (1972)   Delerm and Cirotteau (1973)
(de-epithelialized flap for anchoring)

Front   Side   Side   Back

Flap

Before   After   Before   After   Before   After

McCraw (1974) (circumferential excision)

Back   Front   Back   Perineum

Cutaneous
anchor

Subcutaneous
fat removed

Before   After   Before   After   Before   After   Before   After

Before   After   Vilain (1975)

Vilain (1975)

240

**Incisional history of
hipplasty and thighplasty**

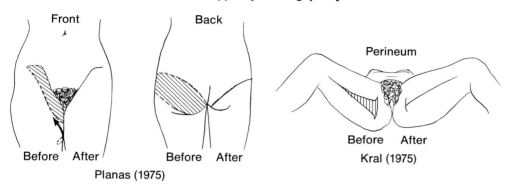

Front   Back   Perineum

Before   After   Before   After   Before   After

Planas (1975)   Kral (1975)

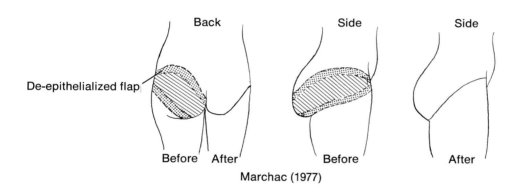

Back   Side   Side

De-epithelialized flap

Before   After   Before   After

Marchac (1977)

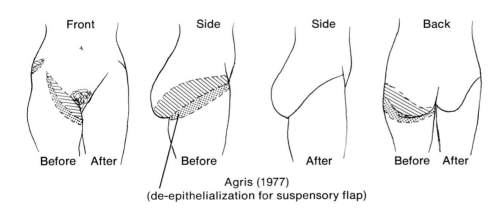

Front   Side   Side   Back

Before   After   Before   After   Before   After

Agris (1977)
(de-epithelialization for suspensory flap)

241

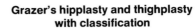

**Grazer's hipplasty and thighplasty
with classification**

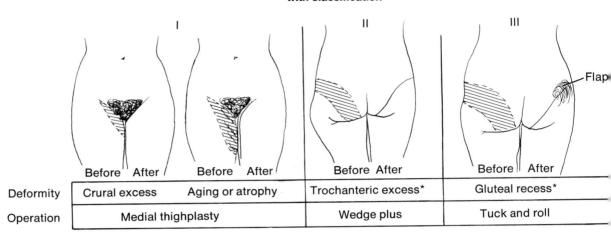

	I		II	III
	Before After	Before After	Before After	Before After
Deformity	Crural excess	Aging or atrophy	Trochanteric excess*	Gluteal recess*
Operation	Medial thighplasty		Wedge plus	Tuck and roll

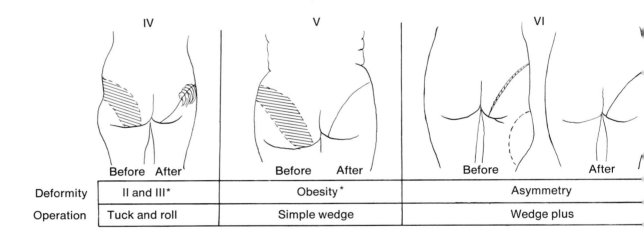

	IV	V	VI
	Before After	Before After	Before After
Deformity	II and III*	Obesity*	Asymmetry
Operation	Tuck and roll	Simple wedge	Wedge plus

	VI	VII
	Before After	Before After
Deformity	Traumatic deformity	Aging or atrophy†
Operation	Tuck and roll	Tuck and pleat

*Crural excess.
†Atrophy.

Incisional history of brachioplasty

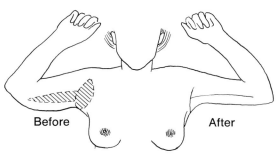

Before   After

McCraw (1974)

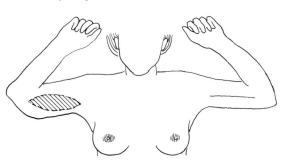

Kelly (1910), Thorek (1942), Berson (1948),
Schörcher (1965), Lewis (1973), Vilain (1975)

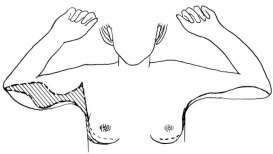

Pitanguy (1975)

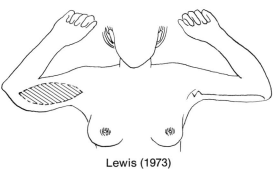

Lewis (1973)
Grazer (1973)

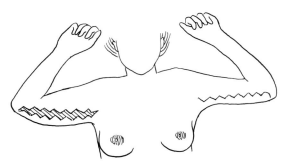

W-plasty (number variable)

Grazer (1972)
Lewis (1973)

the patient in an upright position. Planas[20] described a surgical technique called a crural meloplasty that sweeps the medial thigh tissue superiorly and laterally, bringing the final scars above the public area into the abdominal area. Vilain[22] described and illustrated limited removal of small areas of fat around the knee and above the ankle by way of small incisions and the use of a sharp curette. Baroudi[1] authored an extensive article on dermolipectomy of the upper arm with that included a thorough review of the anatomy of the area. He noted that evaluation of the results of arm dermolipectomy is critical because of the location of the scars.

SURGICAL APPROACHES

Surgery related to the thighs, buttocks, and hips is a relatively new aspect of body contouring. Terms such as "riding britches" syndrome, lipodystrophy, and sagging buttocks[7] have been used in the literature to describe deformities in these areas. Such terminology is lacking in both precision and accuracy. The term *lipodystrophy* implies a disease process,[3] which is a misnomer. The other terms, although graphically describing the deformities, have no standard definitions. The demand for this type of surgery has increased over the past few years for reasons that include improvement in surgical techniques and increased publicity through such avenues as lay magazines, as well as the world's new emphasis on health and appearance.

The greatest objection in thighplasty has been the resultant scar deformity. Some of the early approaches recommended correction with lateral hip incisions.[7,21] Pitanguy,[17] after placing the incision in the gluteal fold and extending it upward to the lateral hip area, used a simple wedge excision with minimal undermining. The scars resulting from the lateral hip and gluteal fold incisions were visible with the patient in a bikini. Although the simple wedge excision, without undermining, is effective in many patients, it does not correct the deformity in others. It is important to develop surgical approaches that confine the incision within the bikini line and still correct the anatomical defect. The area of the infragluteal fold, which is exposed with the average bathing suit (Fig. 8-1), can be called "no-man's-land,"[2] since no final suture line should fall below the lower edge of the swimsuit in the authors' opinion.

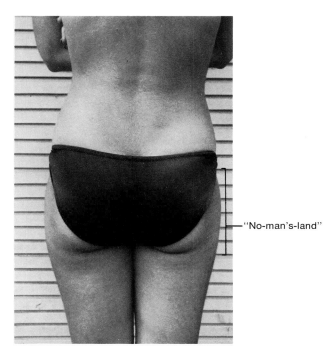

—"No-man's-land"

Fig. 8-1

Types of deformities

An anatomical classification (Figs. 8-2 to 8-4) has been introduced to help standardize the definitions of the various deformities with which the surgeon must cope. Specific surgical approaches to each of the seven basic types of deformities follow. The classification takes into consideration the major anatomical components in and around the hip and thigh areas that contribute to the body's configuration:

Type I, *crural excess*, includes medial thigh fullness, relaxation, and wrinkling. It is usually seen in the middle-aged patient and is the deformity most frequently seen by the authors. Extreme examples of this deformity also occur in patients of advanced age or marked weight loss.

Type II, *trochanteric or riding britches deformity*, is characterized by the fullness in the trochanteric area. Frequently seen in younger age groups, this is the next most frequent deformity.

Type III, *gluteal or supratrochanteric recess*, is characterized by the recess in the medial aspect of the buttocks on the lateral side and is seen primarily in the early middle-aged group.

Type IV, a composite of types II and III, is an aggravated example of type III recession with more fullness over the trochanteric areas.

Type V,* *obesity*, is self-explanatory and is seen at almost any age.

Type VI, *asymmetry*, is either traumatic or congenital in nature and is seen at almost any age.

Type VII, *aging or atrophy*, usually occurs in the older age groups and involves generalized muscle atrophy and excessive skin with loss of adipose tissue. This deformity is also seen with anorexia or other diet starvation syndromes.

---

*The term *cellulite* is often mentioned in the lay press. This dimpling effect of fat is most often seen in type V.

Classification of thigh, hip, and gluteal contour deformity

		Upper gluteal	Medial gluteal	Lower gluteal	Trochanteric	Crural area
Type I **Crural** **excess**	*Skeletal* *Muscle* *Skin* *Adipose*	Normal Normal Normal Normal	Normal Normal Normal Normal	Normal Normal Normal Normal	Normal Normal Normal Normal	Normal Normal Excess Excess
Type II **Trochanteric** **("riding britches")** **deformity**	*Skeletal* *Muscle* *Skin* *Adipose*	Normal Normal Normal Normal	Normal Normal to decreased Normal to excess Normal	Normal Normal to decreased Normal to excess Normal	Normal Normal Excess Excess	Normal Normal Normal to excess Normal to excess
Type III **Gluteal** **(supratrochanteric)** **recess**	*Skeletal* *Muscle* *Skin* *Adipose*	Normal Normal Normal Normal	Normal Normal Excess Deficient	Normal Normal Excess Excess	Normal Normal Normal to +1 Normal to +1	Normal Normal Normal to +1 Normal to +1
Type IV **Composite of** **types II and III**	*Skeletal* *Muscle* *Skin* *Adipose*	Normal Normal Normal Normal	Normal Atrophic Excess Deficient	Normal Normal Excess Excess	Normal Normal Excess Excess	Normal Normal Normal to excess Normal to excess
Type V **Obesity**	*Skeletal* *Muscle* *Skin* *Adipose*	Normal Normal Excess Excess	Normal Normal Excess Excess	Normal Normal Excess Excess	Normal Normal Excess Excess	Normal Normal Excess Excess
Type VI **Asymmetry** **and** **traumatic** **deformity**	*Skeletal* *Muscle* *Skin* *Adipose*	Variable Variable Variable Variable	Variable Variable Variable Variable	Variable Variable Variable Variable	Variable Variable Variable Variable	Usually normal
Type VII **Aging** **or** **atrophy**	*Skeletal* *Muscle* *Skin* *Adipose*	Normal Atrophic Excess Deficient	Normal Atrophic Excess Deficient	Normal Atrophic Excess Deficient	Normal Atrophic Excess Deficient	Normal Deficient Excess Deficient

Fig. 8-2

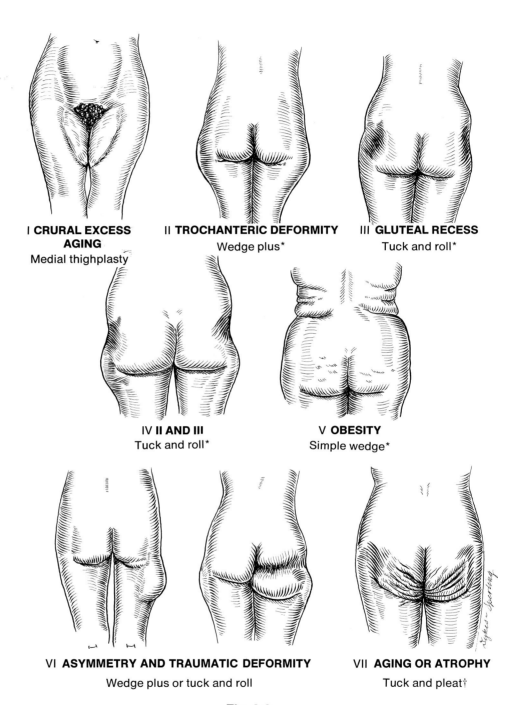

I CRURAL EXCESS
AGING
Medial thighplasty

II TROCHANTERIC DEFORMITY
Wedge plus*

III GLUTEAL RECESS
Tuck and roll*

IV II AND III
Tuck and roll*

V OBESITY
Simple wedge*

VI ASYMMETRY AND TRAUMATIC DEFORMITY
Wedge plus or tuck and roll

VII AGING OR ATROPHY
Tuck and pleat†

Fig. 8-3

*Crural excess.
†Atrophy.

I   II   III

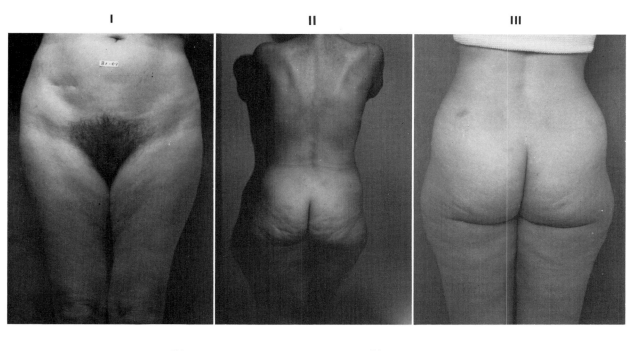

IV   V

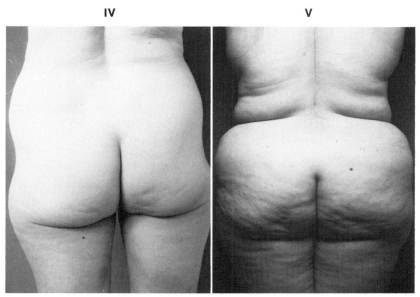

VI   VI   VII

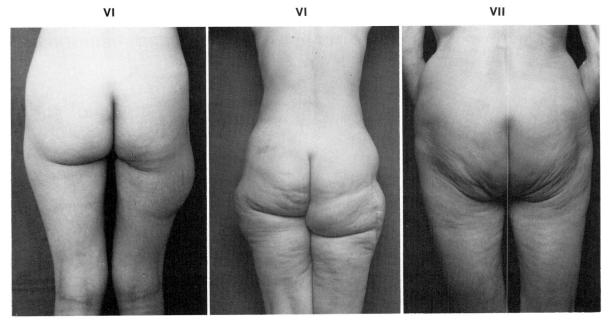

Fig. 8-4

PATIENT SELECTION

As others have pointed out, patient selection is extremely important for patients seeking thigh, hip, and gluteal lipectomies.[11] Proper selection of the patients must involve the desires and objectives of the patient as well as the surgeon's evaluation of the potential benefits and risks. The initial assessment should include a careful history of scar potential and family history of keloid formation, as well as inspection of any preexisting scars. As with the abdominoplasty patient, the patient with a history of diabetes or cardiopulmonary and other metabolic or autoimmune diseases, as well as the obese patient, is a less-than-ideal candidate for these procedures.

The degree of patient motivation is one of the most significant criteria used in patient selection. The patient who is highly motivated is more likely to accept the requirements of the postoperative period and possible complications. Keep in mind what Gorney[8] has said: "When the degree of deformity is small and the degree of anxiety is great, the patient should not be operated upon."

INFORMED CONSENT

It is important that the patient be properly informed of any possible complications, including excessive blood loss, skin loss, fat necrosis, asymmetry, possible deep-vein thrombosis, pulmonary emboli, and the frequent need for secondary procedures (scar revision). It is helpful to show the patient photographs that indicate a wide range of possible results[11] or a film[9,10] on the operative procedure that vividly demonstrates the position and the width of the postoperative scars.

The patients are advised that they will not be able to sit for approximately ten days following surgery. (An exception is the patient with a medial thighplasty, who is allowed to sit postoperatively.) For several days after surgery for deformities of types II through VII, a Foley catheter is used. After its removal, patients should be advised to void in the standing position or in a fracture pan. Following is a description of one of our patient's postoperative experiences with elimination:

> After the catheter was removed I found myself standing over the commode wondering what to do. I tried to urinate standing up, but found my aim wasn't that great. The white carpet didn't appreciate the shower either. After experimenting with a large Dixie cup and trying to bend and aim, the result was disastrous. The aim wasn't good, and the Dixie cup wasn't large enough. The end result, "an apology to malt lovers," was a huge, plastic, 48-ounce cup. Lifting both lids on the commode, I stood with my legs apart (a bit painful at first), and, as I held the cup, I urinated into it . . . very effective. Bowel movements were also done standing. My aim was much better, and I didn't need a cup. Holding onto my walker, which was placed in front of the commode, helped to steady me.

Patients should also be advised that they will experience a great deal of difficulty dressing and climbing in and out of bed. They should be given instructions preoperatively by the nursing personnel and the physical therapist to make their postoperative course as pleasant as possible. Patients are also advised that in the postoperative period they may have areas of discomfort, especially in wearing clothes next to the scars in the crural areas. Many patients find it more comfortable to go without underclothing during this period. Frequently a well-fitting panty girdle with legs is helpful as a support. This discomfort usually ceases after several weeks to several months. Patients should also be advised that a high percentage of these operative procedures will require a secondary scar revision, which is usually performed as an outpatient procedure under local anesthesia.

PREOPERATIVE PLANNING

All criteria and objectives described for abdominoplasty are equally important for patients undergoing hip and thigh contouring. Almost always, more blood is lost in major thighplasties than in abdominoplasties. It is suggested that thighplasty patients begin donating their blood two to three months prior to surgery for storage in the hospital blood bank so that it will be available for autotransfusion.

The evening before surgery, the patients are placed on a low-residue diet, which is continued postoperatively. In addition, all patients are given a cleansing enema prior to surgery.

Preoperative medications, including a broad-spectrum antibiotic, are ordered by the surgeon; the remaining medications are ordered by the anesthesiologist. After an antiseptic shower, the patient is usually marked in a bikini.

On the morning of the day of surgery, the patient should void immediately before entering the operating room if a Foley catheter is not going to be used. The pubic hair is selectively shaved, preferably by the surgeon, immediately before surgery, which avoids potential infections that might result from skin nicks. No localized infections such as furuncles should be present anywhere on the patient's body.

TYPE I: CRURAL DEFORMITIES

To the swimsuit-oriented woman, nothing is more perplexing than sagging of the medial thighs (Figs. 8-5 and 8-7, *A*). This deformity usually occurs in the middle-aged group, becoming more accentuated in the older-aged group, and frequently occurs with weight reduction (Fig. 8-6). When correction can be accomplished by the simple wedge excision (Fig. 8-7, *B*), it can be combined with other aesthetic procedures such as abdominoplasty, breast augmentation, and/or facial aesthetic procedures. When the deformity is exaggerated and requires extension of the surgery into the gluteal area, it should not be combined with abdominoplasty procedures because of possible lymphatic complications. This simple wedge excision lends itself well to either local or general anesthesia.

The patient, in her bikini, is being marked in the standing position in Fig. 8-7, *C*.

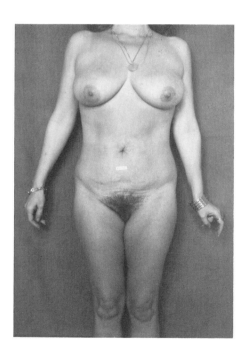

Fig. 8-5

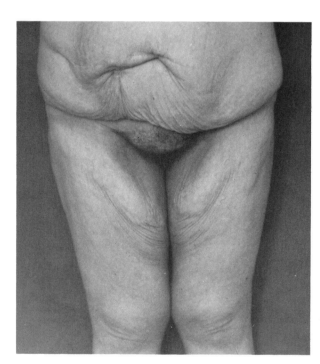

Fig. 8-6

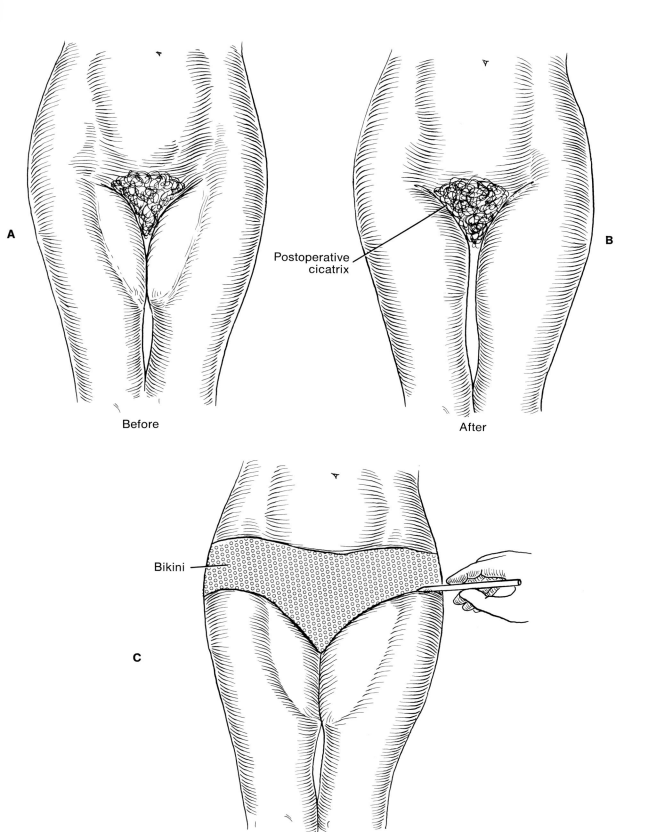

A

Before

B

Postoperative
cicatrix

After

C

Bikini

Marking outline of bikini while patient stands

Fig. 8-7. Type I (crural) deformity.

The patient is prepared with povidone-iodine complex while in the supine position with the legs in the froglike position. After preparation, the legs are covered with sterile Stockinette dressings, which makes abduction and adduction of the thighs convenient for the assistant. Remarking of the patient is done to ensure that the medial segment of the incision lies slightly inside the inguinal fold and extends inferiorly to connect with the sulcus genitofemoralis accessorius (Chapter 3) (Fig. 8-8, *A* to *C*). The amount of resection depends on the amount of excess tissue (Fig. 8-8, *D* and *E*). Care must be taken to avoid removing too much skin which might result in a gaping of the labia majora and minora and pulling down of the cicatrix.

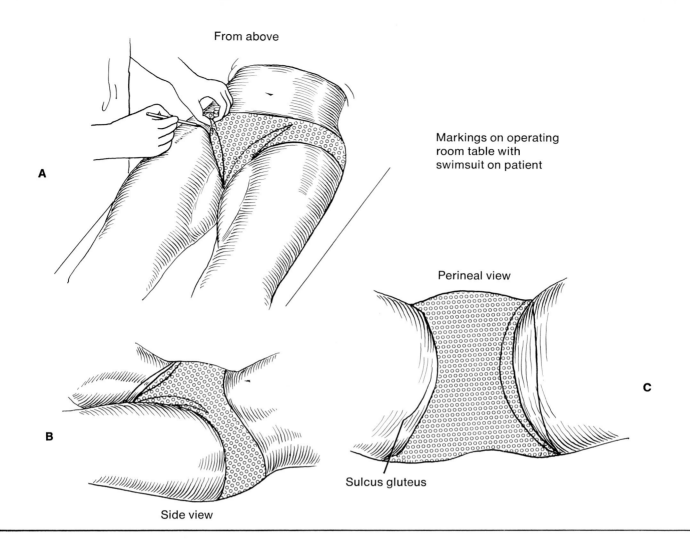

From above

Markings on operating
room table with
swimsuit on patient

A

Perineal view

B

Side view

C

Sulcus gluteus

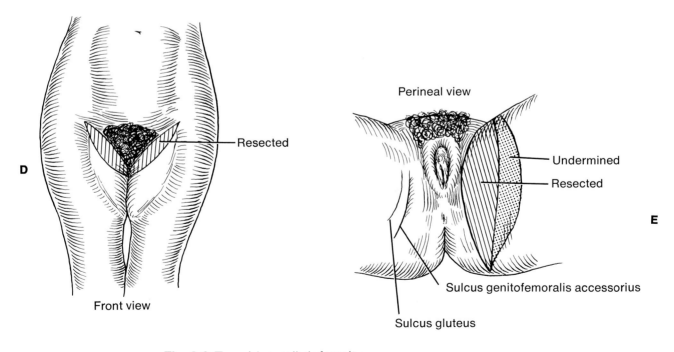

D

Resected

Front view

Perineal view

Undermined

Resected

Sulcus genitofemoralis accessorius

Sulcus gluteus

E

Fig. 8-8. Type I (crural) deformity.

255

Lidocaine (Xylocaine), 0.5%, with 1:200,000 epinephrine (Adrenalin) is injected into the area irrespective of the type of anesthesia plans (Chapter 4). The added epinephrine decreases the intraoperative bleeding. The position of horizontal markings and dog ears is demonstrated in Fig. 8-9.

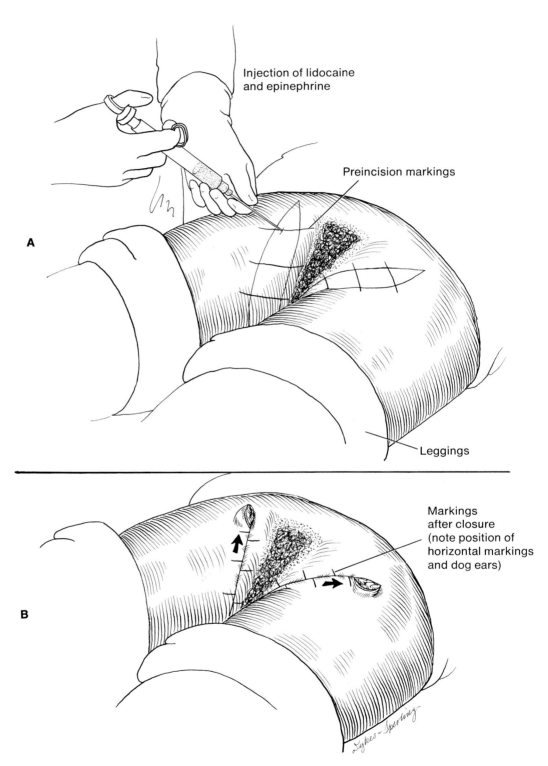

Fig. 8-9. Type I (crural) deformity.

Surgery is begun at the apex of the inguinal area; the ellipse is developed downward with tacking sutures as the surgeon works toward the posterior gluteal area (Fig. 8-10). The assistant can manipulate the legs by adducting and abducting the thighs for better exposure.

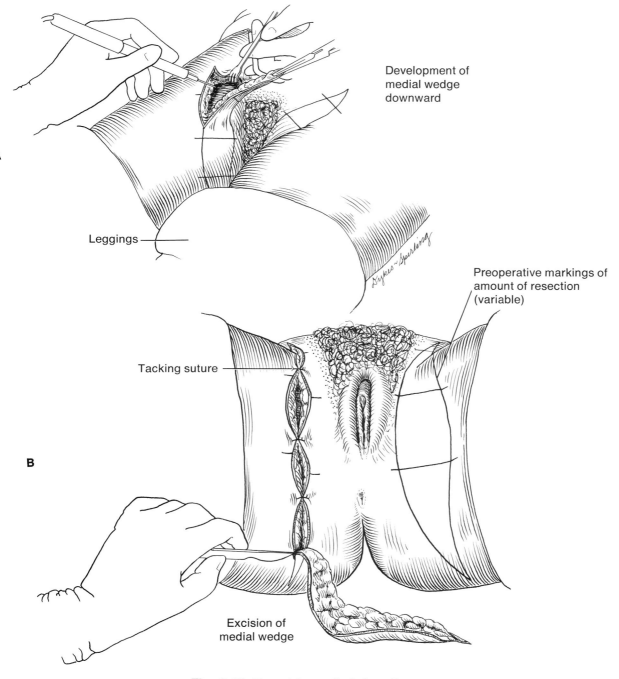

Fig. 8-10. Type I (crural) deformity.

After the ellipse has been excised, shifting of the tissue anteriorly adjusts for the differential lengths of the incision line. It is easier to correct the dog ear deformity in the groin area than in the gluteal area. Closure is accomplished with 3-0 buried Dexon sutures with an occasional 3-0 or 4-0 external nylon suture (Fig. 8-11, *A* and *B*), which may be replaced with a running intercuticular nylon; 1-inch Steri-Strip tapes are optional (Fig. 8-11, *C* and *D*).

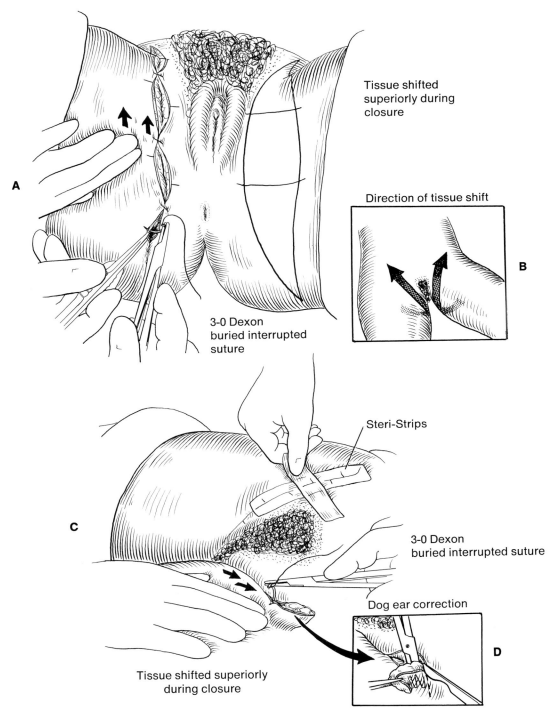

A

Tissue shifted
superiorly during
closure

Direction of tissue shift

B

3-0 Dexon
buried interrupted
suture

Steri-Strips

C

3-0 Dexon
buried interrupted suture

Dog ear correction

D

Tissue shifted superiorly
during closure

Fig. 8-11. Type I (crural) deformity.

Type I case histories

The 46-year-old woman in Fig. 8-12 complained of moderate fullness in both medial thighs, which apparently led to skin irritation from her legs rubbing together. She underwent a medial excision. A modified meloplasty for correction of actinic changes of facial skin was performed at the same time.

The length of the operation was 4 hours. The total estimated blood loss was well under a unit. Postoperative recovery was uneventful. The patient is shown six months after surgery in Fig. 8-13.

Critique: This is a satisfactory result. No change in approach would be recommended.

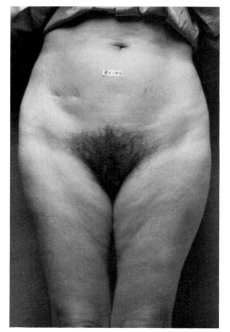

Fig. 8-12

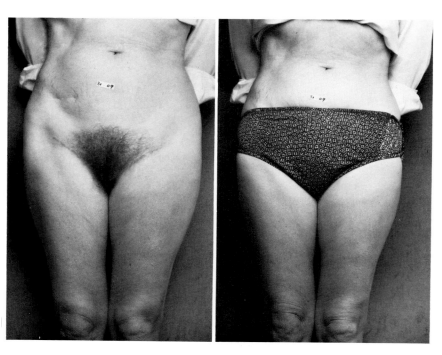

Fig. 8-13

The 43-year-old woman in Fig. 8-14, *A*, was concerned about both an abdominal deformity and the relaxation of her medial thighs. She underwent a combined procedure of a gull-wing abdominoplasty and medial excision. The total operating time was 4 hours, blood loss was minimal, and the postoperative course uncomplicated.

The patient's appearance nine months after surgery is demonstrated in Fig. 8-14, *B*. She can wear a "string" bikini with neither scar visible (Fig. 8-14, *C*).

Critique: This is a satisfactory result, in spite of a hypertrophic abdominoplasty scar. Note the inconspicuous medial thigh scar.

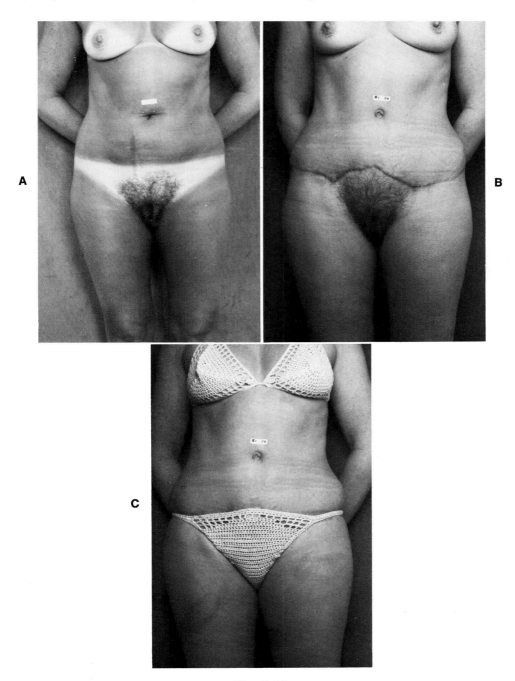

Fig. 8-14

Marked medial thigh relaxation

In the case of marked medial thigh relaxation, a medial ellipse of tissue must be removed from the thigh (Figs. 8-15 and 8-16). The excision may extend all the way to the knee in some cases.

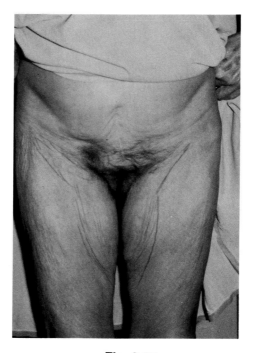

Fig. 8-15

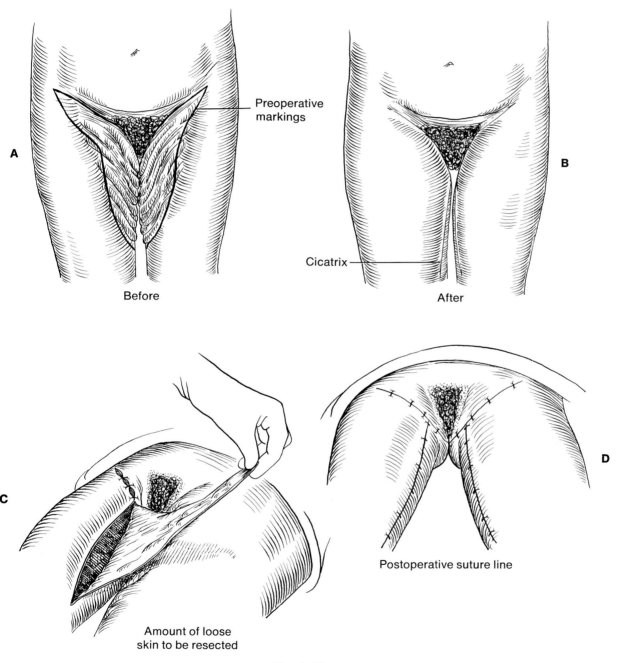

A

Preoperative
markings

Before

B

Cicatrix

After

C

Amount of loose
skin to be resected

D

Postoperative suture line

Fig. 8-16

This 70-year-old woman (Figs. 8-15 and 8-17) had marked medial thigh relaxation, which was treated by medial thigh excision at the same time a brachioplasty was performed.

The total operative time was 3 hours 40 minutes. As discussed in Chapter 6, the brachioplasty was done prior to the thighplasty. Total blood loss was minimal. The postoperative course was complicated by cellulitis and thrombophlebitis of the left leg, which developed fifteen days after surgery and after the initial discharge, necessitating readmission. The patient responded to application of heat to and elevation of the extremity.

The patient's appearance three months after surgery is shown in Fig. 8-18.

Critique: We would now monitor a person of this age undergoing surgery of this extent with a fibrinogen-^{125}I scan before and after surgery.

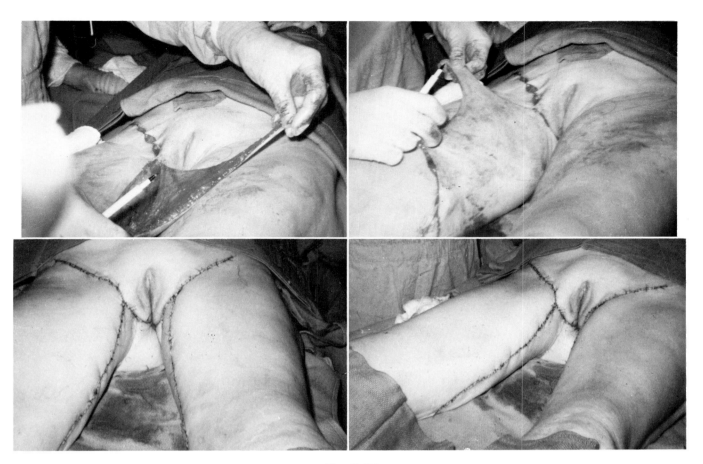

Fig. 8-17

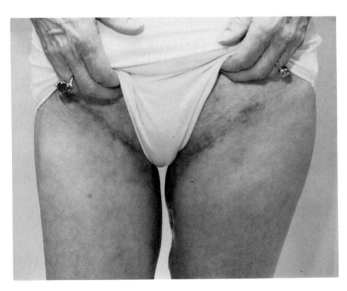

Fig. 8-18

TYPE II: TROCHANTERIC (RIDING BRITCHES) DEFORMITY

The primary deformity in these patients exists directly lateral to the trochanter and can be corrected by a highly placed wedge excision and defatting of the trochanteric fat pad. In most cases this is combined with medial thigh excision.

As shown in Figs. 8-19 and 8-20, *C* to *E,* the patient is marked in the standing position wearing a bikini. (This patient also exhibits some obesity). Resection and undermining of the medial thigh is shown in Fig. 8-21.

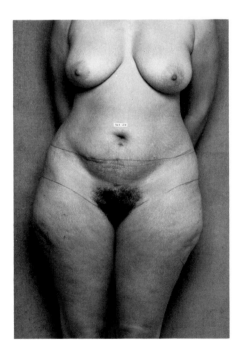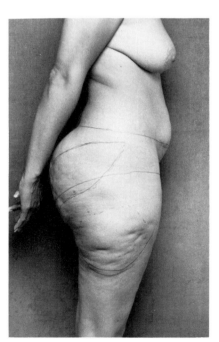

Fig. 8-19

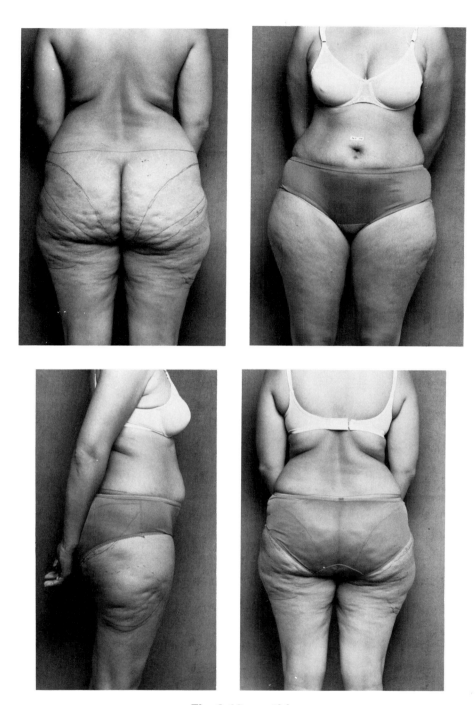

Fig. 8-19, cont'd

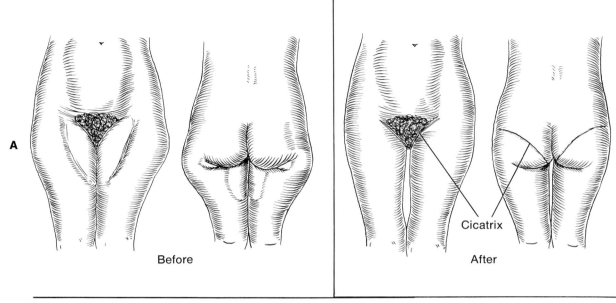

A   Cicatrix

Before   After

Marking bikini outline and deformities while patient stands

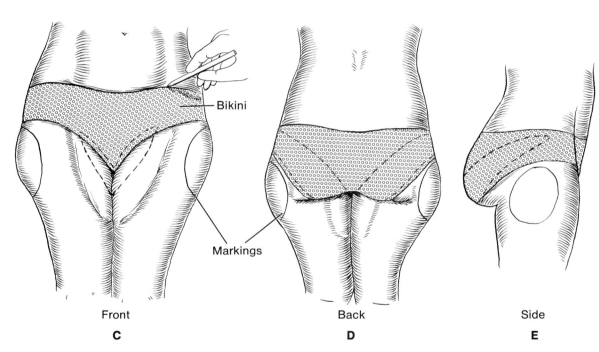

Bikini

Markings

Front   Back   Side

C   D   E

Fig. 8-20. Type II (trochanteric) deformity. **A,** Preoperative appearance. **B,** Postoperative appearance. **C** to **E,** Preoperative marking of the patient in the standing position wearing a bikini.

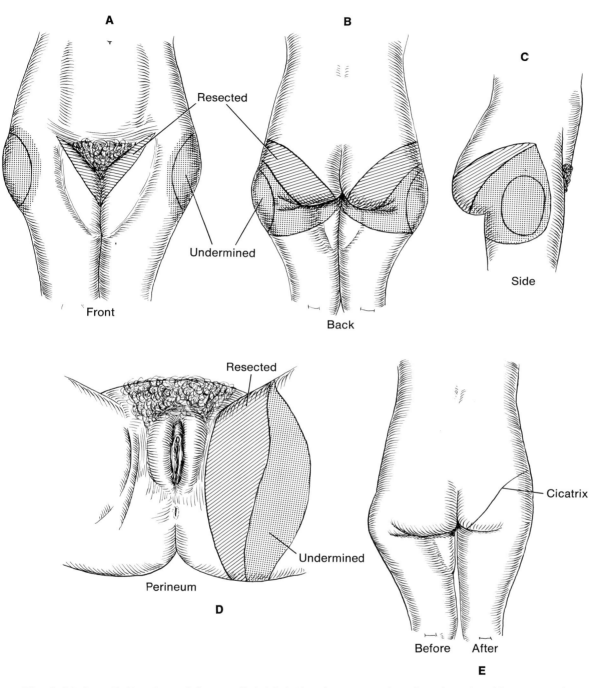

Fig. 8-21. A to **D,** Portion of the medial thigh that is resected and undermined in cases of trochanteric deformity. **E,** Appearance before and after surgery.

When the anterior thighplasty is included, the patient is placed on the operating table in the supine position, and a Foley catheter is inserted at the time of povidone-iodine preparation. The patient is placed in the frog-leg position with sterile leg drapes. Infiltration with 0.5% lidocaine with 1:200,000 epinephrine is used to reduce the intraoperative bleeding (Figs. 8-22 and 8-24, *A*).

The surgical technique (Fig. 8-24, *B* to *D*) for the medial thigh aspect is essentially the same as that for type I defects, with the exception that the medial thigh skin and subcutaneous tissue are rotated from anterior to posterior, which helps to tighten the medial thigh. After completion of the anterior resection (Fig. 8-23), the skin flaps are either wrapped in a sterile towel or resected, and the raw surface is covered with a sterile drape.

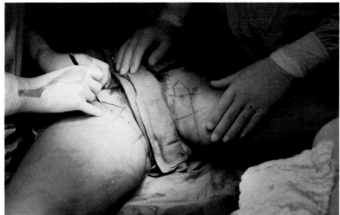 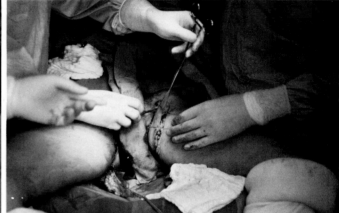

Fig. 8-22

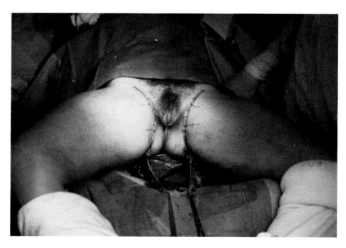

Fig. 8-23

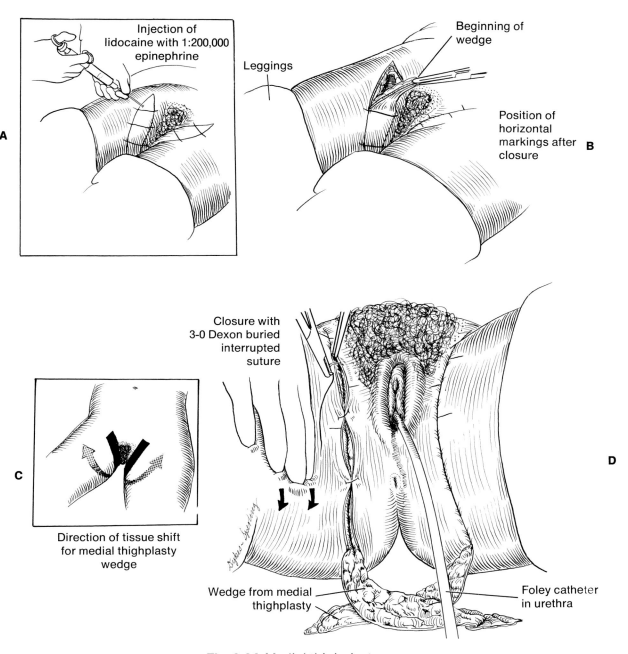

Fig. 8-24. Medial thighplasty.

The patient is then placed in the prone position without contaminating the sterile leggings. Markings are confirmed with the string-compass technique (Fig. 8-26, *A* and *B*). The size of the wedge is marked but not removed until the final steps of the procedure. Additional 0.5% lidocaine with 1:200,000 epinephrine is injected (Figs. 8-25 and 8-26, *C*). In the trochanteric deformity there is usually no supratrochanteric recess (mediogluteal recess); thus augmentation of this area is not necessary.

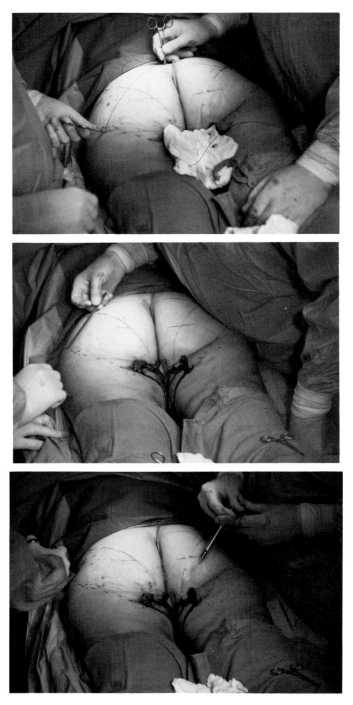

Fig. 8-25

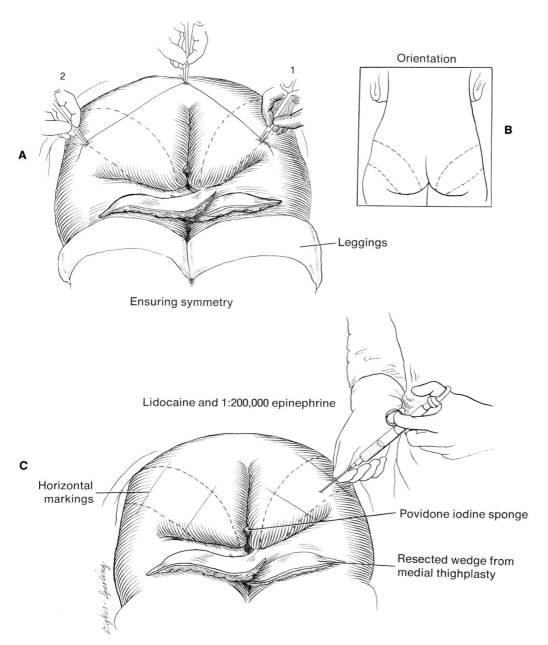

Orientation

B

Leggings

A

Ensuring symmetry

Lidocaine and 1:200,000 epinephrine

C

Horizontal
markings

Povidone iodine sponge

Resected wedge from
medial thighplasty

Fig. 8-26. Type II (trochanteric) deformity.

The incision is made along the superior markings down through the subcutaneous fat to the gluteal area, where the medial resection incision is encountered (Figs. 8-27 and 8-29, *A*, and *B*). At this point, undermining over the infragluteal area and trochanter is accomplished (Figs. 8-28 and 8-29, *C* to *E*).

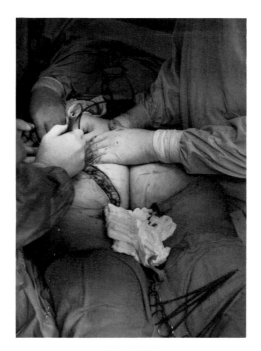

Fig. 8-27

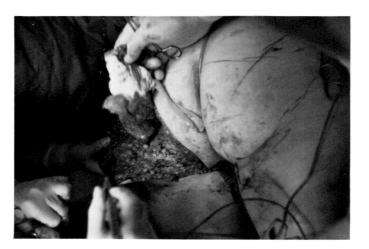

Fig. 8-28

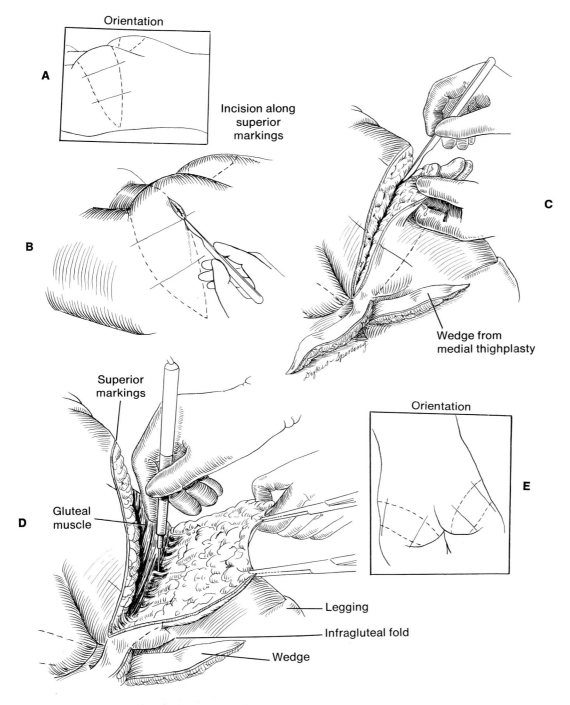

Orientation

A

Incision along
superior
markings

B

C

Wedge from
medial thighplasty

Superior
markings

Orientation

E

Gluteal
muscle

D

Legging

Infragluteal fold

Wedge

Fig. 8-29. Type II (trochanteric) deformity.

Severing all soft tissue septal connections in the infragluteal area is essential to aid in the advancement of the flap and to create a new infragluteal fold (Figs. 8-30 and 8-31, *A* and *B*). Undermining over the trochanter exposes the always-present trochanteric fat pad, which is directly over the trochanteric bursa. With the resection of this fat pad, most of the trochanteric deformity is eliminated (Fig. 8-31, *C* and *D*).

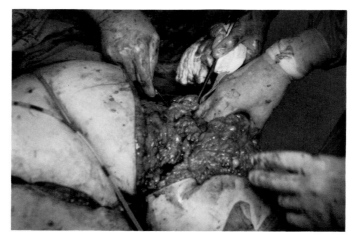

Fig. 8-30

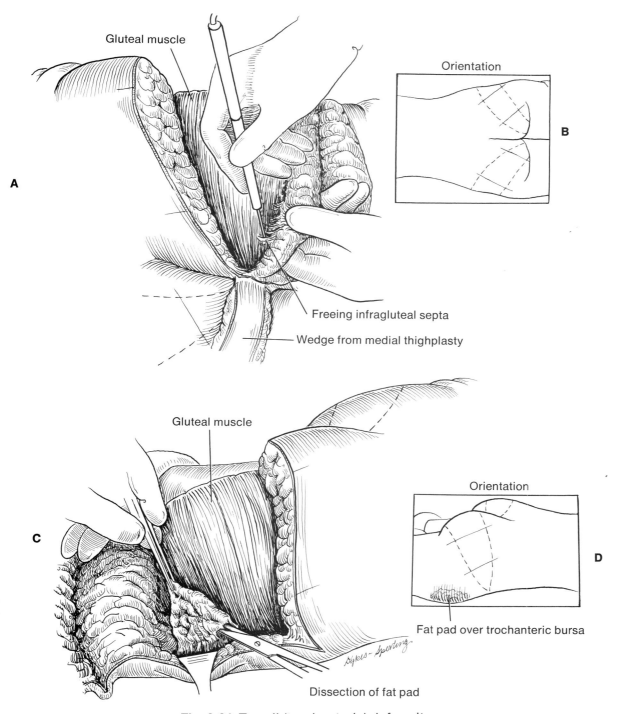

Gluteal muscle

Orientation

B

A

Freeing infragluteal septa

Wedge from medial thighplasty

Gluteal muscle

Orientation

C

D

Fat pad over trochanteric bursa

Dissection of fat pad

Fig. 8-31. Type II (trochanteric) deformity.

After meticulous hemostasis, the flap is pulled up and directed laterally (Fig. 8-32). With the flap pulled taut, incisions are made down to the level of removal. The flap is usually divided into three segments (Figs. 8-33 and 8-34).

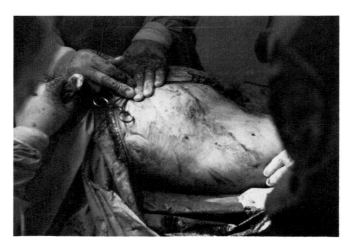

Fig. 8-32

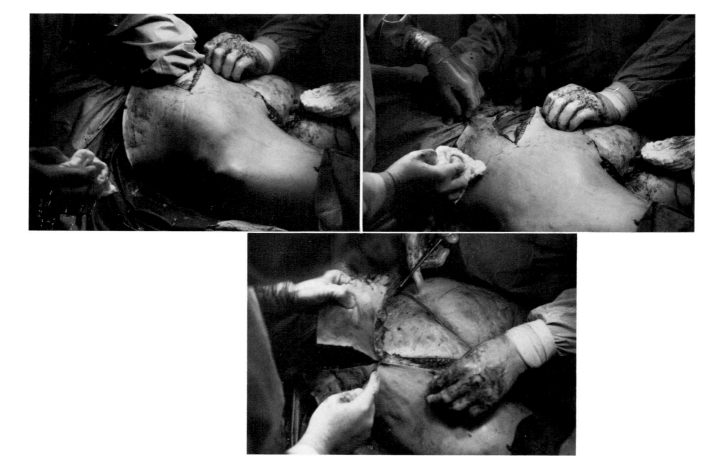

Fig. 8-33

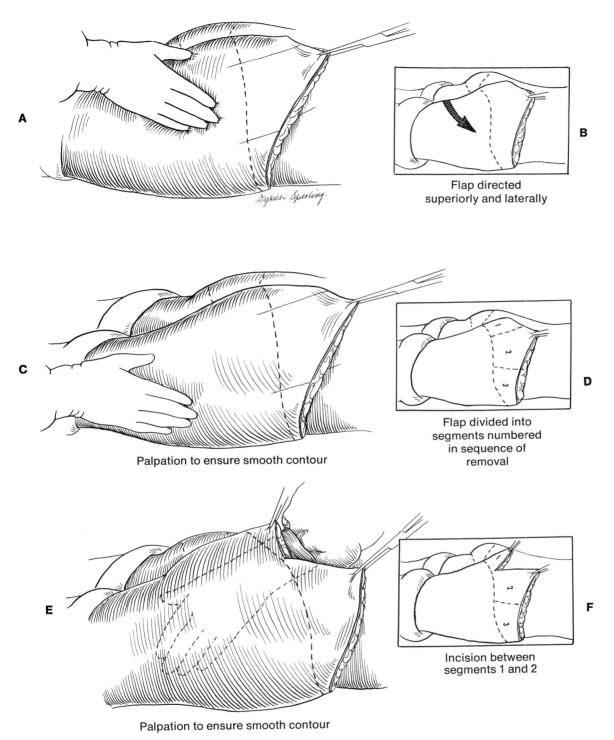

Flap directed
superiorly and laterally

Palpation to ensure smooth contour

Flap divided into
segments numbered
in sequence of
removal

Palpation to ensure smooth contour

Incision between
segments 1 and 2

Fig. 8-34. Type II (trochanteric) deformity.

The fiberoptic-lighted instrument (Fig. 8-35) is used to check hemostasis, if indicated. Each flap is resected separately (Fig. 8-37, *A* and *B*); buried sutures of 2-, 3-, and 4-0 Dexon are used for the deep closure (Figs. 8-36 and 8-37, *C* and *D*).

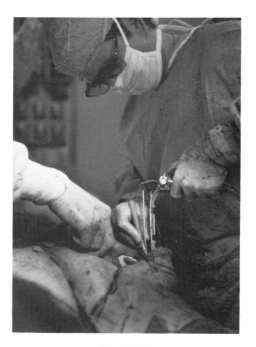

Fig. 8-35

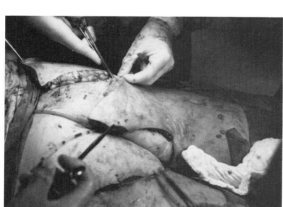 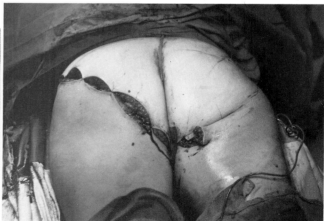

Fig. 8-36

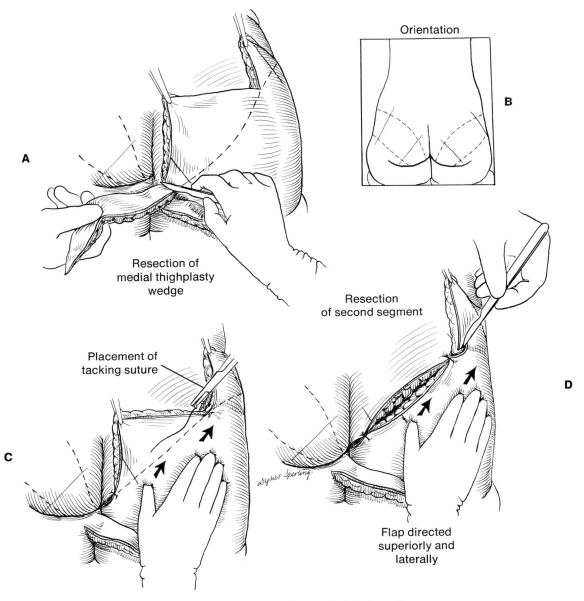

A

Resection of
medial thighplasty
wedge

Orientation

B

Placement of
tacking suture

Resection
of second segment

C

D

Flap directed
superiorly and
laterally

Fig. 8-37. Type II (trochanteric) deformity.

The dog ear is removed laterally by a downward displacement of the incision (Figs. 8-38 and 8-40, *A* to *D*). One or two Jackson-Pratt drains are used to drain the undermined area (Figs. 8-39 and 8-40, *E* and *F*).

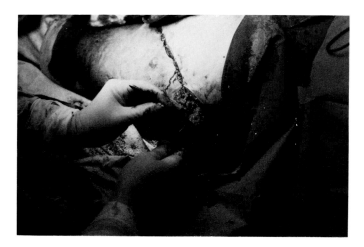

Fig. 8-38

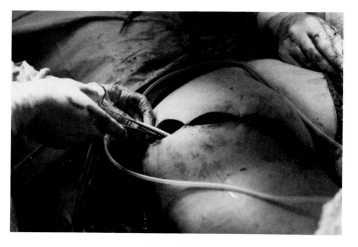

Fig. 8-39

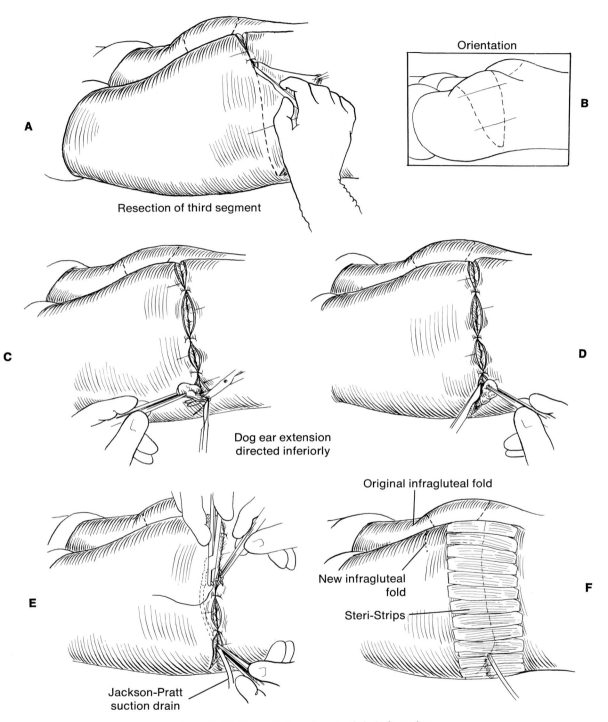

Orientation

A

Resection of third segment

B

C

D

Dog ear extension
directed inferiorly

Original infragluteal fold

New infragluteal
fold

Steri-Strips

E

F

Jackson-Pratt
suction drain

Fig. 8-40. Type II (trochanteric) deformity.

One-inch Steri-Strips are applied over the incision site and reinforced with Elastoplast tapes. The upper thighs and hip areas are then wrapped with Ace bandages (Fig. 8-41).

The patient, in the supine position, is usually rolled over from the operating table to the Nelson bed and extubated.

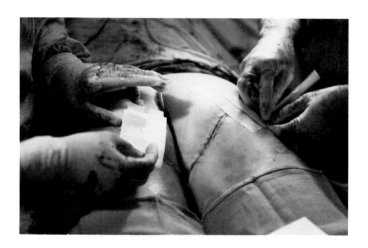

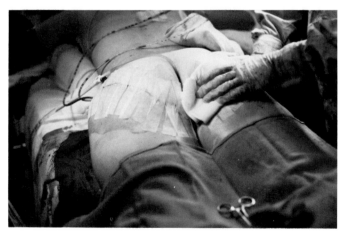

Fig. 8-41

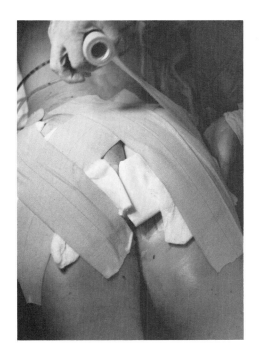

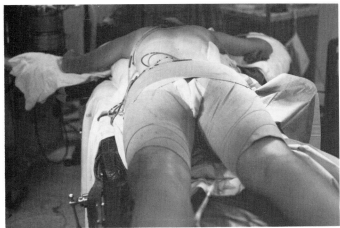

Fig. 8-41, cont'd

Type II case histories

The 29-year-old woman in Fig. 8-42 complained of typical riding britches deformity, which interfered with her appearance in slacks and other sportswear. A reduction thighplasty with undermining was performed. Approximately 2 kg of tissue were resected. Total operating time was 3 hours 20 minutes. The blood loss of 2 units required replacement within the first two days after surgery.

The patient's postoperative course was complicated by the development of a small serous effusion, which was easily aspirated as an outpatient procedure (Fig. 8-43, *A*), and postoperative postural hypotension, which was treated by transfusion in the hospital. Fig. 8-43, *B* to *E,* shows the patient three weeks postoperatively, at which time she returned from California to her home in the Midwest. Note the formation of the new infragluteal fold in Fig. 8-43, *C.* The patient is shown four months after surgery in Fig. 8-43, *F* and *G,* and a year postoperatively in Fig. 8-43, *H* to *J.*

> **Critique:** This was the procedure of choice for this type of deformity. Had the patient lived closer and had the opportunity to donate blood for autotransfusion, the operative blood loss would have been more quickly replaced. The hesitancy to use bank blood is based on the risk of reactions and hepatitis. Caution should be observed with patients who live far from the surgery location, since good follow-up is frequently unavailable elsewhere.
>
> The authors are aware of critical appraisal of these procedures in regard to postoperative appearance, especially gluteal flattening. With time (Fig. 8-43, *H* and *I*) these deformities tend to minimize.

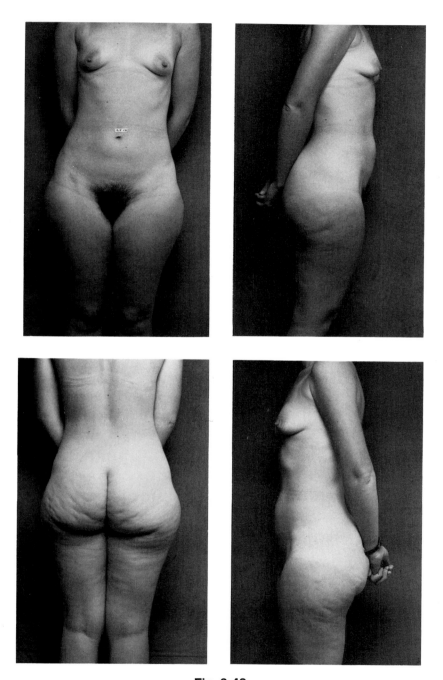

Fig. 8-42

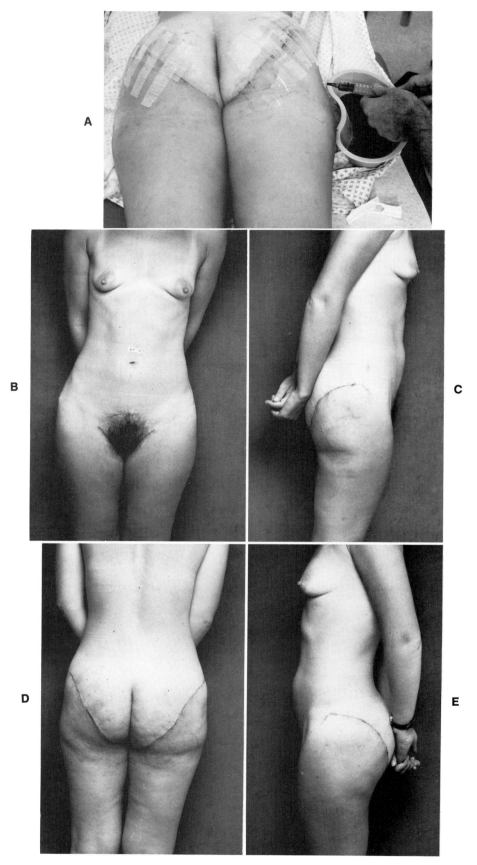

Fig. 8-43

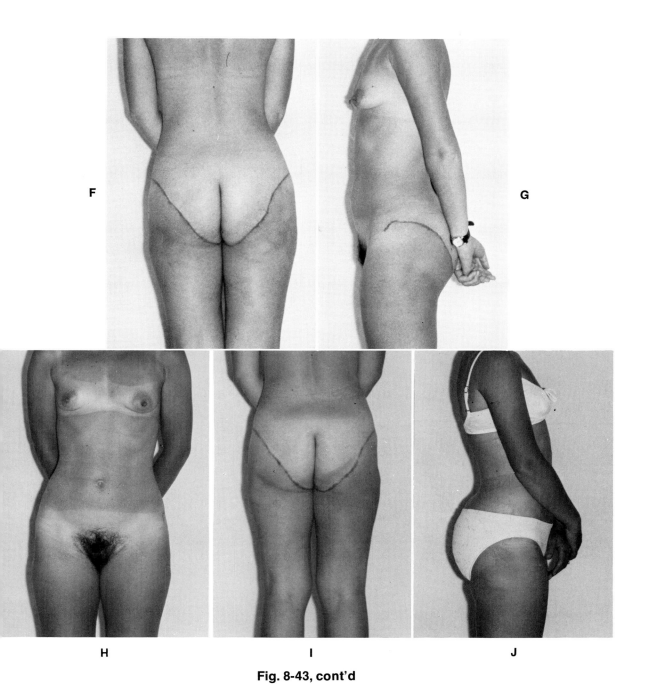

Fig. 8-43, cont'd

TYPE III, GLUTEAL RECESS, AND TYPE IV, COMPOSITE, DEFORMITIES

Deformities of types III and IV have the medial thigh (supratrochanteric) recess in common.

Experience with patients with defects of types III and IV was our stimulus to develop a surgical approach that would enable correction of the contour deformity of the upper hip rather than apparently aggravating it with a simple wedge incision, as was done in the following example of our earlier thighplasties.

Fig. 8-44 demonstrates the type III deformity with the supratrochanteric recess and trochanteric (riding britches) deformity. A simple wedge procedure was performed and included the medial thighs. A total of 1,260 g of tissue was removed (Fig. 8-45). The patient's persistent hollowness after four years is demonstrated in Fig. 8-46.

Cases of types III and IV respond well to the tuck-and-roll thighplasty, which is essentially an inferiorly based flap that is tucked and rolled to fill out the depression. Defatting of the trochanteric fat depends on the amount of trochanteric fullness.

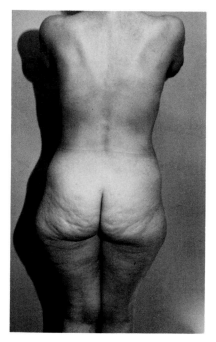

Fig. 8-44

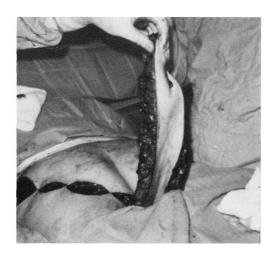

Fig. 8-45

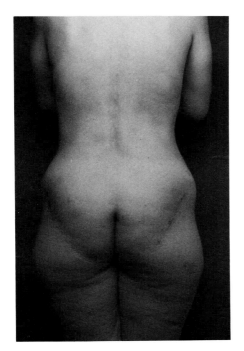

Fig. 8-46

The anterior resection is essentially identical to the procedure described for type II. Figs. 8-47 and 8-48 show the undermined and resected area.

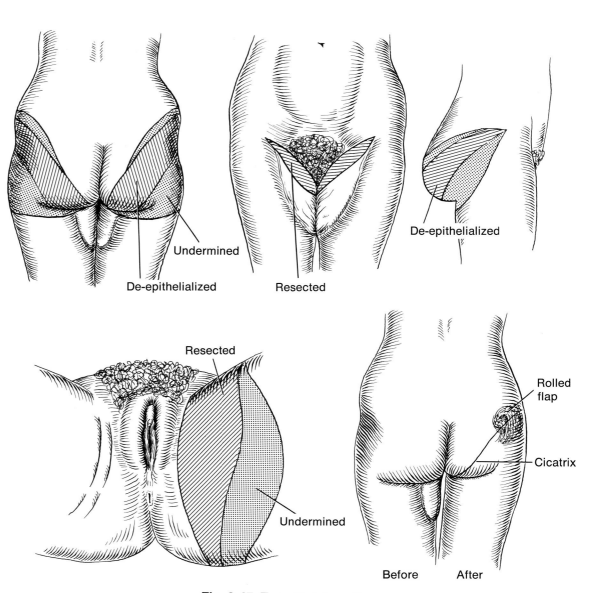

Fig. 8-47. Type III deformity.

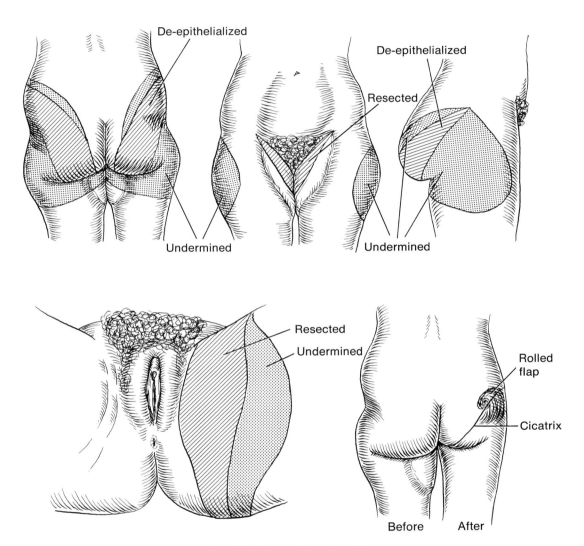

Fig. 8-48. Type IV deformity.

The patient is placed in the supine position, prepared with povidone-iodine solution, and draped with sterile leggings. Infiltration of 0.5% lidocaine with 1:200,000 epinephrine is used to reduce the intraoperative bleeding (Fig. 8-49, *A*). Surgery is begun at the apex of the inguinal area, and the ellipse is developed downward with tacking sutures as the surgeon works toward the posterogluteal area (Fig. 8-49, *B*). A Foley catheter is inserted at the time of surgery or at the completion of the anterior portion of the resection (Fig. 8-49, *C* and *D*). (See Fig. 8-22.)

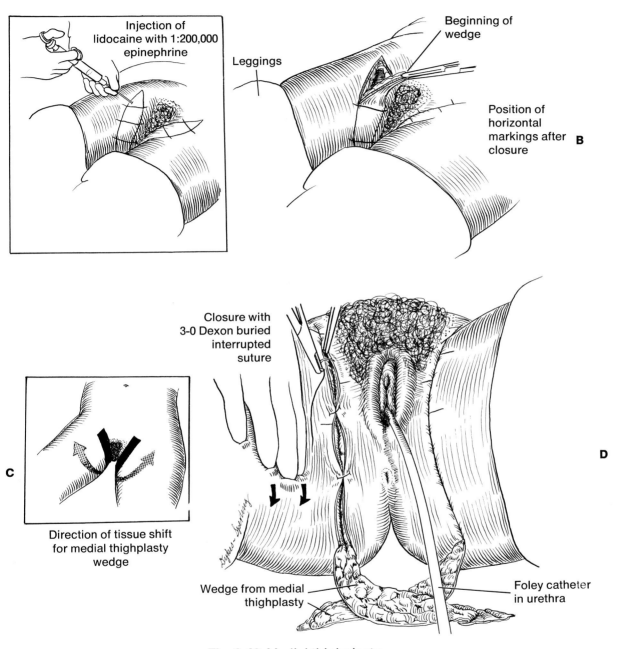

Injection of lidocaine with 1:200,000 epinephrine

Leggings

Beginning of wedge

Position of horizontal markings after closure **B**

Closure with 3-0 Dexon buried interrupted suture

C

Direction of tissue shift for medial thighplasty wedge

Wedge from medial thighplasty

Foley catheter in urethra

D

Fig. 8-49. Medial thighplasty.

The patient is now placed in the prone position, reprepared, and redraped, and the markings are reconfirmed with the string-compass technique (Figs. 8-50 and 8-51, *A* and *B*). Local anesthesia, 0.5% lidocaine with 1:200,000 epinephrine, is injected to decrease intraoperative bleeding (Fig. 8-51, *C*). At this point the tuck-and-roll thighplasty differs from the wedge excision in that the final amount of resection is not determined until the completion of the procedure.

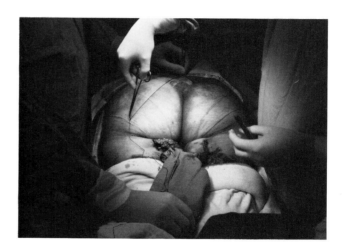

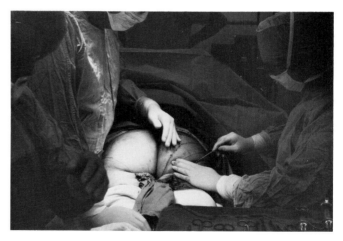

Fig. 8-50

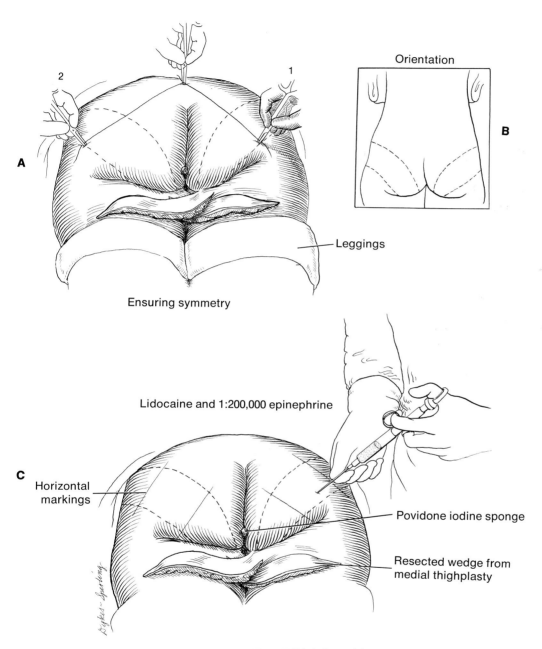

Orientation

B

A

Leggings

Ensuring symmetry

Lidocaine and 1:200,000 epinephrine

C

Horizontal
markings

Povidone iodine sponge

Resected wedge from
medial thighplasty

Fig. 8-51. Types III and IV deformities.

De-epithelialization follows (Figs. 8-52 and 8-54, *A* and *B*). It is not essential that all of the dermis remain behind in the de-epithelialization procedure. After hemostasis (Fig. 8-54, *C* and *D*) an incision is made perpendicularly through the upper portion of the flap down to the gluteal musculature (Figs. 8-53 and 8-54, *E*).

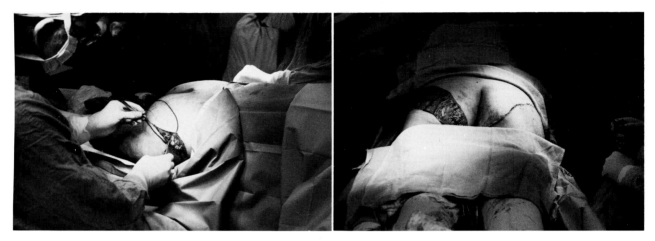

Fig 8-52

Fig. 8-53

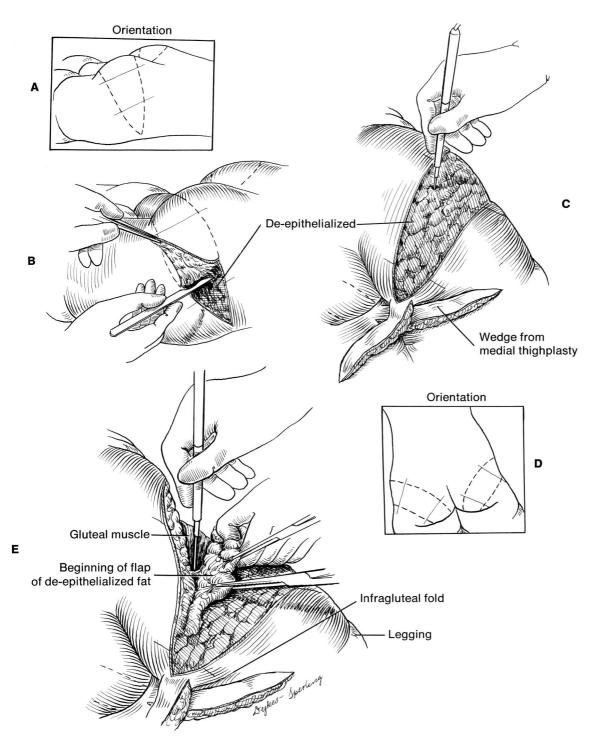

Fig. 8-54. Types III and IV deformities.

After the initial incision is completed as far as the gluteal musculature, an inferiorly based flap is developed (Figs. 8-55 and 8-56, *A* and *B*). It is important to sever the infragluteal septa to allow the posterior thigh tissue to advance superolaterally with creation of a new infragluteal fold (Fig. 8-56, *C*).

Depending on the deformity, either a portion or all of the trochanteric fat pad is removed (Figs. 8-30 and 8-56, *D*).

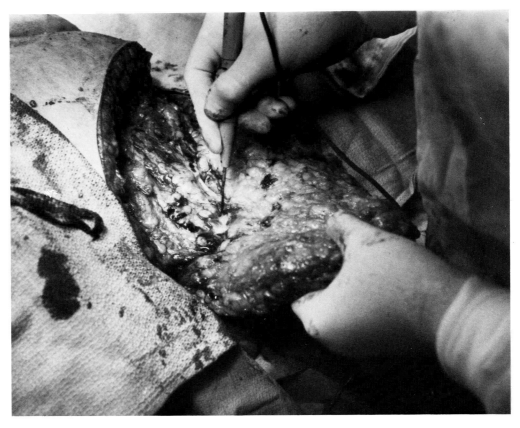

Fig. 8-55

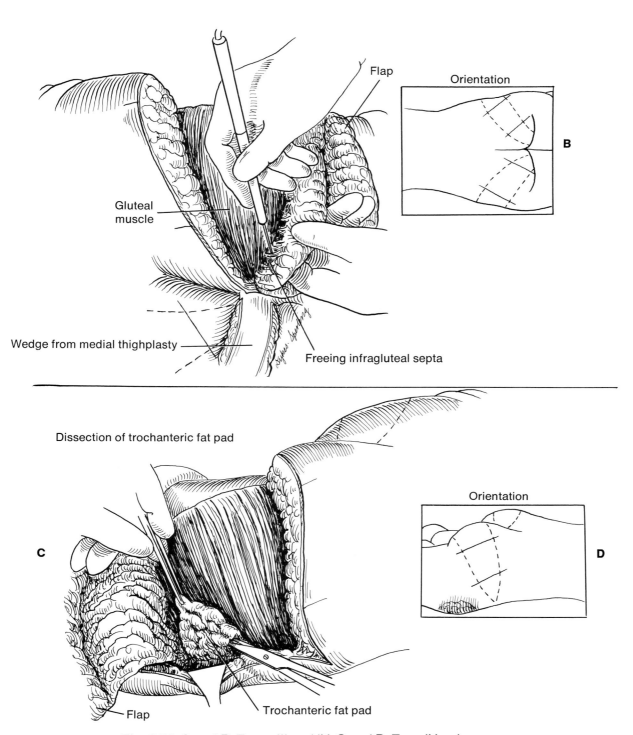

Flap

Orientation

B

Gluteal
muscle

Wedge from medial thighplasty

Freeing infragluteal septa

Dissection of trochanteric fat pad

Orientation

C

D

Flap

Trochanteric fat pad

Fig. 8-56. A and **B,** Types III and IV. **C** and **D,** Type IV only.

The inferiorly based flap is trimmed and contoured (Fig. 8-57), removing the unnecessary portion medially and somewhat less laterally (Fig. 8-59, *A* and *B*).

A superior pocket is developed (Fig. 8-58) in the area above the gluteal depression (Fig. 8-59, *C* and *D*).

Fig. 8-57

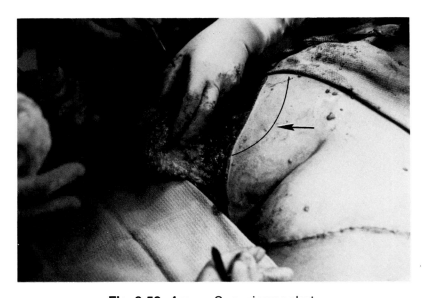

Fig. 8-58. *Arrow,* Superior pocket.

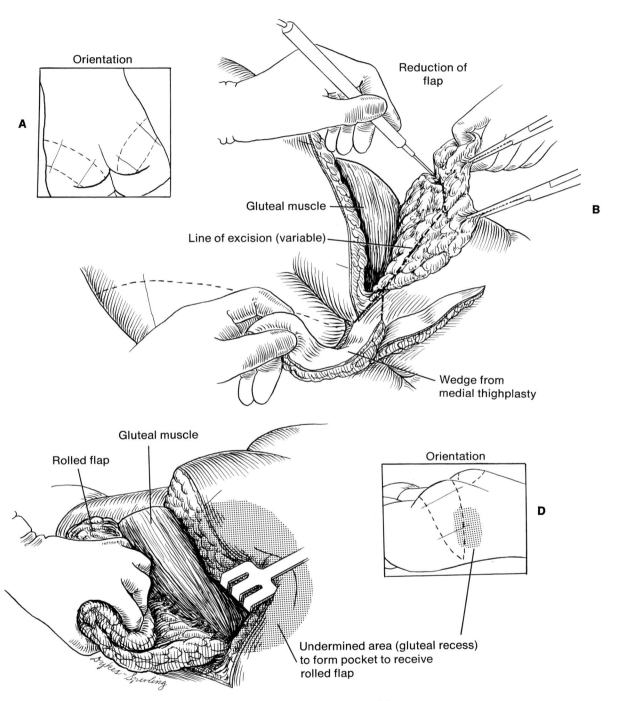

Orientation

A

Reduction of
flap

Gluteal muscle

Line of excision (variable)

B

Wedge from
medial thighplasty

Gluteal muscle

Rolled flap

Orientation

D

Undermined area (gluteal recess)
to form pocket to receive
rolled flap

Fig. 8-59. Types III and IV deformities.

303

The flap is tucked and rolled into the area of apparent tissue discrepancy. The flap is shifted laterally, resulting in a further tightening effect on the upper thigh (Fig. 8-63, *A* and *B*) and creating the dog ear laterally. Closure is begun from medial to lateral (Fig. 8-60), with final tailoring of the inferiorly based flap tissue accomplished (Fig. 8-63, *C* and *D*). The dog ear is removed in an inferior lateral direction (Fig. 8-63, *E* and *F*). Figs. 8-61 and 8-63, *G*, show the rolled flap in place.

Closure is with 3-0 Dexon and interrupted 3-0 and 4-0 nylon sutures. Drainage is accomplished with a silicone suction-drainage system such as the Jackson-Pratt drain (Fig. 8-62).

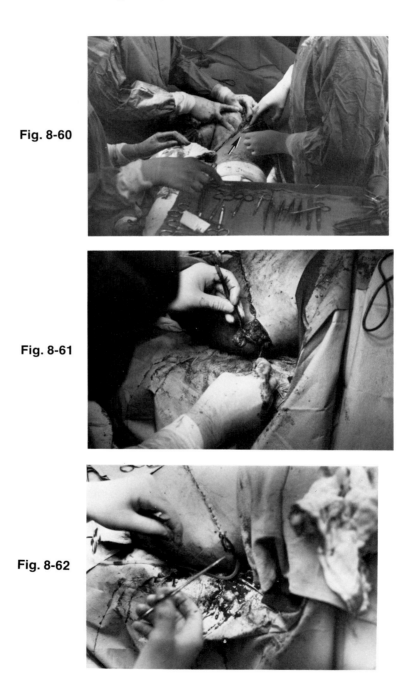

Fig. 8-60

Fig. 8-61

Fig. 8-62

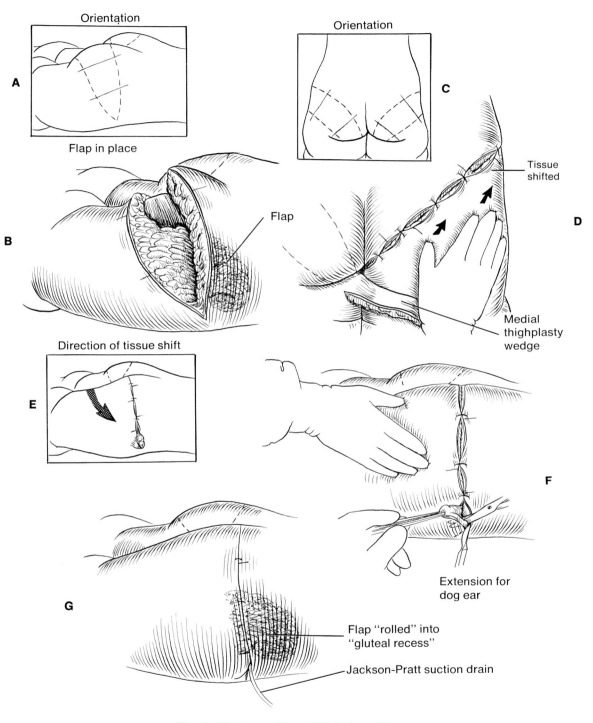

Orientation

Flap in place

A

B

Orientation

C

Flap

Tissue shifted

D

Medial thighplasty wedge

Direction of tissue shift

E

Extension for dog ear

F

G

Flap "rolled" into "gluteal recess"

Jackson-Pratt suction drain

Fig. 8-63. Types III and IV deformities.

The final dressing is with 1-inch Steri-Strips, an ABD dressing, Elastoplast, and a circumferential Ace wrap (Fig. 8-64).

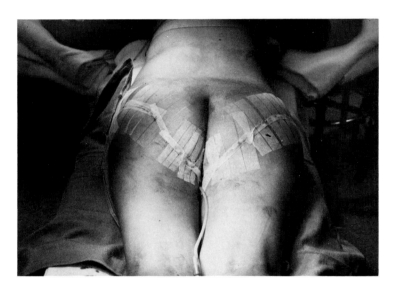

Fig. 8-64

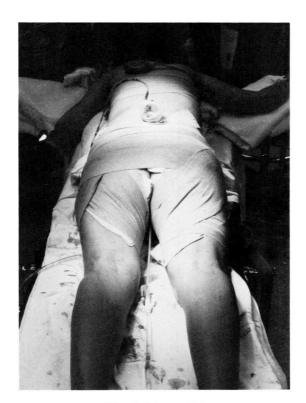

Fig. 8-64, cont'd

Types III and IV case history

This 31-year-old woman complained of unattractive thigh contours, which were most obvious in sports clothes and bathing suits. A tuck-and-roll thighplasty was chosen because of the supratrochanteric recess, which is apparent in preoperative photographs (Fig. 8-65). This case is closest to type III.

Operating time was 4 hours, with a blood loss of less than a unit. The postoperative course was unremarkable. The patient was discharged on a stretcher three days after surgery and recuperated at home. (This patient described her postoperative experience earlier in the chapter.)

The patient is shown a year after surgery in Fig. 8-66.

Critique: The tuck-and-roll thighplasty enables the surgeon to fill out the supratrochanteric recess and thus restore a more "normal" contour to the buttocks. The weakness with this procedure is that it does not provide for a method to support the rolled-in flap; the wound closure is dependent on the skin and dermis alone. Davis[5] indicated that a similiar procedure performed by him resulted in atrophy of the inferior flap after five years.[4] (If all aesthetic procedures would last five years, most surgeons would be happy).

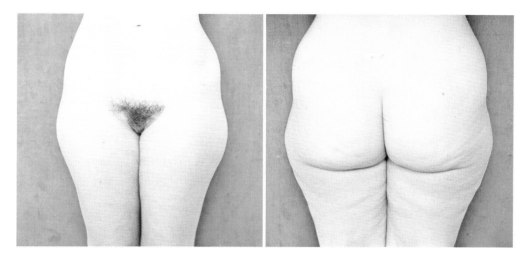

Fig. 8-65

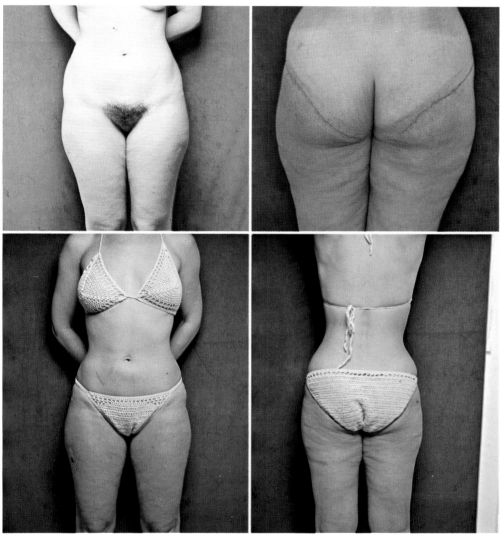

Fig. 8-66

TYPE V: OBESITY

Thigh reduction in the obese patient, because of the amount of resection, usually results in the loss of several units of blood; consequently, it is recommended that the patient donate several units prior to surgery. This surgical procedure is designed to reduce bulk and volume more than to contour. Undermining of the trochanteric area is not recommended in these cases because of the large wedges usually required to reduce the amount of bulk. The incision placement is still in the relatively same high position as that described for types III through VII. Anterior excision such as in type I is frequently recommended for obese patients because of the problem of intertrigo in the crural area (Fig. 8-67). Skin closure, skin advancement, drainage, and dog ear removal is performed in the same way as in the procedures described for types I to IV. Occasionally hip contouring of the upper gluteal area is essential (Figs. 6-63 to 6-66).

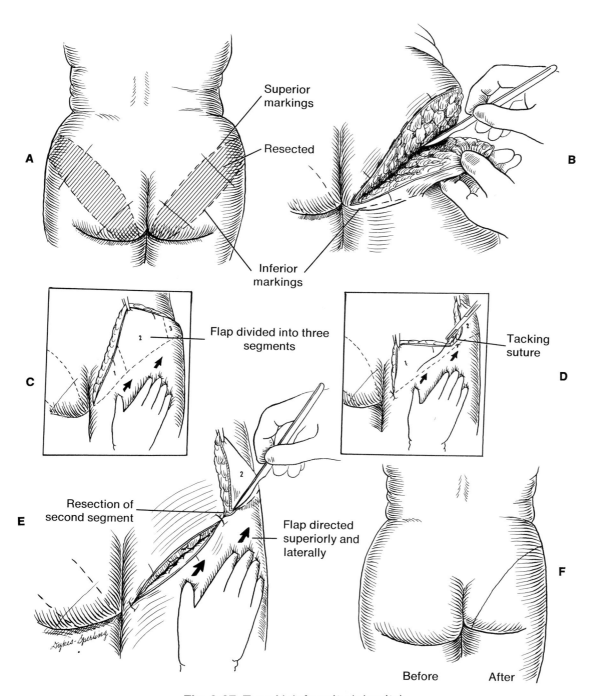

Superior
markings

Resected

Inferior
markings

A

B

C

Flap divided into three
segments

D

Tacking
suture

E

Resection of
second segment

Flap directed
superiorly and
laterally

F

Before   After

Sykes-Sperling

Fig. 8-67. Type V deformity (obesity).

Type V case history

The 41-year-old woman with marked obesity in Fig. 8-68 had had an abdominoplasty (Fig. 6-70, *A*) six months before, which had been complicated by a postoperative pulmonary embolus. Nonetheless, the patient was extremely anxious to have the thighplasty. It was thought that she understood the risks.

After a careful preoperative workup in consultation with the internist who had been managing her anticoagulant therapy after the embolism, it was decided that the thighplasty could be done. Oral anticoagulants were discontinued a week before surgery with subsequent complete coagulation studies. Minidose heparin was begun 3 hours prior to surgery.

Simple wedge excision without undermining of the medial and lateral thighs was performed with a total resection of 3.8 kg of tissue. Total operating time was 4 hours, with a blood loss of 1.2 to 1.8 liters. The patient was ambulated approximately 14 hours postoperatively. While walking approximately 30 hours after surgery, she fainted and fell. Wound dehiscence did not occur, but subsequent wound drainage through the Jackson-Pratt drains was approximately 5 liters during the next several days. The minidose heparin was then discontinued, and the lost blood replaced with 1 liter of whole blood. The patient was discharged fifteen days after surgery. No further sequelae to the fall occurred, and anticoagulation was not reinstituted.

Long-term photographic follow-up is not available.

Critique: As was discussed in Chapter 5, patients with this magnitude of obesity should not be considered for surgery until a significant weight loss has occurred by either diet or bypass surgery.

The motivation exemplified by this patient—that is, the expectation that the surgery would prevent the dissolution of her marriage—was unrealistic; consequently, the surgical results did not meet her needs, although she has been much more comfortable physically since undergoing the surgery. In light of our present understanding of patient motivation, this particular patient should not have undergone surgery. We encouraged her to consider bypass surgery because of her intractable obesity. At the present time, three years after surgery, she states that she weighs 150 pounds (67.5 kg), about 50 pounds (22.5 kg) less than at the time of her surgery.

We have learned from this experience that during first-day ambulation the patient may need a walker and one or two assistants because of the risk of syncope.

For an alternative to this approach, refer to the discussion later in the chapter of secondary thigh contouring in the obese patient, as well as Figs. 6-63 to 6-66.

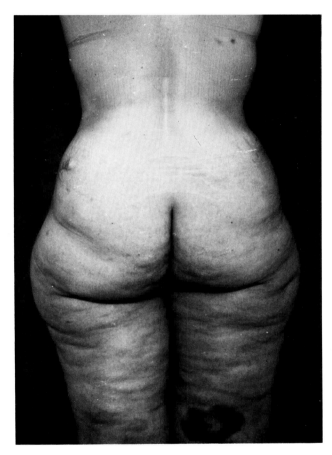

Fig. 8-68

TYPE VI: ASYMMETRY AND TRAUMATIC DEFORMITY

Asymmetry or traumatic deformities of the hip and gluteal area lend themselves to the procedures for deformities of types II through VII. Deformities of the lateral thigh and gluteal area are demonstrated in Fig. 8-69. A combination of techniques may be necessary to assure symmetry.

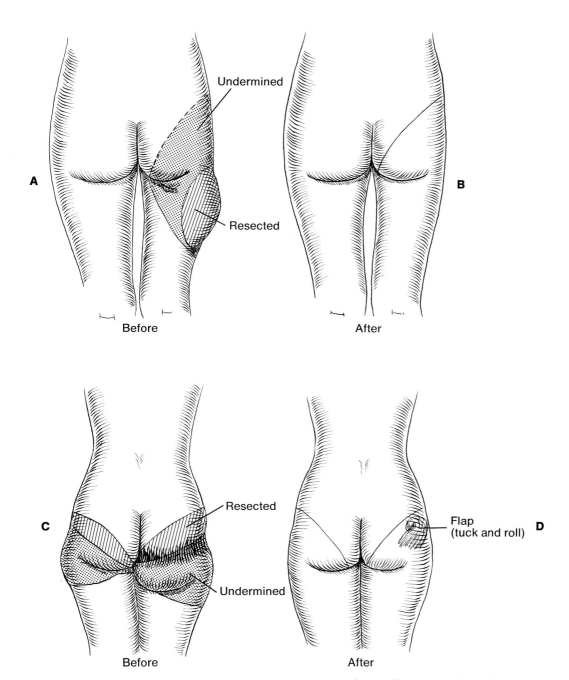

Fig. 8-69. Type VI deformities. **A** and **B,** Asymmetry. **C** and **D,** Traumatic deformity.

Type VI case histories

The 28-year-old woman in Fig. 8-70 sought repair of a riding britches deformity as well as a posttraumatic asymmetry resulting from a hematoma of the right thigh that occurred when she was struck by an automobile a year before.

Initially, bilateral wedge resection was performed high on the buttocks. On the right side 450 g were resected; on the left, 400 g. A curette was used to remove the bulky fat from the lateral deformity area (Fig. 8-71). The patient's traumatic deformity was not completely corrected at the initial surgery. Fig. 8-72 shows the immediate postoperative appearance with the Jackson-Pratt drain in the most dependent portion of the undermined area. At the secondary surgery the drain is inserted through a separate stab wound in contrast to our usual insertion through the suture line.

The first procedure took 3 hours, with a blood loss of less than a unit. The secondary procedure required 1½ hours.

The patient is seen postoperatively in Fig. 8-73.

Critique: The approach used to treat this woman's deformity has become the prototype. This experience provided us with the confidence that wide undermining over the lateral thigh and trochanteric area is possible. This approach has been more successfully used in the two cases that follow.

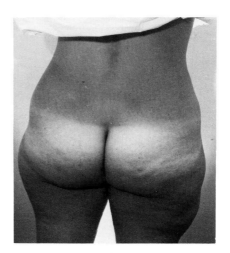

Fig. 8-70

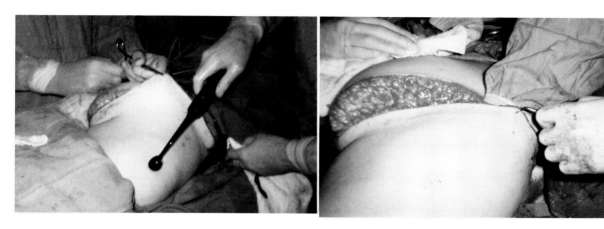

Fig. 8-71

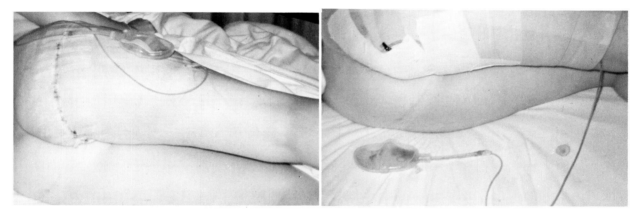

Fig. 8-72

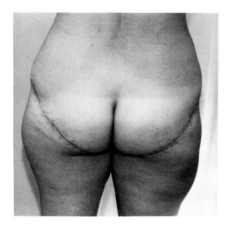

Fig. 8-73

The 23-year-old woman in Fig. 8-74 sustained a crushing injury to her leg while laying a telephone cable two years before seeking surgical repair. The resultant hematoma became organized, leaving the patient with a bulbous deformity of the posterolateral area of the right thigh.

A small wedge excision of buttocks tissue was performed along with deep undermining to expose the deformity, which was then removed by blunt and sharp dissection. The pathological report described the mass as lipomatous in nature. The amount of resection totaled 115 g. Operating time was 1 hour 15 minutes, with minimal blood loss.

The patient's postoperative course was uneventful. Her appearance a month after surgery is shown in Fig. 8-75.

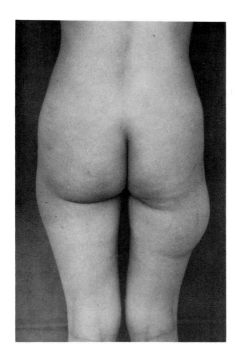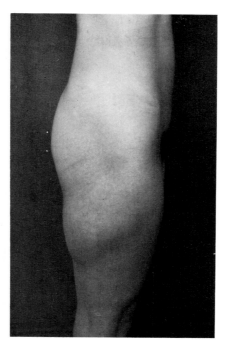

Fig. 8-74

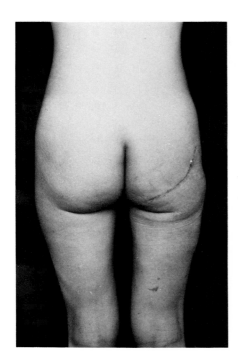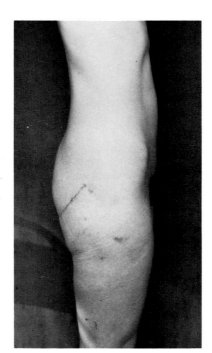

Fig. 8-75

The 39-year-old woman in Fig. 8-76 was injured in an automobile accident twelve years previously, sustaining fractures of the right hip and knee, as well as the pelvis. Numerous surgical procedures, including a total hip replacement, have been required to treat these injuries, which resulted in marked asymmetry and gross trochanteric dystrophy.

Bilateral wedge resection with undermining and removal of trochanteric fat pads was performed, with creation of a new infragluteal fold. A total of 3.2 kg of tissue was removed. The total operating time was 3 hours 15 minutes. Blood loss was approximately 1.5 units, but the blood was not replaced. The postoperative course was uneventful, and the patient left the hospital six days after surgery.

The patient's appearance a month after surgery is demonstrated in Fig. 8-77.

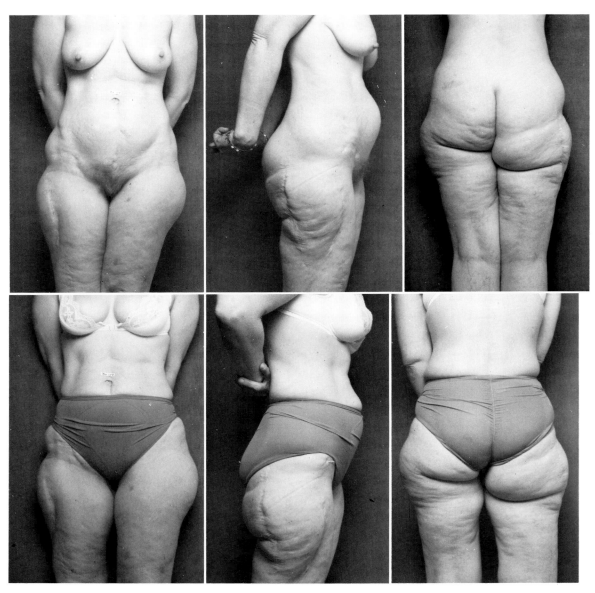

Fig. 8-76

Critique: Because of this patient's many previous surgical procedures in the operative area and the presence of a total hip prosthesis, due consideration was given to the risk of postoperative infection. The orthopedic surgeon was consulted preoperatively. The usual antibiotic coverage with cephalexin monohydrate (Keflex) was carried out.

Although a type II procedure was performed in this case, it is conceivable that in certain asymmetries, a tuck-and-roll thighplasty (types III and IV) might be done on one side, and a wedge resection (type II) with undermining on the other.

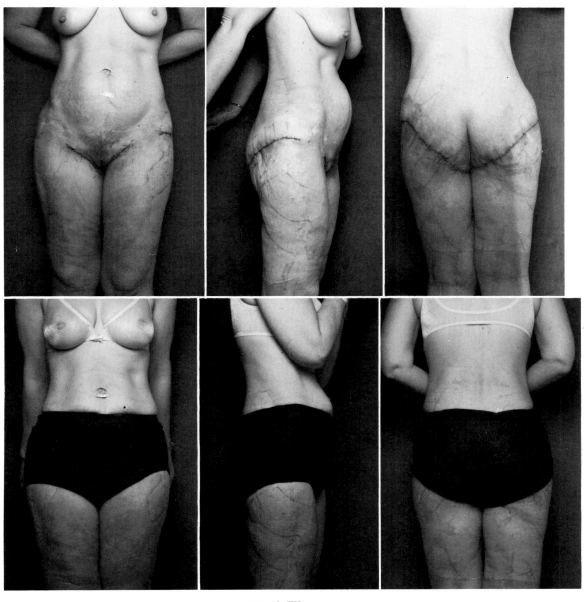

Fig. 8-77

TYPE VII: AGING OR ATROPHY (TUCK AND PLEAT)

With the increase in longevity, the incidence of aging, or atrophic, deformities of the hips and thighs is rising. Occasionally the tuck-and-roll thighplasty may be required for correction of the bulkier deformities with a trochanteric component; however, the majority lend themselves to the following tuck-and-pleat procedure.

Fig. 8-78, *A* and *B,* illustrates the appearance before and after the tuck-and-pleat procedure. The de-epithelialization and undermining is shown in Fig. 8-78, *C* and *D.* The essential mechanism is to reduce the skin envelop and to fill out the contour of the buttocks with existing soft tissue.

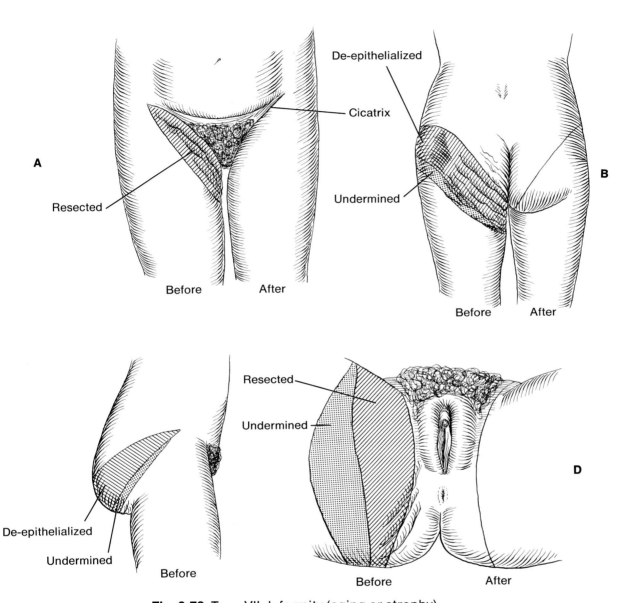

Fig. 8-78. Type VII deformity (aging or atrophy).

The anterior resection, when necessary, is the same as that for cases requiring medial resection in types II to IV, and the posterior procedure is the same up to de-epithelialization (Figs. 8-79 to 8-82).

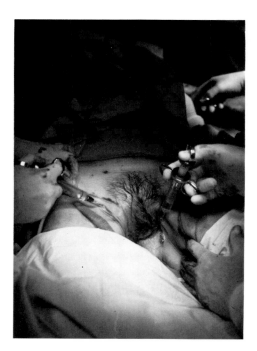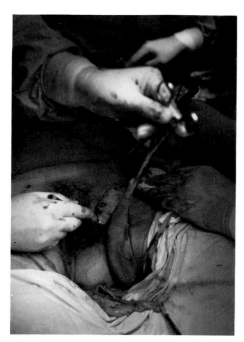

Fig. 8-79

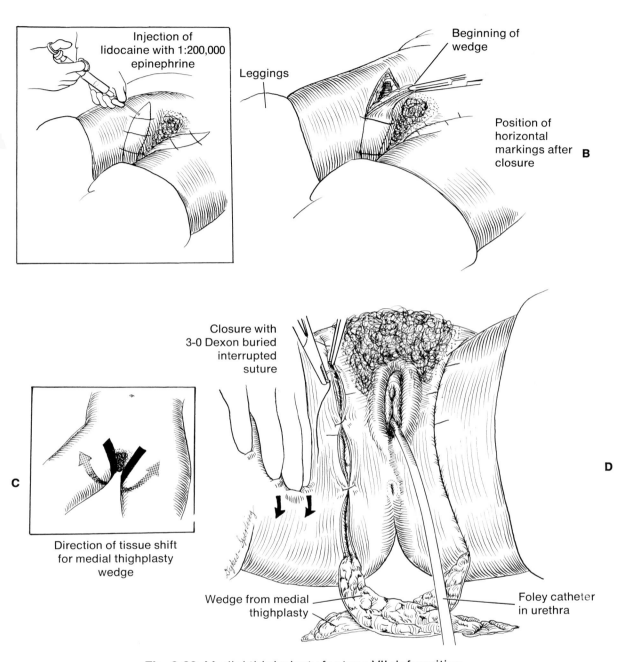

Injection of lidocaine with 1:200,000 epinephrine

Leggings

Beginning of wedge

Position of horizontal markings after closure **B**

Closure with 3-0 Dexon buried interrupted suture

C

Direction of tissue shift for medial thighplasty wedge

Wedge from medial thighplasty

Foley catheter in urethra

D

Fig. 8-80. Medial thighplasty for type VII deformities.

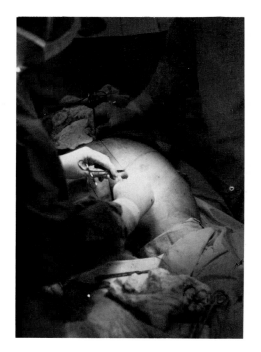
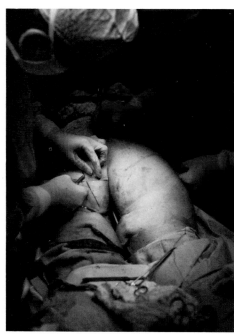
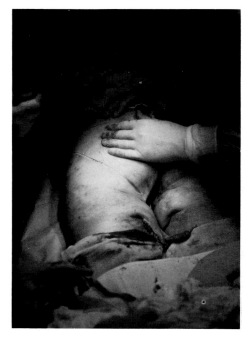
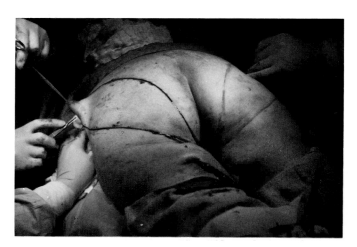

Fig. 8-81

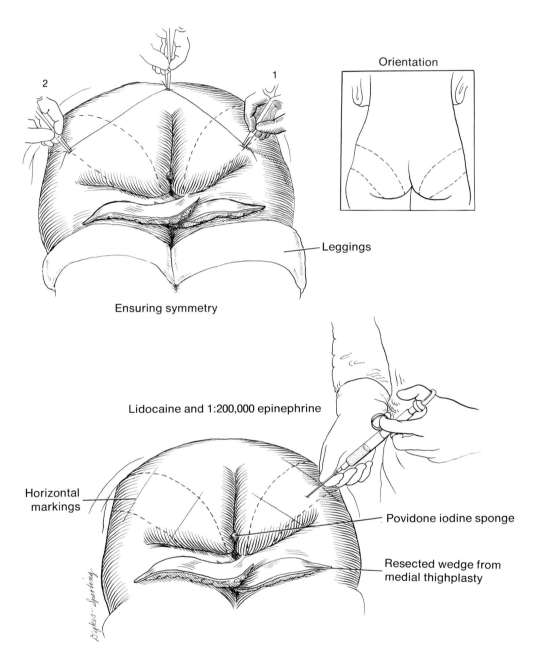

Orientation

2   1

Leggings

Ensuring symmetry

Lidocaine and 1:200,000 epinephrine

Horizontal
markings

Povidone iodine sponge

Resected wedge from
medial thighplasty

Fig. 8-82. Type VII deformities.

After de-epithelialization (Fig. 8-84, *A* and *B*), enough undermining is done at the infragluteal fold area to allow the medial flap tissue and the posterior edge of the posterogluteal thigh area to be shifted anterolaterally (Figs. 8-83 and 8-84, *C* to *F*).

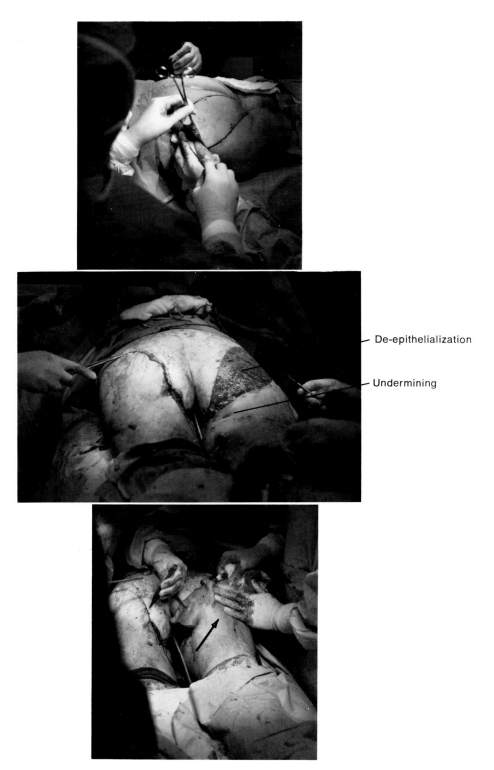

De-epithelialization

Undermining

Fig. 8-83

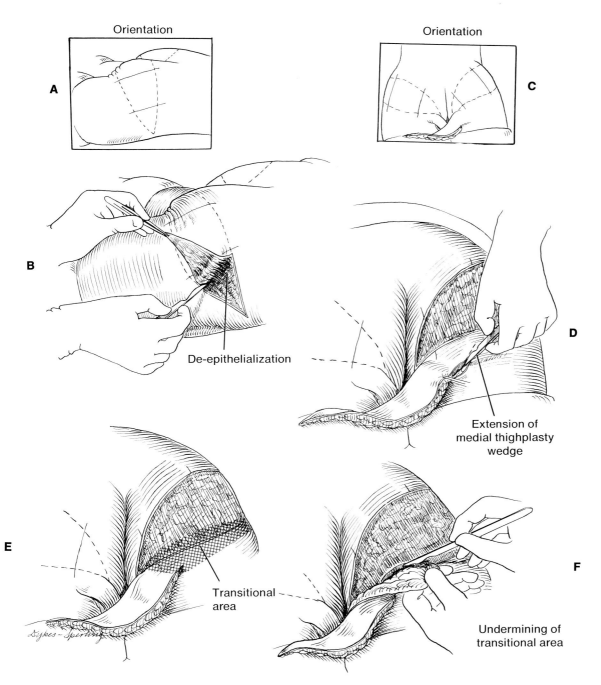

Orientation

A

Orientation

C

B

De-epithelialization

D

Extension of
medial thighplasty
wedge

E

Transitional
area

F

Undermining of
transitional area

Fig. 8-84. Type VII deformities.

After freeing has taken place along the entire inferior segment (Fig. 8-86, *A* and *B*), the anchor suture is placed (Fig. 8-86, *C*) with the medial-to-lateral advancement. The soft tissue is folded on itself and pleated with interrupted 0 chromic catgut sutures (Figs. 8-85 and 8-86, *D* and *E*).

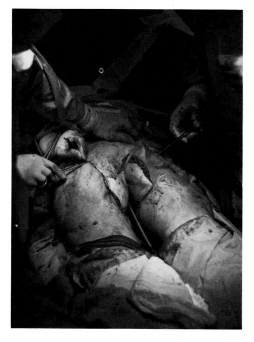 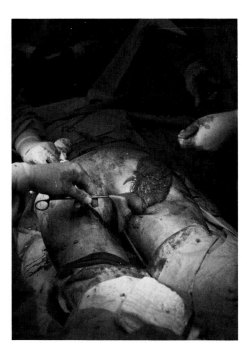

Fig. 8-85

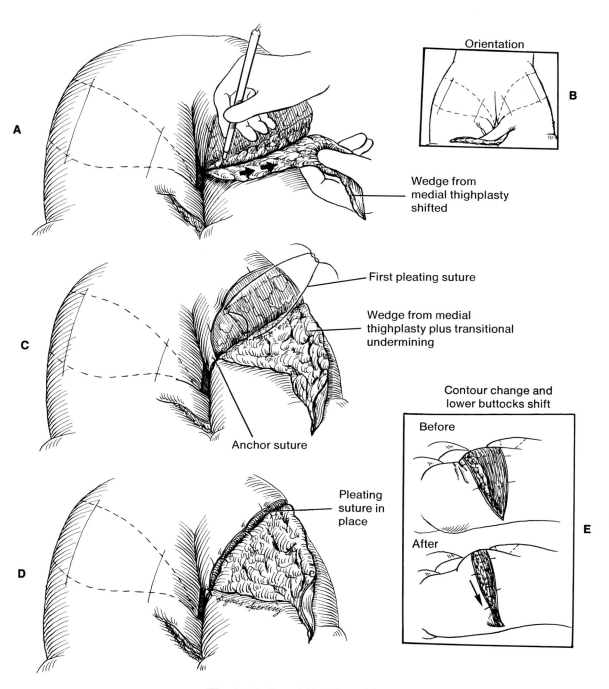

Orientation

B

Wedge from
medial thighplasty
shifted

First pleating suture

Wedge from medial
thighplasty plus transitional
undermining

Anchor suture

Pleating
suture in
place

Contour change and
lower buttocks shift

Before

After

E

Fig. 8-86. Type VII deformities.

The relaxed soft tissue is forced into a tighter configuration by skin closure (Fig. 8-87), which is accomplished with multiple 4-0 Dexon intercuticular sutures, followed by a running 4-0 nylon suture. As the tissue is folded, refer to Fig. 8-85, *B;* the portion of the medial thighplasty segment is resected (Fig. 8-89, *A* to *C*), and the dog ears are removed laterally in a downward direction similar to the procedure described for types II to IV (Figs. 8-88 and 8-89, *D* to *F*).

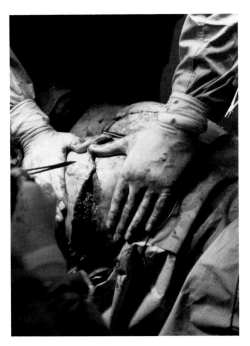

Fig. 8-87

Fig. 8-88

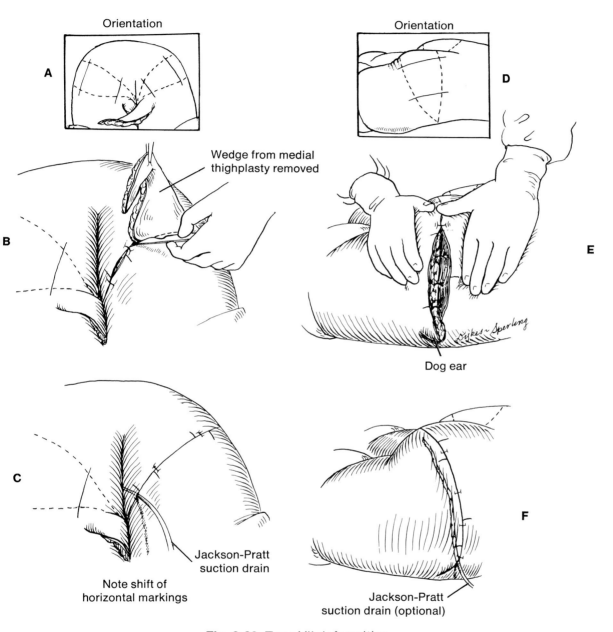

Orientation

A

B

Wedge from medial
thighplasty removed

C

Note shift of
horizontal markings

Jackson-Pratt
suction drain

Orientation

D

E

Dog ear

F

Jackson-Pratt
suction drain (optional)

Fig. 8-89. Type VII deformities.

333

Two Jackson-Pratt drains are used on each side, one in the medial segment and one in the lateral segment. The dressing is similar to that for types II through VI: 1-inch Steri-Strip tapes followed by gauze fluffs and an Elastoplast dressing held in place with two 6-inch Ace wraps beginning from the thighs and wrapping superiorly (Fig. 8-90).

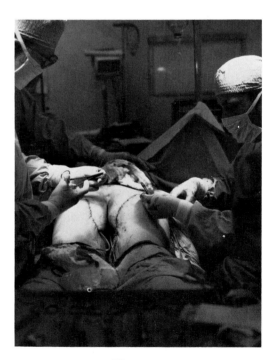

Fig. 8-90

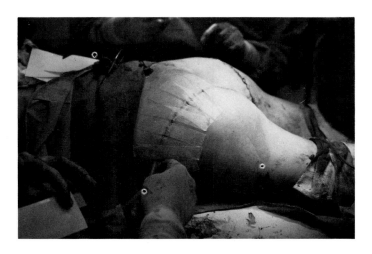

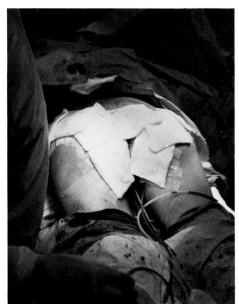
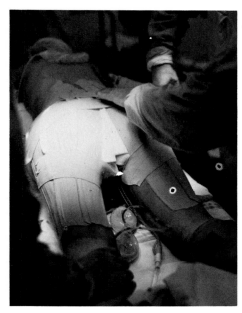

Fig. 8-90, cont'd

Type VII case history

Fig. 8-91 shows a 57-year-old woman who complained of an unattractive appearance caused by loss of muscle tone and subcutaneous tissue in upper arms and thighs. The patient had experienced a pronounced weight loss following a vagotomy and pyloroplasty ten years before. This contributed to her aged appearance, as did the skin damage from lifelong prolonged sun exposure. Brachioplasty, tuck-and-pleat thighplasty, and secondary meloplasty were done as a combined procedure, the order of which is outlined in Chapter 6. Figs. 8-92 and 8-93 show the patient a month postoperatively.

Critique: This patient was well motivated and responded well emotionally and physically. The only disappointment to the patient was lack of improvement in the contouring around her knees. At this time, her surgeon does not believe an isolated procedure in the knee area is safe.

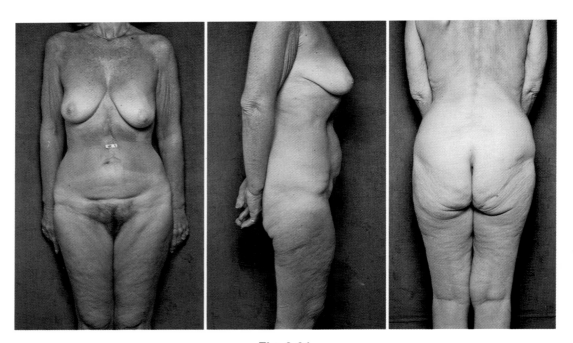

Fig. 8-91

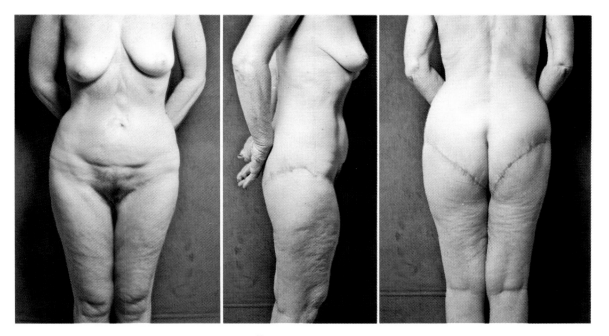

Fig. 8-92

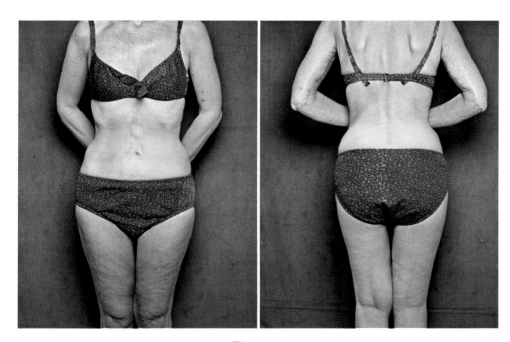

Fig. 8-93

IMMEDIATE POSTOPERATIVE CARE

At the completion of the operative procedure for deformities of types II through VII, the patient remains in the prone position, the Nelson bed (Fig. 8-94) is brought into the operating room, and, while the patient is still intubated, she is rolled from the operating table to the Nelson bed; at this point the anesthesiologist extubates the patient in the supine position. The patient is taken to the recovery room for observation. If the patient's vital signs are stable, it is often helpful to tilt her in the bed several times and encourage her to cough and breathe deeply. It is not unusual for patients to have some degree of hypotension after this surgery. Blood loss is always greater than was estimated. Circulation of the legs should be monitored frequently by checking peripheral pulses, color, and warmth of toes. The Jackson-Pratt bulb drains are checked and emptied every 4 hours or when they become half full; if drainage is excessive, wall suction may be used. The amount of drainage may be variable. The surgeon should be notified if the drainage is greater than 50 ml/hour. The amount of pain these patients experience is quite variable. We recommend the administration of 25 to 50 mg of meperidine (Demerol) every 2 to 3 hours as necessary. Antibiotics are routinely administered for five days after surgery.

It is important to change the patient's position from the supine to the prone several times during the first 24 hours to prevent tissue necrosis.

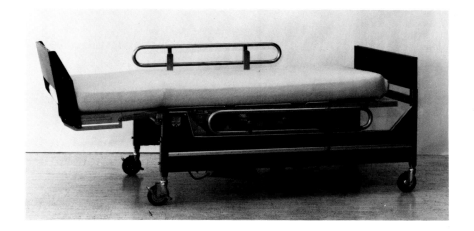

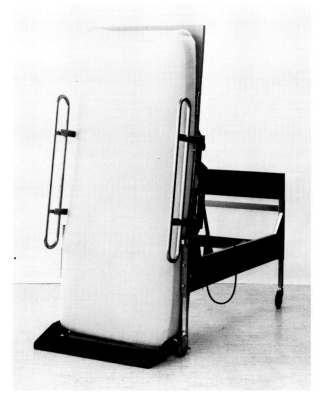

Fig. 8-94

Ambulation

Patients are not always able to stand at first, and they frequently have problems with dizziness, nausea, and fear. The patient must be secured to the bed with straps to prevent falling (Fig. 8-95, *A*). On the first postoperative day the patient is tilted to the 45-degree angle in the Nelson bed; if no evidence of syncope occurs, the patient is placed in the erect position (Fig. 8-95, *B*). If the patient tolerates standing, a wheeled walker is used for the first few steps off the bed and back again (Fig. 8-95, *C*). The patient is encouraged to take short, shuffling steps for the first couple of days (Fig. 8-95, *D*). As she becomes more stable on her feet, she can be weaned from the walker and ambulate with or without assistive devices. Once safely ambulating, usually on the third or fourth day, the patient is taught to enter and exit a regular bed. The simplest way for the patient to exit the bed is to move her body to the edge of the bed. Since the problem of flexion exists not with the knees but with the hips, the patient can place her foot nearest the edge of the bed to the floor and, by using her arms behind her, can halfway roll out of bed onto the floor with both feet without flexing the hips. The catheter is removed two or three days after surgery. An additional aid to urination, which was developed as the result of improvements in the aerospace industry and is called a "Jillsjohn" (Fig. 8-95, *E*), is used by males or females while flying in small planes. It is very helpful for voiding in the standing position.

The drains are usually removed four or five days postoperatively. Frequently, however, a moderate amount of serous drainage occurs, and the drains should remain in place longer. We believe that the drains may be safely removed when drainage is less than 30 ml/24 hours. The patient may shower after the dressings and drains are removed. Sutures are not removed for at least ten to twelve days after surgery and then selectively, depending on the appearance of the incision. The wound is reinforced with tincture of benzoin and 1-inch Steri-Strips. Approximately ten to twelve days after surgery, the patient may begin to sit halfway with the Ace bandage or other suitable support such as a well-fitting long-leg girdle that does not cut or bind the incision line, provided the wounds are healing well.

The first few postoperative weeks are often trying for the patient, who is uncomfortable and unable to sit normally. Once the large dressing has been removed and she can see the resultant change in the thigh and hip contour, the patient obtains some encouragement; however, some residual bruising and edema usually occurs. Friends, relatives, and husbands are helpful during this period and need encouragement and suggestions on managing home activities such as dressing changes and helping the patient in and out of the shower or bathtub.

The patient should be encouraged to resume activities gradually. Most patients are surprised at the fatigue they feel after surgery. All postoperative activity is discussed with the patient before surgery. The discussion needs to be reinforced the first few weeks after surgery when the patient begins to feel discouraged by the fatigue or to feel guilty about not being able to carry out all usual household or social activities. She may need the permission and encouragement of the surgeon to let others help her with essential tasks such as housework. Contrary to most teachings, after the first month or two we encourage sunshine on our suture lines. We also recommend swimming as soon as the patient feels comfortable. Scar revisions, which are usually done six months to a year after surgery as a local outpatient procedure, are frequent, as one would suspect.

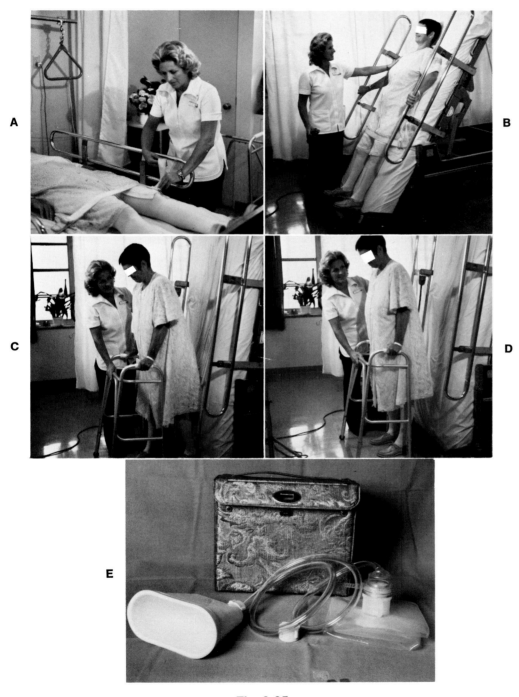

Fig. 8-95

PERSPECTIVE ON THIGHPLASTIES

A review of the literature leads one to believe that hip and thigh contour surgery is performed much less frequently than is abdominoplasty. There certainly must be a reason for this; as we stress in the sections on patient selection and informed consent earlier in this chapter, the possibility of complications is great. Pitanguy has said that undermining over the hip and thigh area should be avoided.[17] In our experience, greater complications have occurred with extensive undermining of the tissues, resulting in tissue loss and fat necrosis. In addition, we have had more blood loss than we anticipated, confirming Hoffman and Simon's[11] observations.

If the surgeon and the patient are prepared to accept the risks, this surgery is justified, provided the surgeon is well founded in the fundamentals of soft tissue surgery. The following case represents a disaster resulting from an office procedure by an untrained surgeon.

The patient, 32 years of age, developed sepsis and necrosis of all the flaps, which was not discovered until five days after surgery. The patient was returned to the office surgery for debridement and kept there for five days. The photographs in Fig. 8-96 were taken at the patient's home by her friend approximately ten days after the disaster.

The patient was seen in consultation with Dr. Robert Miner of Santa Ana, California, at our recommendation. Fig. 8-97 shows the patient four months after the disaster with large areas of granulation tissue. The patient had severe abduction contractures, making it impossible to have sexual intercourse. (The photographs were taken prior to skin grafting.)

We hope that the preceding tragedy will serve as a warning to untrained surgeons who want to do these procedures and to those who are trained and are performing this type of surgery to tread lightly.[4]

Fortunately, secondary surgery often improves the contour (in addition to improving the scar). We are endeavoring to use some of the techniques that we have found useful in abdominoplasty to reduce our complications in thighplasty, including the use of intravenously injected fluorescein and the use of transcutaneous noninvasive monitoring of the Po_2 of the flap.[12]

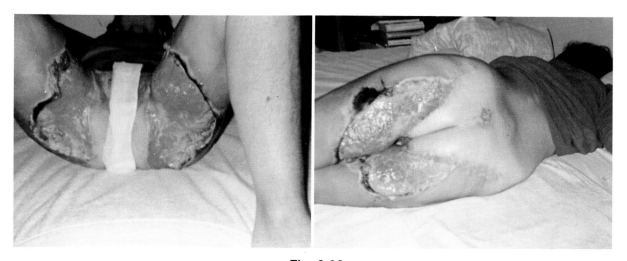

Fig. 8-96

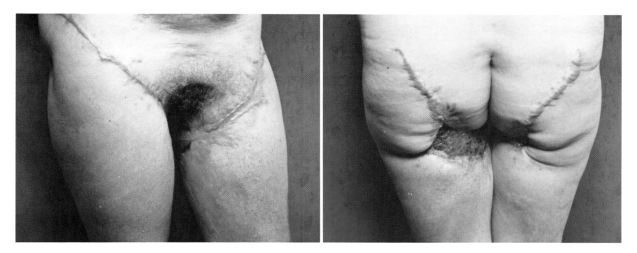

Fig. 8-97

The 54-year-old woman in Fig. 8-98 sought surgical correction of her increasing deformity of hollow upper thighs and marked trochanteric fullness (type III).

A tuck-and-roll thighplasty was performed, with a resection of 530 g of tissue on the left side and 570 g on the right side. The operating time was 4 hours, with a blood loss of 1.2 liters, which was replaced with 2 liters of Ringer's lactated solution.

Four days after surgery, the patient's amount of hemoglobin had decreased to 6.9 g, necessitating whole blood replacement. A urinary tract infection occurred after removal of the urinary catheter. The patient was discharged from the hospital six days after surgery. Thirteen days postoperatively, 175 ml of serous fluid were aspirated from under the left posterior flap. The wounds appeared to be healing without incident until three weeks later, when several small areas of skin and fat necrosis appeared on both sides (Fig. 8-99). Treatment included local debridement and daily use of a whirlpool and administration of povidone-iodine complex and antibiotics. Over the next five months gradual contracture occurred in the size of the defect on the left side, whereas the defect on the right healed completely.

Secondary surgery was required to correct the residual deformity on the left side. The patient is shown after this surgery in Fig. 8-100.

Critique: The correct operation was selected for the patient in light of the improved contour evident after surgery. In our earlier series, patients were allowed to remain in the supine position without occurrence of necrosis. However, with the gradual increase in the amount of undermining in the posterior thigh area, the patient should be turned to the prone position frequently to decrease pressure on the posterior flap.

The drains should be left for three to five days in patients who have extensive undermining rather than for the 48 hours previously recommended.

Blood should be promptly replaced in any patient who loses more than 2 units, since it is possible that a decreased level of hemoglobin may be a contributing factor to localized tissue loss. If the patient has blood available for autotransfusion, the surgeon will be less hesitant to order blood replacement because of the minimal risk of reaction and hepatitis.

The use of fluorescein monitoring and percutaneous Po_2 monitoring may be helpful in predicting potential compromised circulation to skin flaps.[12] The use of a hyperbaric chamber should be considered (Fig. 6-95). The high placement of the gluteal incisions gives the surgeon more latitude than would a lower position. Also, the prolonged healing required was better tolerated by this patient, since she could still wear a bathing suit.

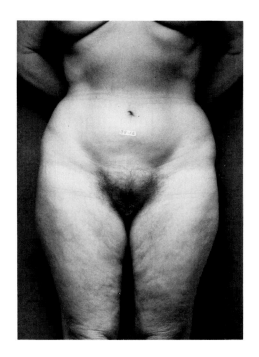

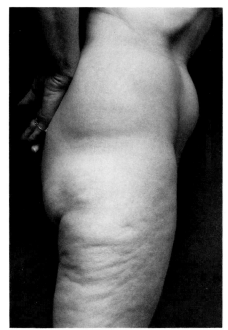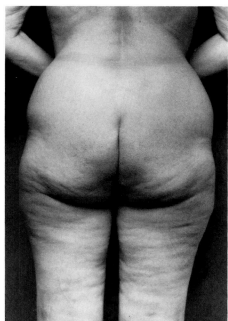

Fig. 8-98

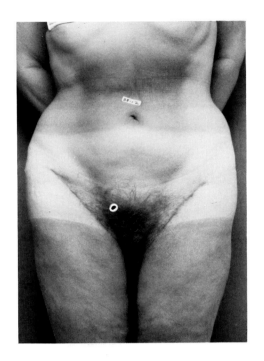

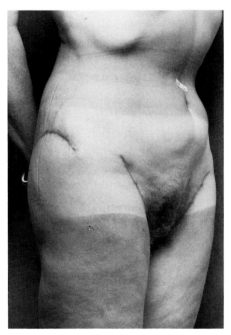 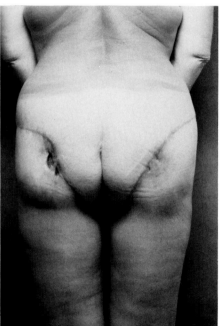

Fig. 8-99

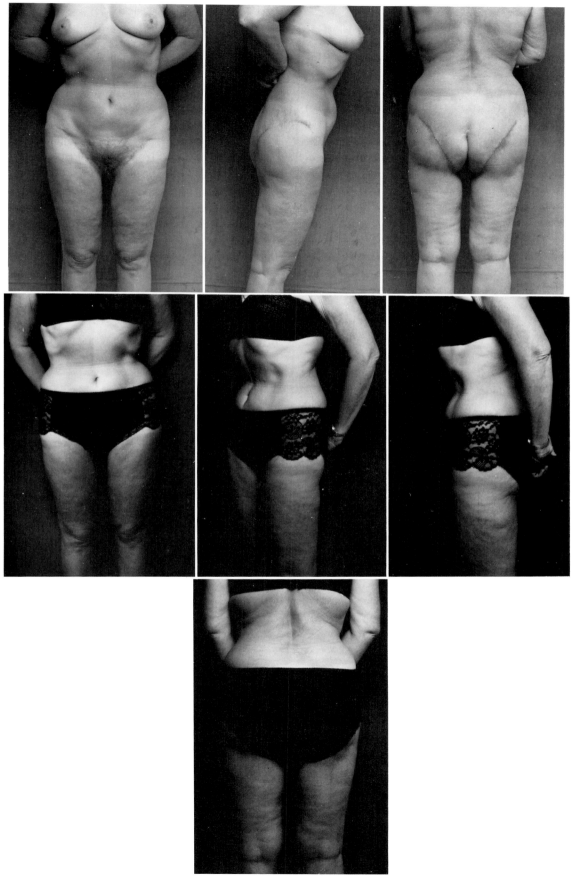

Fig. 8-100

The 36-year-old woman in Fig. 8-101 sought surgical correction of trochanteric deformity. The asymmetry between the right and left thighs resulted from an earlier hip injury.

The tuck-and-roll thighplasty was performed, with resection of approximately 500 g of tissue on each side. The operating time was 4 hours. The blood loss of 1 liter was not replaced. The patient was discharged five days after surgery. On the eleventh postoperative day she required the aspiration of 200 ml of serous drainage from under the left posterior flap. No further complications occurred in the patient's postoperative course. Fig. 8-102 shows the patient's appearance three months after surgery; Fig. 8-103, a year postoperatively.

Critique: As can be seen in Fig. 8-102, the patient still has a slight asymmetry, which should be corrected by a secondary surgery. In more recent cases, we have been able to prevent this asymmetry by more aggressive removal of the trochanteric fat pad. This operation does not correct the problem of bulging of the hip tissue above the top of the bikini (Fig. 8-103), which can be corrected as shown in the next case.

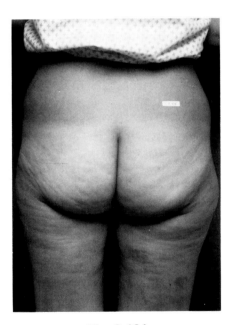

Fig. 8-101

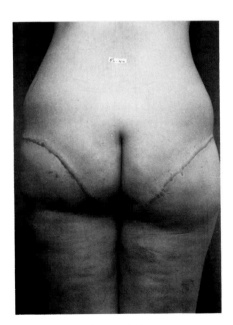

Fig. 8-102

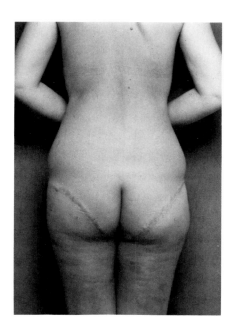

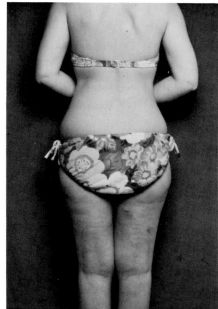 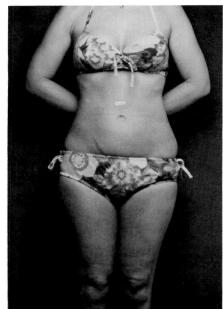

Fig. 8-103

The 56-year-old woman in Fig. 8-104 was in good health but concerned about "sagging all over." A tuck-and-roll thighplasty was performed, as well as a meloplasty and blepharoplasty. A total of 535 g of tissue was removed during the thighplasty. The total operating time was 5 hours 45 minutes. The estimated amount of blood loss was 750 ml. Discharged seven days after surgery, the patient had an uneventful postoperative course. A year later, when the patient sought additional body contouring, a combined procedure of brachioplasty, abdominoplasty, and additional contouring of the thigh areas was done (see Chapter 9 for discussion of the brachioplasty results).

A year after the thighplasty, the patient's hip contour is significantly improved in the anterior view (Fig. 8-105, *A*); a moderate supratrochanteric recess highlights the upper hip bulge (Fig. 8-105, *B*). As can be seen in Fig. 8-105, *C* additional contouring of the hip with removal of the bulge and recess was possible by extending the lateral aspects of the abdominoplasty incisions.

Figs. 8-106 and 8-107 show the patient's appearance a year after brachioplasty, abdominoplasty, and upper thighplasty.

Critique: Multiple combined operative procedures must come under careful scrutiny. Excellent health and motivation are the two major considerations in selecting a patient for a combined procedure. We believe that this careful preoperative evaluation has reduced postoperative problems among our patients.

As illustrated in the film, *The New Image,*[10] techniques such as preparing and draping the patient at the same time and using two surgical assistants allows for independent surgical activity at more than one site at a time, thus reducing the total operating time. For example, the second assistant surgeon follows behind the surgeon and does all fine suturing while the surgeon and first assistant proceed with the next phase.

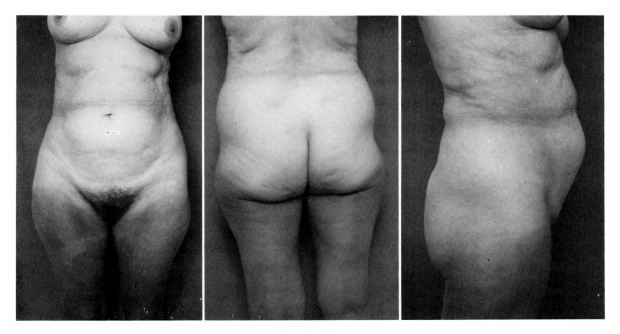

Fig. 8-104

A   B   C

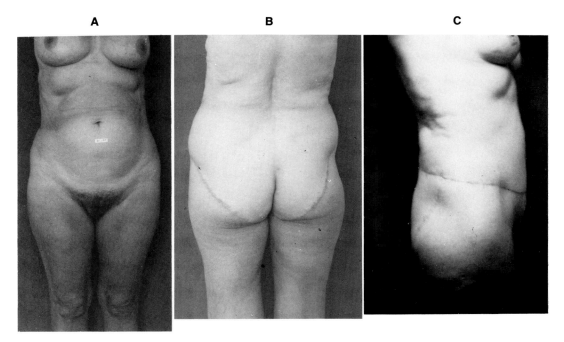

Fig. 8-105

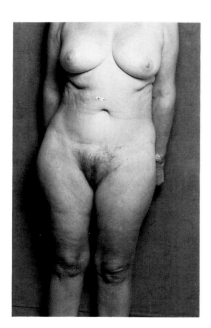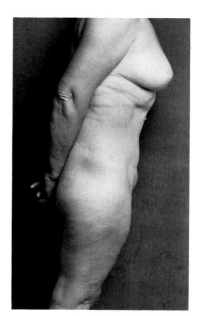

Fig. 8-106

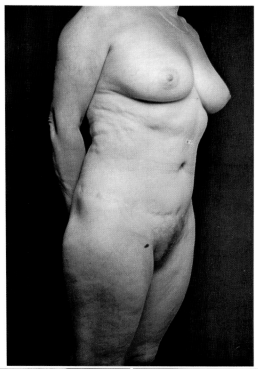

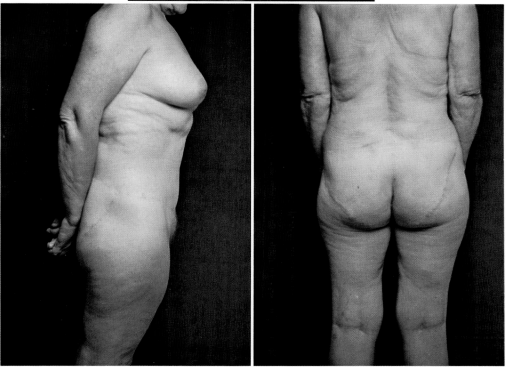

Fig. 8-107

A wedge excision with undermining and removal of the trochanteric fat pad was performed for the 36-year-old woman in Fig. 8-108 (type II). Approximately 1 kg of tissue was removed from each side. The operating time was 3 hours 15 minutes, with an estimated blood loss of 750 to 1,000 ml. Two days after surgery the patient received a unit of whole blood.

On the eighth postoperative day, an area of necrosis was evident along the suture line on the inferior portion of the right flap (Fig. 8-109). The patient was returned to the operating room on the thirteenth postoperative day, and an excision of the necrotic area with a bolster surgical closure was carried out. The pathological report showed a ruptured epidermal cyst. Bacteriological cultures grew out only a few beta-hemolytic streptococci. The patient was then placed on a regimen of clindamycin (Cleocin) for ten days and started on daily whirlpools on the fourth postoperative day. Slow healing by secondary intention occurred (Fig. 8-110). This patient required multiple aspirations of the left thigh for effusion. Administration of 60 ml of hypertonic saline into the effusion site decreased the rate of collection.

The patient is shown in Fig. 8-111 after complete healing.

Critique: Extensive preoperative evaluation of scar history and discussion of possible keloid formation was included in the informed consent for this patient.

As shown by the extent of her "cellulite" deformity, extensive undermining was required and probably contributed to the necrosis. In retrospect the use of fluorescein might have alerted us to the possibility of compromised circulation to the flap, although no evidence of this problem occurred until eight days postoperatively. As previously mentioned, frequent turning to a prone position might decrease the threat of diminished circulation caused by positional pressure.

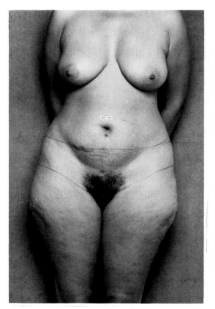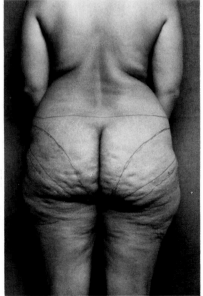

Fig. 8-108

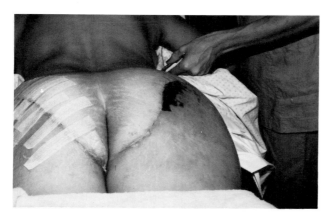

Fig. 8-109

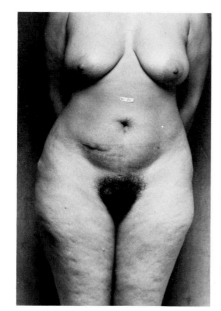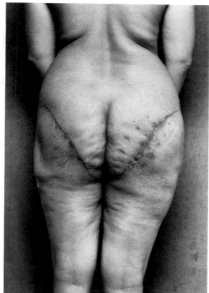

Fig. 8-110

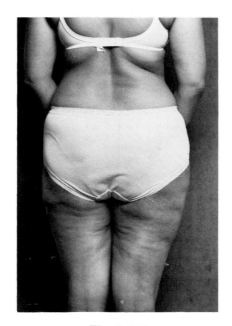

Fig. 8-111

REFERENCES

1. Baroudi, R.: Dermatolipectomy of the upper arm, Clin. Plast. Surg. **2**:485, 1975.
2. Bunnell, S.: Surgery of the hand, ed. 4, Philadelphia, 1964, J. B. Lippincott Co.
3. Clarkson, P.: Lipodystrophies, Plast. Reconstr. Surg. **37**:499, 1966.
4. Courtiss, E. H., editor: Aesthetic surgery: trouble—how to avoid it and how to treat it, St. Louis, 1978, The C. V. Mosby Co.
5. Davis, J.: Personal communication. Lipectomías, course 5B, Second Iberian Plastic Surgical Congress, Guadalajara, Oct., 1978, Centro de la Amistad Internacional de Guadalajara.
6. Delerm, A., and Cirotteau, Y.: Plastie cruro-fémoro-fessière ou circum fessière, Ann. Chir. Plast. **18**:31, 1973.
7. Farina, R., Baroudi, R., Golcman, B., and Castro, O. de: Riding-trousers-like type of pelvicrural lipodystrophy (trochanteric lipomatosis), Br. J. Plast. Surg. **13**:174; [Lipodistrofia pelvi-trocantérica tipo calca de montaría (lipomatose trocantérica)], Hospital (Rio de J.) **57**:717, 1960.
8. Gorney, M.: Psychiatric and medical-legal implications of rhinoplasty, mentoplasty, and otoplasty. In Masters, F. W., and Lewis, J. R., Jr., editors: Symposium on aesthetic surgery of the nose, ears, and chin, vol. 6, St. Louis, 1973, The C. V. Mosby Co.
9. Grazer, F. M.: Tuck and roll, thighplasty, film, Sept., 1976, presented to the American Society for Aesthetic Plastic Surgery, San Francisco, Oct., 1977.
10. Grazer, F. M.: The new image, film presented to the meeting of the American Society of Plastic and Reconstructive Surgeons, Oct., 1977.
11. Hoffman, S., and Simon, B. E.: Experiences with the Pitanguy method of correction of trochanteric lipodystrophy, Plast. Reconstr. Surg. **55**:551, 1975.
12. Huch, A., and Huch, R.: Transcutaneous noninvasive monitoring of pO_2, Hosp. Prac. **11**:43, June, 1976.
13. Lewis, J. R., Jr.: The thigh lift, J. Int. Coll. Surg. **27**:330, 1957.
14. Lewis, J. R.: Correction of ptosis of the thighs: the thigh lift, Plast. Reconstr. Surg. **37**:494, 1966.
15. Lewis, J. R.: Correction of redundancies of the arm: the arm lift. In Body contouring, J. South. Med. Assoc. (in press).
16. McGregor, I. A., and Morgan, G.: Axial and random pattern flaps, Br. J. Plast. Surg. **26**:202, 1973.
17. Pitanguy, I.: Trochanteric lipodystrophy, Plast. Reconstr. Surg. **34**:280, 1964.
18. Pitanguy, I.: Surgical reduction of the abdomen, thigh, and buttocks, Surg. Clin. North Am. **51**:479, 1971.
19. Pitanguy, I.: Correction of lipodystrophy of the lateral thoracic aspect and inner side of the arm and elbow dermosenescence, Clin. Plast. Surg. **2**:477; [Correção lipodistrofia da região lateral do torax, face interna do braço e da dermossenescência do cotovelo], Rev. Bras. Cirurg. **65**:277, 1975.
20. Planas, J.: The "crural meloplasty" for lifting of the thighs, Clin. Plast. Surg. **2**:495, 1975.
21. Schörcher, F.: Kosmetische Operationen, Munich, 1955, J. F. Lehmanns Verlag.
22. Vilain, R.: Some considerations in surgical alteration of the feminine silhouette, Clin. Plast. Surg. **2**:499, 1975.

CHAPTER 9

Brachioplasty

The female arm has been an object of beauty throughout the ages. Although exposure of the arms is accepted in everyday life now, women usually cover up the defect with long sleeves when shapelessness and flacidity occur. Recently, with more emphasis on body surgery, patients are seeking plastic surgical consultation with regard to brachioplasty.[1,2,4,5] (For the history of dermolipectomy of the upper extremities, see pp. 238 to 244.)

PATIENT SELECTION

The patient who seeks correction of changes caused by aging, weight loss, or wrinkling is a good candidate for arm contouring, whereas an obese patient is a poor candidate. It is important to ascertain through a thorough medical history such disorders as Raynaud's disease or other problems that might be related to circulatory defects, as well as any scar potential.

INFORMED CONSENT

The patient should be made aware of the permanent surgical scar deformities, the possible problem of hypertrophic scarring, and the possibility of contracture in the axilla. We prefer to show the patient photographs of acceptable as well as unacceptable results as a means of assisting the patient to develop a realistic outlook.[3] Marking of the proposed incision lines on the patient while she is standing with the arm at a 90-degree angle and the shoulder slightly abducted will allow the patient to see the ultimate position of the scar (Fig. 9-1). Fig. 9-2 illustrates improper placement of an incision.

PREPARATION

We ask our patients to begin showering with pHisoHex several days prior to surgery; the actual skin preparation and shaving is not done until the day of surgery to prevent nicks in the skin that might occur. The anesthesiologist prescribes the preoperative medications; however, the patient is routinely given preoperative antibiotics of the broad-spectrum variety. Our preference is cephalexin if the patient is not allergic to this drug.

PREOPERATIVE CARE AND EDUCATION

Like all surgical patients, those undergoing a brachioplasty need careful orientation to the hospital environment and to preoperative and postoperative care. (Brachioplasty is also feasible as an outpatient procedure in selective cases.) Specific preoperative instructions should include the coughing and deep-breathing exercises, since many of these patients are elderly and more prone to respiratory complications, as well as the postoperative restrictions on moving arms and hands, which may interfere with personal hygiene and self-feeding.

Since brachioplasty can be performed with moderate rapidity, it is frequently combined with other aesthetic procedures (Chapter 6). Specific instructions must include the limitations that the combined procedures may provoke.

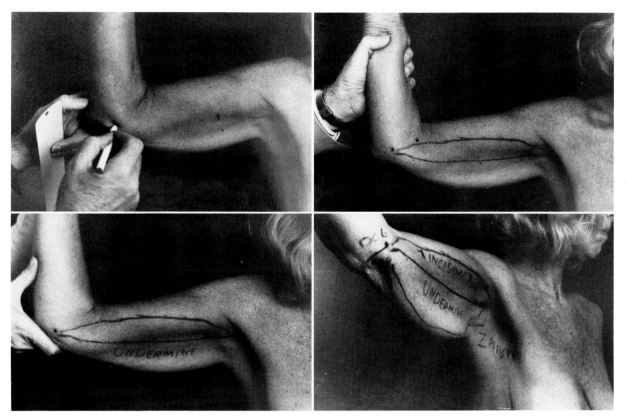

Fig. 9-1

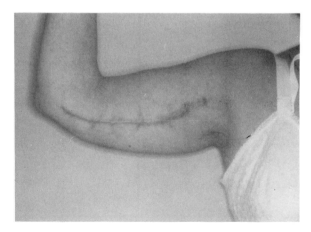

Fig. 9-2

SURGICAL TECHNIQUE
Key to marking

The major landmark for patients undergoing brachioplasty is the medial epicondyle, from which a line roughly parallels the upper surface of the arm and extends to the center of the axilla. This line is the desired location of the postsurgical scar, since it is the most inconspicuous position. To determine the final resting place of the incision line, a curvilinear incision is made from the medial epicondyle to the central point of the axilla. The height of the curvilinear incision can be accurately estimated by placing a finger on the medial aspect of the arm and rotating the skin and soft tissue down to the imaginary line (Fig. 9-3).

Transverse parallel lines marked across the two incision lines (Fig. 9-4) will aid in accurate alignment of the new suture line and prevent shifting of the normal relationships in the arm (Fig. 9-5).

Fig. 9-3

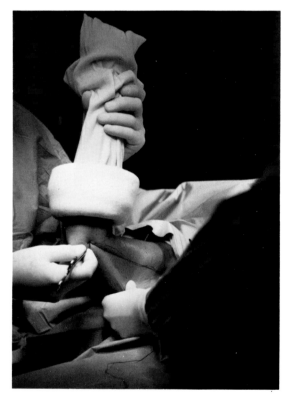

Fig. 9-4

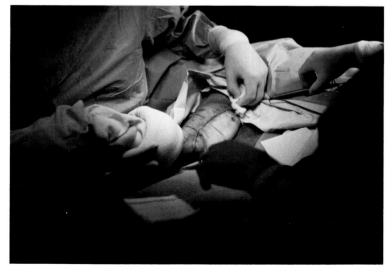

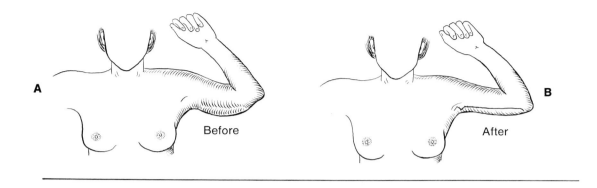

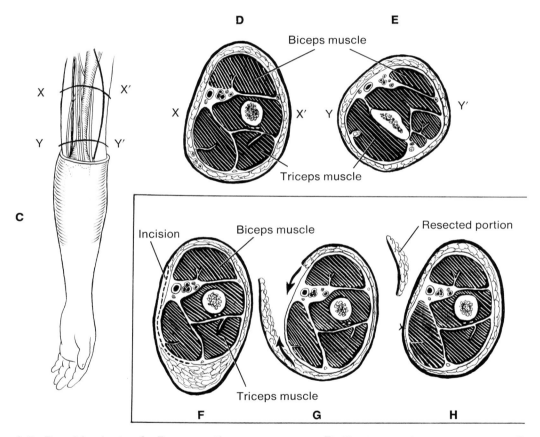

Fig. 9-5. Brachioplasty. **A,** Preoperative appearance. **B,** Postoperative appearance. **C,** Anatomical view of upper arm. **D** to **H,** Cross-sectional view. **F,** Incision. **G,** Traction of the upper and lower segments. **H,** Resected portion is discarded, and segments are sutured in place.

Incision

The patient is positioned with twin armboards. Sterile Stockinette dressings are applied after povidone-iodine preparation and skin marking (Fig. 9-6, *B*). We prefer this technique as opposed to the suspension of the arms above the patient, as described by Guerrero-Santos.[2] The intravenous tubing can be led out through a small opening in the Stockinette dressings, thus eliminating the necessity for running the tubing into the patient's leg. The marking is described with a vertical parallel line splitting up the segmental areas into smaller segments.[1,2] This allows accurate alignment of the new suture line and prevents shifting of the normal relationship of the arm.

The incision is made down through the subcutaneous fat to the bicipital groove (Fig. 9-6, *A*). Care must be taken not to injure the medial brachial cutaneous, the accessory, and branches of the second and third intercostal nerves that all traverse the operative field[2] (Chapter 3). The flap is developed inferiorly in the direction of the triceps muscle (Fig. 9-6, *C*).

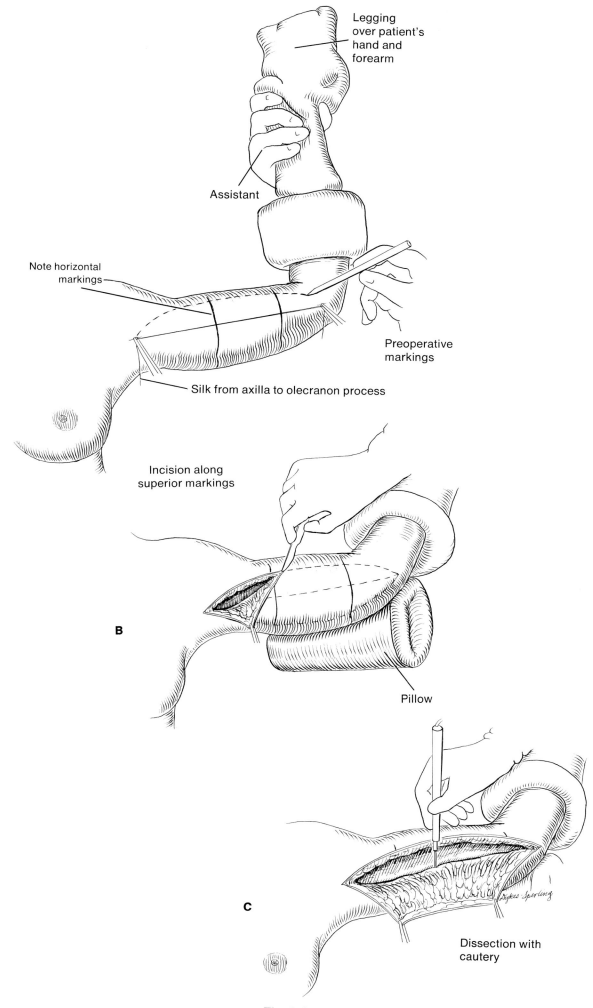

A

Legging over patient's hand and forearm

Assistant

Note horizontal markings

Preoperative markings

Silk from axilla to olecranon process

B

Incision along superior markings

Pillow

C

Dissection with cautery

Fig. 9-6

Resection

Undermining is performed only where the tissue is going to be removed (Fig. 9-8, *A*). After adequate hemostasis has been achieved and the flap has been developed, the assistant places several Kocher clamps to elevate the tissue superiorly (Figs. 9-5, *F* to *H*, 9-7, and 9-8). The vertical incisions are made with adjustment of the tension on the suture lines, allowing for final placement of the incision line as determined preoperatively (Fig. 9-8, *C*). After suturing of the three or four segments, resection is completed, and each segment is weighed for comparison with those from the opposite arm.

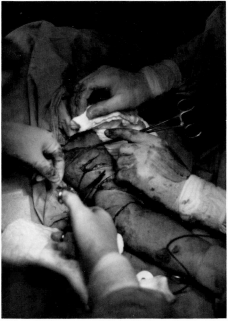

Fig. 9-7

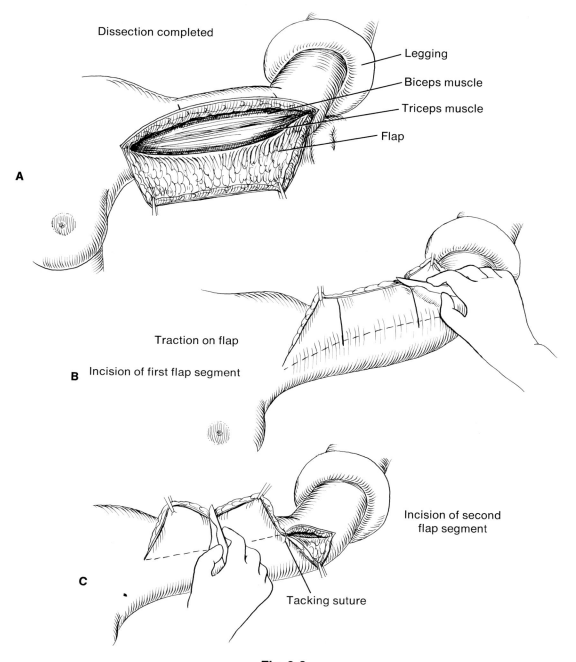

Dissection completed

Legging

Biceps muscle

Triceps muscle

Flap

A

Traction on flap

Incision of first flap segment

B

Incision of second
flap segment

C

Tacking suture

Fig. 9-8

Fig. 9-11, *A*, shows the resection of flap segments. At the elbow the resultant dog ear is removed laterally by extending the incision toward the olecranon process (Fig. 9-11, *B*). The arm is then abducted and elevated to place tension in the axilla to determine the direction of the Z-plasty, which will be designed to conform to the axillary configuration (Figs. 9-9 and 9-11, *B*). The flaps are incised, transposed, inset, and sutured with 3-0 and 4-0 Dexon or Vicryl (Figs. 9-10 and 9-11, *C*).

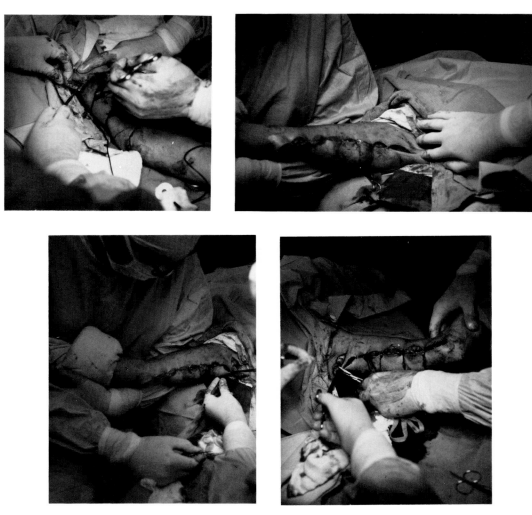

Fig. 9-9

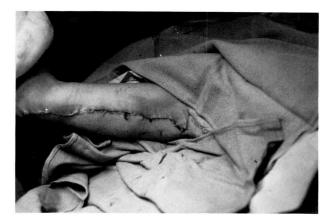

Fig. 9-10

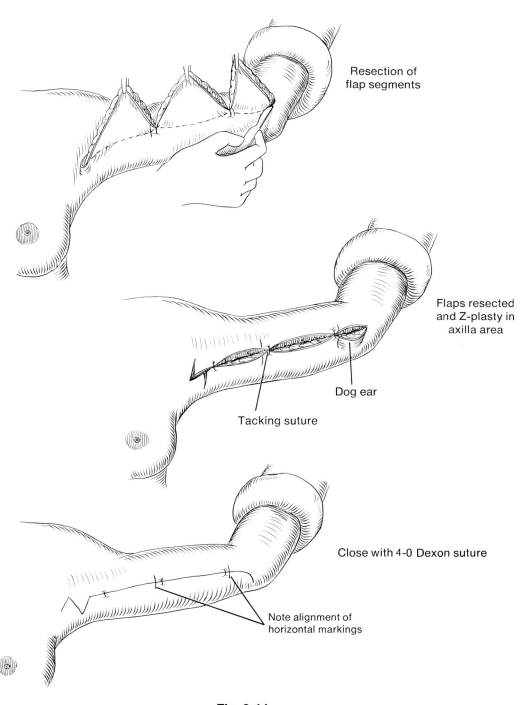

Resection of
flap segments

Flaps resected
and Z-plasty in
axilla area

Dog ear

Tacking suture

Close with 4-0 Dexon suture

Note alignment of
horizontal markings

Fig. 9-11

Closure

Final suture closure is accomplished with intercuticular 5-0 Prolene pull-out sutures. The suture line is reinforced with ½- or 1-inch Steri-Strip closures (Fig. 9-12). The arm is then wrapped with a soft dressing such as Kerlex (Fig. 9-13). (The patient is in the prone position for additional surgery of the thighs.)

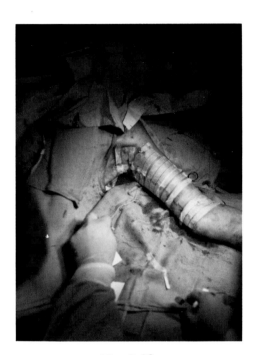

Fig. 9-12

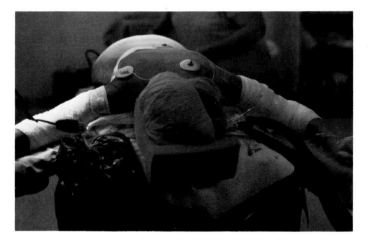

Fig. 9-13

POSTOPERATIVE CARE

Postoperatively the arms are placed in the elevated position on pillows with close observation of the circulation in the arms and hands. The patient is encouraged to open and close the hands frequently after surgery to stimulate circulation and is advised that there will be a tight feeling for several weeks. Since no drains are used, close observation is required. If unusual bleeding or signs of decreased circulation through the peripheral arm and hand are noted by increasing complaints of tightness of the dressing, the surgeon should be notified immediately.

On the first postoperative day, the physical therapist or nurse begins range-of-motion exercises. On the second day after surgery the arm dressings are usually removed and the wound inspected. The patient is allowed to increase the range of motion and is usually discharged on the second postoperative day; with combined surgery, the major procedure dictates the time of discharge. Sutures are usually removed on the tenth day after surgery. The wound is reinforced with Steri-Strips. The patient is allowed to shower 48 hours after surgery with the Steri-Strips in place. Normal activities such as driving may be resumed approximately ten days after surgery, but actions such as lifting or pulling should be avoided for four to six weeks after brachioplasty. Because of benefits to their final appearance, we recommend that patients expose their scars to the sun two to three months after surgery.

ALTERNATE INCISIONS AND COMBINED PROCEDURES

Alternate incisions range from multiple small Z-plasties to the W-plasty, of which the following case is an example.

The 71-year-old woman in Fig. 9-14 sought surgical correction of redundant subcutaneous tissue and skin of the upper arms and thighs, for which a thighplasty was performed in combination with a bilateral brachioplasty. Multiple W-shaped incisions were used (Fig. 9-15). The total operating time was 3 hours 30 minutes; blood loss was less than 1 unit. The patient was discharged on the twelfth day after surgery. The brachioplasty wounds healed without incident. She developed a postoperative thrombophlebitis of the left leg, which responded to treatment with elevation and heat. Fig. 9-16 shows the patient a year after surgery; Fig. 9-17, five years postoperatively.

Critique: For this patient's age the surgical result was satisfactory, although we do not recommend this as a routine procedure.

Fig. 9-14

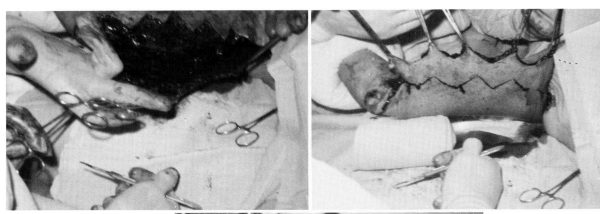

Fig. 9-15

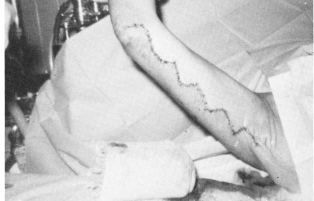

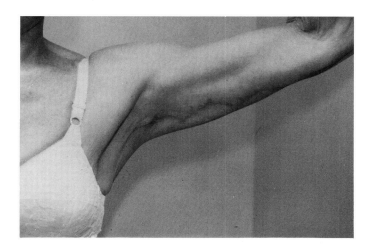

Fig. 9-16

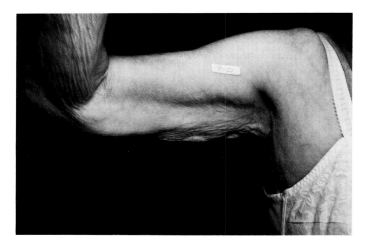

Fig. 9-17

The preoperative appearance of a 58-year-old woman who underwent a bilateral brachioplasty in combination with an abdominoplasty and upper thigh contouring procedures (Figs. 8-104 to 8-107) is shown in Fig. 9-18.

Fig. 9-19 shows the improvement in arm contouring two months after surgery; Fig. 9-20, a year postoperatively.

Critique: The surgery was uneventful, and the results were satisfactory to the patient.

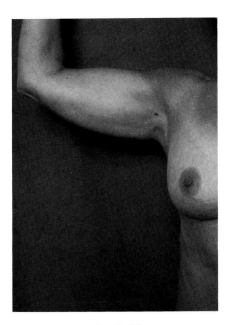

Fig. 9-18

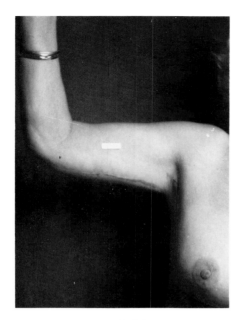

Fig. 9-19

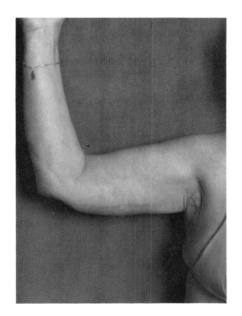

Fig. 9-20

Fig. 9-21 is of a 57-year-old woman who sought brachioplasty in conjunction with thighplasty and meloplasty. She had lost weight after a vagotomy and pyloroplasty (Figs. 8-91 to 8-93).

The patient's appearance two months after surgery is shown in Fig. 9-22.

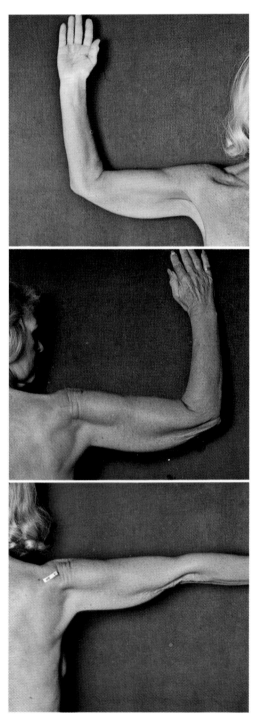

Fig. 9-21

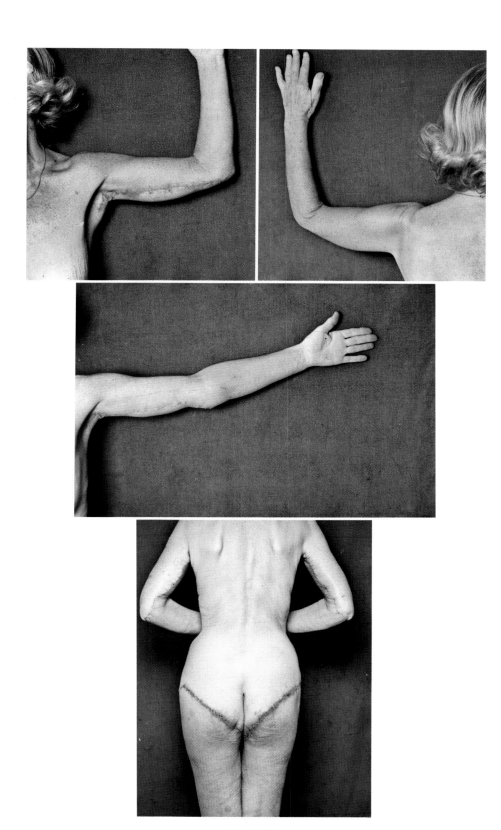

Fig. 9-22

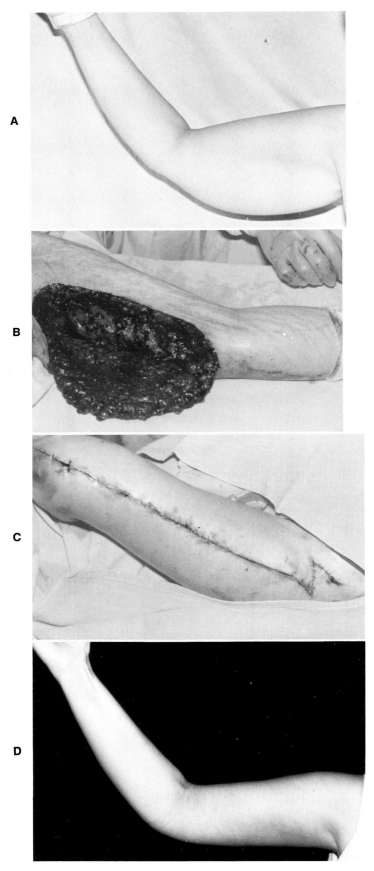

Fig. 9-23. Brachioplasty with Z-plasty in 48-year-old woman. **A,** Preoperative appearance. **B,** Surgery. **C,** Incision with the small Z-plasty. **D,** Postoperative result. (Surgery performed by B. M. Achauer, M.D., at University of California, Irvine, with one of the authors as attending surgeon.)

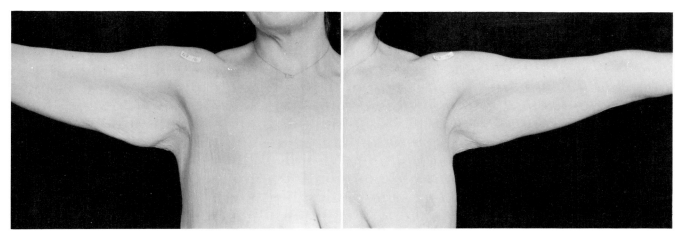

Fig. 9-24. This patient, who had undergone a bypass operation as a result of excess weight, was left with a great deal of flabby skin after losing weight. She underwent an abdominoplasty and brachioplasty two years after the bypass surgery. (Surgery completed with V. Polish, M.D., resident staff member at University of California, Irvine.)

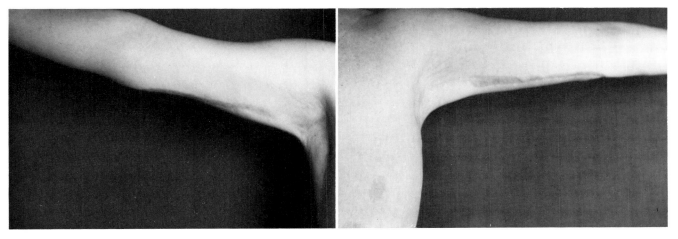

Fig. 9-25. Widening of scars two years after brachioplasty.

REFERENCES

1. Baroudi, R.: Dermatolipectomy of the upper arm, Clin. Plast. Surg. **2:**485, 1975.
2. Guerrero-Santos, J.: Arm-lift. In Courtiss, E. H., editor: Aesthetic surgery: trouble— how to avoid it and how to treat it, St. Louis, 1978, The C. V. Mosby Co.
3. Hoffman, S., and Simon, B. E.: Experiences with the Pitanguy method of correction of trochanteric lipodystrophy, Plast. Reconstr. Surg. **55:**551, 1975.
4. Lewis, J. R.: Atlas of aesthetic plastic surgery, Boston, 1973, Little, Brown & Co.
5. Pitanguy, I.: Correction of lipodystrophy of the lateral thoracic aspect and inner side of the arm and elbow dermosenescence, Clin. Plast. Surg. **2:**477; [Correção lipodistrofia da região lateral do torax, face interna do braço e da dermossenescência do cotovelo], Rev. Bras. Cirurg. **65:** 277, 1975.

CHAPTER 10

Counterpoint and prediction

The search through the literature for greater insight into the human's self-image has led to some obscure subject matter. The appraisal of another's purposes and motives is often grossly misleading and in total error. The large amount of time spent on many subjects that appeared to produce so little for this book was nevertheless a loom from which greater understanding developed. The reason that the primitive person sought the witch doctor or the body painter is believed to be intimately related to why the modern person seeks the plastic surgeon. The stimulus that makes an individual want to change appearance was looked for in as many places as can be imagined. Also sought was the antithesis of this approach: the reasons why some condemn others' trying to modify themselves. Interestingly, the psychological psychiatric literature that approached the subject of human change by surgery referred only to the face. Even multidisciplinary groups, in discussing, debating, and classifying the issues of medical ethics and the morality of body modification, concern themselves only with cosmetic surgery of the face or organ transplantation. Only in cases in which plastic surgeons are co-authors or the psychiatrist or psychologist and others have been working with plastic surgeons is concern revealed about patients who desire and obtain alteration of parts of their bodies other than the face.

In exploring the history of dermolipectomy, we were exposed to many surgeons whose comprehension of their surgical responsibilities and awareness of the potential problems as compared to the current state of the surgical art was unanticipatedly astute and laudable. As with every branch of learning, the potential for abuse and misuse always exists. No amount of admonition can persuade the overeager, insensitive surgeon with monetary motives from performing the wrong surgery or operating on the wrong patient. Nowhere in medicine is the potential for wrongdoing any greater than with the patient who, in eagerness to be shed of a deformity, real or imagined, will accept the persuasiveness of the plastic surgeon as fact. Patient welfare is the necessary core and law base of all medical practice. It is no less and undoubtedly more important when the plastic surgeon is involved. There are no religious or moral connotations of such a dictum. Common sense pointedly underlines the continued need for patient confidence in the physician; history has verified this assumption repeatedly.

When basic surgical principles are forgotten or when concern for the patient's welfare is sublimated to economic needs of the surgeon, resulting disasters are inevitable.

Many problems and complications plague the best of surgeons under the most ideal of circumstances. However, we submit that total dedication to every patient's welfare, backed by excellent training and proper surgical techniques, is a minimal standard that must be rigidly adhered to by all plastic surgeons. The relationship between the levels of skin flap undermining in all phases of dermolipectomy and the resulting massive skin loss has not been understood. Multiple wrongly placed scars of the uncaring surgeon have created permanent deformities. The misuse of outpatient surgery for problems for which hospitalization is a basic requirement has resulted in the most dire consequences.

Of all the areas in cosmetic surgery that are offered to the public for relief of nonpathological deformity, whether real or imagined, dermolipectomy offers the greatest potential for ultimate problems. Some new concepts have been introduced that may or may not stand the test of time. With safeguards, the results seem to justify their introduction at this current level of dermolipectomy. Change and progress is inevitable. What is done today may not be what is done tomorrow. Speculating on the future is a hazardous but intriguing venture. Predictions are usually made based on observations of what occurred in the past. The following estimates should be taken as intended: as pure conjecture and nothing more.

NOW AND IN THE NEAR FUTURE

With the increasing liberation of women, the emphasis on body shape will continue to be on slimmer, more boyish figures. Surgery to reduce hips, breasts, limbs, and torsos will continue for as long as the current state of economic affluence exists. This tendency will permit women more sexually alluring clothes with greater body exposure on one hand but also will enhance the use of masculine attire by the "liberated" woman if desired. In a similar manner, the permissive society allows the man to wear the more colorful and less rugged clothing of the woman. This is characteristic of an affluent society. Surgery to attain the slim body form will continue to flourish, as will all cosmetic surgery. A progressively greater understanding of body fluid physiology, the micro-anatomy of all tissues, as well as the pathological process of aging will continue to broaden the scope of cosmetic surgery. The search for understanding human behavior will continue and will be equally frustrating in its inability to convert research to positive results.

At this time, it appears that disintegration of the present high standards of plastic surgery training and responsibility to the welfare of patients will inevitably be responsive to existing political pressures. However, the worldwide inflation and economic recession that now looms on the horizon portends decreases in elective cosmetic surgery. Outside the United States are areas of armed conflict in which cosmetic surgery is minimal at most. Depending on the reached level and duration of economic depression, the standards for body form will probably change. Because of the current rapid means of communication, no particular economic state is apt to persist at a relatively even level for decades or even several years as it did in the past. This, of course, precludes worldwide armed conflict and all it implies. Major conflict of any kind always requires the service of plastic surgeons. Other than the general educational and technical advances, cosmetic surgery itself will be in a state of limbo. With the return of affluence, the concern for self-image and aesthetic surgery will again reach its present and possibly greater heights.

Bibliography

AGING

Barrows, C. H., Jr., Yiengst, M. J., and Shock, N. W.: Senescence and metabolism of various tissues of rats, J. Gerontol. **13**:351, 1958.

Birren, J.: Handbook of aging and the individual, Chicago, 1959, University of Chicago Press.

Björntorp, P.: Effects of age, sex and clinical conditions on adipose tissue cellularity in man Metabolism **23**:1091, 1974.

Björntorp, P., Bengtsson, C., Blohmé, G., et al.: Adipose tissue fat cell size and number in relation to metabolism in randomly selected middle-aged men and women, Metabolism **20**:927, 1971.

Bortz, E. L.: The dual nature of aging, J. Am. Geriatr. Soc. **8**:753, 1960.

Bortz, E. L.: Medicine's stake in our older population, Rocky Mt. Med. J. **57**:25, 1960.

Bouissou, H., et al.: Cutaneous aging: its relation with arteriosclerosis and atheroma. In Robert, L., and Robert, B., editors: Aging of connective tissues–skin, Basel, Switzerland, 1973, S. Karger, AG.

Brown, R. G.: Family structure and social isolation of older persons, J. Gerontol. **15**:170, 1960.

De Gorgio, A.: The influence of light on the aging skin, G. Gerontol. **4**:563, 1956.

Forbes, G. B., and Hursh, J. B.: Age and sex trends in lean body mass calculated from K^{40} measurements, Ann. N.Y. Acad. Sci. **110**:255, 1963.

Friedfeld, L.: Geriatrics, medicine and rehabilitation, J.A.M.A. **175**:595, 1961.

Gitman, L.: Endocrines and aging, Springfield, Ill., 1967, Charles C Thomas, Publisher.

Gurdin, M.: Surgery for the aging face, Med. Aspects Hum. Sex. **5**:46, 1971.

Havighurst, R. J., and Albrecht, R.: Older people, New York, 1953, Longmans, Green & Co., Inc.

Hayflick, L.: Aging human cells, Triangle **12**:141, 1973.

Manganotti, G.: Contributo allo studio dei fenomeni di senescenza della cut umana. Relazione a V Cong. Naz. Soc. Ital. Gerontol. Atti, suppl. 5, p. 9, 1955.

Norris, A. N., Shock, N. W., and Yiengst, M. J.: Age changes in heart rate and blood pressure responses to tilting and standardized exercise, Circulation **9**:521, 1953.

Pierard, J., et al.: L'élastose sénile. In Congrès des dermatogistes et syphillograph du langue français: Maladies du tissu élastique cutané, Paris, 1968, Masson & Cie, Editeurs.

Robert, B., and Robert, L.: Aging of connective tissue. In Robert, L., and Robert B., editors: Aging of connective tissues–skin, Basel, Switzerland, 1973, S. Karger, AG.

Robert, B., and Robert, L.: Le vieillissement du tissu conjonctif, Triangle **14**:163, 1974.

Robert, L.: Le tissu conjonctif et la médecine moderne, Concours Méd., suppl. 4, p. 3, 1975.

Robert, L.: Rapport sur le symposium européen du tissu conjonctif de Padoue, Sept. 1974, Concours Méd., suppl. 4, p. 8, 1975.

Shock, N. W.: Current concepts of the aging process, J.A.M.A. **175**:108, 1961.

Shock, N. W., Watkin, D. M., and Yiengst, M. J.: Nutritional aspects of aging. In Metabolic aspects of aging: report of the Third Congress of the International Association of Gerontology: Old age in the modern world, Edinburgh, 1955, E. & S. Livingstone, Ltd.

Shock, N. W., and Yiengst, M. J.: Age changes in acid-base equilibrium of blood of males, J. Gerontol. **5**:1, 1950.

Silvestri, U.: On the histochemistry of senile skin [In tema di istochimica della cute senile], G. Gerontol. **8**:243, 1960.

Townsend, P.: The family life of old people,

London, 1957, Routledge & Kegan Paul, Ltd.

Vidik, A.: Rheology of skin with special reference to age related parameters and their possible correlations to structure. In Robert, L., and Robert, B., editors: Aging of connective tissues–skin, Basel, Switzerland, 1973, S. Karger, AG.

Vilain, R., and Monsaingeon, J.: Rapport du XI colloque international de dermo-chirurgie sur le vieillissement de la peau, Ann. Chir. Plast. **18:**92, 1973.

Wollaeger, E. E., Comfort, M. W., Weir, J. F., and Osterberg, A. E.: Total solids, fat and nitrogen in feces; study of normal persons and of patients with duodenal ulcer on test diet containing large amounts of fat, Gastroenterology **6:**83, 1946.

Wollaeger, E. E., Comfort, M. W., and Osterberg, A. E.: Total solids, fat and nitrogen in feces: study of normal persons taking test diet containing moderate amount of fat; comparison with results obtained with normal persons taking test diet containing large amount of fat, Gastroenterology **9:**272, 1947.

Woodruff, D. S., and Birren, J. E.: Aging: scientific perspectives and social issues, New York, 1975, Van Nostrand Reinhold Co.

ANATOMY

Crock, H. V.: The blood supply of the lower limb bones in man, Edinburgh, 1967, E. & S. Livingstone, Ltd.

Elbaz, J. S., and Dardour, J. C.: Anatomy and physiology of the arteries and veins of the abdominal wall. In Marchac, D., editor: Transactions of the Sixth International Congress of Plastic and Reconstructive Surgery, Paris, 1975, Masson & Cie, Editeurs.

Elbaz, J. S., Dardour, J. C., and Ricbourg, B.: Vascularization artérielle de la paroi abdominale, Ann. Chir. Plast. **20:**19, 1975.

Elbaz, J. S., and Zumer, L.: Maternité et préjudices esthétiques, Dos. Obstét. **2:**16, 1974.

Felstein , I.: A change of face and figure, London, 1971, Constable & Co., Ltd.

Fujino, T.: Contribution of the axial perforator vasculature to circulation in flaps, Plast. Reconstr. Surg. **30:**125, 1967.

Gardner, E., Gray, D., and O'Rahilly, R.: Anatomy, ed. 2, Philadelphia, 1963, W. B. Saunders Co.

Georgiadis, N., and Katsas, A.: Topography of fat in the sacroiliac region, Plast. Reconstr. Surg. **49:**110, 1972.

Gould, G. M., and Pyle, W. M.: Anomalies and curiosities of medicine, Philadelphia, 1897, W. B. Saunders Co.

Grant, B.: Grant's method of anatomy, Baltimore, 1965, The Williams & Wilkins Co.

Haddad, C. M.: Ensaios sôbre a rêde arterial da parede ântero-lateral do abdomen. Estudo radiológico, Rev. Assoc. Med. Bras. **14:**255, 1968.

Herrlinger, R.: History of medical illustration from 1600 to 1970, New York, 1970, Medicina Rara Antiquity Editions, Ltd.

Hewes, J. W.: Communication of sexual interest: an anthropological view, Med. Asp. Hum. Sex. **7**(1):66, 1973.

Kurtz, R., and Prestera, H.: The body reveals, New York, 1976, Harper & Row, Publishers.

Lopez, A.: Préjudices osseux et musculaires, Dos. Obstét. **2:**26, 1974.

O'Malley, C. D., and Saunders, J.: Leonardo da Vinci on the human body, New York, 1952, Henry Schuman, Inc., Publishers.

Pierard, J., et al.: Le tissu élastique cutané normal. In Congrès des dermatogistes et syphillograph du langue français: Maladies du tissu élastique cutané, Paris, 1968, Masson & Cie, Editeurs.

Poirer: Traité d'anatomie humaine, vol. II, Paris, 1902, Bartels.

Quain, J., and Wilson, W.: Vessels of the human body, New York, 1837, Appleton.

Richer, P. M.: L'art et la médecine, Paris, 1902, Gaultier & Cie.

Rouvière, H.: Anatomía human descriptiva y topográfica, Madrid, 1926, Baily-Baillière, S.A.

Rouvière, H.: Anatomie des lymphatiques de l'homme, Paris, 1932.

Sheldon, W. H.: Atlas of men. A guide for somatotyping the adult male at all ages, New York, 1954, Gramercy Publishing Co.

Sheldon, W. H., Stevens, S. S., and Tucker, W. B.: Varieties of human physique, New York, 1940, Harper & Brothers.

Snell, R. S.: Atlas of clinical anatomy, Boston, 1978, Little, Brown & Co.

Testut, L.: Traité d'anatomie humaine, Paris, 1848-1849, Doin.

Testut, L., and Billet, H.: Atlas de disección por regiones, Barcelona, 1953, Salvat, S. A.

Testut, L., and Jacob, O.: Traité d'anatomie topographique, Paris, 1909, Octave Doin, Editeur.

Testut, L., and Jacob, O.: Anatomia topografica, Turin, Italy, 1933, Unione Tipografico Editrice Torinese.

Thorek, P.: Anatomy in surgery, Philadelphia, 1951, J. B. Lippincott Co.

Tillaux, P.: Anatomía humana topográfica, Mexico, 1948, Editora Nacional.

ANESTHESIA

Adriani, J.: Nerve blocks: a manual of regional anesthesia for practitioners and students of medicine, Springfield, Ill., 1954, Charles C Thomas, Publisher.

Adriani, J.: Selection of anesthesia: the physiological and pharmacological basis, Springfield, Ill., 1955, Charles C Thomas, Publisher.

Bouchet, N., and Le Brigand, J.: Anesthésie et réanimation, Paris, 1957, Flammarion & Cie.

Davison, M. H. A.: Pentamethonium iodide in anesthesia, Lancet 1:252, 1950.

Daw, E. F., Didier, E. P., and Theye, R. A.: Controlled hypotension, Surg. Clin. North Am. 45:1003, 1965.

De Castro, J.: In Colloque international d'ostende sur la neuroleptanalgésie, Agressologie 3:95, 1962.

De Castro, J., and Mundeleer, P.: Anesthésie sans barbituriques: la neuroleptanalgésie, Anesth. Analg. (Paris) 16:1022, 1959.

De Castro, J., and Mundeleer, P.: Anesthésie sans sommeil: "neuroleptanalgésie," Acta Chir. Belg. 58:689, 1959.

De Castro, J., and Mundeleer, P.: Die Neuroleptanalgesie, Anaesthesist 11:3, 1962.

De Castro, J., Mundeleer, P., and Bauduin, T.: Evaluation critique de la ventilation et de l'équilibre acide-base sous neuroleptanalgésie, Ann. Anesthesiol. Fr. 3:425, 1964.

Deligne, P.: The importance of pyrrolamidol in anesthesiology; its application in surgery of the head (neurosurgery, O.R.L., ophthalmological, stomatological, plastic and esthetic surgery) [Interêt du pyrrolamidol en anesthésiologie; ses applications en chirurgie de la tête], Montpellier Med. 55:389, 1959.

Dobkin, A. B.: Neuroleptanalgesics: a comparison of the cardiovascular, respiratory and metabolic effects of innovan and thiopentone plus methotrimeprazine, Br. J. Anaesth. 35:694, 1963.

Doutriaux, J.: Association Palfium. Taractan en anesthésiologie, J. S. Medicales de Lille, No. 2, 1962.

Enderby, G. E. H.: Controlled circulation with hypotensive drugs and posture to reduce bleeding in surgery; preliminary results with pentamethonium iodide, Lancet 1:1145, 1950.

Enderby, G. E. H.: Postural ischaemia and blood pressure, Lancet 1:185, 1954.

Enderby, G. E. H.: Halothane and hypotension, Anaesthesia 15:25, 1960.

Enderby, G. E. H.: A report on mortality and morbidity following hypotensive anaesthetics, Br. J. Anaesth. 33:109, 1961.

Fenili, O., Francesconi, G., and Fregi, V.: Indicazioni dell'anestesia peridurale segmentaria in chirurgia plastica ricostruttiva, Riv. Ital. Chir. Plast. 5:185, 1973.

Foldes, F. F.: Muscle relaxants in anesthesiology, Springfield, Ill., 1957, Charles C Thomas, Publisher.

Foldes, F. F., Kepes, E. R., Kronfeld, P. P., et al.: A rational approach to neuroleptanesthesia, Anesth. Analg. (Cleve.) 45:642, 1966.

Foldes, F. F., Swerdlow, M., and Siker, E. S.: Narcotics and narcotic antagonists; chemistry, pharmacology and applications in anesthesiology and obstetrics, Springfield, Ill., 1964, Charles C Thomas, Publisher.

Gaveau, T., and Viars, P.: Étude de l'utilisation de phénopéridine et de déhydrobenzpéridol associés en chirurgie périphérique, Anesth. Analg. (Paris) 23:927, 1966.

Gemperli, M., and Gruninger, B.: Analyse des gaz du sang après neuroleptanalgésie type II, Anesth. Analg. (Paris) 21:101, 1964.

Goodman, L. S., and Gilman, A. Z., editors: The pharmacological basis of therapeutics; a textbook of pharmacology, toxicology, and therapeutics for physicians and medical students, ed. 3, New York, 1965, The Macmillan Co., Publishers.

Hanquet, M.: Manuel d'anesthésiologie, Paris, 1973, Masson & Cie, Editeurs.

Huguenard, P., and Jacquenaud, P.: Exposés d'anesthésiologie, Paris, 1966, Masson & Cie, Editeurs.

Huguenard, P.: La notion de protection en anesthésie réanimation. Rapport au XIX Congrés Français d'Anesthesie, Lyon, France, 1969.

Janssen, P. A. J.: Communication au premier congrès européen d'anesthésiologie, Vienna, 1962, Chir. Scand. 133:467, 1967.

Laver, M. B.: A time to measure, Anesthesiology 45:114, 1976.

Mazzia, U. D. B., Roy, B. S., and Antusio, J. F., Jr.: The use of a thiophanium derivative for controlled hypotension in intracranial operation, Ann. Surg. **143**:81, 1956.

Nilsson, E., and Janssen, P.: Neuroleptanalgesia—an alternative to general anaesthesia, Acta Anesthesiol. Scand. **5**:73, 1961.

Noël, A.: Die aesthetique Chirurgie und ihre soziale Bedeutung, Leipzig, 1932, Johann Ambrosius Barth Verlag.

Organe, G.: Change and progress in anaesthesia, Proc. R. Soc. Med. **43**:181, 1949.

Paton, W. D. M., and Zaimis, E.: Clinical potentialities of certain bisquaternary salts causing neuromuscular and ganglionic block, Nature **162**:810, 1948.

Sadove, M. S., Wyant, G. M., and Gleave, G.: Controlled hypotension; study on arfonad (RO 2-2222), Anaesthesia **8**:175, 1953.

Sadove, M. S., Wyant, G. M., Gleave, G., and Bucy, P. C.: Controlled hypotension, J. Neurosurg. **11**:143, 1954.

Simkoff, A. A.: Interêt et limites d'une technique de neuroleptanalgésie au cours de l'insuffisance rénale. Thesis, Paris, 1969, Faculté de Médecine de Paris.

Simkoff, A. A., and Cohen, A. S.: De la place de l'hypotension contrôlée en odonto-stomatologie, Rev. Belge Med. Dent. **29**:419, 1974.

Simkoff, A. A., and Elbaz, J. S.: L'hypotension contrôlée, une technique d'anesthésie injustement méconnue en chirurgie plastique, Ann. Chir. Plast. **19**:353, 1974.

Viars, P., and Gaveau, T.: Réflexion sur l'emploi de la phénopéridine, Anesth. Analg. (Paris) **25**:163, 1968.

Viars, P., and Guidicelli, F.: Justification pharmacologique de l'emploi des analgésiques centraux en anesthésiologie: rapport au 18 Congrès Français d'anesthesie, Nantes, France, 1968.

Viars, P., and Subacher, J.: Les interférences, risques thérapeutiques, et incompatibilités médicamenteuses, Paris, 1973, Arnette.

Wood-Smith, F. G., Vickers, M. D., and Stewart, H. C.: Drugs in anaesthetic practice, ed. 4, Sevenoaks, Kent, England, 1973, Butterworth & Co. (Publishers), Ltd.

Wylie, W. D. T.: Anaesthesia for surgery of the ears, nose, throat and mouth. In Wylie, W. D. T., and Churchill-Davidson, H. C.: A practice of anaesthesia, ed. 3, London, 1972, Lloyd-Luke (Medical Books), Ltd.

ANTIBIOTICS

Alexander, J., and Altemeier, W. A.: Penicillin prophylaxis of experimental staphylococcal wound infections, Surg. Gynecol. Obstet. **120**:243, 1965.

Altemeier, W. A., Culbertson, W. R., and Hummel, R. P.: Surgical considerations of endogenous infections—source, types, and methods of control, Surg. Clin. North Am. **48**:227, 1968.

Burke, J.: The effective period of preventive antibiotic action in experimental incisions and dermal lesions, Surgery **50**:161, 1961.

Burke, J.: Preoperative antibiotics, Surg. Clin. North Am. **43**:665, 1963.

Hoeprich, P.: New antimicrobics for the treatment of infections caused by gram-negative bacilli, Med. Clin. North Am. **48**:255, 1964.

Martin, W. J.: Newer antimicrobial agents having current or potential clinical application, Med. Clin. North Am. **48**:255, 1964.

Martin, W. J.: Newer penicillins, Med. Clin. North Am. **51**:1107, 1967.

Todd, J. C.: Wound infection: etiology, prevention, and management, including selection of antibiotics, Surg. Clin. North Am. **48**:787, 1968.

ART

De Wulf, M.: Art and beauty, St. Louis, 1950, B. Herder Book Co.

Eichenberg, F.: The art of the print, New York, 1976, Harry N. Abrams, Inc., Publishers.

Hamlyn, P.: The drawings of Holbein, London, 1966, Drury House.

Herrlinger, R.: History of medical illustration from 1600 to 1970, New York, 1970, Medicina Rara Antiquity Editions, Ltd.

Janson, H. W., et al.: A history of art and music, Englewood Cliffs, N.J., 1968, Prentice-Hall, Inc.

Kuh, K.: The open eye; in pursuit of art, New York, 1971, Harper & Row, Publishers.

Kurth, W.: The complete woodcuts of Albrecht Dürer, New York, 1937, Arden Book Co.

Rousselot, J.: Medicine in art, New York, 1960, McGraw-Hill Book Co.

Squire, G.: Dress, art, and society, London, 1974, Studio Vista.

Vilain, R.: De la silhouette et des chirurgiens ou l'art médical de la silhouette, Nouv. Presse Med. **4**:1217, 1975.

Von den Steinen, K.: Die Marquesaner und ihre Kunst, New York, 1969, Hacker Art Books.

BLOOD, BLEEDING DISORDERS, AND THROMBOEMBOLIC PHENOMENA

Adams, E.: Postoperative thrombocytosis, Arch. Intern. Med. **73:**329, 1944.

Adams, T., Schulz, L., and Goldberg, L.: Platelet function abnormalities in the mycloproliferative disorders, Scand. J. Haematol. **13:**215, 1974.

Alexander, B.: Estimation of plasma prothrombin by the one-stage method. In Tocantins, L. M., and Kazal, L. A., editors: The coagulation of blood: methods of study, New York, 1955, Grune & Stratton, Inc.

Baar, H.: The stickiness of platelets, Lancet **2:**775, 1941.

Bancroft, F. W., Stanley-Brown, M., and Chargaff, E.: Postoperative thrombosis and embolism, Ann. Surg. **106:**868, 1937.

Barrow, E. M., and Graham, J. B.: Von Willebrand's disease. In Tocantins, L. M., and Kazal, L. A., editors: Blood coagulation, hemorrhage and thrombosis; methods of study, ed. 2, New York, 1964, Grune & Stratton, Inc.

Bergquist, G.: Über postoperative Thrombosen. Vorläufige Mitteilung, Acta Chir. Scand. **83:**415, 1940.

Bick, R., Adams, T., and Schmalhorst, W.: Bleeding times, platelet adhesions and aspirin, Am. J. Clin. Pathol. **65:**69, 1976.

Bizzozero, J.: Ueber einen neuen Formbestandtheil des Blutes und dessen Rolle bei der Thrombose und der Blutgerinnung, Virchows Arch. (Pathol. Anat.) **90:**251, 1882.

Borchgrevink, C. F.: A method for measuring platelet adhesiveness in vivo, Acta Med. Scand. **168:**157, 1960.

Borchgrevink, C. F., Egeberg, O., Godal, H., and Hjort, P. F.: The effect of plasma and Cohn's fraction I on the Duke and Ivy bleeding times in von Willebrand's disease, Acta Med. Scand. **173:**235, 1963.

Bouma, B. N., Wiegerink, Y., Sixma, J. J., et al.: Immunological characterization of purified anti-haemophilic factor A (factor VIII) which corrects abnormal platelet retention in von Willebrand's disease, Nature [New Biol.] **236:**104, 1972.

Bowie, E. J. W.: Platelet abnormalities in von-Willebrand's disease, Ann. N.Y. Acad. Sci. **201:**400, 1972.

Bowie, E. J. W., and Ambrus, J. L.: Hematologic reviews, New York, 1968, Marcel Dekker, Inc.

Bowie, E. J. W., Didisheim, P., Thompson, J. H., Jr., et al.: The spectrum of von Willebrand's disease, Thromb. Diath. Haemorrh. **18:**40, 1967.

Bowie, E. J. W., Owen, C. A., Jr., Hansen, R. J., et al.: Electronic method for quantitation of bleeding time, Am. J. Clin. Pathol. **58:**255, 1972.

Bowie, E. J. W., Owen, C. A., Jr., Thompson, J. H., et al.: Platelet adhesiveness in von Willebrand's disease, Am. J. Clin. Pathol. **52:**69, 1969.

Bowie, E. J. W., Owen, C. A., Jr., Thompson, J. H., Jr., et al.: A test of platelet adhesiveness, Mayo Clin. Proc. **44:**306, 1969.

Bowie, E. J. W., and Owen, C. A., Jr.: Some factors influencing platelet retention in glass bead columns including the influence of plastics, Am. J. Clin. Pathol. **56:**479, 1971.

Bowie, E. J. W., and Owen, C. A., Jr.: The value of measuring platelet "adhesiveness" in the diagnosis of bleeding disease, Am. J. Clin. Pathol. **60:**302, 1972.

Brambel, C. E., and Loker, F. F.: Significance of variations of prothrombin activity of diulte plasma, Proc. Soc. Exp. Biol. Med. **53:**218, 1943.

Brecher, G., Schneiderman, M., and Cronkite, E. P.: The reproducibility and constancy of the platelet count, Am. J. Clin. Pathol. **23:**15, 1953.

Chan, J. Y. S., Owen, C. A., Jr., Bowie, E. J., et al.: Von Willebrand's disease "stimulating factor" in porcine plasma, Am. J. Physiol. **214:**1219, 1968.

Chumnijarakij, T., and Poshyachinda, V.: Postoperative thrombosis in Thai women, Lancet **1:**1357, 1975.

Cohn, J. E., and Shock, N. W.: Blood volume studies in middle-aged and elderly males, Am. J. Med. Sci. **217:**388, 1949.

Coller, B. S., and Zuker, M. D.: Reversible decrease in platelet retention by glass bead columns (adhesiveness) induced by disturbing the blood, Proc. Soc. Exp. Biol. Med. **136:**769, 1971.

Copley, A. L., and Houlihan, R. B.: On the mechanism of plately agglutination, Fed. Proc. **4:**173, 1945.

Cronberg, S.: Investigations in haemorrhagic disorders with prolonged bleeding time but normal number of platelets with special reference to platelet adhesiveness, Acta Med. Scand. Suppl. **486:**1, 1968.

Dausset, J.: Las anemias hemolíticas adquiridas, Día Méd. (B. Aires), p. 1488, June, 1951.

Dawbarn, R. Y., Earlam, F., and Howel Evans, W.: The relation of the blood platelets to thrombosis after operation and parturition, J. Pathol. Bacteriol. **31**:833, 1928.

Erickson, B. N., Williams, H. H., Avrin, I., and Lee, P.: The lipid distribution of human platelets in health and disease, J. Clin. Invest. **18**:81, 1939.

Fonio, A., and Schwenderner, J.: Die Thrombozyten des menschlichen Blutes und ihre Beziehung zum Gerinnungs- und Thrombosevorgang, Bern, Switzerland, 1942, Hans Huber.

Frick, P. G.: Hemorrhagic diathesis with increased capillary fragility caused by salicylate therapy, Am. J. Med. Sci. **231**:402, 1956.

Friedman, L. L., Bowie, E. J., et al.: Familial Glanzmann's thrombasthenia, Proc. Staff Meet. Mayo Clin. **39**:908, 1964.

Gaarder, A., Jonsen, J., Laland, S., et al.: Adenosine diphosphate in red blood cells as a factor in the adhesiveness of human blood platelets, Nature **192**:531, 1961.

Glanzmann, E.: Hereditare haemorrhagische Thrombasthenie: ein Beitrag zur Pathologie der Blutplättchen, Jahrb. Kinderk. **88**:1, 1918.

Harrison, S. J. G., and Mitchell, J. R. A.: The influence of red blood cells on platelet adhesiveness, Lancet **2**:1163, 1966.

Hellem, A. J.,: The adhesiveness of human blood platelets in vitro. Scand. J. Clin. Lab. Invest. **12**:(Suppl. 51):1, 1960.

Hellem, A. J., Borchgrevink, C. F., and Ames, S. B.: The role of red cells in haemostasis, Br. J. Haematol. **7**:42, 1961.

Hellem, A. J., and Owren, P. A.,: The mechanism of the hemostatic function of blood platelets, Acta Haematol. (Basel) **31**:230, 1964.

Hellem, A. J., and Stormorken, H.: Platelet adhesion—aggregation reaction and its clinical significance. In Poller, L., editor: Recent advances in blood coagulation, London, 1969, J. & A. Churchill, Ltd.

Herndon, J. H.,,and Riseborough, E. J.: Fat embolism—pathophysiology, symptomatology and management, J. Trauma **11**:673, 1971.

Holmsch, H., and Weiss, H. J.: Further evidence for a deficient storage pool of adenine nucleotides in platelets from some patients with thrombocytopathia "storage pool disease," Blood **39**:197, 1972.

Hurn, M., Baker, N. W., and Mann, F. D.: Variations in prothrombin and antithrombin in patients with thrombosing tendencies, Am. J. Clin. Pathol. **17**:709. 1947.

Ingram, G. I. C., Kingston, P. J., Leslie, J., et al.: Four cases of acquired von Willebrand's syndrome, Br. J. Haematol. **21**:189, 1971.

Ivy, A. C., Shapiro, P. F., and Melnick, P.: The bleeding tendency in jaundice, Surg. Gynecol. Obstet. **60**:781, 1935.

Jacques, L. B., Fidlar, E., et al.: Silicones and blood coagulation, Can. Med. Assoc. J. **55**:26, 1946.

Kadish, A. N.: Coagulation of the blood in lusteroid tubes; a study of normal persons and patients with arterial or venous thrombosis, Am. Heart J. **34**:212, 1947.

Kakkar, V. V. The problems of thrombosis in the deep veins of the leg, Ann. R. Coll. Surg. Engl. **45**:257, 1969.

Kristenson, A.: Beobachtungen über die Thrombozytenzahl bei klinischer Venenthrombose, Acta Med. Scand. **69**:453, 1928.

Larrieu, M. J., Caen, J. P., Meyer, D. O., et al.: Congenital bleeding disorders with long bleeding time and normal platelet count, Am. J. Med. **45**:354, 1968.

Lewis, J. H., and Didsheim, P.: Differential diagnosis and treatment in hemorrhagic disease, A.M.A. Arch. Intern. Med. **100**:157, 1957.

Lozner, E., Taylor, F. N. L., and MacDonald, H.: The effect of foreign surfaces on blood coagulation, J. Clin. Invest. **21**:241, 1942.

Meyer, D., and Larrieu, M. J.: L'analyse des fonctions plaquettaires: mesure de l'adhésivité des plaquettes au verre sur sang total (méthode de Salzman), Rev. Fr. Etud. Clin. Biol. **12**:736, 1967.

Meyer, D., and Larrieu, M. J.: In vivo and vitro studies of platelet adhesiveness to glass beads in von Willebrand's disease. In Transactions of the Twelfth Congress of the International Society of Hematology (Abstract WW9), New York, 1968, International Society of Hematology.

Meyer, D., Larrieu, M. J., Maroteaux, P., et al.: Biological findings in von Willebrand's pedigress: implications for inheritance, J. Clin. Pathol. **20**:1904, 1967.

Mielke, C. H., Kaneshiro, M. M., Maher, L. A., et al.: The standardized normal Ivy bleeding time and its prolongation by aspirin, Blood **34**:204, 1969.

Milstone, J. H.: Activation of prothrombin by platelets plus globulin, Proc. Soc. Exp. Biol. Med. **68**:225, 1948.

Mollitt, D. L., Gartner, D. J., and Madura, J. A.: Bedside monitoring of heparin therapy, Am. J. Surg. **135**:801, 1978.

Moolten, S. E.: Studies on extractable factors in the spleen and other organic sources which influence the blood platelet count, J. Mt. Sinai Hosp. N.Y. **12**:866, 1945.

Moolten, S. E., and Vroman, L.: The adhesiveness of blood platelets in thromboembolism and hemorrhagic disorders. I. Measurement of platelet adhesiveness by the glass-wool filter, Am. J. Clin. Pathol. **19**:701, 1949.

Morawitz, P., and Jurgens, R.: Gibt es eine Thrombasthenie? Munch. Med. Wochenschr. **77**:2001, 1930.

Moses, C.: The effect of digitalis, epinephrine, and surgery on the response to heparin, J. Lab. Clin. Med. **30**:603, 1945.

Mosley, J. W.: The surveillance of transfusion-associated viral hepatitis, J.A.M.A. **193**:91, 1965.

Newman, M. M., Hamstra, R., and Block, M.: Use of banked autologous blood in elective surgery, J.A.M.A. **218**:861, 1971.

Nicolaides, A. N., editor: Thromboembolism; etiology, advances in prevention and management, Baltimore, 1975, University Park Press.

Normann, E.: Wie verhalten sich die Thrombozyten nach operativen behandelten Krankheitsfallen und bei der Entstehung postoperativer Thrombose, Dtsch. Z. Chir. **212**:166, 1928.

Nye, S. W., Grahem, J. B., and Brinkhous, K. M.: The partial thromboplastin time as a screening test for the detection of latent bleeders, Am. J. Med. Sci. **243**:279, 1962.

Nygaard, K. K., and Brown, G. E.: Essential thrombophilia. Report of 5 cases, Arch. Intern. Med. **59**:82, 1937.

O'Brien, J. R.: The adhesiveness of native platelets and its prevention, J. Clin. Pathol. **14**:140, 1961.

O'Brien, J. R.: Effect of salicylates on human platelets, Lancet **1**:779, 1968.

O'Brien, J. R., and Heywood, J. B.: Some interactions between human platelets and glass: von Willebrand's disease compared with normal, J. Clin. Pathol. **20**:56, 1967.

Ollgaard, E.: On the agglutination of the blood platelets under normal and pathological conditions, Acta Med. Scand. **115**:1, 1943.

Ottaviani, P., et al.: L'adesività delle piastrine, in vitro e in vivo, nelle leucemie in rapporto con il loro contenuto di ATP e ADP, Profr. Med. Roma **20**:46, 1964.

Owen, C. A., Jr., Bowie, E. J. W., et al.: The diagnosis of bleeding disorders, London, 1969, J. & A. Churchill, Ltd.

Owen, C. A., Jr., and Thompson, J. H., Jr.: Soybean phosphatides in prothrombin—consumption and thromboplastin—generation tests, Am. J. Clin. Pathol. **33**:197, 1960.

Pachter, R., et al.: Bleeding, platelets and macroglobulinemia, Am. J. Clin. Pathol. **31**:467, 1959.

Papayannis, A. G., Wood, J. K., and Israels, M. C. G.: Factor VIII levels, bleeding times, and platelet adhesiveness in patients with von Willebrand's disease and their relatives, Lancet **1**:418, 1971.

Pittman, M. A., Jr., and Graham, J. B.: Glanzmann's thrombopathy: an autosomal recessive trait in one family, Am. J. Med. Sci. **247**:292, 1964.

Potts, W. J., and Pearl, E.: A Study of the platelet count on the coagulation time of plasma and whole bood following operation, Surg. Gynecol. Obstet. **731**:492, 1941.

Praga, C., Malisardi, P., Pollini, C., et al.: Bleeding time and antiaggregating drugs: a controlled study in elderly patients, Thromb. Res. **3**:13, 1973.

Quick, A. J.: Studies on the enigma of the hemostatic dysfunction of hemophilia, Am. J. Med. Sci. **214**:272, 1947.

Quick, A. J.: Hemorrhagic disease, Philadelphia, 1957, Lea & Febiger.

Quick, A. J.: Salicylates and bleeding: the aspirin tolerance test, Am. J. Med. Sci. **252**:265, 1966.

Quick, A. J.: Hemostasis and thrombosis: a new look, Minn. Med. **50**:1333, 1967.

Quick, A. J.: Bleeding problems in clinical medicine. Philadelphia, 1970, W. B. Saunders Co.

Quick, A. J.: The hemorrhagic diseases and the pathology of hemostasis, Springfield, Ill., 1974, Charles C Thomas, Publisher.

Rocko, J. M., et al.: The safety of low dose heparin prophylaxis, Am. J. Surg. **135**:798, 1978.

Rossi, E. C., and Green, D.: A study of platelet retention by glass bead columns (platelet adhesiveness in normal subjects), Br. J. Haemotol. **23**:47, 1972.

Salzman, E. W., and Britten, A.: In vitro correction of defective platelet adhesiveness in von Willebrand's disease (abstr.), Fed. Proc. **23:**239, 1964.

Salzman, E. W.: Measurements of platelet adhesiveness: A simple in vitro technique demonstrating an abnormality in von Willebrand's disease, J. Lab. Clin. Med. **62:**724, 1963.

von Seemen, H., and Binswanger, H.: Über allgemein Veränderungen, besonders des Blutes, nach chirurgischen Eingriffen und ihre Bedeutung für Entstehung und Bekampfung der mittelbaren Operationsschädigungen, Dtsch. Z. Chir. **209:**157, 1928.

Shapiro, S.: Hyperprothrombinemia, a premonitory sign of thromboembolization, Exp. Med. Surg. **2:**103, 1944.

Sherry, S., and Scriabine, A., editors: Platelets and thrombosis, Baltimore, 1974, University Park Press.

Strauss, H. S., and Bloom, G. E.: Von Willebrand's disease. Use of a platelet-adhesiveness test in diagnosis and family investigation, N. Engl. J. Med. **273:**171, 1965.

Stubbe, L.: The role of aspirin in causing iron-deficiency anemia. In Dixon, A. S. J., Martin, P. K., Smith, M. J. H., and Wood, D. H. H., editors: Salicylates: an international symposium, London, 1963, J. & A. Churchill, Ltd.

Sutor, A. H., Bowie, E. J. W., Thompson, J. H., Jr., et al.: Bleeding from standardized skin punctures. Automated technique for recording time intensity and patten of bleeding, Am. J. Clin. Pathol. **55:**541, 1971.

Symposium: fat embolism syndrome, Contemp. Surg. **9:**49, July, 1976.

Tuft, H. S., and Rosenfield, R. E.: Significance of the accelerated reaction in determination of prothrombin time of diluted plasma, Am. J. Clin. Pathol. **17:**704, 1947.

Walsh, J. J., Bonnar, J., and Wright, F. W.: A study of pulmonary embolism and deep leg vein thrombosis after major gynecological surgery using labelled fibrinogen-phlebography and lung scanning, J. Obstet. Gynaecol. Br. Commonw. **81:**311, 1974.

Weiss, H. J.: Aspirin ingestion compared with bleeding disorders—search for a useful platelet antiaggregant, Blood **35:**333, 1970.

Weiss, H. J.: The pharmacology of platelet inhibition, In Spaet, T. H., editor: Progress in hemostasis and thrombosis, vol. I, New York, 1972, Grune & Stratton, Inc.

Weiss, H. J., Aledort, L. M., and Kochwa, S.: The effect of salicylates on the hemostatic properties of platelets in man, J. Clin. Invest. **47:**2169, 1968.

Weiss, H. J., and Rogers, J.: Thrombocytophathia due to abnormalities in platelet release reaction—studies on six unrelated patients, Blood **30:**187. 1972.

Welch, W. H.: Thrombosis. In Papers and addresses, vol. I. Pathology: preventive medicine, Baltimore, 1920, Johns Hopkins Press.

Wharton, J. T.: On the state of the blood and the blood vessels in inflammation ascertained by experiments, injections and observations by the microscope, Buy's Hosp. Rep. **7:**1, 1851.

von Willebrand, E. A., and Jürgens, R.: Ueber eine neue Bluterkrankheit. Die konstitutionelle Thrombopathie, Klin. Wochenschr. **12:**414, 1933.

Windfeld, P.: Beiträge zur Kenntnis der postoperativen Blutveränderungen, Acta Chir. Scand. **70**(suppl. 25):1, 1933.

Wingerson, L.: To prevent clots that kill, Med. World News, p. 61, Feb. 7, 1977.

Wintrobe, M. M.: Clinical hematology, ed. 5, Philadelphia, 1961, Lea & Febiger.

Wright, H. P.: The adhesiveness of blood platelets in normal subjects with varying concentrations of anticoagulants, J. Pathol. Bacteriol. **53:**255, 1941.

Wright, H. P.: Changes in the adhesiveness of blood platelets following parturition and surgical operations, J. Pathol. Bacteriol. **54:**461, 1942.

Zahn, F. W.: Untersuchungen über Thrombose: Bildung der Thromben, Virchows Arch. (Pathol. Anat.) **62:**81, 1875.

Zimmerman, B., Ratnoff, O. D., and Powell, A. E.: Immunologic differentiation of classic hemophilia (factor VIII deficiency) and von Willebrand's disease, J. Clin. Invest. **50:**244, 1970.

Zucker, M. B.: In vitro abnormality of the blood in von Willebrand's disease correctable by normal plasma, Nature **197:**601, 1963.

COSTUME

Artez, G.: The elegant woman, New York, 1932, Harcourt, Brace & Co.

Boucher, F.: 20,000 years of fashion, New York, 1978, Harry N. Abrams, Inc.

Contini, M.: Fashion from ancient Egypt to the present day, New York, 1965, Crescent Books.

Davenport, M.: The book of costume, New York, 1940, Crown Publishers, Inc.

Garland, M.: The changing form of fashion, New York, 1970, Praeger Publishers, Inc.

Kemper, R.: A history of costume, New York, 1977, Newsweek Books.

Kohler, C.: A history of costume, New York, 1963, Dover Publications, Inc.

Langner, L.: The importance of wearing clothes, New York, 1969, Hastings House.

Laver, J.: Costume, New York, 1963, Hawthorn Books, Inc.

Laver, J.: Modesty in dress, Boston, 1969, Houghton Mifflin Co.

McClellan, E.: Historic dress in America, 1607, New York, 1977, Arno Press.

McConathy, D., with Vreeland, D.: Hollywood costume, New York, 1976, Harry N. Abrams, Inc.

Treasures acquired from Metro-Goldwyn-Mayer (catalog), vol. 5, Los Angeles, 1970, David Weisz Co.

Warwick, E., et al.: Early American dress; the Colonial and Revolutionary periods, New York, 1965, Benjamin Blom, Inc.

Wilcox, R. T.: Five centuries of American costume, New York, 1963, Charles Scribner's Sons.

Wilcox, R. T.: The dictionary of costume, New York, 1969, Charles Scribner's Sons.

GENERAL AND PLASTIC SURGERY

Aronsohn, R. B., and Epstein, R. A.: The miracle of cosmetic plastic surgery, Los Angeles, 1970, Sherbourne Press.

Babcock, W. W.: A textbook of surgery for students and physicians, ed. 2, Philadelphia, 1935, W. B. Saunders Co.

Babcock, W. W.: Principles of practice of surgery, Philadelphia, 1944, Lea & Febiger.

Bankoff, G.: The story of plastic surgery, London, 1943, Faber & Faber, Ltd.

Barsky, A. J., and Kahn, S.: Principles and practice of plastic surgery, New York, 1964, McGraw-Hill Book Co.

Bell, J.: Health and beauty, Philadelphia, 1838, E. L. Carey & A. Hart.

Berson, M. I.: Atlas of plastic surgery, ed. 2, New York, 1963, Grune & Stratton, Inc.

Bickham, W. S.: Operative surgery, Philadelphia, 1924, W. B. Saunders Co.

Blocksma, R., and Braley, S.: Implantation materials. In Grabb, W. C., and Smith, J. W., editors: Plastic surgery: a concise guide to clinical practice, Boston, 1968, Little, Brown & Co.

Burian, F.: The plastic surgery atlas, New York, 1968, The Macmillan Co.

Cannaday, G. E.: Some of the uses of the cutis graft in surgery, Am. J. Surg. 59:409. 1943.

Cannaday, G. E.: An additional report on some of the uses of cutis graft material in reparative surgery, Am. J. Surg. 67:238, 1945.

Converse, J. M., editor: Reconstructive plastic surgery, Philadelphia, 1964, 1977, W. B. Saunders Co.

Conway, H., and Stark, R. B.: Plastic surgery at the New York Hospital one hundred years ago, New York, 1953, Paul B. Hoeber, Inc.

Davis, J. S.: Plastic surgery, its principles and practice, New York, 1919, P. Blakiston's Son & Co.

Hazards of cosmetic surgery (editorial), Br. Med. J. 1:381, 1967.

Favire, J.: La chirurgie esthétique et le médecin practicien, Gaz. Hop. 23:55, 1972.

Foged, J., and Jacoby, O.: Surgical therapy of pendulous abdomen, Ugeskr. Laeger 110:1311, 1948.

Fomon, S.: Cosmetic surgery, principles and practice, Philadelphia, 1960, J. B. Lippincott Co.

Fonseca Ely, J.: Cirurgia plástica, São Paulo, Brazil, 1964.

Gibson, T.: Modern trends in plastic surgery, vol. 2, London, 1966, Butterworth & Co. (Publishers), Ltd.

Gillies, H., and Millard, H.: Principles and art of plastic surgery, vol. 2, Boston, 1957, Little, Brown & Co.

Hoffmeister, F. S.: Studies on timing of tissue transfer in reconstructive surgery, Plast. Reconstr. Surg. 19:283, 1957.

Hollander, E.: Plastik und Medizin, Stuttgart, 1912, Verlag von Ferdinand Enke.

Hollander, E.: Plastische (kosmetische) operation kritische Darstelling ihres gegenwärtigen Standes, Neue Dtsch. Klin. 9:1.

Joseph, J.: Nasenplastik und sonstige Gesichtsplastik. Nebst einem Angang über Mammaplastik und einige weitere Operationen aus dem Gebiete der äusseren Körper-plastik. Ein Atlas und Lehrbuch, Leipzig, 1931, Curt Kabitzch.

Kaplan, I.: The scope of plastic surgery, Jerusalem, 1972, Academic Press, Inc.

Kolle, F. S.: Plastic and cosmetic surgery, New York, 1911, D. Appleton & Co.

La Barre, H.: Plastic surgery, beauty you can

buy, New York, 1970, Holt, Rinehart & Winston, Inc.

Lewis, J. R.: Lower extremity and buttocks. In Atlas of aesthetic plastic surgery, Boston, 1973, Little, Brown & Co.

Maltz, M.: Evolution of plastic surgery, New York, 1946, Froben Press, Inc.

Maltz, M.: Doctor Pygmalion—the autobiography of a plastic surgeon, New York, 1953, Thomas Y. Crowell Co.

Matthews, D. N.: The plastic surgeon's problems and responsibilities in aesthetic surgery. In Marchac, D., editor: Transactions of the Sixth Congress of Plastic and Reconstructive Surgeons, Paris, 1975, Masson & Cie, Editeurs.

May, H.: Reconstructive and reparative surgery, Philadelphia, 1947, F. A. Davis Co.

Miller, C. C.: The surgical reduction of the nasal tip of excessive length, Ala. Med. J., p. 620, 1906.

Miller, C. C.: Surgical treatment of hump nose, Med. Brief **34**:160, 1906.

Miller, C. C.: Cosmetic surgery of the face, Int. J. Surg. **20**:311, 1907.

Miller, C. C.: External canthotomy and section of the fibers of the orbicularis palpebrarum for minimizing "crow's-feet," St. Louis Clin. **20**:213, 1907.

Miller, C. C.: The eradication by surgical means of the nasolabial lines, Ther. Gaz. **31**:676, 1907.

Miller, C. C.: Semilunar excision of the skin at the outer canthus for the eradication of "crow's-feet," Am. J. Dermatol., p. 483, 1907.

Miller, C. C.: Subcutaneous division of the fibers of the orbicularis muscle for overcoming "crow's-feet," Med. Times, p. 207, 1907.

Miller, C. C.: Subcutaneous section of the facila muscles to eradicate expression lines, Am. J. Surg., p. 235, 1907.

Miller, C. C.: The correction of featural imperfections, Chicago, 1907, Oak Printing Co.

Miller, C. C.: The cure of rupture by paraffin injections, Chicago, 1908, Oak Printing Co.

Miller, C. C.: The limitations and the use of paraffin in cosmetic surgery, Wis. Med. Rec. **11**:277, 1908.

Miller, C. C.: Cosmetic surgery. The correction of featural imperfections, Philadelphia, 1924, F. A. Davis Co.

Miller, C. C., and Miller, F.: Folds, bags and wrinkles of the skin about the eyes and their eradication by simple surgical methods, Med. Brief **35**:540, 1907.

O'Brien, B. M.: Replantation and reconstructive microvascular surgery. II, Ann. R. Coll. Surg. Engl. **58**:171, 1976.

Passot, R.: Chirurgie esthetique pure. Techniques et résultats, vol. XXII, Paris, 1931, Gaston Doin.

Posse, R. P.: Cirugía estíteca, Buenos Aires, 1946.

Reich, J.: The evolution of thought concerning the justification of aesthetic plastic surgery, Aesthet. Plast. Surg. **2**:183, 1978.

Reich, J.: Aesthetic judgement in the surgery of appearance, Aesthet. Plast. Surg. **1**:35, 1976.

Rosenthal, S.: Cosmetic surgery: a consumer's guide, Philadelphia, 1977, J. B. Lippincott Co.

Seitchik, M. W., and Kahn, S.: The effects of delay on the circulatory efficiency of pedicled tissue. A review, Plast. Reconstr. Surg. **33**:16, 1964.

Skoog, T.: Plastic surgery. New methods and refinements, Stockholm, 1974, Almquist & Wiksell International.

Smith, F. W., and Baker, S.: Doctor, make me beautiful, New York, 1973, David McKay Co., Inc.

Stark, R. B.: Plastic surgery, New York, 1962, Harper & Row, Publishers.

Wilson, J. G.: The patient with disease of the skin—subcutaneous tissue. In Moidel, H. C., editor: Nursing care of the patient with medical-surgical disorders, New York, 1976, McGraw-Hill Book Co.

Zeno, L.: Cirugía plástica, Buenos Aires, 1943, El Ateneo.

HISTORY

Ceram, C. W.: Hands on the past, New York, 1966, Alfred A. Knopf, Inc.

Conway, H., and Stark, R. B.: Plastic surgery at the New York Hospital one hundred years ago with biographical notes on Gordon Buck, New York, 1953, Paul B. Hoeber, Inc.

Gould, G. M., and Pyle, W. M.: Anomalies and curiosities of medicine, Philadelphia, 1897, Saunders.

Hollander, E.: Die Medizin in der klassischen Malerei, Stuttgart, 1912, Verlag von Ferdinand Enke.

Major, R. H.: A history of medicine, vols. 1 and 2, Springfield, Ill., 1954, Charles C Thomas, Publisher.

Maltz, M.: Evolution of plastic surgery, New York, 1946, Froben Press.

Miller, C. C.: The surgical reduction of the nasal tip of excessive length, Ala. Med. J., p. 620, 1906.

Miller, C. C.: Surgical treatment of hump nose, Med. Brief **34:**160, 1906.

Miller, C. C.: Cosmetic surgery of the face, Int. J. Surg. **20:**311, 1907.

Miller, C. C.: The eradication by surgical means of the nasolabial lines, Ther. Gaz. **31:**676, 1907.

Miller, C. C.: External canthotomy and section of the fibers of the orbicularis palpebrarum for minimizing "crow's-feet," St. Louis Clin. **20:**213, 1907.

Miller, C. C.: Semilunar excision of the skin at the outer canthus for the eradication of "crow's-feet," Am. J. Dermatol., p. 483, 1907.

Miller, C. C.: Subcutaneous division of the fibers of the orbicularis muscle for overcoming "crow's-feet," Med. Times, p. 207, 1907.

Miller, C. C.: Subcutaneous section of the facial muscles to eradicate expression lines, Am. J. Surg., p. 235, 1907.

Miller, C. C.: The correction of featural imperfections, Chicago, 1908, Oak Printing Co.

Miller, C. C.: Cosmetic surgery. The correction of featural imperfections, Philadelphia, 1924, F. A. Davis Co.

Miller, C. C.: The cure of rupture by paraffin injections, Chicago, 1908, Oak Printing Co.

Miller, C. C.: The limitations and the use of paraffin in cosmetic surgery, Wis. Med. Rec. **11:**277, 1908.

Miller, C. C., and Miller, F.: Folds, bags and wrinkles of the skin about the eyes and their eradication by simple surgical methods, Med. Brief **35:**540, 1907.

Ploss, H. H., Bartels, M., and Bartels, P.: Woman—an historical, gynaecological and anthropological compendium (Dingwall, E. J., editor), London, 1935, William Heinemann, Ltd.

Regnault, P.: The history of abdominal dermolipectomy, Aesthet. Plast. Surg. **2:**113, 1978.

Robin, G.: Dr. Suzanne Noël. Dictionnaire national des contemporains, vol. I, Paris, 1936, La Jeunesse.

Rogers, B. O.: A brief history of cosmetic surgery, Surg. Clin. North Am. **51:**265, 1971.

Siebert, I.: Women in the ancient Near East, New York, 1974, Abner Schram.

Stark, R.: The history of plastic surgery in wartime, Clin. Plast. Surg. **2:**509, 1975.

Tagliacozzi, G.: Quoted in Maltz, M.: Evolution of plastic surgery, New York, 1946, Froben Press.

Vilain, R.: Woman's figures: yesterday, today, tomorrow, Quest. Med. **27:**1351, 1974.

Vogel, V. J.: American Indian medicine, Norman, 1970, University of Oklahoma Press.

OBESITY AND BYPASS PROCEDURES

Benedetti, A., and Zerbini, E.: Adiposità e funzione respiratoria, Prog. Med. **14:**355, 1958.

Benedetti, A., and Zerbini, E.: La funzione respiratoria nel obesità patologica, Rass Fisiopat. Clin. **30:**119, 1958.

Bertezene, F.: Thérapeutiques inutiles ou dangereuses dans la cure de l'obésité, Cah. Med. Lyon. **46:**9, 1970.

Björntorp, P.: Effects of age, sex and clinical conditions on adipose tissue cellularity in man, Metabolism **23:**1091, 1974.

Björntorp, P., Bengtsson, C., Blohmé, G., et al.: Adipose tissue fat cell size and number in relation to metabolism in randomly selected middle-aged men and women, Metabolism **20:**927, 1971.

Björntorp, P., and Sjöström, L.: Number and size of adipose tissue fat cells in relation to metabolism in human obesity, Metabolism **20:**703, 1971.

Bondar, G. F., and Pisesky, W.: Complications of small intestinal short-circuiting for obesity, Arch. Surg. **94:**707, 1967.

Bouchon, J. P., and Couderc, F.: Obésités, Perfect. Prive Pract., p. 46, 1970.

Bray, G. A.: Clinical management of the obese patient, Postgrad. Med. **51:**125, 1972.

Bruch, H.: Obesity and sex, Med. Asp. Hum. Sex. **3:**42, 1969.

Buchwald, H., and Varco, R.: A bypass operation for obese hyperlipidemic patients, Surgery **70:**62, 1971.

Canning, H., and Mayer, J.: Obesity: an analysis of attitudes, knowledge and weight control in girls, Res. Q. **39:**894, 1968.

Casalis, G. A.: Lipectomy as a cure for adiposity and menstrual irregularity; notes on two cases, J. Obstet. Gynaecol. Br. Emp. **21:**34, 1912.

Castle, H. E.: Obesity and its surgical treatment by lipectomy, Ann. Surg., **54:**706, 1911.

Chlouverakis, C., and Hojnicki, I.: Lipectomy in obese hyperglycemic mice (obob), Metabolism **23:**133, 1974.

Clarkson, P.: Lipodystrophies, Plast. Reconstr. Surg. **37**:499, 1966.

Clarkson, P., and Jeffs, J.: The contribution of plastic surgery to the treatment of obesity. In Modern trends in plastic surgery, London, 1966, Butterworth & Co. (Publishers), Ltd.

Dercum, F. X., and McCarthy, D. J.: Autopsy in a case of adiposus dolorosa, Am. J. Sci. **124**:994, 1902.

Desjardins, P.: Résection de la couche adi d'obésité extrème (lipectomie). Rapport par Dartigues, Paris Chir. **3**:466, 1911.

Drastic cures of obesity (editorial), Lancet **1**: 1094, 1970.

Duncan, G. G., Jensen, W. K., Fraser, R. I., and Cristofori, F. C.: Correction and control of intractable obesity, J.A.M.A. **181**: 309, 1962.

Dwyer, J. I.: Psychosexual aspects of weight control and dieting behavior in adolescents, Med. Asp. Hum. Sex. **7**(3):82, 1973.

Faust, I. M., Johnson, P. R., and Hirsch, J.: Adipose tissue regeneration following lipectomy, Science **197**:301, 1977.

Foged, J.: Operative treatment of abdominal obesity especially pendulous abdomen, Br. J. Plast. Surg. **1**:274, 1949.

Galtier, M.: Surgical therapy of obesity of the abdominal wall with ptosis [traitement chirurgical de l'obésité de la paroi abdominale avec ptose], Mem. Acad. Chir. **81**:341, 1955.

Galtier, M.: L'obésité de la paroi abdominale avec ptose. Traitement chirurgical, Presse Med. **70**:135, 1962.

Georgiadis, N., and Katsas, A.: Topography of fat in the sacroiliac region, Plast. Reconstr. Surg. **49**:110, 1972.

Gray, G., and Jones, H.: A case of diffuse symmetric lipomatosis, Plast. Reconstr. Surg. **23**:547, 1959.

Gray, H.: Mammoth obesity: an anthropometric study, Stanford Med. Bull. **8**:106, 1950.

Handley, J. H.: Diabetics, overweight: U.S. problems, J. Am. Diet. Assoc. **32**:417, 1956.

Hinderer, U. T.: Tratamiento quirúrgico de la obesidad abdominal (dermolipectomías), Ann. Acad. Med. Quir. Esp. **51**:3, 1966-1967.

Hirsch, J., and Han, P. W.: Cellularity of rat adipose tissue: effects on growth, starvation and obesity, J. Lipid Res. **10**:77, 1969.

Humberd, C. D.: Extreme obesity, J. Missouri Med. Assoc. **33**:265, 1936.

Hussels, I. E.: Progressive lipodystrophy, Birth Defects **7**:229, 1971.

Iturraspe, M. C.: Tratamiento quirúrgico de la obesidad, Rev. Assoc. Med. Argent. **66**:340, 1952.

Johnson, P. R., and Hirsch, P. W.: Cellularity of adipose depots in six strains of genetically obese mice, J. Lipid Res. **13**:2, 1972.

Jones, C. M., Culver, P. J., Drummey, G. D., and Ryan, A. E.: Modification of fat absorption with an emulsifying agent, Ann. Intern. Med. **29**:1, 1948.

Jones, L. J., and Boines, G. J.: Rehabilitation in obese by lipectomy, Del. Med. J. **18**:161, July, 1946.

Kamper, M. J., Galloway, D., and Ashley, F.: Abdominal panniculectomy after massive weight loss, Plast. Reconstr. Surg. **50**:441, 1972.

Kaufmann, J. H., and Weldon, H. W.: Intussusception, a late complication of small bowel bypass for obesity, J.A.M.A. **202**:1147, 1967.

Kennedy, G. C.: The role of depot fat in the hypothalamic control of food intake in the rat, Proc. R. Soc. Lond. [Biol.] **140**:578, 1952.

Kessering, U. K., and Meyer, R.: A suction curette for removal of excessive local deposits of subcutaneous fat, Plast. Reconstr. Surg. **62**:305, 1978.

Kiene, V. S.: Plastic surgery for abdominal adiposity, Zentralbl. Chir., p. 92, 1967.

Knittle, J. L.: Nombre et taille des cellules adipeuses du sujet obèse, Triangle **14**:4, 1974.

Knittle, J. L., and Ginsberg-Fellner, F.: Effect of weight reduction on in vitro adipose tissue lipolysis and cellularity in obese adolescents and adults, Diabetes **21**:754, 1972.

Larkin, C. N.: Lipectomy for abdominal fat, Conn. Med. J. **7**:706, 1950.

Liebelt, R. A., Ichinoe, A. S., and Nocholson, N.: Regulatory influences of adipose tissue on food intake and body weight, Ann. N. Y. Acad. Sci. **131**:559, 1965.

Lupo, G., et al.: Adiposus nosography in lipomatosis and lipodystrophy in light of present criticism, Plast. Reconstr. Surg. **57**:683, 1976.

Mabry, C. C., and Hollingsworth, D. R.: Failure of hypophysectomy in generalized lipodystrophy, J. Pediatr. **81**:990, 1972.

MacLean, L. D.: The extreme pendulous abdomen and its surgical treatment by a new three flap operation, Surg. Gynecol. Obstet. **28**:190, 1919.

Mann, G. V.: The influence of obesity on health, N. Engl. J. Med. **291**:178, 225, 1974.

Masson, J. K.: Lipectomy: the surgical removal of excess fat, Postgrad. Med. **32:**381, 1962.

Maxwell, J. G., Richards, R. C., and Albo, D., Jr.: Fatty degeneration of the liver after intestinal bypass for obesity, Am. J. Surg. **176:**648, 1968.

McCraw, L. H.: Surgical rehabilitation after massive weight reduction. Case report, Plast. Reconstr. Surg. **53:**349, 1974.

Meyerowitz, B. R., et al.: From massive weight loss to abdominal panniculectomy, R. N. **37:**1, 1974.

Moore, M. E., Stunkard, A., and Srole, L.: Obesity, social class, and mental illness, J.A.M.A. **181:**962, 1962.

Moriet: Radical cure of obesity, Ann. Med. Phys. Anvers. **10:**285, 1912.

Morris, R. T.: Surgery of the obese, Mon. Cycl. Med. Bull. **3:**641, 1910.

Muhlbauer, W. D.: Plastic surgery in the treatment of obesity [die plastisch-chirurgische Behandlung der Fettleibigkeit], Munch. Med. Wochenschr. **117:**745, 1975.

Palmer, B., et al.: Skin reduction plasties following intestinal shunt operations for treatment of obesity, Scand. J. Plast. Reconstr. Surg. **9:**47, 1975.

Passot, R.: Correction esthétique des adiposités localisées. Chirurgie esthétique pure, vol. XXII, Paris, 1931, Gaston Doin.

Payne, J. H., and DeWind, L. T.: Surgical treatment of obesity, Am. J. Surg. **118:**141, 1969.

Payne, J. H., DeWind, L. T., and Commons, R. R.: Metabolic observations in patients with jejunocolic shunts, Am. J. Surg. **106:**273, 1963.

Payne, J. H., DeWind, L., Schwab, C. E., et al.: Surgical treatment of morbid obesity. Sixteen years of experience, Arch. Surg. **106:**432, 1973.

Printen, K. J., and Mason, E. E.: Gastric surgery for relief of morbid obesity, Arch. Surg. **106:**428, 1973.

Rockey, A. E.: Surgical operations on the obese and the advantage of preparatory fasting, Northwest Med. **3**(NS):241, 1911.

Rosenthal, P., Blava, C., Spencer, H., and Zimmerman, H. J.: Liver morphology and function tests in obesity and during total starvation, Am. J. Dig. Dis. **12:**198, 1967.

Rosnard, N.: Cellulite, New York, 1973, Beauty & Health Publishing Corp.

Roucher, F.: Contribution de la chirurgie plastique au traitement de l'obésité, Grenoble, France, 1969, E. P. U.

Sanders, R.: The plastic surgical treatment of obesity, Proc. R. Soc. Med. **68:**664, 1975.

Schemmel, R., Mickelsen, O., Pierce, S. A., Johnson, J. T., and Schirmer, R. G.: Fat depot removal, food intake, body fat and fat depot weights in obese rats, Proc. Soc. Exp. Biol. Med. **136:**1269, 1971.

Schwartz, A. W.: Technique for excision of abdominal fat, Br. J. Plast. Surg. **27:**44, 1974.

Scott, H. W., Jr., Dean, R., Shull, H. J., et al.: Considerations in use of jejunoileal bypass in patients with morbid obesity, Ann. Surg. **177:**723, 1973.

Scott, H. W., Jr., Sandstead, H. H., Brill, A. B., Burko, H., and Younger, R. K.: Experience with a new technique of intestinal bypass in the treatment of morbid obesity, Ann. Surg. **174:**560, 1971.

Seltzer, C. C., and Mayer, J.: Body build obesity—who are the obese? J.A.M.A. **189:**677, 1964.

Seltzer, C. C., and Mayer, J.: A simple criterion of obesity, Postgrad. Med. **38:**A101, 1965.

Seltzer, C. C. and Mayer, J.: Body build (somatotype) distinctiveness in obese women, J. Am. Diet. Assoc. **55:**454, 1969.

Short, J. J.: Extreme obesity followed by therapeutic reduction of 239 pounds, J.A.M.A. **111:**2196, 1938.

Simkin, B.: Urinary 17-ketosteroid and 17-ketogenic steroid excretion in obese patients, N. Engl. J. Med. **264:**94, 1961.

Sjöström, L., Björntorp, P., and Vrana, J.: Microscopic fat cell size measurements on frozen-cut adipose tissue in comparison with automatic determinations of osmium-fixed fat cells, J. Lipid Res. **12:**521, 1971.

Sjöström, L., Smith, U., Krotkiewski, M., et al.: Cellularity in different regions of adipose tissue in young men and women, Metabolism **21:**1143, 1972.

Sokolova, L. A.: Free adipo-dermal grafts in the surgical treatment of progressive lipodystrophy, Acta Chir. Plast. **14:**157, 1972.

Sokolova, L. A.: Lipodermal grafts in the surgical treatment of progressive lipodystrophy, Plast. Reconstr. Surg. **52:**686, 1973.

Steinkamp, R. C., Cohen, N. L., Gaffey, W. R., McKey, T., Bron, G., Sui, W. E., Sargent, T. W., and Isaacs, E.: Measures of body fat and related factors in normal adults. A simple clinical method to estimate body fat and lean body mass, J. Chronic Dis. **18:**1291, 1965.

Stunkard, A. J., and Mendelson, M.: Disturbances in body image of some obese persons, Am. Diet. Assoc. **38:**328, 1961.

Talamas-Vasquez, J.: Abdominal lipectomy for obesity, Prensa Med. Mex. **11:**69, 1946.

Tamerin, J. A.: Surgical repair of the obese abdomen, Diab. Obes. Rev. **1:**26, Jan., 1936.

Taylor, L. M., Beahrs, O. H., and Fontana, R. S.: Benign symmetric lipomatosis, Proc. Staff Meet. Mayo Clin. **36:**1961.

Tennant, C. E.: Lipectomies in the obese when operating for intra-abdominal lesions, Denver Med. Times **34:**43, 1914-1915.

Vilain, R.: Chirurgie raisonnable de l'obésité. Entretiens de Bichat. Chirurgie et specialités, Paris, 1958, L'Expansion Scientifique Français.

Vilain, R.: Plastique chirurgicale de l'obésité, Vie Méd. **46:**10, 1523, 1965.

Vilain, R.: Surgical correction of steatomeries, Clin. Plast. Surg. **2:**467, 1975.

Vilain, R.: Le traitement des steatoméries chez la femme, Ann. Chir. Plast. **20:**135, 1975.

Vilain, R., Dardour, J. C., and Bzowski, A.: De-epithelialized flaps in the treatment of scars, abdominal excess of skin and subtrochanteric steatomeries, Paris (undated), Hospital Boucicaut.

Wells, H. G.: Adipose tissue, a neglected subject (Fenger lecture), J.A.M.A. **114:**2177, 2284, 1940.

Willoughby, D. P.: An extraordinary case of obesity, Hum. Biol **14:**166, 1942.

Winkelman, N. Z., and Eckel, J. L.: Adiposis dolorosa (Dercum's disease), J.A.M.A. **85:** 1935, 1925.

Wood, L. C., and Chremos, A. N.: Negative results—treating obesity by "short-circuiting" the small intestine, J.A.M.A. **186:**63, 1963.

Zucker, L. M., Cruce, L. M., and Hirsch, J.: Cellularity of adipose depots in the genetically obese Zucker rat, J. Lipid Res. **12:**706, 1971.

PHYSIOLOGY

Bonica, J.: The management of pain, Philadelphia, 1953, Lea & Febiger.

Borgstrom, B., et al.: Studies of intestinal digestion and absorption in the human, J. Clin. Invest. **36:**1521, 1957.

Crock, H. V.: The blood supply of the lower limb bones in man, Edinburgh, 1967, E. & S. Livingstone, Ltd.

Elbaz, J. S., and Dardour, J. C.: Anatomy and physiology of the arteries and veins of the abdominal wall. In Marchac, D., editor: Transactions of the Sixth International Congress of Plastic and Reconstructive Surgery, Paris, 1975, Masson & Cie, Editeurs.

Elbaz, J. S., Dardour, J. C., and Ricbourg, B.: Vascularisation artérielle de la paroi abdominale, Ann. Chir. Plast. **20:**1, 19, 1975.

Elman, R., and Read, J.: Nutritional recovery following removal of all but three fat of jejunum and half of colon, J. Missouri Med. Assoc. **42:**145, 1945.

Faust, I. M., Johnson, P. R., and Hirsch, J.: Noncompensation of adipose mass in partially lipectomized mice and rats, Am. J. Physiol. **231:**538, 1976.

Faust, I. M., Johnson, P. R., and Hirsch, J.: Surgical removal of adipose tissue alters feeding behavior and the development of obesity in rats, Science **197:**393, 1977.

Folch, J. M.: The regulation of adiposity in the mouse: the relationship between caloric intake and compensatory thypertrophy. Doctoral thesis, Ithaca, N.Y., 1973, Cornell University.

Fujino, T.: Contribution of the axial perforator vasculature to circulation in flaps, Plast. Reconstr. Surg. **30:**125, 1967.

Goss, R. J.: Adaptive growth, London, 1964, Logos.

Hewes, J. W.: Communication of sexual interest: an anthropological view, Med. Asp. Hum. Sex. **7**(1):66, 1973.

Jordan, P. H.: Physiology of the small intestine, Surg. Gynecol. Obstet. **124:**1331, 1967.

Kety, S. S.: Measurement of regional circulation by the local clearance of radioactive sodium, Am. Heart J. **38:**321, 1949.

Kremen, A. J., Linner, J. H., and Nelson, C. H.: An experimental evaluation of the nutritional importance of proximal and distal small intestines, Ann. Surg. **140:**430, 1954.

Lopez, A.: Préjudices osseux et musculaires, Dos. Obstét. **2:**26, 1974.

Mabry, C. C., and Holingsworth, D. R.: Failure of hypophysectomy in generalized lipodystrophy, J. Pediatr. **81:**990, 1972.

Meyerowitz, B. R., and Nelson, R.: Measurement of the velocity of blood in lower limb veins with and without compression, Surgery **56**:484, 1964.

Mitz, V., Elbaz, J. S., and Vilde, F.: Etude des fibres élastiques dermiques au cours d'opérations plastiques du tronc, Ann. Chir. Plast. **20**:31, 1975.

Payne, J. H., DeWind, L. T., and Commons, R. R.: Metabolic observations in patients with jejunocolic shunts, Am. J. Surg. **106**:273, 1963.

Pierard, J., et al.: Le tissu élastique cutané normal. In Maladies du tissu élastique cutané, Paris, 1968, Masson & Cie, Editeurs.

Pire, J. C.: Les complications respiratoires des grandes éventrations. Thesis, Paris, 1968, Faculté de Médecine de Paris.

Todd, W. R. Dittlebrandt, M., Montague, J. R., and West, E. S.: Digestive absorption in a man with three feet of small intestine, Am. J. Dig. Dis. **7**:295, 1940.

Ubiglia, G. P., and Pastacaldi, P.: Nuovo metodo di addominoplastica estetica, Riv. Ital. Chir. Plast. **9**:257, 1977.

West, E. S., Montague, J. R., and Judy, F. R.: Digestion and absorption in a man with three feet of small intestine, Am. J. Dig. Dis. **5**:690, 1938.

PSYCHOLOGY, PSYCHIATRY, AND BODY IMAGE

Abeles, M. M.: Postoperative psychosis, Am. J. Psychiatry **94**:2287, 1938.

Adamson, J. D., Hershberg, D., and Shane, F.: The psychic significance of parts of the body in surgery, Psychiatry **8**:137, 1977.

Apton, A. A.: Your mind and appearance, New York, 1951, Citadel Press.

Arnheim, R.: Visual thinking, London, 1969, Faber & Faber, Ltd.

Baker, W. Y., and Smith, L. N.: Facial disfigurement and personality, J.A.M.A. **112**:301, 1939.

Barsky, A. J.: Psychology of the patient undergoing plastic surgery, Am. J. Surg. **65**:238, 1944.

Barsky, A. J.: Psychosomatic medicine and plastic surgery. In Cantor, A. J., and Foxe, A. N., editors: Psychosomatic aspects of surgery, New York, 1956, Grune & Stratton, Inc.

Bettman, A. G.: The psychology of appearances, Northwest Med. **28**:182, 1929.

Bonica, J.: The management of pain, Philadephia, 1953, Lea & Febiger.

Burk, J.: A psychological approach to cosmetic surgery in women: self-consistency, Dissertation Abstr. Int. **36**:5859, 1976.

Cobb, S., and McDermott, N. T.: Postoperative psychosis, Med. Clin. North Am. **22**:569, 1938.

Courtiss, E. H., editor: Aesthetic surgery: trouble—how to avoid it and how to treat it, St. Louis, 1978, The C. V. Mosby Co.

Debaere, P. A.: Psychologie de l'obèse. Candidat à lipectomie. Doctoral thesis, Lille, France, 1975.

Depaulis, J.: Les problèmes psychologiques posés par la chirurgie plastique, Bordeaux Med. **9**:775, 1976.

Deutsch, H.: Psychology of women, New York, 1944, Grune & Stratton, Inc.

Dicker, R. L., and Syracuse, V. R.: Consultation with a plastic surgeon, Chicago, 1975, Nelson-Hall Co.

Dunbar, F.: Psychosomatic diagnosis, New York, 1943, Paul B. Hoeber, Inc.

Dwyer, J. I.: Psychosexual aspects of weight control and dieting behavior in adolescents, Med. Asp. Hum. Sex. **7**(3):82, 1973.

Edgerton, M. T.: Plastic surgeon's obligations to the emotionally disturbed patient (editorial), Plast. Reconstr. Surg. **55**:81, 1975.

Edgerton, M. T., and Jacobson, W. E., and Meyer, E.: Surgical-psychiatric study of patients seeking plastic (cosmetic) surgery: ninety-eight consecutive patients with minimal deformity, Br. J. Plast. Surg. **13**:136, 1960.

Edgerton, M. T., and Knorr, N. J.: Motivational patterns of patients seeking cosmetic (aesthetic surgery), Plast. Reconstr. Surg. **48**:551, 1971.

Fiedler, L.: Freaks, myths and images of the secret self, New York, 1978, Simon & Schuster, Inc., Publishers.

Fisher, S.: Extensions of theory concerning body image and body reactivity, Psychosom. Med. **21**:142, 1959.

Fisher, S., and Albercrombie, J.: The relationship of body image distortions to body reactivity gradients, J. Pers. **26**:320, 1958.

Fisher, S., and Cleveland, S. E.: An approval to physiological reactivity in terms of a body image schema, Psychol. Rev. **64**:26, 1957.

Fisher, S., and Cleveland, S. E.: Body image and personality, Princeton, N.J., 1958, D. Van Nostrand Co., Inc.

Franklyn, R. A., with Gould, H.: The art of staying young, New York, 1964, Frederick Fell, Inc.

Frazier, C. A.: Is it moral to modify man? Springfield, Ill., 1973, Charles C Thomas, Publisher.

Gardiner, L. E.: Faces, figures and feelings, London, 1959, Robert Hale, Ltd.

Garland, M.: The changing face of beauty, New York, 1957, Barrows & Co., Inc.

Gifford, S.: Cosmetic surgery and personality change: a review and some clinical observations. In Goldwyn, R. M.: The unfavorable result in plastic surgery, Boston, 1972, Little, Brown & Co.

Goldstein, D. L.: Psychology of the prospective plastic surgery patient, J. Med. Soc. 66:647, 1969.

Goldwyn, R. M.: The unfavorable result in plastic surgery, Boston, 1972, Little, Brown & Co.

Graham, L., and Conley, E.: Evaluation of anxiety and fear in adult surgical patients, Nurs. Res. 20:113, 1971.

Hill, G., and Silver, A. G.: Psychodynamic and esthetic motivations for plastic surgery, Psychosom. Med. 12:345, 1950.

Hinderer, U. T.: Problemas psicológico y psiquiátrico en el paciente de cirugía plástica, Rev. Esp. Psicot. Anal. 1:31, 1968.

Jacobson, W. E., Edgerton, M. T., Meyer, E., Canter, A., and Slaughter, R.: Psychiatric evaluation of male patients seeking cosmetic surgery, Plast. Reconstr. Surg. 26:356, 1960.

Jacobson, W. E., Meyer, E., and Edgerton, M. T.: Psychiatric contributions to the clinical management of plastic surgery patients, Postgrad. Med. 29:513, 1961.

Jefferson, R. S.: The psychiatric assessment of candidates for cosmetic surgery, J. Natl. Med. Assoc. 65:411, 1976.

Jung, C.: Man and his symbols, Garden City, N.Y., 1964, Doubleday & Co., Inc.

Knorr, N. J., Edgerton, M. T., and Hoppes, J. E.: The "insatiable" cosmetic surgery patient, Plast. Reconstr. Surg. 40:285, 1967.

Knorr, N. J., Hoopes, J. E., and Edgerton, M. T.: Psychiatric-surgical approach to adolescent disturbance in self-image, Plast. Reconstr. Surg. 41:248, 1968.

Kramer, C. Y.: Extension of multiple range tests to group means with unequal numbers of replications, Biometrics 12:307, & Cie, Editeurs.

Lewin, M. L.: The collaboration between the psychologist, the psychiatrist and the surgeon in plastic surgery. In Marchac, D., editor: Transactions of the Sixth International Congress of Plastic and Reconstructive Surgery, Paris, 1975, Masson & Cie, Editeurs.

Lindermann, E.: Observations on psychiatric sequelae to surgical operations in women, Am. J. Psychiatry 98:132, 1941.

Linn, L.: Psychiatric aspects of plastic surgery. In Bellak, L., editor: Psychology of physical illness, New York, 1952, Grune & Stratton, Inc.

Linn, L., and Goldman, I.: Psychiatric observation concerning rhinoplasty, Psychosom. Med. 11:307, 1949.

Macgregor, F. C.: Transformation and identity. The face and plastic surgery, New York, 1974, Quadrangle/The New York Times Book Co.

Macgregor, F. C., and Schaffner, G.: Screening patients for nasal plastic operations, Psychosom. Med. 12:227, 1950.

Matton, G.: Function, aesthetic problems and psyche in plastic surgery [functie, esthetiek en psyche in de plastiche], Hulkunde-Klin. Plast. Hulk. Rijksuniv. Gent. T. Geneesk 28:287, 1972.

Menninger, K. A.: Somatic correlations with the unconscious repudiation of feminity in women, J. Nerv. Ment. Dis. 89:514, 1939.

Menninger, K. A.: Somatic correlations with the unconscious repudiation of feminity in women, Bull. Menninger Clin. 3:106, 1939-1940.

Meyer, E.: Psychiatric aspects of plastic surgery. In Converse, J. M., editor: Reconstructive plastic surgery, Philadelphia, 1964, W. B. Saunders Co.

Meyer, E., et al.: Motivational patterns in patients seeking elective plastic surgery. I. Women who seek rhinoplasty, Psychosom. Med. 22:193, 1960.

Meyer, E., and Edgerton, M.: Abstracts of papers presented before the meeting of the Johns Hopkins Medical Society, Bull. Johns Hopkins Hosp. 100:234, 1957.

Meyer, E., and Mendelson, M.: Psychiatric consultations with patients on medical and surgical wards. Patterns and processes, Psychiatry 24:197, 1961.

Mitchell, A.: No man despairs, London, 1958, George G. Harrap & Co., Ltd.

Nicoletis, C.: Morphologie et psychologie, Psychosom. Med. 21:101, 1972-1973.

Olley, P. C.: Psychiatric aspects of cosmetic surgery, Mod. Perspect. Psychiatry 7:491, 1976.

Penn, J.: The right to look human—an autobiography, New York, 1974, McGraw-Hill Book Co.

Pitanguy, I., Jaimovick, C. A., and Schwartz,

S.: Evaluation of the psychological and psychiatric aspects in plastic surgery, Rev. Bras. Cirurg. **66**(3-4):120, 1976.

Powell, G. E., Tutton, S. J., and Stewart, R. A.: The differential stereotyping of similar physiques, Br. J. Soc. Clin. Psychol. **13**:421, 1974.

Reich, J.: The surgery of appearance: psychological and related aspects, Med. J. Aust. **2**:5, 1969.

Rosen, V. H.: The role of denial in acute postoperative affective reactions following removal of body parts, Psychosom. Med. **12**: 356, 1950.

Rozner, L.: Attitudes to cosmetic surgery, Med. J. Aust. **2**:8, 513, September, 1973.

Sachs, B. C.: This bosom business. I. Changing emphasis on the breasts, Med. Asp. Hum. Sex. **3**(4):49; II. Cosmetic aids and surgery, Med. Asp. Hum. Sex. **3**(5):14, 1969.

Schilder, P.: The image and appearance of the human body: studies in the constructive energies of the psyche, Psyche Monographs, no. 4, London, 1935, Kegan Paul, Trench, Trubner & Co., Ltd.

Schireson, H. I.: As others see you, New York, 1838, The Macaulay Co.

Seidenberg, R.: Psychosexual adjustment of the unattractive woman, Med. Asp. Hum. Sex. **7**(5):5, 1973.

Sheldon, W. H., Stevens, S. S., and Tucker, W. B.: Varieties of human physique, New York, 1940, Harper & Brothers.

Shemken, F.: Borderline states, J. Nerv. Ment. Dis. **123**:466, 1956.

Stepner, A. L.: Borderline case presenting paranoid and obsessive features, J. Hillside Hosp. **1**:103, 1952.

Stern, K., Doyon, D., and Racine, R.: Preoccupation with the shape of the breast as a psychiatric symptom in women, Can. Psychiatr. Assoc. J. **4**:243, 1959.

Straith, C. L.: Plastic surgery: its psychological aspects, J. Mich. State Med. Soc. **31**:13, 1932.

Stunkard, A. J., and Mendelson, M.: Characteristics of disturbances in body image of some obese persons, Am. Diet. Assoc. **38**:328, 1961.

Szasz, T. S.: Pain and pleasure, New York, 1957, Basic Books, Inc.

Taylor, B. W., Litin, E. M., and Litzow, T. J.: Psychiatric considerations in cosmetic surgery, Mayo Clin. Proc. **41**:608, 1966.

Thompson, W. E.: Retirement and family relationships, presented at the meeting of the American Sociologocial Society, Chicago, Sept., 1959.

Thomson, H. W.: Preoperative selection and counseling of patients for rhinoplasty (editorial), Plast. Reconstr. Surg. **50**:174, 1972.

Thomson, J. A., Jr., Knorr, N. J., and Edgerton, M. T., Jr.: Cosmetic surgery: the psychiatric perspective, Psychosomatics **19**(1):7, 1978.

Titchener, J. L., and Levine, M.: Surgery as a human experience, New York, 1960, Oxford University Press, Inc.

Updegraff, H. S., and Menninger, K. A.: Some psychoanalytic aspects of plastic surgery, Am. J. Surg. **25**:554, 1934.

Washburn, A. C., and Carns, M. L.: Postoperative psychosis suggestions for prevention and treatment, J. Nerv. Ment. Dis. **82**:508, 1935.

Wolberg, A. R.: "Borderline" patient, Am. J. Psychother. **6**:694, 1952.

Zalon, J., with Block, J. L.: I am whole again, New York, 1978, Random House, Inc.

SKIN

Allen, A. C.: The skin: a clinicopathologic treatise, St. Louis, 1954, The C. V. Mosby Co.

Allografts: epithelial dividends, Med. World News **14**:5, 1973.

Bailey, A. J., and Robins, S. P.: Development and maturation of the crosslinks in the collagen fiber of the skin. In Robert, L., and Robert, B., editors: Aging of connective tissues–skin, Basel, Switzerland, 1973, S. Karger, AG.

Bern, H. A.: Histology and chemistry of keratin formation, Nature **1974**:509, 1954.

Bonting, S. J. L., Jr.: Cysteine, cystine, and methionine in the skin of young and adult rats, Biochim. Biophys. Acta **6**:183, 1950.

Brown, H.: The mineral content of human skin, J. Biol. Chem. **75**:789, 1927.

De Gorgio, A.: The influence of light on the aging skin, G. Gerontol. **4**:563, 1956.

Franco, T.: A cicatrização da ferida cirurgia, Folha Med. **57**:213, 1968.

Goldbaum, R. W., Piper, W. W., and Campbell, D. W.: A comparison of 3 histochemical stains for the demonstration of protein bound sulfhydryl groups in normal human skin, J. Invest. Dermatol. **23**:375, 1954.

Kraus, E.: Implantation of skin flaps into peritoneum to study the possibility of a functional adaptation of the skin, Arch. Mikroanat. **79**:332, 1912.

Lewis, J. R.: Surgery of scars, New York, 1964, McGraw-Hill Book Co.

Little: Acne vulgaris with keloids, Proc. R. Soc. Med. Dermatol. Sect. **3**:107, 1909-1910.

Mescon, H., and Flesch, P.: Modification of Bennett's method for the histochemical demonstration of free sulfhydryl groups in skin, J. Invest. Dermatol. **18**:261, 1952.

Montagna, W.: The structure and function of skin, ed. 2, New York, 1962, Academic Press, Inc.

Morris, D.: Extensive acne with scars and keloid, Br. J. Dermatol. **21**:329, 1909.

Penn, J.: The removal of "cross-hatch" scars, Plast. Reconstr. Surg. **25**:73, 1960.

Ross, R.: Pathways of radioactive collagen loss from skin grafts, Surg. Gynecol. Obstet. **1**:138, 1974.

Rudolph, R., and Klein, L.: Pathways of radioactive collagen loss from skin grafts, Surg. Gynecol. Obstet. **138**:55, 1974.

Schatz, H.: Sloughing of skin following flourescein extravasation, Ann. Ophthalmol. **10**:625, 1978.

Silvestri, U.: On the histochemistry of senile skin, G. Gerontol. **8**:243, 1960.

Vidik, A.: Rheology of skin with special reference to age related parameters and their possible correlations to structure. In Robert, L., and Robert, B., editors: Aging of connective tissues–skin, Basel, Switzerland, 1973, S. Karger, AG.

Vilain, R., Dardour, J. C., and Bzowski, A.: De-epithelialized flaps in the treatment of scars, abdominal excess of skin and subtrochanteric steatomeries, Paris (undated), Hospital Boucicaut.

Wilson, J. G.: The patient with disease of the skin–subcutaneous tissue. In Moidel, H. C., editor: Nursing care of the patient with medical-surgical disorders, New York, 1976, McGraw-Hill Book Co.

Zoltan, J.: Techniques for ideal wound healing. In Cicatrix optima, Baltimore, 1977, University Park Press.

SURGICAL TECHNIQUES: ABDOMEN, EXTREMITIES, AND BUTTOCKS

Acquaviva, D. E., and Bourret, P.: Cure des éventrations par plaques de nylon, Presse Med. **56**:892, 1948.

Agris, J.: Use of dermal fat suspension flaps for thigh and buttock lifts, Plast. Reconstr. Surg. **59**:817, 1977.

Aievoli, E.: Plastiche ed operazioni ortomorfiche sulle parti addominali, Incurabili (Napoli) **30**:121, 1915.

Aknan, C.: Un étude de 500 hernies par incision, J. Int. Coll. Surg. **37**:125, 1965.

Albertango. A. G.: Dermolipectomia, Ann. Chir. **21**:151, 1956.

Allansmith, R.: An excision of abdominal fat apron, A.M.A. Arch. Surg. **80**:327, 1960.

Allshorn, A. H.: On protuberant abdomen. An outline of its causes and treatment, London, 1875, Houlston & Son.

Andrews, J. M.: Nova ténica de lipectomía abdominal e onfaloneoplástica. In Transactions of the Third Latin American Congress of Plastic Surgery, 1956.

Antoni, F. P.: Técnica de Moreston-Caballos adaptada al tratamiento de las hernias umbilicales, eventraciones medias y abdomen fláccido, Prensa Med. Argent. **56**:502, 1969.

Apfelberg, D. B., Maser, M. R., and Lash, H.: Two unusual umbilicoplasties, Plast. Reconstr. Surg. **64**:268, 1979.

Artaud, L., et al.: Les greffes de derme dans le traitement des éventrations, Marseille Chir. **4**:251, 1952.

Artz, C., and Hardy, J.: Le complicanze in chirurgia e lor trattamento, Padua, Italy, 1963, Piccin Editore.

Asbell, N.: Giant panniculus adiposus abdominis, Arch. Surg. **107**:901, 1973.

Ashbell, T. S.: Intraabdominal and pelvic surgery without visible scars, Med. J. **149**:51, 1976.

Aston, S. J., and Pickrell, K. L.: Reconstructive surgery of the abdominal wall. In Converse, J. M., editor: Reconstructive plastic surgery, ed. 2, Philadelphia, 1977, W. B. Saunders Co.

Ausset: Le gros ventre flasque, Gaz. Med. Liege **9**:380, 1896-1897.

Azevedo, A.: Conficção da cicatriz umbilical nas abdominoplastias, Rev. Bras. Cirurg. **66**:353, 1976.

Babcock, W. W.: The correction of the obese and relaxed abdominal wall with special reference to the use of buried silver chain, Am. J. Obstet. **74**:596, 1916.

Babcock, W. W.: Disease of women and children, Am. J. Obstet. Gynecol. **74**:596, 1916.

Babcock, W. W.: Plastic reconstruction of the female breasts and abdomen, Am. J. Surg. **43**:260, 1939.

Baker, T. J., Gordon, H. L., and Mosienko, P.:

A template (pattern) method of abdominal lipectomy, Aesthet. Plast. Surg. **1:**167, 1977.

Bankoff, G.: A new method of lipectomy for abdominal obesity, Am. J. Surg. **80:**564, 1950.

Baron, H. C.: The surgical treatment of panniculus adiposus abdominis, Gen. Pract. **22:**130, 1974.

Baroudi, R.: Management of the umbilicus in abdominoplasty, presented at the meeting of the American Society for Aesthetic Plastic Surgery, Newport Beach, Calif., March, 1973.

Baroudi, R.: Dermatolipectomy of the upper arm, Clin. Plast. Surg. **2:**485, 1975.

Baroudi, R.: Umbilicalplasty, Clin. Plast. Surg. **2:**431, 1975.

Baroudi, R.: Syllabus for the Instructional Course of Body Sculpture, San Francisco, 1978, American Society for Aesthetic Plastic Surgery.

Baroudi, R., Keppke, E. M., and Tozzi-Netto, F.: Abdominoplasty, Plast. Reconstr. Surg. **54:**161, 1974.

Barraya, L., and Dezeuze, J.: Chirurgie abdominale, réparations pariétales et dermolipectomies. Nouvel ombilic, Mem. Acad. Chir. **93:**473, 1967.

Barraya, L., and Nakpane, E.: Abdomen molluscus—abdomen pendulum reparation. Nouvel ombilic, Presse Med. **76:**2287, 1968.

Barrile, N.: Cirugía plástica de los ventrosos, Semana Med. **111:**997, 1957.

Barsky, A. J., and Kahn, S.: Principles and practice of plastic surgery, Baltimore, 1950, The Williams & Wilkins Co.

Bazy, L.: La "laparoplastie" (méthode de Morestin), Rev. Gen. Clin. Ther. **27:**2, 1913.

Beck, C.: Pendulous abdomen, cure by removal of excess fat and obliteration of ventral hernias, Surg. Clin. **1:**731, 1917.

Belin, R. P., Stone, N. P., Fischer, R. P., et al.: Improved technique of panniculectomy, Surgery **59:**222, 1966.

Bellero, V., et al.: Abdominoplasty: physiorespiratory surgery and esthetic problems, Plast. Reconstr. Surg. **56:**356, 1975.

Berman, J. K., et al.: Massive resection of the intestine, J.A.M.A. **135:**918, 1947.

Biesenberger, H.: Eine neue Methode der Mammaplastik, Zentralbl. Chir. **55:**2382, 1928.

Biesenberger, H.: Zur Reduktion des Fett-Hängebauches, Zentralbl. Chir. **63:**1399, 1936.

Blonk, J. C.: Behandling van hangbuik, Bl. Hyg. Ther. Amst. **2:**71, 1900.

Bocchiotti, G., and Colonna, U.: Innesti adiposi e dermo adiposi, Minerva Chir. **28:**1018, 1973.

Booth, C. C.: The metabolic effects of intestinal resection in man, Postgrad. Med. J. **37:**7, 1961.

Borges, A. F.: Reconstruction of the umbilicus, Br. J. Plast. Surg. **28:**75, 1975.

Bourgeon, R., Borelli, J., and Lanfranchi, J.: L'utilisation des prosthèses de Mersilène dans le traitement des éventrations post-opératoires, Ann. Chir. **26:**541, 1972.

Bourrel, P., et al.: Dermolipectomies abdominales et cruro jambières. À propos de vingt et une observations, Soc. Med. Chir. Hop. **5:**215, 1966.

Bouterie, R. L.: Reflected fascial flaps for the repair of large abdominal defects, J. Intern. Surg. **61:**300, 1976.

Bowen, W. H.: Successful resection of 8 feet of small bowel in a boy for gangrene due to torsion of mesentery, Clin. J. **68:**117, 1939.

Bowen, W. L.: Massive resection of small intestine, Am. J. Surg. **58:**438, 1942.

Brown, R. G., Vasconez, L. O., and Jurkiewicz, M. J.: Transverse abdominal flaps and the deep epigastric arcade, Plast. Reconstr. Surg. **55:**416, 1975.

Bruck, H.: A method of reconstructing the whole abdominal wall, Br. J. Plast. Surg. **9:**108, 1956.

Brucke, H. G., and Mulbi, G.: Erfahrungen mit der Pitanguy'schen Reithosenplastick, Cosmetologia **10:**33, 1970.

Brugnion, J. P.: Plastie cutanée lors des éventrations, Med. Hyg. **29:**635, 1971.

Brunn, von: Ueber die plastische Deckung von defecten intraperitonealer Hohlorgane, Berl. Klin. Wochenschr. **41:**24, 1904.

Buchwald, H., and Varco, R.: Partial ileal bypass for hypercholesterolemia and atherosclerosis, Surg. Gynecol. Obstet. **124:**1231, 1967.

Bullitt, J. B.: Retrenchment of lipomatous abdominal wall combined with operation for radical cure of umbilical hernia, Ann. Surg., p. 663, 1900.

Burker, K.: Eine einfache Methode zur Gewinnung von Blutplättchen, Zentralbl. Physiol. **17:**137, 1903.

Buschke, A., Joseph, A., and Birkenfeld, W.: Leitfaden der Kosmetik, Berlin, 1932, Walter de Gruyter & Co.

Callia, W. E. P.: Dermolipectomia abdominal

(operation de Callia). Fascicule tireclufilm realisé par Benedito J. Duarte, São Paulo, Brazil, 1965, Centre Cinématographique Carlo Erba.

Callia, W. E. P.: Uma plastica para cirurgia geral, Med. Hosp. **1**:40, 1967.

Cannady, G. E.: The use of cutis graft in the repair of certain types of incisional herniae and other conditions, Ann. Surg. **115**:775, 1942.

Caronni, E. P.: Dettagli de tecnica per la lipectomia abdominale a fini estetici, Riv. Ital. Chir. Plast. **6**:345, 1974.

Carvahlo, C. G. S., Baroudi, R., and Keppke, E. M.: Anatomical and technical refinements for abdominoplasty, Aesthet. Plast. Surg. **1**:217, 1977.

Castanares, S., and Goethal, J.: Abdominal lipectomy; a modification in technique, Plast. Reconstr. Surg. **40**:378, 1967.

de Castle, H. E.: A recent case of lipectomy, Calif. State J. Med. **11**:58, 1913.

de Castro, C.: Abdominoplastias de retina, J. Bras. Med. **30**:103, 1976.

de Castro, C.: Study of surgical association of abdominoplasty with other procedures, J. Bras. Ginecol. **83**:137, 1977.

Castro, C., and Daher, M.: Simultaneous reduction mammaplasty and abdominoplasty, Plast. Reconstr. Surg. **61**:36, 1978.

Cervený, J.: Reconstruction of the abdominal wall at venter pendulus, Acta Chir. Plast. **16**:178, 1974.

Chachava, M. K., and Gotsiridze, T. I.: Plastic surgery in pendulous abdomen, Vestn. Khir. **107**:89, 1972.

Chaimowitz, M. A.: Mesenteric vascular occlusion, South African Med. J. **12**:567, 1947.

Chlouverakis, C., and Hojnicki, I.: Lipectomy in obese hyperglycemic mice (obob), Metabolism **23**:133, 1974.

Christensen, N. A., Musgrove, J. E., and Wollaeger, E. E.: Extensive resection of bowel for occlusion of superior mesenteric artery: report of case with postoperative studies of function of gastro-intestinal tract, Proc. Staff Meet. Mayo Clin. **25**:449, 1950.

Claoué, C.: Chirurgie plastique abdominale: cure chirurgicale de ptose cutanée abdominal, ventre en tablier, Paris, 1940, Norbert Maloine.

Claoué, C.: Abdominal plastic surgery [Cirugía plástica abdominal. Tratamiento quirúrgico de la ptosis cutánea abdominal], Clin. Lab. **64**:81, 1957.

Clarkson, P.: Lipodystrophies, Plast. Reconstr. Surg. **37**:499, 1966.

Codazzi-Aguirre, J. A.: Somatocaliplastia. In Transactions of the Second Latin American Congress of Plastic Surgery, Buenos Aires, 1942.

Coffey, R. C.: Plastic surgery of the abdominal wall, Grenzgeb. Med. Chir. **18**:776, 1908.

Coffey, R. C.: Plastic surgery of the abdominal wall, Surg. Gynecol. Obstet. **10**:90, 1910.

Cogswell, H. D.: Massive resection of small intestine, Ann. Surg. **127**:377, 1948.

Coleman, E. P., and Bennett, D. A.: Massive intestinal resection, Am. J. Surg. **59**:429, 1943.

Costagliola, M.: Abdomen pendulum et éventrations monstreux, Ajaccio, France, 1970, Société Française de la Chirurgie Plastique.

Courtiss, E. H., editor: Aesthetic surgery: trouble—how to avoid it and how to treat it, St. Louis, 1978, The C. V. Mosby Co.

Dantlo, R.: Transplantation de derme pour la cure des éventrations, Presse Med. **50**:680, 1946.

Dartigues, L.: Les disgraces et deficiences de la morphologie humaine. In Chirurgie réparatrice, plastique et esthétique de la poitrine et de l'abdomen, Paris, 1936, R. Lepine.

Debaere, P. A.: Chirurgie morphologique abdominale. Doctoral thesis, Lille, France, 1975.

Delerm, A., and Cirotteau, Y.: Plastie cruro-fémoro-fessière ou circum fessière, Ann. Chir. Plast. **18**:31, 1973.

De Muth, W. E., and Rottenstein, H. S.: Death associated with hypocalcemia after small bowel short-circuiting, N. Engl. J. Med. **270**:1239, 1964.

Denk, W.: Zur Pathologie und Therapie der Bruche der vorderen Bauchwand, Arch. Klin. Chir. **93**:711, 1910.

Depaulis, M. J.: La chirurgie des "abdomen pendulum"—réflexions sur une série de 20 cas, J. Med. Bordeaux Sud-Ouest **144**:697, 1967.

Deroutnau, A.: Les plasties abdominales. Medical thesis, Toulouse, France, 1973.

De Santis, U. M. J., Panyza, J. C., and Oris, D. R.: A combined abdominocrural dermolypectomy, Cir. Plast. Argent. **1**:26, 1977.

Desjardins, P.: Résection de la couche adi d'obésité extrème (lipectomie). Rapport par Dartigues, Paris Chir. **3**:466, 1911.

Detár, M.: Plastic repair of pendulous abdomen, Gyogyaszat. **80**:558, 1940.

Detrie, P.: L'opère abdominal: les suites normales et compliqués de la chirurgie abdominale, Paris, 1970, Masson & Cie, Editeurs.

Devernoix de Bonnefon, M. R.: Chirurgie du ventre en tablier par l'incision en T renversé, Arch. Hosp. **27**:4, 111, 1955.

Devernoix de Bonnefon, M. R.: Chirurgie du ventre en tablier par l'incision en T renversé, Concours Méd. **78**:2587, 1956.

Dogo, G.: Trapianto libero di derma nel riparo di ernie post-operatorie, Riv. Ital. Chir. Plast. **2**:105, 1973.

Douglas, W., et al.: An experience in aesthetic buttocks augmentation, Clin. Plast. Surg. **2**:471-476, 1975.

Doyen, E. L.: Traité de thérapeutique chirurgie et de la technique opérative, Paris, 1911, Norbert Maloine.

Drew, E. J.: Removal of panniculus adiposus, J.A.M.A. **229**:391, 1974.

Dubou, R., and Ousterhout, D. K.: Placement of the umbilicus in an abdominoplasty, Plast. Reconstr. Surg. **61**:291, 1978.

Ducourtioux, J. L.: Technique and indications for crural dermolipectomies, Ann. Chir. Plast. **17**:204, 1972.

Dufourmentel, C.: Chirurgie réparatrice et corrective, Paris, 1939, Masson & Cie, Editeurs.

Dufourmentel, C., and Mouly, R.: Chirurgie plastique. Plasties abdominales, Paris, 1959, Flammarion & Cie.

Dummont, A., and Van Der Ghinst, M.: L'utilisation de la greffe de peau totale dans la cure des hernies et des éventrations. Resultats cloignés. Enseignement a tirer de deux réinterventions, Acta Chir. Belg. **48**:456, 1959.

Ehrenfeld, H.: Ein neues plastisches Verfahren zur Behebung des Hängebauches, Zentralbl. Chir. **63**:566, 1936.

Elbaz, J. S.: Les plasties abdominales, Immex Spec. Ann., p. 711, May, 1972.

Elbaz, J. S.: Abdominal plastic surgery—horseshoe technique [á propos des plasties abdominales. Technique du fer à cheval], Ann. Chir. Plast. **19**:155, 1974.

Elbaz, J. S.: Panel (secrétariat) des abdominoplasties. In Marchac, D., editor: Transactions of the Sixth International Congress of Plastic and Reconstructive Surgery, Paris, 1975, Masson & Cie, Editeurs.

Elbaz, J. S., and Falguel, G.: Chirurgie plastique de l'abdomen, Paris, 1977, Masson & Cie, Editeurs.

Erwald, R., and Rieger, A.: Tantalum mesh in hernial repair, Acta Chir. Scand. **119**:55, 1960.

Farina, R.: Cirurgia plastica e reparadora, São Paulo, 1965, Grafica.

Farina, R., Baroudi, R., Golcman, B., and Castro, O. de: Riding-trousers-like type of pelvicrural lipodystrophy (trochanteric lipomatosis), Br. J. Plast. Surg. **13**:174; [lipodistrofia pelvi-trocantérica tipo calca de montaria (lipomatose trocantérica)], Hospital (Rio de J.) **57**:717, 1960.

Faust, I. M., Johnson, P. R., and Hirsch, J.: Adipose tissue regeneration following lipectomy, Science **197**:391, 1977.

Fernández, J. C., and Iturraspe, M. C.: Dermolipectomía vertical en el delantal grasoso, Día Méd. (B. Aires) **23**:1483, 1951.

Fernández, J. C.: Dermolipectomía vertical del abdomen, Semana Med. **120**:431, 1962.

Fernández, J. C., and Iturraspe, M. C.: Lipectomía del abdomen, Bol. Trab. Soc. Argent. **22**:591, 1961.

Fey, B., Mocquot, P., Oberlin, S., Quenu, J., Truffert, P., David, M., Iselin, M., and Puech, P.: Traité de technique chirurgicale, Paris, 1952, Masson & Cie, Editeurs.

Fischl, R.: Vertical abdominoplasty, Plast. Reconstr. Surg. **51**:139, 1973.

Flesch-Thebesius, M., and Weinsheimer, K.: Die Operation des Hängebauches, Chirurg **3**:841, 1931.

Foged, J.: Operative treatment of abdominal obesity especially pendulous abdomen, Br. J. Plast. Surg. **1**:274, 1949.

Fogh, A. P.: Repair of monstrous ventral hernia with buried dermis of whole skin grafts, Acta Chir. Scand. **126**:455, 1963.

Foucher, J., Foucher, G., and Colin-Foucher, E.: Les crinoplaques. Technique, indications et résultats, Mem. Acad. Chir. **96**:618, 1970.

Fournier, M.: Lipectomía abdominal, Cir. Cir. **21**:433, 1953.

Francesconi, G., et al.: Complicanze nella dermolipectomia addominale, Riv. Ital. Chir. Plast. **5**:455, 1973; Plast. Reconstr. Surg. **56**:355, 1975.

Franco, T.: A cicatrização da ferida cirurgia, Folha Med. **57**:213, 1968.

Franco, T.: Abdominoplasty in association with intracavity surgeries, Rev. Bras. Cirurg. **61**:5, 1971.

Freeman, B.: Panel des abdominoplasties. In Marchac, D., editor: Transactions of the Sixth International Congress of Plastic and Reconstructive Surgery, Paris, 1975, Masson & Cie, Editeurs.

Frist, J.: Die Operation des Hängebauches, Wien. Klin. Wochenschr. **34**:226, 1921.

Frist, J.: Plastic operation for pendulous abdomen and pendulous breasts, Med. Klin. **23:**1269, 1927.

García, F. I., and Dargallo, J.: El neumo subcutáneo en el tratamiento del abdomen péndulo, J. Med. Clin. **19:**325, 1952.

Galtier, B. C., Quandalle, P., Florin, M., and Faillon, J. M.: Le traitement des éventrations postoperatoires par plaque de Mersilène, Lille Chir., p. 13, 1968.

Galtier, M.: Traitement chirurgical de l'obésité de la paroi abdominale avec ptose [surgical therapy of obesity of the abdominal wall with ptosis], Mem. Acad. Chir. **81:**341, 1955.

Galtier, M.: L'obésité de la paroi abdominale avec ptose. Traitement chirurgical, Presse Med. **70:**135, 1962.

Garvoglia, M., et al.: L'innesto libero dermoadiposo autologo nel trattamento del laparocele post operatorio, Minerva Chir. **31:**993, 1976.

Gauthier, R.: Des larges excisions de tissu adipeux chez les obèses (large excisions of fatty tissue in obesity), Paris, 1895.

Giegerich, R. L.: Unsere Erfahrungen mit der freien Kutisplastik nach Rehn zum Verschluss grosser Bauchwandbrüche, Zentralbl. Chir. **76:**881, 1951.

Glicenstein, J.: Les difficultés du traitement chirurgical des dermodystrophies abdominales, Ann. Chir. Plast. **20:**147, 1975.

Glicenstein, J.: Chirurgie esthétique de l'abdomen, Vie Med. **2:**27, 3214, 1972.

Goldenberg, B.: Dermolipectomía abdominal, Día Méd. (B. Aires) **36:**618, 1951.

Goldwyn, R. M.: The unfavorable result in plastic surgery, Boston, 1972, Little, Brown & Co.

Gonzáles-Ulloa, M.: Circular lipectomy with transposition of the umbilicus and aponeurolytic technique, Cirurgía **27:**394, 1959.

Gonzáles-Ulloa, M.: Belt lipectomy, Br. J. Plast. Surg. **13:**179, 1960.

Gonzáles-Ulloa, M., and Flores, S.: Total rehabilitation of the female body from deformities due to the obstetrical neglect syndrome, Gazz. Sani. (Milano) **19**(3):105, 1970.

Gosset, J.: Bandes de peau totale comme matériel de suture autoplastique en chirurgie, Mem. Acad. Chir. **75:**277, 1969.

Gould, A. P.: A clinical lecture on the surgery of the abdominal wall, Br. Med. J. **2:**1517, 1911.

Graser, E.: Zur Technik der Radikaloperation grosser Nabel-und Bauchwandhernien, Arch. Klin. Chir. **80:**324.

Grazer, F. M.: Use of fiberoptic bundles in plastic surgery, Plast. Reconstr. Surg. **48:**28, 1971.

Grazer, F. M.: Abdominoplasty, Plast. Reconstr. Surg. **51:**617, 1973.

Grazer, F. M.: Plastic operation on the abdomen, Calif. Med. **119:**64, Aug., 1973.

Grazer, F. M.: Instructional course summaries of the Educational Foundation, San Francisco, 1976-1978, American Society of Plastic and Reconstructive Surgeons.

Grazer, F. M., and Goldwyn, R. M.: Abdominoplasty assessed by survey, with emphasis on complications, Plast. Reconstr. Surg. **59:**513, 1977.

Grazer, F. M., and Goldwyn, R. M.: Esthetic surgery. In McCoy, F. J., editor: Year book of plastic and reconstructive surgery, 1978, Chicago, 1978, Year Book Medical Publishers, Inc.

Grazer, F. M., and Klingbeil, J. R.: Abdominoplasty. In Courtiss, E. H., editor: Aesthetic surgery: trouble—how to avoid it and how to treat it, St. Louis, 1978, The C. V. Mosby Co.

Grazer, F. M., Klingbeil, J. R., and Mattiello, M.: Long-term results of abdominoplasty, Boston, 1980, Little, Brown & Co. (in press).

Grazer, F. M., and Krugman, M. E.: A new triaxial fiberoptic soft tissue retractor, Aesthet. Plast. Surg. **2:**161, 1978.

Guerrero-Santos, J.: Lipectomies, presented at the Second Annual Symposium on Aesthetic Plastic Surgery, Mexico, Oct., 1973, University of Guadalajara.

Guerrero-Santos, J.: Lipectomies: arms, abdomen, and thighs. Study session section I, Annual Meeting of the Educational Foundation of the American Society of Plastic and Reconstructive Surgeons, Houston, Oct., 1974.

Guerrero-Santos, J.: Arm-lift. In Courtiss, E. H., editor: Aesthetic surgery: trouble— how to avoid it and how to treat it, St. Louis, 1978, The C. V. Mosby Co.

Haberer, von: Offizielles Protokoll der k.k. Gesellschaft der Aerzte in Wien, Wien. Klin. Wochenschr. **21,** 1908.

Haberland, H. F. O.: Advances in plastic surgery (abdomen), Zentralbl. Chir. **63:**154, 1963.

Hagerty, R. F., Hawk, J. C., Jr., Boniface, K., et al.: Resection of massive abdominal panniculus adiposus, South. Med. J. **67**:984, 1974.

Harkins, H. N.: Cutis grafts: clinical and experimental studies on their use as reinforcing patch in repair of large ventral and incisional herniae, Ann. Surg. **122**:996, 1945.

Harrison, R. J., and Booth, C. C.: Massive resection of the small intestine after occlusion of superior mesenteric artery, Gut **1**:237, 1960.

Hartel, P.: Erfahrungen mit der abdominalen Dermolipektomie nach Pitanguy. In Bohmer, H.: Plastische Chirurgie des Kopfes und Halsbereiches unter der weiblichen Brust 5 Tagg., Verein Dtsch. Plast. Chir. Munich **301**, 1974; Stuttgart, 1975, Georg Thieme Verlag KG.

Haymond, H. E.: Massive resection of small intestine; analysis of 257 collected cases, Surg. Gynecol. Obstet. **61**:693, 1935.

Hinderer, U. T.: Tratamiento quirúrgico de la obesidad abdominal (dermolipectomías), Ann. Acad. Med. Quir. Esp. **51**:3, 1966-1967.

Hinderer, U. T.: The dermolipectomy approach for augmentation mammaplasty, Clin. Plast. Surg. **2**:359, 1975.

Hoffman, S., and Simon, B. E.: Experiences with the Pitanguy method of correction of trochanteric lipodystrophy, Plast. Reconstr. Surg. **55**:551, 1975.

Hohf, R.: Combined surgical procedures, Surg. Clin. North Am. **50**:13, Feb., 1970.

Holman, C. C.: Survival after removal of twenty feet of intestine, Lancet **2**:597, 1944.

Horton, C., Georgiade, N., Campbell, F., Masters, F., and Pickrell, K.: The behavior of split thickness and dermal grafts in the peritoneal cavity, Plast. Reconstr. Surg. **12**:269, 1953.

Igarzabal, J. E.: Pendulous abdomen, surgical therapy, Semana Med. **1**:1361, 1938.

Interlandi, G.: Nota di tecnica operatoria per la cura dell'addome pendulo complicato da sventramento sopra-pubico, Minerva Chir. **29**:208, 1974.

Iturraspe, M. C.: Resultados de la dermolipectomía abdominal vertical, Bol. Trab. Soc. Argent. Cir. **13**:648, 1952.

Iturraspe, M. C.: Tratamiento quirúrgico de la obesidad, Rev. Assoc. Med. Argent. **66**:340, 1952.

Iturraspe, M. C.: Dermolipectomía vertical del abdomen, Semana Med. **121**:1071, 1962.

Ivanissevich, O.: Dermolipectomía. Técnica de Vélez Diez Canseco, Semana Med. **118**:535, 1961.

Jackson, I. T., and Downie, P.: Abdominoplasty—the waistline stitch and other refinements, Plast. Reconstr. Surg. **61**:180, 1977.

Jackson, J. A., and Steeper, J. R.: Operative excision of giant panniculus adiposus, J. Int. Coll. Surg. **15**:85, 1951.

Jacques, W. S.: Abdominoplasty, R. Amrigs **20**:75, 1976.

Jensenius, H. C.: Results of experimental resections of the small intestine on dogs, Copenhagen, 1945, Nyt. Nordisk Forlag Arnold Busck.

Jerauld, F. N. C., and Washburn, W. W.: Extensive resection of small intestine, J.A.M.A. **92**:1827, 1929.

Julliard, A. F.: Les grands épanchements permanents dans la lipectomie antérieure, Ann. Chir. Plast. **21**:267, 1976.

Jurgens, R., and Naumann, W.: Klinische und experimentelle Untersuchungen über Funktionen der Blutplättchen, Dtsch. Arch. Klin. Med. **172**:248, 1931.

Juri, J., Juri, C., and Raiden, G.: Reconstruction of the umbilicus in abdominoplasty, Plast. Reconstr. Surg. **63**:580, 1979.

Juzbasic, D.: L'utilisation des plasties dermiques, notamment dans le traitement des pertes de substance de la paroi abdominale et dans la chirurgie générale, Lyon Chir. **62**:641, 1966.

Kamper, M. J., Galloway, D., and Ashley, F.: Abdominal panniculectomy after massive weight loss, Plast. Reconstr. Surg. **50**:441, 1972.

Kaufmann, J. H., and Weldon, H. W.: Intussusception, a late complication of small bowel bypass for obesity, J.A.M.A. **202**:1147, 1977.

Keeley, J. L., and Schairer, A.: Mechanical methods of improving exposure in abdominal operations, Surg. Clin. North Am. **48**:91, Feb., 1968.

Kelly, H. A.: Report of gynecological cases (excessive growth of fat), Bull. Johns Hopkins Hosp. **10**:197, 1889 (case 3).

Kelly, H. A.: Excision of the fat of the abdominal wall lipectomy, Surg. Gynecol. Obstet. **10**:229, 1910.

Kemper, G. W. H.: Pendulous abdomen, Am. Pract. **19**:30, 1879.

Kiene, V. S.: Plastic surgery for abdominal adiposity, Zentralbl. Chir., p. 92, 1967.

Kiffner, E., Knote, G., and Bohmert, H.: Dermolipektomien zur Beseitigung überschüssiger Haut und lokaler Fettgewebsan-sammlung, Fortschr. Med. **94**:2020, 1976.

Kirchmayr, L.: Construction of a cosmetic umbilicus in an umbilical hernia [über Nabel-Plastik bei Umbilikarnen], Zentralbl. Chir. **51**:1403, 1924.

Kirianoff, T. G.: Making a new umbilicus when none exists, Plast. Reconstr. Surg. **61**:603, 1978.

Koechlin, C.: Les plasties abdominales, Rev. Med. Suisse Romande **94**:981, 1974.

Koontz, A. R.: An operation for large inci-sional epigastric hernias, Surg. Gynecol. Obstet. **114**:117, 1962.

Kral, J.: Surgical reduction of adipose tissue hypercellularity in man, Scand. J. Plast. Reconstr. Surg. **9**:140, 1975.

Kraus, F.: Implantation of skin flaps into peritoneum to study the possibility of a functional adaptation of the skin, Arch. Mikroanat. **79**:332, 1912.

Kremen, A. J., Linner, J. H., and Nelson, C. H.: An experimental evaluation of the nutritional importance of proximal and distal small intestine, Ann. Surg. **140**:430, 1954.

Kurzweg, F. T.: Pulmonary complications following abdominal surgery, Am. Surg. **9**:967, 1953.

Kuster, K.: Operation bein Hängebrust und Hängeleib, Monatsschr. Geburtshilfe Gy-naekol. **73**:316, 1926.

Labry, R., and Duroux, P. E.: Opérations de dégraissage de la paroi abdominale, Lyon Chir. **46**:230, 1956.

Laburthe-Tolra, Y., and Chomé, J.: La greffe libre de peau totale fraîche retournée. Son utilisation dans le comblement des pertes de substance de la paroi abdominale, J. Chir. **100**:399, 1970.

Lagiche, G., and Vandenbussche, F.: Indica-tions, contre-indications et résultats de la technique de Callia dans le traitement des ptoses cutanées abdominales avec ou sans surcharge graisseuse, Ann. Chir. Plast. **16**:37, 1971.

Lagrot, F.: Traitement des éventrations, E. M. C. **40**:165.

Lagrot, F., Micheau, Costagliola, M., et al.: À propos des dermolipectomies abdominales, Bordeaux Chir. **3**:221, 1970.

Landouzy: Refashioning the abdominal wall, Arch. Med. Pharm. Mil. **52**:81, 1908.

Largeau, J. R.: The surgery of the abdominal wall, Gaz. Med. Paris **11.s.I**:63, 135, 1898.

Larkin, C. N.: Lipectomy for abdominal fat, Conn. Med. J. **7**:706, 1950.

Lasala, A. J.: Lipectomy with conservation of umbilicus (Flesch-Thebesius-Weinsheimer operation) in therapy of pendulous abdo-men, Prensa Med. Argent. **28**:408, 1941.

Lekieffre, J.: Chirurgie esthétique de l'abdo-men, Gaz. Med. Fr. **75**:2605, 1968.

Lemerle, G., and Vilain, R.: Eviscerations, Concours Med. **93**:1910, 1971.

Lewis, J. R., Jr.: The thigh-lift, J. Int. Coll. Surg. **27**:330, 1957.

Lewis, J. R.: Correction of ptosis of the thighs: the thigh-lift, Plast. Reconstr. Surg. **37**:494, 1966.

Lewis, J. R.: Corrective surgery of the abdo-men, buttocks, arms and thighs. In Sym-posium on Youth and Beauty, sponsored by the Education Foundation of the American Society of Plastic and Reconstructive Sur-geons, Philadelphia, 1970, Temple Univer-sity Health Sciences Seminar.

Lewis, J.: Surgical contouring by removal of fat. In Lende, S. M., editor: Cosmetic surgery: what it can do for you, 1971, MS Award Books.

Lewis, J. R.: The abdominoplasty. In Body contouring, J. South. Med. Assoc. (in press).

Lewis, J. R.: Correction of redundancies of the arm: the arm-lift. In Body contouring, J. South. Med. Assoc. (in press).

Lewis, J. R.: Foreward, In Lewis, J. R., editor: Aesthetic surgery of trunk and extremities, Clin. Plast. Surg. **2**:345, 1975.

Lewis, L. A., Turnbull, R. B., Jr., and Page, I. H.: "Short-circuiting" of the small intes-tine. Effect on concentration of serum cho-lesterol and lipoproteins, J.A.M.A. **182**:77, 1962.

Lewis, L. A., Turnbull, R. B., Jr., and Page, I. H.: Effects of jejunocolic shunt on obes-ity, serum, lipoproteins, lipids and electro-lytes, Arch. Intern. Med. **117**:4, 1966.

Lexer, E.: Die gesamte Wiederherstellungs-chirurgie (along with ed. 2 of Wiederstel-lungschirurgie), Leipzig, 1931, Johann Ambrosius Barth Verlag.

Linder, A. M., Jackson, W. P. U., and Linder, G. C.: Small gut insufficiency following in-testinal surgery. III. Further clinical and autopsy studies of a man surviving for 3½ years with seven inches of small intestine, South Afr. J. Clin. Sci. **4**:1, 1953.

Loeffler, M. Odtworzenie powłock brzusznych w leczeniu otyłości, Pol. Przegl. Chir. **35**:211, 1963.

MacLean, N. J.: Technique for the repair of postoperative abdominal hernias, Trans.

West. Surg. Assoc. **27**:49, 1917; Surg. Gynecol. Obstet. **83**:200, 1946.

MacLean, L. D.: The extreme pendulous abdomen and its surgical treatment by a new three flap operation, Surg. Gynecol. Obstet. **28**:190, 1919.

Malbec, E. F.: Lipectomía abdominal, técnica operatoria, Prensa Med. Argent. **35**:1251, 1948.

Manchanda, R. L., Singh, R., and Singh, H.: An unusual abdominal flap, Br. J. Plast. Surg. **19**:372, 1966.

Mantero, R., and Rossi, F. G.: Trattamento di laparocele piu volte recidivato con affondamento di limbo cutaneo pedunculoato, Riv. Ital. Chir. Plast. **4**:341, 1972.

Marchac, D.: La cutaneo—lipectomie tessière pour correction de la culotte de cheval, Nouv. Presse Med. **6**:1387, 1977.

Marchal, G., Lapeyrie, H., and Amar, E.: Sur un procède de plastie cutanée dans la paroi abdominale, Montpellier Chir. **10**:315, 1964.

Marinow, I.: À propos de la cure autoplastique des hernies et des éventrations par l'emploi de bandes de peau totale, Thèses Paris **687**:56, 1955.

Mars, J.: Contribution à l'étude du traitement des éventrations et des hernies recidivantes de la paroi abdominale avec auto-greffe dermique, Cir. Cir. **22**:268, 1954.

Martini: Notre experience de l'emploi d'implantation de peau totale dans la cure des hernies recidivés et des éventrations, Boll. Mem. Soc. Tosco. Umbra. Chir. **10**:1, 1949.

Martins, L. C.: Lipectomia abdominale, Riv. Ital. Chir. Plast. **8**:289, 1976.

Masson, J. K.: Lipectomy: the surgical removal of excess fat, Postgrad. Med. **32**:481, 1962.

Mateos, F.: Lipectomía abdominal, Cir. Cir. **21**:433, 1953.

Maxwell, J. G., Richards, R. C., and Albo, D. Jr.: Fatty degeneration of the liver after intestinal bypass for obesity, Am. J. Surg. **1976**:648, 1968.

May, H., and Spann, R. G.: Cutis grafts for repair of incisional and recurrent hernias, Surg. Clin. North Am. **28**:517, 1948.

Maylard, A. E.: Direction of abdominal incisions, Br. Med. J. **2**:895, 1907.

McCabe, W. P., and Kelly, A. P.: Panniculectomy following intestinal bypass, Br. J. Plast. Surg. **27**:346, 1974.

McCraw, L. H.: Surgical rehabilitation after massive weight reduction. Case report, Plast. Reconstr. Surg. **53**:349, 1974.

McGregor, I. A., and Morgan, G.: Axial and random pattern flaps, Br. J. Plast. Surg. **26**:202, 1973.

Mendelson, B. C., and Mason, M. D.: Silicone implants for contour deformities of the trunk, Plast. Reconstr. Surg. **50**:535.

Meyer, H. W.: Acute superior mesenteric artery thrombosis; recovery following extensive resection of small and large intestines, Arch. Surg. **53**:298, 1946.

Meyerowitz, B. R., et al.: From massive weight loss to abdominal panniculectomy, R.N. **37**:1, 1974.

Meyerowitz, B. R., Bruber, R. P., and Laub, D. R.: Massive abdominal panniculectomy, J.A.M.A. **224**:408, 1973.

Millard, D. R., Piggot, R., and Zies, P.: Free skin grafting of full thickness defects of abdominal wall, Plast. Reconstr. Surg. **43**:569, 1969.

Mir y Mir, L.: Lipectomia abdominal, Actas Riun. Policlin. **20**:49, 1966.

Mitz, V., Elbaz, J. S., and Vilde, F.: Étude des fibres élastiques dermiques au cours d'opérations plastiques du tronc, Ann. Chir. Plast. **20**:31, 1975.

Moore, H. G., and Harkins, H. N.: The surgical correction of panniculus adiposus abdominis, Surgery **34**:728, 1953.

Morestin, A.: Laparoptosis and laparoplasty, Bull. Mem. Soc. Chir. Paris **39**(NS):1114, 1913.

Morestin, A.: La restauration de la paroi abdominale par résection étendue des téguments et de la graisse sous cutanée et le plissement des aponeuroses superficielles envisagé comme complement de la cure radicale des hernies ombilicales. Thesis, Paris, 1912, Faculté de Médecine de Paris.

Morgan, A. P., and Moore, F. D.: Jejunoileostomy for extreme obesity, Ann. Surg. **1966**:75, 1967.

Morini, S.: Body sculpture, New York, 1972, Dell Publishing Co., Inc.

Mornard, P.: La résection esthétique du ventre en tablier avec transplantation de l'ombilic. In Pauchet, V.: La pratique chirurgicale illustrée, vol. XVI, Paris, 1930, Gaston Doin.

Morris, R. T.: Surgery of the obese, Mon. Cycl. Med. Bull. **3**:641, 1910.

Mouzas, G. L., and Yeadon, A.: Does the choice of suture material affect the incidence of wound infection? Br. J. Surg. **62**:952, 1975.

Moynihan, B.: Abdominal operations, Philadelphia, 1914, W. B. Saunders Co.

Muhlbauer, W. D.: Plastic surgery in the treatment of obesity [die plastisch-chirurgische Behandlung der Fettleibigkeit], Munch. Med. Wochenschr. **117**:745, 1975.

Noël, A.: La chirurgie esthétique, son rôle social, Paris, 1926, Masson & Cie, Editeurs.

Oechlecker, F.: Die Nabelbruchoperation mit ausgedehnter Fettexcision, Zentralbl. Chir. **38**:388, 1911.

O'Connor, C. M.: Abdominal dermolipectomy. A modified technique, Prensa Med. Argent. **55**:969, 1968.

Palmer, B., et al.: Skin reduction plasties following intestinal shunt operations for treatment of obesity, Scand. J. Plast. Reconstr. Surg. **9**:47, 1975.

Passot, R.: Chirurgie esthétique pure. Techniques et résultats, Paris, 1930, Gaston Doin.

Pate, J. C.: Massive resection of small intestine excision of 12 feet 6 inches, with recovery, J. Fla. Med. Assoc. **29**:28, 1942.

Pauchet, V.: Cure de la hernie ombilicale chez les obèses après amaigrissement. Lipectomie et omphalectomie. In La pratique chirurgicale illustrée, vol. VII, Paris, 1925, Gaston Doin.

Pauchet, V.: Abdominoplasty, Clinique **7**:421, 1912.

Payne, J. H., and DeWind, L. T.: Surgical treatment of obesity, Am. J. Surg. **118**:141, 1969.

Payne, J. H., DeWind, L. T., and Commons, R. R.: Metabolic observations in patients with jejunocolic shunts, Am. J. Surg. **106**:273, 1963.

Payne, J. H., DeWind, L., Schwab, C. E., et al.: Surgical treatment of morbid obesity. Sixteen years of experience, Arch. Surg. **106**:432, 1973.

Perel, L.: Plasties abdominales, Bull. Fed. Gynecol. Obstet. Fr. **20**:495, 1968.

Peskova, H.: Plastic operations of abdominal wall, Acta Chir. Plast. **8**:127, 1966.

Peters, L.: Resection of the pendulous fat abdominal wall in cases of extreme obesity, Ann. Surg. **33**:220, 1901.

Petrina, N., and Mercadante, T.: L'uso delle reti di tantalio, acciaio e nylon nella chirurgia riparatrice della parte abdominale, Minerva Chir. **10**:747, 1955.

Pfannenstiel, H.: Ueber die Vortheile des suprasymphysisen Fascienquerschnitts für die gynaekologischen Koeliotomien, zugleich ein Beitrag zu der Indikationsstellung der Operationwege, Samml. Klin. Vorts (Gynaekol.) **268**:1735, 1900.

Picaud, A. J., and Sabatier, P. H.: D'une technique de lipectomie qui garde ses indications précises, Turin, Italy, 1973, XXIII Congrès national de la Société italienne de chirurgie plastique et reconstructive.

Pick, J. F.: Surgery of repair, vol. 2, Philadelphia, 1949, J. B. Lippincott.

Pick, J. F.: Cirugía reparadora, Barcelona, 1955, Salvat Editores S. A.

Pickrell, K. L.: Reconstructive surgery of the abdominal wall and back. In Converse, J. M., editor: Reconstructive plastic surgery, vol. 5, Philadelphia, 1964, W. B. Saunders Co.

Pire, J. C.: Les complications respiratoires des grandes éventrations. Thesis, Paris, 1968, Faculté de Médecine de Paris.

Pitanguy, I.: Trochanteric lipodystrophy, Plast. Reconstr. Surg. **34**:280; [Lipodistrofia trocanteriana], Rev. Bras. Cirurg. **47**:69, 1964.

Pitanguy, I.: Abdominal lipectomy—an approach to it through an analysis of 300 consecutive cases, Plast. Reconstr. Surg. **40**:384, 1967.

Pitanguy, I.: Abdominoplastias, Hospital (Rio de J.) **71**:1541, 1967.

Pitanguy, I.: Vantaggi dell'impiego di contenzione gessata nelle plastiche addominali, Minerva Chir. **22**:595, 1967.

Pitanguy, I.: Surgical reduction of the abdomen, thighs, and buttocks, Surg. Clin. North Am. **51**:479, 1971.

Pitanguy, I.: Techniques for trunk and thigh reductions. In Hueston, J. M., editor: Transactions of the Fifth International Congress of Plastic and Reconstructive Surgeons, Melbourne, 1971, Butterworth & Co. (Publishers), Ltd.

Pitanguy, I.: Dermolipectomies crurales, Ann. Chir. Plast. **17**:40, 1972.

Pitanguy, I.: Thigh lift and abdominal lipectomy. In Goldwyn, R. M.: The unfavorable result in plastic surgery, Boston, 1972, Little, Brown & Co.

Pitanguy, I.: Lipectomy. In Grabb, W. C., and Smith, J., editors: Plastic surgery, ed. 2, Boston, 1973, Little, Brown & Co.

Pitanguy, I.: Present aspects in abdominal lipectomy, Rev. Bras. Cirurg. **64**:149, 1974.

Pitanguy, I.: Abdominal lipectomy, Clin. Plast. Surg. **2:**401, 1975.

Pitanguy, I.: Correction of lipodystrophy of the lateral thoracic aspect and inner side of the arm and elbow dermosenescence, Clin. Plast. Surg. **2:**477; [Correção lipodistrofia da região lateral do torax, face interna do braco e da dermossenescência do cotovelo], Rev. Bras. Cirurg. **65:**277, 1975.

Pitanguy, I.: Dermolipectomy of the abdominal wall, thigh, buttocks, and upper extremity. In Converse, J. M., editor: Reconstructive plastic surgery, vol. 7, ed. 2, Philadelphia, 1977, W. B. Saunders Co.

Pitanguy, I., et al.: Dermolipectomies crurais, evolução e variações de uma técnica pessoal, Rev. Bras. Cirurg. **61:**237, 1971.

Pitanguy, I., et al.: Resultados desfavoráveis em cirurgia plástica, Bol. Cirurg. Plast. **61:**125, 1972.

Pitanguy, I., et al.: Aspectos atuais des lipectomias abdominais, Bol. Cir. Plast. Rev. Bras. Cirurg. **19:**149, 1974.

Planas, J.: Communications, Jerusalem, 1974, Second Congress of the International Society of Aesthetic Plastic Surgery.

Planas, J.: The "crural meloplasty" for lifting of the thighs, Clin. Plast. Surg. **2:**495, 1975.

Planas, J.: Introduction of breast implants through the abdominal route, Plast. Reconstr. Surg. **57:**434, 1975.

Planas, J.: The "vest over pants" abdominoplasty, Plast. Reconstr. Surg. **61:**694, 1978.

Potter, H. P., Jr., and Bassett, D. R.: Extensive jejunoileal resection, Pa. Med. **69:**27, 1966.

Printen, K. J., and Mason, E. E.: Gastric surgery for relief of morbid obesity, Arch. Surg. **106:**428, 1973.

Prisleau, W. H.: Symposium on abdominal surgery; massive resection of small intestine; report on two cases, Ann. Surg. **119:**372, 1944.

Prudente, A.: Dermolipectomía abdominal com conservação de cicatrix umbilical. In Transactions of the Second Latin American Congress of Plastic Surgery, Buenos Aires, 1942-1943, Guillermo, Kraft.

Psillakis, J. M.: Abdominoplasty: some ideas to improve results, Aesthet. Plast. Surg. **2:**205, 1978.

Quenu, J.: Chirurgie de l'abdomen, ed. 8, Paris, 1949, Masson & Cie, Editeurs.

Quenu, J., Loygue, J., Perrotin, J., Dubost, C., and Moreaux, J.: Opérations sur les parois de l'abdomen et sur le tube digestif, Paris, 1967, Masson & Cie, Editeurs.

Raffaele, A. P., Poggi, D., A., and Bases, L.: El enfisema subcutáneo como tiempo previo a las lipectomies, Bol. Trab. Soc. Argent. Cir. **10:**73, 1949.

Rao-Subba, Y. V.: Augmentation mammaplasty and abdominoplasty in one stage, Plast. Reconstr. Surg. **43:**148, 1969.

Rebello, C.: Plástica de abdomen, Folha Med. **56:**51, 1968.

Rebello, C., and Franco, T.: Abdominoplasty through a submammary incision, Int. Surg. **62:**462, 1977.

Regnault, P.: Abdominal dermolipectomy, microfilm, New York, 1972, International Society of Aesthetic Plastic Surgery.

Regnault, P.: Abdominal lipectomy, a low W incision, microfilm, New York, 1972, International Society of Aesthetic Plastic Surgery.

Regnault, P.: Abdominal dermolipectomies, Clin. Plast. Surg. **2:**411, 1975.

Regnault, P.: Abdominoplasty by the W technique, Plast. Reconstr. Surg. **55:**265, 1975.

Regnault, P.: Syllabus: Abdominal dermolipectomy and body sculpture, San Francisco, 1977, Education Foundation, American Society of Plastic and Reconstructive Surgeons.

Regnault, P., and Alfara, A.: Lipodystrophie céphalo-thoracique de Barraquez-Simons, presentation d'un cas, Union Med. Can. **96:**286, 1967.

Reich, J.: The surgical improvement in appearance of the female body, Med. J. Aust. **2:**767, 1974.

Rene, L.: La laparoplastie, Gaz. Med. Fr. **60:**1247, 1953.

Ribeiro, L.: Inclusão da protesis de Cronin por via areolar e abdominal. In Transactions of the Second Argentine Congress of Aesthetic Surgery, Buenos Aires, 1974.

Richard, E. F.: A mechanical aid for abdominal panniculectomy, Br. J. Plast. Surg. **18:**336, 1965.

Rives, J.: Les grandes éventrations, Mem. Acad. Chir. **99:**547, 1973.

Rives, J.: Les pieces en Dacron et leur place dans la chirurgie des hernies de l'aine, Ann. Chir. **22:**159, 1968.

Rockey, A. E.: Surgical operations on the obese and the advantage of preparatory fasting, Northwest Med. **w**(NS):241, 1911.

Rojas, G. H.: Consideraciones acerca de lipectomía abdominal circular, dermolipectomía circular combinada con lipectomía de la parte posterior-inferior del tronco, 1975 (newspaper article).

Rojas, G. H.: Dermolipectomía circular, primeros doce casos practicados en Venezuela, II Simposium Internacional de Cirugía Estética, Buenos Aires, Sept., 1974.

Rose, D. J., Edwards, and Reid, C. A.: L'innesto cutaneo nel trattamento delle ernie recidive e degli sventramenti, Lyon Chir. **70:**65, 1974.

Rosenblatt, S.: El obeso frente al quirúrgico, Prensa Med. **28:**2153, 1941.

Rousselin, L.: Les greffes libres de peau dans la cure chirurgicale des éventrations, Lyon Chir. **38:**486, 1943.

Ryan, R. F.: Which patient needs the abdominoplasty? (letter), Plast. Reconstr. Surg. **59:**842, 1977.

Sabatier, P. H., and Borelli, J. P.: L'utilisation des prothèses intra-peritonéales dans le traitement des éventrations. In Communication au 6. Congrès International de Chirurgie Plastique, Paris, 1975.

Sampolinski, A.: Pendulous abdomen, its surgical correction, Am. J. Surg. **69:**262, 1945.

Schepelmann, E.: Über Bauchdeckenplastiken mit besonderer Berücksichtigung des Hängebauches, Bruns Beitr. Klin. Chir. **3:**372, 1918.

Schepelmann, E.: Preservation of the navel in the operation on a pendulous abdomen, Zentralbl. Gynaekol. **48:**2289, 1924.

Schörcher, F.: Kosmetische Chirurgie, Munich, 1953, J. F. Lehmanns Verlag.

Schörcher, F.: Kosmetische Operationen, Munich, 1955, J. F. Lehmanns Verlag.

Schrimpf, H.: The operation of the pendulous abdomen with conservation of the navel. In Transactions of the First International Congress of Plastic Surgeons, Stockholm, 1955.

Schrimpf, H.: Hängebauchplastik, Z. Geburtshilfe Gynaekol. **142:**11, 1954.

Schruddle, J.: Lipectomy and lipexhaeresia in the area of the lower extremities (author's transl.) [Lipektomie und Lipexhaerese im Bereich der unteren Extremitäten], Langenbecks Arch. Chir. **345:**127, Nov., 1977.

Schulz, C.: Mittels Grenzgebiete, Med. Chir. **18:**776, 1908.

Schultze: Die Rekonstruktion der Bauchdecken, Zentralbl. Chir. **40:**268, 1913.

Schurter, M., Letterman, G., and Teimourian, B.: Dermolipectomy, a surgical adjunct to the treatment of obesity, J. Am. Med. Wom. Assoc. **19:**769, 1964.

Schutt, J. P.: Lipectomy with case report, Northwest Med. **16:**118, 1917.

Schwartz, A. W.: Technique for excision of abdominal fat, Br. J. Plast. Surg. **27:**44, 1974.

Scott, H. W., et al: Experience with a new technic of intestinal bypass operations in treatment of massive obesity, Ann. Surg. **174:**560, 1971.

Scott, H. W., Jr., and Law, D. H., IV: Clinical appraisal of jejunoileal shunt in patients with morbid obesity, Am. J. Surg. **117:**246, 1969.

Secail, J.: Sur deux cas de cure d'éventration par greffe dermique, Soc. Chir. Toulouse **28,** Feb., 1948.

Seror, J., Stoppa, R., Dvilali, G., and Issad, H.: Cure autoplastique des éventrations par lambeau de peau indue, Presse Med. **73:**489, 1965.

Serson, D.: Planeamiento geométrico para la dermolipectomía abdominal, Rev. Esp. Cir. Plast. **4:**37, 1971; abstracted, Plast. Reconstr. Surg. **48:**605, 1971.

Serson, D., and Martins, L.: Cirugía plástica abdominal, Ars Curandi **16,** Feb., 1970.

Serson, D., and Martins, L. C.: Geometric planning for abdominal dermolipectomy. In Owens, N., and Stephenson, K. L., editors: The year book of plastic and reconstructive surgery, Chicago, 1970, Year Book Medical Publishers, Inc.

Serson, D., and Martins, L. C.: Dermolipectomía abdominal, abordage geométrico, Rev. Lat. Am. Cir. Plast. **16:**13, 1972.

Shackelford, R. T., and Bickham, W. S.: Callander surgery of the alimentary tract, Philadelphia, 1961, W. B. Saunders Co.

Shallenberger, W. H.: Abdominal lipectomy (report of two cases), Bull. Johns Hopkins Hosp. **249:**410, 1911.

Sherman, C. D., Jr., et al.: Clinical and metabolic studies following bowel bypassing for obesity, Ann. N.Y. Acad. Sci. **131:**614, 1965.

Shibata, H. R., Mackenzie, J. R., and Long, R. C.: Metabolic effects of controlled jejunocolic bypass, Arch. Surg. **95:**413, 1967.

Sibila, C. E.: Hernia umbilical y grandes lipectomías, Semana Med. **1:**774, 1939.

Smith, L.: Excision of panniculus adiposus, J. Med. Assoc. Ga. **28:**193, 1939.

Sokolova, L. A.: Free adipo-dermal grafts in the surgical treatment of progressive lipodystrophy, Acta Chir. Plast. **14:**157, 1972.

Sokolova, L. A.: Lipodermal grafts in the surgical treatment of progressive lipodystrophy, Plast. Reconstr. Surg. **52:**686, 1973.

Somalo, M.: Dermolipectomía circular del tronco, Semana Med. **1:**1435, 1940.

Somalo, M.: Dermolipomatomía circular del tronco, Cong. Latino-americano Cir. Plast. II, Arch. Chir. Exp. **1:**404, 1941.

Somalo, M.: Dermolipectomía abdominal. In Transactions of the First Latin American Congress of Plastic Surgery, vol. II, São Paulo, 1941.

Somalo, M.: Circular dermolipectomy of trunk in obesity, Med. Argent. Cir. Clin. Exp. **6:**540, 1942.

Somalo, M.: Dermolipectomía ventral cruciforme; "incisión en golondrina," Prensa Med. Argent. **33:**75, 1946.

Spadafora, A.: Abdomen péndulo, dermolipectomía anterolateral baja (técnica personal), Prensa Med. Argent. **49:**494, 1962.

Spadafora, A.: Abdomen adiposa y péndulo: dermolipectomía: iliaco-inguino-pubiana, Prensa Univ. (B. Aires) **114:**1839, 1965.

Spadafora, A., and Durand, A. S.: Demolipectomy: anterolateral low reconstruction of umbilicus, Plast. Reconstr. Surg. **55:**509, 1975.

Spadafora, A., Rios, R. T., and de los Rios, E.: Inguinocrural cutaneous flaccidity, Plast. Reconstr. Surg. **49:**233, 1972; [flaccidez cutánea inguinocrural], Prensa Med. Argent. **58:**1393, 1971.

Spadafora, A., and Torres San Marco, J. M.: Cirugía de obesidad, flaccidez cutánea y envejecimiento, Buenos Aires, 1974, López Liberos Editores.

Spaulding, A. E.: Operation for the relief of a pendulous abdomen, St. Paul Med. J. **3:**674, 1901.

Spencer, F. H.: Lipectomy for abdominal fat, J. Surg. **27:**387, 1913.

Spina, V.: Abdomen péndulo, An. Paul. Med. Cir. **64:**425, 1952.

Spischarny, I. K.: Muscle plastic for defective abdominal wall, Zentralbl. Chir. **36:**329, 1909.

Statti, M. B., and Loyarte: Dermolipectomies complémentaires, Semana Med. **67:**117, 1960.

Steffen, I.: Die operative Korrektur des Hängebauches, Zentralbl. Gynaekol. **99:**1077, 1977.

Stolz, M.: Weinhold's abdominoplasty, Zentralbl. Gynaekol. **34:**229, 1910.

Stoppa, R.: Un procédé personnel de plastie à la peau dans la cure de certaines grosses éventrations, Ann. Fr. Chir. **19:**63, 1961.

Straham, A. W. B.: Hernia repair by whole skin grafts with report of 413 cases, Br. J. Surg. **38:**276, 1951.

Subba, R.: Abdominoplasty and augmentation mammaplasty, Plast. Reconstr. Surg. **43:**148, 1969.

Szczawiński, A., Oknińska, H., and Dreszer, S.: Plastic operations for pendulous abdomen in obese subjects, Pol. Med. J. **11:**922, 1972; [Operacje plastyczne obwisłej powłoki brzusznej u otyłych], Pol. Przegl. Chir. **43:**1317, 1971.

Szpilman, M.: Surgical correction of female body contour, J. Bioscoc. Ginecol. **82:**399, 1976.

von Szymanowski, J., and Uhde, C. W. F.: Handbuch der operativen Chirurgie, Brunswick, Germany, 1870, Verlag von Friedrich Vieweg & Sohn.

Tafalla, and Pena, M.: Abdominal dermolipectomy (Spanish), Cir. Plast. Ibero Latinoam. **3:**62, 1977.

Tai, Y., and Hasegawa, H.: A transverse abdominal flap for reconstruction after radical operations for recurrent breast cancer, Plast. Reconstr. Surg. **53:**52, 1974.

Talamas-Vasquez, J.: Abdominal lipectomy for obesity, Prensa Med. Mex. **11:**69, 1946.

Tamerin, J. A.: Surgical repair of the obese abdomen, Diab. Obes. Rev. **1:**26, Jan., 1936.

Tennant, C. E.: Lipectomies in the obese when operating for intra-abdominal lesions, Denver Med. Times **34:**43, 1914-1915.

Thomeret, G.: Prothèse et traitement des hernies récidivées. Entretiens de Bichat, Paris, 1967, L'Expansion Scientifique Français.

Thomeret, G.: La lipectomie circulaire. Nouvelle pratique chirurgicale illustrée, Paris, 1971.

Thompson, N.: The subcutaneous dermis graft: clinical and histologic study in man, Rec. Surg. **26:**1, 1960.

Thorek, M.: Possibilities in the reconstruction of the human form, N.Y. Med. J. Rec. **116:**572, 1922.

Thorek, M.: Esthetic surgery of pendulous breast, abdomen and arms in females, Ill. Med. J. **58:**48, July, 1930.

Thorek, M.: Plastic reconstruction of the

female breasts and abdomen, Am. J. Surg. **43**:268, 1939.

Thorek, M.: Modern surgical technique, 1-vol. war ed. Philadelphia, 1942, J. B. Lippincott Co.

Thorek, M.: Plastic surgery of the breast and abdominal wall, Springfield, Ill., 1942, Charles C Thomas, Publisher.

Ubiglia, G. P., and Pastacaldi, P.: Nuovo metodo di abdominoplastica estetica, Riv. Ital. Chir. Plast. **9**:257, 1977.

Ugland, O. M.: Hengebuk, T. Norsk. Laegeforen. **88**:1677, 1968.

Vandenbussche, F., et al.: Abdominal lipectomy: morphological indications and choice of operative technique. In Transactions of the Sixth International Congress of Plastic and Reconstructive Surgery, Paris, Aug. 24-29, 1975.

Vandenbussche, F., and Lagiche, G.: À propos d'une technique de dermo-lipectomie abdominale. Indications, résultats, analyse critique, Lille Chir. **26**(4-5):177, 1971.

Vandenbussche, F., Meresse, B., and Lagiche, G.: Chirurgie des excédents cutanéo-graisseux corporels (41 cas). Communication au Congrès Italien de Chirurgie Plastique à Turin, Septembre 1973, Riv. Ital. Chir. Plast. **3**:369, 1973.

Van Hook, W.: Laparoplasty by a new method, Surg. Gynecol. Obstet. **28**:598, 1919.

Van Hook, W.: Reconstruction of the abdominal wall and the principles involved, Railway Surg. (Chicago) **26**:31, 1919-1920.·

Vernon, S.: Umbilical transplantation upward and abdominal contouring in lipectomy, Am. J. Surg. **94**:490, 1957.

Vesco: Zur Reduction des Bauchdeckenfettes, Wien. Klin. Wochenschr., p. 155, 1914.

Vilain, R.: À propos de la chirurgie réparatrice de la paroi abdominale, Bull. Mem. Soc. Chir. Paris **54**:290, 1964.

Vilain, R.: Chirurgie réparatrice à visée esthétique de la paroi abdominale, Concours Méd. **87**:6213, 1965.

Vilain, R.: De la silhouette et des chirurgiens ou l'art médical de la silhouette, Nouv. Presse Med. **4**:1217, 1975.

Vilain, R.: Some considerations in surgical alteration of the feminine silhouette, Clin. Plast. Surg. **2**:499, 1975.

Vilain, R.: Surgical correction of steatomeries, Clin. Plast. Surg. **2**:467, 1975.

Vilain, R.: La technique dite "en soleil couchant" dans les dermodystrophies abdominales, Ann. Chir. Plast. **20**:239, 1975.

Vilain, R.: Le traitement des stéatoméries chez la femme, Ann. Chir. Plast. **20**:135, 1975.

Vilain, R., Dardour, J. C., and Bzowski, A.: De-epithelialized flaps in the treatment of scars, abdominal excess of skin and subtrochanteric steatomeries, Paris (undated), Hospital Boucicaut.

Vilain, R., and Dubousset, J.: Techniques et indications de la lipectomie circulaire: à propos de 150 interventions, Ann. Chir. **18**:289, 1964.

Vilain, R., Elbaz, J., Singier, P., and Gueriot, J.: Étude critique des complications des laparotomies, Ann. Chir. **21**:262, 1967.

Vilain, R., and Soyer, R.: Traitement chirurgical des éventrations, Ann. Chir. **18**:277, 1964.

Voloir, P.: Travail basé sur les techniques de Morel Fatio et de R. Vilain. Opérations plastique sus-aponévrotiques sur la paroi abdominale antérieure. Thesis no. 365, Paris, 1960, Faculté de Médecine de Paris.

Walzel-Wiesentreu, P.: Resection of abdominal fat in operations for umbilical hernias and for hernias of linea alba [Bauchfettresektion bei Operationen von Nabelbruchen und Hernien der Mittellinie Erwachsener], Arch. Klin. Chir. **136**:221, 1925.

Weckesser, E. C., et al.: Extensive resection of the small intestine, Am. J. Surg. **78**:706, 1949.

Weinhold, S.: Bauchdeckenplastik, Zentralbl. Gynaekol. **38**:1332, 1909.

Weisman, R. E.: Surgical palliation of massive and severe obesity, Am. J. Surg. **125**:437, 1973.

Wernicke, G. R.: Tratamiento quirúrgico de la sobrecarga grasa abdominal, Prensa Med. Argent. **44**:39, 1957.

Winninger, A. L.: Mobilisation de la sangle abdominale par désinsertion iliaque des muscles larges, Nouv. Presse Med. **4**:3005, 1975.

Wood, L. C., and Chremes, A. N.: Negative results—treating obesity by "short-circuiting" the small intestine, J.A.M.A. **86**:63, 1963.

Wright, J. E., Hennessy, E. J., and Bissett, R. L.: Wound infection: experience with 12,000 sutured surgical wounds in a general hospital over a period of 11 years, Aust. N.Z. J. Surg. **41**:107, 1971.

Wybert, A.: Greffe invertie et propéritonéal de peau totale dans le traitement chirurgical des éventrations et hernies, Mem. Acad. Chir. **79,** 1954.

Yanov, V. N.: Use of elliptical incisions and plastic reconstruction in cases of combination of diastasis of rectus muscles, umbilical hernia and relaxation of the abdominal wall (Russian), Khirurgiia (Mosk.) **50:**99, 1974.

Zagdoun, M., and Sordinas, A.: L'utilisation des plaques de nylon dans la chirurgie des hernies inguinales, Mem. Acad. Chir. **747:** 1959.

Zagdoun, J., and Zumir, I.: Le traitement chirurgical des distensions de l'aine, Mem. Acad. Chir. **93:**370, 1967.

Zagdoun, J.: Traitement des hernies inguinales récidivées, Rev. Prat. **19**(5):370, 1969.

Zoltan, J.: Abdominal skin reduction. In cicatrix optima, Baltimore, 1977, University Park Press.

Zook, E. G.: The massive weight loss patient, Clin. Plast. Surg. **2:**457, 1975.

TATTOOING, SCARIFICATION, AND BODY PAINTING

Buncke, J. H., Jr.: Tattoos. In Grabb, W. C., and Smith, J. W., editors: Plastic surgery: a concise guide to clinical practice, Boston, 1968, Little, Brown & Co.

Hambly, W. D.: The history of tattooing and its significance, London, 1925, H. F. & G. Witherby.

Mapp, O., artist: Personal communication, New Zealand, 1979.

Mead, M.: Cultural stability in Polynesia, New York, 1969, AMS Press.

Morse, A. L.: The tattooists, San Francisco, 1977, Albert L. Morse Publications.

Parry, A.: Tattoo, New York, 1933, Simon & Schuster, Inc.

Robley, M. G.: Moko or Maori tattooing, London, 1896, Chapman & Hall, Ltd.

Teit, J. A.: Tattooing and face and body painting of the Thompson Indians of British Columbia, facsimile ed., Seattle, 1972, The Shorey Book Store.

Von den Steinen, K.: Die Marquesaner and ihre Kunst, vols. I and II, New York, 1969, Hacker Art Books.

Webb, S.: Heavily tattooed men and women, New York, 1975, McGraw Hill Book Co.

Willodeen, Chafferson, and Handy: Tattooing in the Marquesas, Honolulu, 1922, Bernice P. Bishop Museum; reprinted by Kraus Reprint Co., Millwood, N.Y., 1978.

Zucker, H.: Tattooed women and their mates, New York, 1955, Andre Levy.

Index